THE PENGUIN BOOK OF

Oral Poetry

EDITED BY RUTH FINNEGAN

ALLEN LANE

Allen Lane
Penguin Books Ltd,
17 Grosvenor Gardens, London SW1W OBD

First published in 1978

Copyright © Ruth Finnegan, 1978

ISBN 0 7139 1030 5
Set in Monotype Ehrhardt

Printed in Great Britain by
Lowe & Brydone Printers Ltd, Thetford, Norfolk

For Rachel, Kathleen, and Brigid

CONTENTS

Introduction   1

Poems from thirteen cultures   11

Gond   13

Dear as the moon   17

Moon of the earth   17

Sleeper rise   17

Red beauty   18

Song of poverty   18

Love songs: A selection of *dadaria* songs   18

O girl, you torment me . . .   19

Pearly beads   19

Come laugh with me   20

A man's need   20

Come to me   20

So close should be our love   21

My heart burns for him   21

Longing   21

The arrow of desire   22

O faithless thorn   22

Water-girl   22

The well: Two songs   23

Flowers   23

My cobra girl   23

Shoes are made to fit the feet . . .   24

O little well   24

The stars are thundering   24

The shattering of love   25

There is no rest . . .   25
In my dreams I searched for you   25
My love is playing . . .   26
Flute player   26
Love and music   26
Like ripples on the water   26
She is not for me   27
Easy as a bat   27
Tonight at least, my sinner   27
Blue calf   28
The right true end   28
The bride's farewell: Two songs   28
Let me go   29
The new wife   30
Song of longing   30
Once I played and danced in my parents' kingdom   31
Old age   31
Be not proud of your sweet body   32
A conceited man   32
Elephants may parade before your house   33
About to die   33
Death   33
What is man's body?   34
The depths of sorrow   34
This earthen body   34
Who can tell?   35
Debt   35
The ever-touring Englishmen . . .   35
The roadmenders' song   35
What matter?   36

Mongol   37

Benediction for the felt   43

Eulogy to the bow and arrow   45

Benediction for the tent   46

Title of a swift horse   51

From a satirical poem about drink, *by Chimediin Jigmed*   53

For the cultural campaign, *by Chimediin Jigmed*   56

Prince Sumiya   58

Siilenboor   63

The speckled horse . . .   64

A cigarette   65

The white, orphaned camel kid . . .   66

Toroi Bandi   67

Are you glad ?   67

The 'word' of an antelope caught in a trap, *by Sandag*   68

The 'word' of a watch-dog, *by Sandag*   69

The 'word' of a wolf encircled by the hunt, *by Sandag*   70

Malay   72

Parting   78

In the heart of the hills . . .   78

Jealousy   78

Unique among girls   78

Entwined   79

Red ants   79

May I be beautiful   79

Music   80

I, lord of all mortals!   80

Love charm   81

Of Iron am I   81

Invitation to a spirit   82

Tin-ore	83
Sri Rama's raiment	83
Dawn	85
Storm at sea	86
Wind	86
Om	86
Invocation before the rice harvest	87
Take up the pen . . .	88
Parting at dawn: Three *pantuns*	88
Kisses	88
The disdainful mistress	89
You drop a pearl . . .	89
Invitation	89
And tomorrow wend our ways	89
Or ever God created Adam	90
. . . Till the sea runs dry	90
Regret	90
A little cheat!	90
The lost	91
Ave atque vale	91
White as paper a-sail in the air . . .	91
Breakers over the sea	91
The meaning of love	92
Two young maids . . .	92
The loves of the birds	92
Taunt	93
The opium den	93
A bully	93
Sanctimony	93
A battle of similes	94
'O that my love were in my arms'	95

Open the door   96
The lover's prayer   96
Sick unto death of love   96
Remember thou me   96
Song of a sick child   97

Somali   98

Battle pledge   101
A denunciation, *by Mahammed Abdille Hassan*   102
To a friend going on a journey, *by Mahammed
    Abdille Hassan*   102
Our country is divided, *by Faarah Nuur*   103
The limits of submission, *by Faarah Nuur*   103
Poet's lament on the death of his wife, *by Raage Ugaas*   104
An elder's reproof to his wife, *by Abdillaahi Muuse*   105
To a dictatorial sultan   106
To a faithless friend, *by Salaan Arrabey*   106
Lament for a dead lover, *by Siraad Haad*   107
A woman sings of her love   107
Fortitude   107
The best dance   108
As camels who have become thirsty . . . the poet's lament,
    by Ilmi Bowndheri   108
Modern love poems   110
Prayer for rain, *by Sheikh Aqib Abdullahi Jama*   113
The Suez crisis   115
Women and men, *by Hassan Sheikh Mumin*   116
Colonialism, *by Cabdullaahi Qarshe*   117
Independence   119

Zulu   120

Shaka   126
Senzangakhona   129
Praises of Henry Francis Fynn   132
War song   134
Praise of a train   134
Baboon   134
Old age   134
I thought you loved me   135
My money! O, my money!, *by Mavimbela*   135
Jojina, my love   136
Those were the days   136
Was it all worth while?   137
Take off your hat . . .   137
Lucky lion!   138
Home   138
Lament for Mafukuzela   138
Satan is following me . . .   139
Dove's song in winter   139
Teasing song, *by Princess Magogo*   140
Work song, *by Raymond Mazisi Kunene*   140
You are lying, O missionary . . ., *by Raymond Mazisi Kunene*   141
Come in, *by Isaiah Shembe*   141
Dance hymn, *by Isaiah Shembe*   141
I am the beginning, *by Isaiah Shembe*   142
Let Zulu be heard, *by Isaiah Shembe*   142
The springtime of the earth . . ., *by Isaiah Shembe*   143

Yoruba   144

Obatala, the creator   149

Eshu, the god of fate   150

Oshun, the river goddess   150

Alajire   151

Praises of the king of Oyo   152

Praise of Ibikunle   153

Dirge for Fajuyi, *by Omobayode Arowa*   154

Wisdom is the finest beauty of a person . . .   156

Oracle: *Iwori wotura*   157

Tiger   157

Death killed the rich . . .   158

The time of creation has come   159

Ifa   159

The lying Muslims   159

Let the dead depart in peace   160

Election songs   160

Kob antelope   161

Salute to the elephant, *by Odeniyi Apolebieji*   161

Leopard   163

Python   163

Mayor of Lagos   164

Variety: Why do we grumble?   164

Money! money!   165

Hunger   166

Women   166

Quarrel   167

Children's poems: 167
        Hunger   167

        Song of abuse   167

Praise of a child   168

Irish   169

Translations from Gaelic

O Virgin   175
Hell   175
A hundred thousand welcomes   176
Thoughts of God   176
I place myself . . .   177
Welcome O great Mary, *by Alice O'Gallagher*   178
A fragrant prayer . . ., *by Biddy Crummy*   178
When your eyes . . .   179
Thanksgiving after Communion   179
A low prayer, a high prayer . . .   180
O King of the world . . .   189
The merry jovial beggar, *by Peter Casey*   181
How well for the birds . . .   181
Ringleted youth of my love . . .   182
My grief on the sea . . ., *by Biddy Cussrooee*   183
From a beggarman's song   184
From a lament for Una, *by Tomas Costello*   184

Composed in English

No place so grand   184
The wearing of the green, *by Dion Boucicault*   185
Famine song   186
The moon behind the hill   186
No Irish need apply   187
I once lov'd a boy . . .   188
I know where I'm going . . .   189
Ballinderry   190
Must I go bound?   191
The green autumn stubble   191

St Kevin   192

In memoriam, *by Padraig de Brun*   193

A new song on the taxes   194

'Are ye right there, Michael?' A Lay of the
     Wild West Clare, *by Percy French*   196

Lisnagade   198

The ould Orange flute, *by Nugent Bohem*   198

Cushendall   200

From a faction song   200

Belfast linen   200

The dream   201

Lullaby. O men from the fields . . ., *by Padraic Colum*   203

Pueblo   204

Rains for the harvest   208

Song of the sky loom   208

Rain magic song   209

The willows by the water side   209

Shadows   210

Lost love   210

Regret and refusal   210

I wonder how my home is   211

Disillusion   211

Scalp dance song   212

Dead on the war path   212

Songs in the turtle dance at Santa Clara   212

The cloud-flower lullaby   213

Corn-blossom maidens, *by Masahongva*   214

Yellow butterflies, *by Koianimptiwa*   214

Butterfly maidens, *by Lahpu*   215

Flute song, *by Masaveimah and Kavanghongevah*   216

Now from the east, *by Masahongva*   216

The rainbow   217

Song of the blue-corn dance   218

The earthquake   218

The taboo woman   219

The songs   219

Our earth mother   220

Corn-grinding song   221

The sunrise call   222

Sunset song   223

Uru-tu-sendo's song   223

Eskimo   224

Solitary song   229

The sun and the moon and fear of loneliness   229

Song of caribou, musk oxen, women, and men who
                  would be manly   230

Hunger   231

Hymn to the air spirit   232

Dead man's song, dreamed by one who is alive,
                  by Paulinaoq   233

Men's impotence   235

Morning prayer, *by Aua*   236

The mother's song   236

Personal song, *by Arnatkoak*   236

I should be ashamed, *by Uvlunuaq*   237

I am but a little woman . . ., *by Kivkarjuk*   239

Bear hunting, *by Aua*   239

Walrus hunting, *by Aua*   240

Musk oxen, *by Igjugarjuk*   240

The gull, *by Nakasuk*   241

The ageing hunter, *by Avane*   241

The song of the trout fisher, *by Ikinilik*   242

Remembering, *by Akjartoq*   243

My breath, *by Orpingalik*   244

It is hard to catch trout, *by Piuvkaq*   247

The joy of a singer, *by Piuvkaq*   247

Great grief came over me, *by Aleqaajik*   248

Accusation, *by Utahania*   248

Mocking song against Qaqortingneq, *by Piuvkaq*   249

Take your accusation back!, *by Kittaararter*   251

Song of joy, *by Uvavnuk*   251

Spirit song   252

Darkened in the soul, *by Napa*   252

Invocation, *by Nakasuk*   253

Song of Sukkaartik, the assistant spirit, *by Ajukutooq*   253

The old man's song   254

Hawaiian   255

Born was the island   259

Old creation chant   259

The Kumulipo: A creation chant (extracts), *by Keaulumoku*   260

The water of Kane   268

Altar prayers   269

Ending   270

Prayer of the fishing net   270

O Kane, O Lono of the blue sea . . .   271

O thirsty wind   272

The rain   272

The Kona Sea   273

Praise song for King Kalakaua   273

Invocation for a storm   274

A stormy day   274

The ocean is like a wreath, *by Kuapakaa*   275

Song, *by Kaiama*   276

A skilful spearman!   277

Anklet song   277

The rainbow stands red . . . A tiring song   277

Laieikawai's lament after her husband's death   278

Cold and Heat   278

The beloved's image   279

Love by the water-reeds   279

Fathomless is my love, *by Kalola*   280

Resemblance   280

Love is a shark   281

My sweetheart in the rippling hills of sand . . .,
        by Princess Likelike (?)   281

Albatross, *by Lele-io-Hoku*   282

Puna's fragrant glades, *by Princess Lili'u-o-ka-lani*   282

The glory of Hanalei is its heavy rain . . .,
        by Alfred Alohikea   283

Hilo, Hanakahi, rain rustling *lehua* . . .   284

The sea! O the sea!   284

I'm going to California, *by Bina Mossman*   285

Sure a poor man   285

Piano at evening, *by Palea*   286

The leper, *by Ka-'ehu*   287

Behold, *by Mary Kawena Pukui*   289

Prayer on making a canoe   289

Maori   290

The six periods of creation   294

The creation   295

Chant to Io, *by Tiwai Paraone*   297

The creation of man   298

Ruaumoko – the earthquake god, *by Mohi Turei*   299

Landfall   300

Whispering ghosts of the west . . .   300

Song of longing   301

Disturb me not . . .   301

Give me my infant now, *by Te-whaka-io-roa*   302

A sentinel's song, *by Rarawa Kerehoma*   302

Love dirge   303

Dirge sung at death   303

Song of despair, *by Rangiaho*   304

The mist over Pukehina   305

Lament for Taramoana, *by Makere*   305

Lament, *by Matangi Hauroa*   307

O beautiful calm . . ., *by Tu-kehu and Wetea*   308

Oh, how my love with a whirling power . . ., *by Tu-kehu
    and Wetea*   309

A mourning song for Rangiaho, *by Te Heuheu Herea*   310

Hitler, frothy-mouth   311

Canoe-hauling chant, *by Apirana Ngata*   311

Fishing song   313

A song of sickness, *by Hine Tangikuku*   314

Government!, *by Tuta Nihoniho*   314

We object . . .   316

Lullaby, *by Nohomaiterangi*   316

Lament for Apirana Ngata, *by Arnold Reedy*   317

Seaweed, seaweed, *as sung by Hannah Tatana*   317

The breeze is blowing . . .   318

Australian Aborigines of Arnhem Land   319

Songs from the Djanggawul cycle   328

Song 1   328

Song 4   329

Song 6   330

Song 7   331

Song 8   331

Song 10   332

Song 11   333

Song 12   334

Song 18   334

Song 21   335

Song 22   337

Song 24   337

Song 27   339

Song 30   340

Song 33   341

Song 51   341

Song 57   342

Song 67   342

Song 84   343

Song 92   344

Song 135   346

Song 144   346

Song 166   347

Song 172   348

Song 174   348

Song 182   349

Snails, *as sung by Liagarang*   349

Yellow cloud, *as sung by Liagarang*   350

The blowflies buzz, *by Djalparmiwi*   350
All you others, eat, *by Djurberaui*   351
Sail at the mast head . . .   352
Three Songs from the Moon-Bone cycle: 352
       The birds   352
       New Moon   353
       The Evening Star   354

       English   356

Chain gang blues   360
Jeff Buckner, *by Frank Beddo*   360
I's gonna shine . . .   361
Dey got each and de udder's man   361
Judgement day   361
I work all day long for you . . .   362
If you see my mother . . ., *by Mack Maze*   363
The peeler's lament   363
Bow down your head and cry   365
The preacher and the slave, *by Joe Hill*   366
Two hoboes   367
They can't do that   368
Down in the valley . . .   369
Drill man blues, *by George Sizemore*   370
The Donibristle Moss Moran disaster, *by J. Ferguson*   371
I'll have a collier for my sweetheart, *by William Oliver*   372
Robens' promised land, *by George Purdom*   373
The Lake of the Caogama, *by Lennox Gavan*   374
Have courage, my boy, to say no!, *by L. M. Hilton*   375
To the pines . . .   376
Ballad of the D-Day Dodgers   376
Plane wreck at Los Gatos, *by Woody Guthrie*   378

Pastures of plenty, *by Woody Guthrie*   379

Jesus Christ, *by Woody Guthrie*   380

O God of Bethel . . ., *by Philip Doddridge and John Logan*   381

Children's poems: 382
    1952   382
    Salome   382
    School dinners   382

Song of a Hebrew, *by Dannie Abse*   383

I'm through with you   383

For no one, *by John Lennon and Paul McCartney*   384

Eleanor Rigby, *by John Lennon and Paul McCartney*   385

Epic and Narrative Poetry   387

New coasts and Poseidon's son, from *The Odyssey*,
    by Homer (early Greek)   389

Beowulf's fight with Grendel's mother, from *Beowulf*
    (early English)   407

The story of Bamsi Beyrek of the grey horse, from *The
    Book of Dede Korkut*, by Dede Korkut
    (medieval Turkish)   413

Zong Belegt Baatar (Mongol)   430

Blood Marksman and Kureldei the Marksman (Tatar)   445

The golden sea-otter, from *Kutune Shirka*, by Wakarpa
    (Ainu)   463

Tip-of-the-Single-Feather, by Velema (Fijian)   473

Ballad of the Hidden Dragon (medieval Chinese)   493

Acknowledgements   511

Sources of poems   516

Index of titles and first lines   527

Index of authors   547

INTRODUCTION

The great extent and richness of the oral poetry of the world is almost totally unknown to most lovers of poetry. It is often wholly unrecognized that unwritten poetry can offer much that, at its best, can parallel the written poetic forms so much more familiar to those of us brought up in a literate culture. Yet to look to *written* literature alone for one's poetic experience means excluding a vast quantity of the beautiful and perceptive poetry that can be found within the field of unwritten literature. It has been common for such poetry to be ignored, even by those interested in exploring the wider ranges of the poetic imagination, and for readers of poetry to have no chance to experience the delights of, say, Gond love songs, Eskimo meditative and personal poetry, the condensed witty Malay *pantun*, or the complex symbolism of Australian Aboriginal song-cycles. This lack of recognition is partly due to the common convention – I would say prejudice – that only written or 'respectable' literature is worth consideration. But it is also because of the plain fact that most of this oral poetry is effectively inaccessible to the general reader: it is to be found mainly in specialist publications or in locally issued and by now often unobtainable books, or buried in out-of-the-way journals. The purpose of this anthology is thus to make some of this memorable poetry easily available in English translation to the general reader.

The question of just what is meant by 'oral' in this anthology needs a word of explanation, for the term is not self-evident. Briefly, oral poetry is *unwritten* poetry. It very often takes the form of a song, or of verse in some way musically accompanied, and ranges from brief couplets like the 'miniature' Somali *balwo* lyrics or the 'songs of protest' of American or English coal-miners, to elaborate epic poems many thousands of lines long.

The context that often springs to mind when 'oral poetry' is mentioned is of some remote village far off the beaten

track with the indigenous people – non-literate and unindustrial-
ized – engaged in performing some local song or piece of traditional
verse, and an outside observer recording or writing it down, later
to transcribe and translate it at home for the benefit of a wider
audience. This picture perhaps approximates more or less to the
context of some of the poems included here: those, for instance, of
the remote Gond peasants of Central India in the 1930s, the Fijian
poet Velema's heroic poem about Tip-of-the-Single-Feather, and
perhaps some of the earlier Eskimo, Maori, and Zulu poems. But
nowadays of course the 'pure' and 'primitive' model of non-
literate peoples so beloved of the romantics is becoming less and
less in accord with the reality. Most oral poetry this century (and
in some places earlier too) is likely to be produced by people who
have at least some contact, however indirect, with the wider world
in general – and with writing and its products in particular. The
result is a continual and fruitful interplay between oral and written
forms of literary expression.

It has become clear that, for this and other reasons,
'oral' literature cannot be totally separated from written literature
in any absolute sense. The common criteria for 'orality' too –
those of oral composition, transmission, and performance – are
relative and elusive ones which may well conflict with each other,
for a poem may be orally composed then later transmitted in
writing, or perhaps written initially but then performed and cir-
culated by oral means. In fact many of the poems often widely
regarded as 'oral' – many ballads, for instance, and so-called 'folk
songs' – have also appeared at some point in printed or written
form. This means that it is in practice impossible to draw up a
precise and indisputable definition of 'oral', one which would make
the delimitation of 'oral' from written poetry a clear-cut matter.

However, though exact definition of 'oral poetry' may
not be feasible, it is only fair to say that in this volume I am taking
a fairly wide approach to what can be counted as 'oral'. I am not
insisting, in other words, that a poem must have been in every
respect composed, transmitted, and performed orally, without any
significant contact with writing, for it to count as 'oral'. Probably
many of the poems included here would qualify as oral, even on a
fairly narrow definition. But, adopting my wider approach, I have
also included some possibly marginal categories, those where the

poems may not be 'oral' in *every* respect. With certain of the epic poems, for instance, the original composition has been claimed by scholars to be 'oral', even though their later transmission to us has been through the written word; this is the justification for including extracts here from *Beowulf* and *The Odyssey*. In other cases the original composition may not have been oral, but the primary means of delivery and circulation certainly are. Hence the inclusion here of a number of modern English and Irish poems, and of verse broadcast over the radio. On my wide definition of 'oral', I consider this oral-delivery aspect significant enough to include these cases and present them as instances of oral poetry, parallels to the poems produced – like, say, the poetry of the Gonds or the Australian Aborigines – in a primarily non-industrial context. Indeed looking at these instances from urban and industrial contexts has the useful result of bringing home to us that oral poetry in the wider sense is far from being the exclusive possession of remote and long-ago peoples only, but is a living art form in the modern world – and one that is likely to expand and develop yet further with our increasing reliance on the at least partially 'oral' media of radio and television.

Deciding the scope and coverage of this anthology was not an easy matter. The obvious policy, at first sight, was to try to make the collection 'representative' in some sense, or at least to pick examples from a very wide range of peoples from all over the world. But there was a problem. When one has little bits and pieces from all over the place, it is almost impossible to gain any real rapport with any of the 'bits'. There may be a few lyrics which, even in translation, immediately appeal irrespective of time or place. But, for the most part, the poetry of an unfamiliar people is difficult for a foreign reader to grasp if there is no opportunity of looking at a reasonable selection (rather than the odd piece or two) and thus acquiring some 'feel' for the accepted genres and modes of expression. At the same time some knowledge of the social and cultural background is a great help in appreciating foreign poetry. In the case of anthologies of poetry from another culture this is usually conveyed by a general introduction to the whole volume. But, if poems are included from all over the world, this kind of introductory material is clearly impossible, even if all the more necessary.

In the end therefore I settled on a more selective approach. The major part of this anthology (excluding, that is, the final section on epic and narrative poetry) concentrates on the poetry of just thirteen peoples or cultures. This means that each of the thirteen can be prefaced by a brief introductory comment giving an outline of the background, and it also gives readers the opportunity – if they wish – of getting acquainted in some depth with the local poetic forms and symbols. This selective approach also means that I did not feel forced to include this or that poem (perhaps only available in re-translation from a translation into some other European language) just so that some particular area of the world could be represented by *something*, but could concentrate on those peoples whose poetry had been extensively recorded and well translated into English. This gives, in my opinion, a more illuminating and worthwhile collection of poetry than would be possible through a more superficial gallop through the world.

Though the selection does not therefore aim to be comprehensive, it can perhaps be claimed that it is not *totally* unrepresentative of the peoples of the world. The coverage in fact comprises peoples of many different kinds. It includes, for example, groups with varying modes of livelihood from the primarily hunting and gathering economies of the Eskimo or Australian Aborigine, pastoralism of the Somali or subsistence agriculture of the Gond, to the rich agricultural urbanism of the Yoruba or the industrial way of life of Irish and English poets. In cultural terms too there is great diversity, ranging from groups in which there is no professional role of poet at all to those in which poets fill official and specified positions – the Zulu *imbongi* or praise-singer at court for instance – or undergo long and esoteric training for their roles, as in the traditional Maori 'school of learning'. Most of the great world religions too appear in one form or another among the poetic traditions represented here, as well as more localized cults; and political systems range from the small-scale and 'stateless' organization of the traditional Eskimo or Australian Aborigine to the great historic states of the Yoruba and the current involvement of so many of the cultures here in the institutions of the modern nation state. Geographically the groups chosen are widely scattered throughout the world. *Some* attempt has therefore been made to achieve some kind of geographical and cultural balance in the selection – giving a range which has the interesting result of suggesting strongly that the development of the poetic imagination is not the prerogative of just any *one* type of society as defined in economic, cultural, or religious terms.

But obviously many other factors besides an impossible attempt at 'representativeness' had to be considered in the selection – the prime one being the availability of a recorded corpus of oral poetry in good English translations – and the collection makes no claim to be comprehensive and truly representative.

It must be remembered therefore that many cultures of the world, equally rich in poetry, do not appear in this volume, and that, even for those included, only a small selection of their poetry could eventually be chosen. This volume, it must be stressed again, is an *anthology*, a selection of flowers, not a definitive and comprehensive collection.

The obvious category of poetry for inclusion in an anthology of this kind seems at first sight to be epigrammatic and lyric verse – the love songs, for instance, in which so many cultures seem to abound. This category is of course well represented here, and is likely to exert an immediate appeal – notably perhaps the Gond love songs and Malay *pantuns*. But these are far from being the only category of oral poems, and it seemed right also to include some of the more 'difficult' and protracted verse forms. If these are perhaps less instantly attractive than some of the shorter love songs, an anthology could only be the poorer for not including, say, the impressive 'Dead man's song' or 'My breath' (from Eskimo poetry), the solemn and formal Mongol 'Benediction for the tent', or the long Zulu and Yoruba praise poems to outstanding leaders and warriors. So longer poems – formal, panegyric, ceremonial, or cosmological – as well as shorter lyric forms sometimes appear in the selections from the thirteen central cultures. In addition there is a final section on epic and narrative poetry which gives a selection of specially chosen longer poems, in full or in part, to complement the earlier groups. This is perhaps not the most usual type of poem to include in a general anthology; but epic and narrative poems form such a major part of oral literature – and many of them are so impressive and picturesque in their own right – that it would be a mistake to let the conventions of earlier anthologizers stand in the way of their inclusion here.

The poems presented are both easy and difficult to appreciate. Easy, because so many of them evoke the common concerns of human beings everywhere – love, death, sorrow, uncertainty, self-knowledge – and, in doing so, can speak across the gulfs of differing ages and cultures. But they can present difficulties too. So often the nuances and references in a poem can only be appreciated with some understanding of a cultural background which may be totally unfamiliar to us. This is a difficulty that cannot be completely solved, but some attempt to meet it has been made by the provision of introductory accounts to each of the thirteen peoples represented, giving some information on the cultural and social background involved, the way poetry is practised, and, where possible, some account of the role of the poets and the locally recognized poetic genres. Similar – though briefer – notes preface each of the longer poems in the final section of the book. These introductory accounts are necessarily short – and specialists will doubtless find them all too schematic – but they do present one important dimension of the poems. They are thus included here not as an exercise in scholarship but as an important aid to an appreciation of the poems. It was once the convention to present oral literary forms as mere 'texts', without any contextual material at all. But it is now more widely recognized that for oral poetry, perhaps even more than for written forms, some understanding of the social and cultural context is essential.

In the body of the anthology each poem is given with its title, poet if known, and any essential notes. This seems the obvious format, but in this case still needs a little explanation.

Oral poems do not usually have titles. Titles are, in fact, a convention for the presentation of *written* rather than *oral* poetry. But, since we *do* have this convention for poetry on a written page, texts without a title look rather odd, and I have therefore included titles here. In many cases these titles have been already supplied by the collector or translator (whether or not based on guidance from the original poet is usually not divulged); in others I have added the titles myself, usually taking them from some phrase within the poem or occasionally (as for instance with the Malay 'Invocation before the rice harvest') from a description of the circumstances of the poem in the original source.

The name of the poet also presents complications. The

composition of an oral poem is often not a once-and-for-all action. It is then hard to say just who the 'real' author is, and in what sense; for in a way every singer and performer can equally be regarded as the 'author' in so far as he contributes – as he often does – to the form and detailed exposition of the poem. The attributions of authorship here must not therefore be regarded as absolute. They are taken from the information given by the collector of the poem, and a closer examination might reveal that some names are of the initial composer, some of the current performer, and some reflections of local beliefs about a perhaps fictional author or a character in an associated story – and that these authors may sometimes blend into each other. Often, unfortunately, not even this much is known, since for many years it was the convention to emphasize the 'tribal' and anonymous nature of all non-literate and non-industrial institutions, including oral poetry; even when the poet/performer was known to the collector, his name was simply not recorded. Hence the absence of a poet's name in so many of the poems here.

Only brief and essential notes are given with each poem, usually none at all. Often a complete understanding would demand far more, but this would have meant overburdening the text with commentary and, quite apart from the consequence of having to exclude poems to make way for the notes, it would have resulted in a very forbidding volume. I think enough has been given for the poems to come across *as* poems, even though I have resisted the temptation to try to elucidate every obscure reference. The sources for each poem are given on pp. 516–26, and if further information is sought it can often be found by consulting the authorities mentioned there.

The translations are clearly varied in form and intent. There are many different ways to translate poetry, and perhaps most of them are represented here. The only things they have in common are: first, that they manage (in my opinion, that is) to communicate in some sense as *poetry*; and second, that they are all, I hope, relatively dependable translations. I must in honesty admit that I am not in a position to check their accuracy with the originals, but I have by and large tried to go to reputable sources, and have avoided obvious rewritings or versions 'after the manner' of the Zulu or Pueblo or whoever. I have also normally avoided double translation (say, a French translation re-translated into English without reference to the original text), the only major exception to this being Eskimo poems (often taken from standard English translations from the original reports in Danish – some of these translations being accredited by the original authors), and the translation of the Tatar 'Blood Marksman and Kureldei the Marksman', whose status is explained in the introductory note to that poem.

The line divisions in the poems appear as they are given by the translators and/or collectors, who presumably based these on their own informed assessment of the natural breaks in the original poem during its oral performance. Once again this is a relative rather than an absolute matter in oral poetry.

In their actual performance many of these poems were sung, and a full scholarly presentation would have to include a transcription of the music – and indeed of the complete vernacular text. This has not been attempted here, partly because such material is sometimes not available in published form, but mainly because it would be out of place in an anthology of this sort, designed to bring a number of oral poems, as living poetry rather than musical transcriptions or scholarly texts, to a wider public.[1]

If some or any of the poems in this volume help to introduce readers to a few of the delights and insights of oral poetry – the productions of poets like the Somali Faarah Nuur, or Eskimo Orpingalik or the anonymous Gond leper who composed 'What is man's body?' – then the many hours spent searching through unfamiliar publications to complete this anthology will have been well worth while. I hope that others will feel, as I do, that the poems here need no defence or apology, and can stand comparison without condescension with many of the riches of written

1. Full references to the sources have been given at the end of the volume and I hope that those interested in following up any points will turn to these sources. Specialists will note that, though the translations have not been tampered with in the sense of 'editing', certain data had perforce to be omitted or simplified (for example, the omission of special phonetic symbols and diacritical marks in the reproduction of some proper names). These points can be checked by consulting the original sources given.

poetry. But I think too that a further important point emerges from a collection like this, which is that many of the older notions about the communal, unself-conscious nature of so-called 'primitive' society can no longer stand up to examination. How can one continue to regard non-literate people as unreflecting after reading Eskimo poems or the vastly complex symbolism of some Australian Aboriginal poetry? And can 'lack of individual expression' really be taken as a characteristic of non-industrial social forms in the face of Makere's 'Lament for Taramoana' or Ikinilik's 'Song of the trout fisher' or Sandag's wonderful 'Words' that try to articulate in poetry the experiences not only of humanity but of the animals human beings encounter? It seems extraordinary that, even now, so many sociologists as well as popular writers continue to present a unitary picture of unchanging, non-individualistic and communal 'tribal' society, when it is so clear, from examples like the poems printed here, that individual poets of oral, as of written, verse can encapsulate their literary imagination in beautiful and personal words – taking advantage of the opportunities presented to them in the recognized poetic genres of their cultures. It is clear too from these poems that non-literate societies and their poetic traditions are far from unitary but can take manifold and varied forms. There are certainly many basic continuities between the several cultures represented here, as between both oral and written literature; but at the same time one of the striking lessons from an anthology like this is surely the remarkable richness and diversity of the human imagination in its many different forms of expression throughout the world.

Many different individuals and organizations helped in the compilation of this volume. To all of them I am most sincerely grateful. They are, I fear, too many to list separately in full, but I must mention particularly the libraries of the Open University, the School of Oriental and African Studies of the University of London, the Royal Anthropological Institute, and the British Museum. I am also especially grateful to Professor Ronald Berndt for advice on the Australian Aborigine section and for his kindness in reading and commenting on the introductory notes to that section, to Peter Ryan for comments on the Eskimo section, and to Professor C. R. Bawden for his magnificent Mongol translations. I was greatly helped throughout by the encouragement and advice so generously given by Dr B. W. Andrzejewski, as also by the stimulus (perhaps not always as fully welcomed at the time as it should have been!) of my husband, David Murray, and my three daughters Rachel, Kathleen, and Brigid.

POEMS FROM THIRTEEN CULTURES

GOND

In the 1930s, when most of these poems were recorded, the remote Gond peasants of Central India lived a poverty-stricken and hungry existence: 'one of the poorest peoples on earth' according to the translators here. Yet the Gonds have a proud history. From the fourteenth century they ruled as rich and powerful kings over the highlands of central India, still known locally as the Gondwana. But their kingdoms crumbled before invaders in the eighteenth century, and, their power and wealth gone, the Gonds were scattered into the remote hills and forests. By the twentieth century they had become subsistence cultivators settled in small villages and winning a precarious living through their primitive agricultural techniques or perhaps working for a pittance in the forest or on the roads. But the poverty of their material life is far from entailing any poverty of spirit or of poetic sensibility. Two of their admirers who spent many years collecting and translating the songs printed here wrote: 'They triumph over their poverty with a heroic merriness of spirit. . . . All the time they are singing, making a living poetry that is never written down, but re-created day by day in the very spirit of delight, sung under the bright moon or in the glow of a great log fire, to the crash of drums, the music of anklet and bangle, and the delicate movements of the feet. . . . These poems are a window into the Gond's mind and heart.'

The Gonds from whom these songs were recorded are spread through the Maikal hills and the forests around Mandla. In this area of central India there is great mixture of languages and people whose cultures blend and are shared together. Some of the songs here are by members of the Pardhan group, a sub-caste of bards and musicians who live with the Gonds, and others originated from the Baiga people and have been taken over by the Gonds. But by and large they can all be called Gond songs.

Many of the poems here are dance songs. For the Gond,

dancing is of constant interest. Villages hold dancing matches against each other and many of the rituals throughout the year are accompanied by dancing. Each dance has its associated songs, perhaps the most poetic of them being those for the great *karma* dance common to so many peoples of India. Men and women dancers rival each other in the composition of songs, and are carried away in the ecstatic rapture of the dance. Many of the most beautiful of their poems about love or death are in fact *karma* dance songs, a large proportion of them composed by members of the Pardhan sub-group.

There are also the satiric songs that the Gonds call *sajani*. These are mocking songs reflecting quarrels or complaints about, say, the rapacity of landlords or, as in 'A conceited man', the pride of the rich. Others again, like 'Debt' and 'The roadmenders' song', speak of the sufferings of hunger and back-breaking labour. These poems are most commonly sung sitting round the fire at night and tend to be longer and more discursive than the dance songs. In them one encounters the kind of detached and satirical comment on contemporary life and ways which was once thought to be the prerogative of literate civilizations.

There are few or no purely religious songs. For the Gonds, though influenced like all Indian peoples by Hinduism, are not notably a religious people. They have stories about the gods but little faith in their benevolence. In any case, they claim, when the railway came all the gods took the train and left for the big cities!

To an English reader, perhaps the most beautiful of the poems here will be the love songs. Their directness and intensity recall Elizabethan love-poetry, and in reading them one is reminded more than once of Donne's

> Whoever loves, if he do not propose
> The right true end of love, he's one that goes
> To sea for nothing but to make him sick.

'For the Gond, romantic love is a necessity,' write the translators. 'The life of the body is naturally of enormous importance to him. Life without a girl is wasted. The finest house is dark if there is no wife to illuminate it.' The love songs are the more heart-felt in that, among the Gond, men and women usually marry for love – or rather they choose their life-partners for love. Official marriages take place, but the women enjoy much freedom and often live with two or three men before they finally choose with whom to settle down. But the corollary of this frequent changing of marriage partners – in one village, for instance, the divorce rate was said to be over 50 per cent – is a deep experience of the sorrows as well as joys of inconstancy in love: the poems abound with references to heartbreak, betrayal, and the deceitfulness of lovers – 'His words are as ripples on the water.' The subject of the love songs is thus not just a topic for imaginative fantasy but a matter of real moment in everyday life and experience. The forms of the love songs are various. Some are in fact dance songs, others are expressed in the condensed form of the *dadaria*: rhymed couplets which are often sung antiphonally between two lovers.

The poems are sung on many occasions. As has been said, the dance is one of the most common contexts for song, but they are also performed by people at work in field or forest, by travellers resting at night, by villagers around the fires in the evening, or by groups of girls going to the bazaar together. They are an important part of love-making too. Lovers sing to each other – particularly in the form of the brief *dadaria* couplets – and many a proposal has been made in song, or seduction or elopement arranged. Poems are also used for taunting enemies, or for competitions between two sides (for instance at weddings).

The names of the composers are not given in the two collections which form the basis of the selection here. It is clear, however, that the majority of the poems are composed by individuals. All the Pardhan *karma* dance songs, for instance, were composed by four women from one household, the house of a leper. Two were the leper's wives, one his sister, the fourth his niece, herself married to a leper. It is small wonder, as the translators point out, that sorrow and mortality should be such prominent themes: 'death is certain, and the loneliness of death when we must travel onward alone. For the body of man is no more than a spark quenched by rain, a straw devoured by fire, a bubble of water broken by the wind. Love passes, separation is inevitable. Man sows his seed in a hard land.' Many of the songs are composed in the experience of the dance, perhaps most often by women, though even here the excitement and emotion does not free the composer from the stylistic conventions of particular dance-song forms. Others are apparently composed in a more reflective and detached mood. The poems of mourning are often sung by a bereaved lover or friend or relative on the day of the death, reflecting the spontaneous expression of heart-felt emotion and at the same time the conventional forms and imagery.

Translation, as always, has presented difficulties. Finding it impossible to reproduce *both* the formal style and the imagery, the translators decided not to attempt to convey the form, but rather concentrate on a literal translation so as to present the poem as a system of images. This follows the same principle as that adopted by Arthur Waley in translating Chinese poetry, holding 'images to be the soul of poetry'. As the translators here write: 'We have tried to represent the original meaning as literally as possible, within the limits of the demands of poetry, and we have been scrupulous in introducing no word or image that is unrepresented in the original.'

The original form therefore does not come through here. The refrains which are so typical a feature do not appear, nor do the frequently repeated ejaculations and meaningless phrases that go with the dance songs and help to fill out the rhythm. The music too is, of course, missing. Still, it is hard not to be convinced by the beauty of the translations here that the images do indeed somehow represent the soul of the poems. Images recur throughout the poems, above all the images of love – giving us new and changing and yet age-old insights, with each poem adding further to the experience of the last. Reading through these poems one feels one has gained some real understanding, from however distant a viewpoint, of the culture and inner experience of the Gonds as they pursue their livelihood in their villages scattered through the hills and forests of central India – in villages which to their inhabitants can be 'dear as the moon'.

Dear as the moon

To you this little village is dear as the moon,
And from the great city you have dragged me away.
Here if you want paper you must tear up your clothes,
For ink you must use the *kazal*[1] from your eyes.
Yet to you this little village is dear as the moon.

Moon of the earth

Your body might have come from the loins of a prince.
Lovely are you as the milky heart of a coconut.
Your body captures the mind with its beauty,
And my life lives within your life.
In the dark clouds there are nine lacs of stars:
The sun and the moon have begun to sink,
And you have come instead as moon of the earth.

Sleeper rise

O sleeper rise, if thou would'st see
At midnight the fig burst into flower.[2]

The feet adorned with rings are beautiful.
Look at her throat, the necklace circling it

The anklets make the ankles beautiful.

From the toes I will remove the rings.

How shall I know if our thoughts agree, O friend?

O sleeper rise, if thou would'st see
At midnight the fig burst into flower.

1. Eye-shadow made from lamp black.
2. Since no one has ever seen the fig flower, it is said to
bloom only at midnight.

Red beauty

Her red cloth is like the lightning
When first I saw you my life ached for you
O proud girl, what shall I do with you?
My enemy
Where did that red cloth come from?
Where did the gay-coloured jacket come from?
As soon as I saw you
My life ached for you, my enemy.

Song of poverty

O swan, come slowly from the sky,
And drink this cooling water from my hands.
When you are wealthy you have many friends,
But the poor man is ever companionless.
O swan, come slowly from the sky,
And drink this cooling water from my hands.

Love songs

A selection of *dadaria* songs. These are among the most
spontaneous and popular of Gond song forms and are often sung anti-
phonally between a pair of lovers or two competing sides in a competition
or conflict, with each verse expecting an answer. They are usually in
rhymed couplet form.

The sugar-cane is just a cubit high
But soon it will be taller than a man
Boy, do not be anxious
You will soon be grown and ready.
*

Your throat looks bare without its beads
My bed is lonely without my girl.
*

She was but a cubit tall
Today the sugar-cane is high as a man
With his hands above his head
She was my friend from childhood
And I have made her wise in love.
*

If you go into the river, it whirls you round
I saw her in my dream, but I woke and the bed was
    empty.
*

Looking, looking, my eyes broke open
I could not say a word and she has gone away.
*

A dried-up lemon gives no juice
My husband says not a word and my mind is withering.

O girl, you torment me . . .

O girl, you torment me, you are so deceiving
And you stand there beautiful as the moon
Yet as a deer is snared and killed
So will I snare you, for I have caught a thousand so.

Pearly beads

You have brought pearly beads
And tied them in your hair
But now stop dancing in my eyes
Or I will tie you round my neck.

Come laugh with me

O come, my body is alone, come laugh with me, come talk with
    me.
Bring mind to mind: clasp heart to heart.
What of the future? I care not for the past.
O come, beloved; come, laugh with me,
Come, talk with me. My body is alone.

A man's need

You can make a tidy leaf-pot out of sarai leaves,
But you can't make a pot with the leaf of the tamarind.
Life with a kept girl is like that.
Yet without a girl, life is useless.
Otherwise what would I do with this lustful body of mine?
As you cannot mix salt with sugar,
So a man cannot fall asleep without a girl.

Come to me

Jump over the wall and come to me,
And I will give you every happiness.
I will give you fruit from my garden,
And to drink, water of Ganges.
Jump over the wall and come to me.
I will give you a bed of silk,
And to cover you a fair, fine-woven cloth.
Only jump over the wall and all delight shall be yours.

So close should be our love

The mangoes grow in clusters,
O laden is the tamarind.
As near as seed to fruit,
So close should be our love.

My heart burns for him

Raja, my heart is mad for you
I have gone mad for you
But you have left the warm bed in my house
Where will you find such warmth outside?
You have left me all alone
You would eat roots and fruit outside
Come, my madman, let us go together to the forest.

Green is the green hill
Yellow are the bamboos
Green is the kalindar creeper
Karanda flowers are in my hair
Where in the forest will I find my Raja?
My heart burns for him
Where in the forest will I find my madman?

Longing

You play the flute
Of young bamboo
How tenderly you handle
The stops with your five fingers
Putting it in your mouth
Bringing the wind out from within
How is it you cannot hear
Your loved yoke-fellow?

The arrow of desire

His teeth are white as curds
His eyes are full of sin
His face is beautiful as a wild creeper
His eyes are full of sin
I am only a bit of cucumber
He is the ghee
To make it palatable
He is the arrow
But he has not destroyed me
His arrow has become the pillar of my house.

O faithless thorn

O faithless thorn
He has my heart no longer
Yet for his sake I no more see
Mother or brother or any friends
O faithless thorn.

Water-girl

O water-girl![3] with tinkling anklets
That sounded under the dark mango tree
O water-girl! your pot of bronze
Is shining in the setting sun
Your lips are dry and thirsty as my heart
O water-girl! with swaying hips
Go to bring water from the lonely well
Fear not the dark, I'll go with you
My heart is thirsty, water-girl.

3. A girl is thought to be at her most attractive and graceful
carrying the heavy water-pots on her head from the well.

The well: Two songs

Cool in summer's heat
Warm in winter's cold
Is the water in the well
And the body of my love.

In my garden is a well
And round it hang the mangoes
How deep and cool my well is!
But you are deeper far in love
The sun beats down and you are thirsty
But you care not for my water
You know the deep love of the heart.

Flowers

Blossom is in her hair
Beautiful is it as the plantain flower
Some flowers bloom in the dawning
Some flowers bloom at the dead of night
The flower of holiness
Blooms in the morning and in the evening
At midnight blooms the flower of sin.

My cobra girl

You are coming very slowly, why do you delay
        O my black cobra?[4]
I have brought you anklets, measured to your feet
        Why do you delay, O my black cobra?

4. A woman is often compared to a snake in poetry because
'Once she desires a man, she chases him and bites him, thus making him
love her. . . . To love a girl is like poison in the body'.

I have brought you a sari, measured to your body
    Why do you delay, O my black cobra?
I have brought you armlets, measured to your arms
    Why do you delay, O my black cobra?
You are coming very slowly, why do you delay
    O my black cobra?

Shoes are made to fit the feet . . .

The girl may not be quite so philosophical as she sounds, for she knows that if she dislikes her husband she can probably run away with someone else!

Shoes are made to fit the feet;
The horse must suit the rider;
But my parents will choose my husband by their taste, not by
    mine.
Yet it is my fate and not theirs that is wrapped up in the
    husband.
Alas! Alas! But what does it matter?
Life is but a bubble on the water that is broken by the wind.

O little well

O little well, you give no water.
Your youth is past.
Think well, your youth is ended.

The stars are thundering

The stars are thundering in the sky.
Among the ant-hills the cobra roars.
Under the earth the cobra's mate is nodding.
And the eagle dances across the sky.

The shattering of love

As in a pot the milk turns sour,
As silver is debased,
So the love I won so hardly
Has been shattered since you have betrayed me.

There is no rest . . .

There is no rest for her, and sleep has left her bed.
Sleepless she sweeps her court,
But on her own heart lies the dust.
For the comrade of her life has left her,
And there is pain in her heart,
There is no rest for her, and sleep has left her bed.

In my dreams I searched for you

The wind and the rain are beating down.
Take shelter or your clothes will be drenched.
The rain is falling, falling.
       In all my dreams I searched for you,
       But I did not find even the echo of your steps.

I have built a fence by the road-side,
I have made a fence for my garden.
Where have you hidden, thief of my heart?
       In all my dreams I searched for you,
       But I did not find even the echo of your steps.

I have cut tall bamboos; I have cut short bamboos.
Large are the hollows of the dwarf bamboos.
The thief who crouched behind my fence has hidden in those
    hollows.
       In all my dreams I searched for you,
       But I did not find even the echo of your steps.

My love is playing . . .

My love is playing on a fiddle
He is hiding behind a tree
O broken and blind may be the eyes
Of any girl that looks at him.

Flute player

The young flute player
Pipes on the river bank
All my desire is resting in his flute
And house and court no more content me
Let them be burnt with fire
Those bamboos that make the flute.

Love and music

He comes from the house as lightning flickers in the sky
His hair is tied in a knot on one side
He stands shining in the court
What is he doing standing in the court?
What is the boy doing? He is shining like the lightning
He is standing on tip-toe playing on the flute
He leaps in the air as he beats on his drum
Come, let us go and listen to his flute.

Like ripples on the water

He talks and talks
His words are as ripples on the water
You know and I know
That such talkers are deceivers

They think of others' loves
And forget their own
He is like a rippling wave
That passes by.

She is not for me

O my soul be patient, she is very beautiful
But this lovely treasure belongs to another
How wonderful she is! When you see her your mouth waters
But she is not for you. Be patient
Ah! she has come out of the house
She peeps out from the veranda
Tears fill my eyes, for she is not for me.

Easy as a bat

To kill a bat is easy
With a bit of split bamboo
Take her in a ditch and tickle her
Stranger, as you go along
Take her in a ditch
Easy as a bat.

Tonight at least, my sinner

O my sinner, let us spend this night together
My mind whispers, Come, let us run away
But I am afraid of that long journey
I look at you and long to live with you for ever
But at least, my sinner, we will spend tonight together.

Blue calf

Blue calf tethered
With a coloured rope
My heart dwells
In your begging-bowl[5]
Stay, my madman,
Stay a night until
Our enemy the cock shall crow.

The right true end

My madman bathes in the golden tank
Gold gold the water rises
On the waves the peacock dances
My heart my heart is far away
On a journey with my friend
Like a blue colt my madman dances
Neighing hiyo hiyo
On the waves the peacock dances
And my madman bathes in the golden tank
Gold gold the water rises.

The bride's farewell: two songs

O brother, as you've given me so much
From me take this blessing
Eat and drink in your house
Live for age after age
And for a hundred thousand years
May your court be beautiful as moonlight
May it always be clean with fresh cow-dung
Let there be cows and bullocks put together

5. A begging-bowl is a common sexual symbol.

May you grow old with your yoke-fellow of equal age
May your house be full of sons and their wives
Though your fate is written in another land
Let us meet fifty-two times in a year
If we live let us meet often
In this treacherous world
Even the iron bar gets rusted
What faith then can we put in human life?
I am all alone, my brother
If you forget me
Who will there be to ask after me?

How fine is my brother with his creaking shoes
And the blue bow in his hand
Brother, as you care for the shoes on your feet
Care for me as well
You have tethered the cow under your tree
But you have let the calf wander alone
To a stranger's land.
The cow is moaning under the tree
The calf has gone to a stranger's land.

Let me go

'Who will pay for the milk I gave you?
Who now will help you on your way?'

'My father will help me on my way
I will pay for the milk you gave me
But let me go, mother, do let me go
To my wife's country.'

'What is your father-in-law's country like?
What sort of man is he?'

'There are many mango trees
But few tamarinds
It is a land of flowing water
My mother-in-law is a holy shrine
My father-in-law is Ganges and Jamna.'

'For ten months I held you in my womb
Yet you never praised me so
For four days you stayed with your father-in-law
And yet you praise him so.'

'Let me go, mother, let me go
To my wife's country.'

The new wife

The song is sung by the first wife.

Rust destroys the wheat
She has destroyed your love for me
How I long to cover you
As the moon is hid by clouds
How I long to take you
All to myself
As a mother takes her child.

Song of longing

A wife sings about her unfaithful husband. The desire to
possess a man completely is characteristic of Gond women.

Could I remove the stones from the river?
Could I steal the beauty from your face?
Could a silver ring turn into copper?
Another's wife cannot content you
For she is brief as the twilight
I will hide you, hide your very name
So I may have you ever for myself.

Once I played and danced in my parents' kingdom

The song is sung by a girl who was not content with her happiness in her own family but found sorrow by following her own will. Her excommunication from her own people is symbolized by old age.

Old age has come, my head is shaking
Sitting on a stool my mind repents too late
I have no mother now, no brother and no family
No one will take me into their home
Sitting on a stool I think
Too late, I think again
Life has become sorrow
More than can be borne
O earth, break open and take me in.
In my parents' kingdom
I played and danced
But in my own kingdom there is sorrow
O earth, break open and take me in.

Old age

It is considered both meritorious and exciting to plant trees. The Gond who does this generally has a great desire to perpetuate his name, and looks forward to a prosperous old age. In the poem the old man who planted mango and tamarind trees in his youth finds himself jealous of the vigour of their fresh green leaves and compares it to the lack of strength and life in his own limbs.

How young I was
When I planted the mango
And the tamarind
And still their leaves are full of life
But there is none in my old body.

Be not proud of your sweet body

Be not proud of your sweet body
The moon and sun were proud and met disaster
For eclipses catch them
Be not proud of your sweet body.

Be not proud of your young body
The fish in the water were proud
And they too came to trouble
For the net has covered them
Be not proud of your young body.

Be not proud of your swift body
The deer in the forest were proud
But they too came to trouble
For the Bahelia sets traps for them
Be not proud of your swift body.

Be not proud of your fair body
The birds in the woods were proud
And they too came to trouble
For a great wind came and blew them away
Be not proud of your fair body.

A conceited man

He is walking in the road,
As proud as any king.
He looks down on everyone,
For his house is full of riches.
        If you don't bow down to someone,
        God Himself will humble you.

Elephants may parade before your house

One day you'll have to go to the City of the Dead.
Elephants and horses may parade before your house,
But when the slave that bears your life away halts at your door,
There will be no friend or ally to help you in that hour.
But you will have to go and knock at the House of the Dead.

About to die

He had no friend,
He had no disciple,
He reached a forest-covered mountain:
There he found a man who looked at him with crooked eyes.
And he said to him, Do not look at me so crookedly.
I can spend the rest of my days as before without a friend.
Tomorrow or the day after, I shall die,
And on my breast grass will grow.
This life only remains in the body for two days,
So do not look at me with your crooked eyes.

Death

Death will make entry into your body which is so beautiful.
O brother, in this sweet life will come separation.
Every vein in my body weeps for you.
My mind repeats, Death is near;
And my heart broods on this sadness.
O death will come to your body, your body which is beautiful
    to me.

What is man's body?

What is man's body? It is a spark from the fire
It meets water and it is put out.
What is man's body? It is a bit of straw
It meets fire and it is burnt.
What is man's body? It is a bubble of water
Broken by the wind.

The depths of sorrow

The depths of sorrow in tears have not been measured
The mountains and the hills will pass away
Like flooded rivers and streams, tears may flow
But what your destiny has given you must accept
Brother, were I a tear-drop I would fall like flooded waters
For the deep limits of sorrow's tears are not yet found.

This earthen body

Take a golden comb
Bathe in shining water
Look at your body in the glass
The body is made of earth
It will be mingled with earth again
Were it made of bell-metal
You could change it for another
Were it made of copper
You could change it for another
But no man can change
His earthen body.

Who can tell?

She goes with her pot for water
But who can tell the sorrow of her heart?

Debt

There is a halo round the moon
The sun is in eclipse
My debts surround my life
And nothing can save me
No one will give us *badhi*
No one will give us *dedhi*
No one will lend us anything
There is a halo round the moon
The sun is in eclipse.

The ever-touring Englishmen . . .

The ever-touring Englishmen have built their bungalows
All over our sweet forest
They drive their trains with smoke
O look at them, how they talk on wires to one another
With their wires they have bound the whole world together for
       themselves.

The roadmenders' song

     A *sajani* song sung by roadmenders in Balaghat. The first
stanza is sung by the men, the second by the women.

Hungry and thirsty we break these stones in the heat of the sun.
The chips of stone fly up and batter our naked bodies.

Our life is empty and useless.

Our naked bodies shine with sweat, the tears flow from our eyes.

Sometimes the chips of stone pierce the flesh, and the blood
      flows.

Those who have plenty of money gorge themselves with food,
            and live peacefully at home.

But it is when the heat is greatest that we have the heaviest work.

The ground burns beneath our feet: the sky blazes above.

The hot wind scorches our faces: why cannot we escape?

Sometimes the young men and girls die by the roadside,

Yet my sinful life will not leave me.

O mother, how long must I break these stones?

I am tired of living any longer.

In the cold days when all are warm in bed,

Then I must be breaking stones on the frosty ground.

In the night sleep comes not because of the cold.

All this I do and what do I get for it?

Only two annas for a long day's toil.

All this I do for my children's sake to keep them alive.

My flesh wastes away with this suffering: only my bones remain.

O that I might die quickly, and return to earth in a different
            form!

Hungry and thirsty we break these stones in the cold of winter.

What matter?

Liquor, you turn us into kings
What matter if the world ignores us?
The Brahmin lives by his books
The Panka boys run off with Panka girls
The Dhulia is happy with his basket
The Ahir with his cows
But one bottle makes a Gond a Governor
What matter if the Congress ignores us?

MONGOL

The homeland of the Mongols is the extensive plateau in eastern Central Asia which lies on either side of the Gobi desert and which, very roughly speaking, separates China on its north-western side from the Soviet Union. Many Mongols do, however, live in Inner Mongolia, on the Chinese side of the political frontier, while Buriat and Kalmuck Mongols are found in the USSR. Mongolia is a land of varied and striking scenery, with snowy mountain ridges, lakes and rivers, wooded hills, grassy plains, and deserts. The sky is blue for a great part of the year, and the broad open spaces are dotted with flocks of sheep and herds of horses and camels. The basic way of life has traditionally been that of the nomadic, horse-riding shepherd. The typical Mongol dwelling is the felt-covered tent. Its construction and nomenclature vary in detail from place to place, but it conforms to a basic pattern. It is furnished according to a recognized scheme of arrangement. This feeling for regularity and formality in everyday life is given expression in the poem 'Benediction for the Tent'.

The historical background to Mongol literature is equally significant. The Mongol nation was the creation of Genghis Khan (1162–1227). He and his immediate successors built up a vast but short-lived empire. The imperial epoch has left less of an imprint upon Mongol literature than might have been expected. Didactic and ritual literature especially look back to this time, showing Genghis Khan as a deified ancestor and as a Promethean initiator. There is only one truly important work of literature dating from the thirteenth century, the *Secret History of the Mongols*. This is an account, part saga, part chronicle, of the origins and doings of the Mongols from their anthropomorphic beginnings up to the death of Genghis Khan, and contains, embedded in it, fragments of what must be rather older oral poetry. After the disintegration of the empire in the late fourteenth century, Mongolia was for over 200 years the scene of civil wars and campaigns against foreign enemies. To this era we may trace the origin of the heroic epic. From the late sixteenth century until quite recently the Mongols lived under the spell of Tibetan lamaism. This was deliberately introduced as a missionary religion, and brought about fundamental changes in the language, social organization, material culture, literature, and beliefs of the Mongols. From the second half of the seventeenth century until 1911 the Mongols were subjects of the Manchu dynasty which controlled China, and the inhabitants of Inner Mongolia have remained to this day subjects of China. Chinese culture never had the same impact as did that of Tibet, but nevertheless it left its mark. In the present century all parts of Mongolia have once again experienced profound change. Outer Mongolia, now the Mongolian People's Republic, has since 1924 been a socialist state under the protection of the USSR, while the Mongols of Inner Mongolia have been brought to socialism along the road shown by Mao's China.

Some of the literary forms beloved of the Mongols, especially their ceremonial poetry, have survived political and cultural changes. The formulaic structure of such poems permits the variations in text which are made necessary by contemporary developments. Thus one may today come across poems of circumstance such as the eulogy for the winning horse which are essentially hardly different at all from eulogies composed some twenty-five years ago in which the name of Stalin was prominent, and even from earlier poems from the pre-revolutionary era. However, traditional literary forms are necessarily competing nowadays with acclimatized forms such as the short story and the novel, which, rather than the epic, are the main vehicle of narrative.

The peculiar circumstances of their way of life have no doubt helped to determine which genres the Mongols were to favour and which they were to neglect. As a nomadic people largely independent of towns, they never developed, until the present day, a dramatic art in the generally accepted sense. Ambitious plays were indeed performed, but these were either mystery plays in the Tibetan tradition put on by the larger lamaseries, or Chinese plays staged in the Chinese theatres at Urga and elsewhere. Printing was a monopoly of the lamaseries or of Chinese printing-houses in Peking which catered for the religious trade, so that secular literature was transmitted either in manuscript or else by word of mouth. The Mongols have excelled in lyric and epic verse, in ceremonial poetry and poetry of circumstance. The horse, the constant companion of the nomad, is a favourite theme of lyric verse, and so is nature, all important to the Mongol in his rugged yet cherished surroundings. The Mongols have a fine sense of occasion, which finds expression even today in poetical accompaniments, recited or sung, to acts of public and private life. Music has always been closely associated with verse. Literacy is more or less universal nowadays, and written literature, indigenous and translated, appears to be displacing the traditional oral literature. Yet a tradition of performance still persists. Even today it is possible to hear old epic poems recited or sung, and prose tales recited by expert story-tellers, while there are numerous amateur performers who can sing the traditional folk songs, among them the characteristic 'long songs' which make considerable demands on the voice.

Two features above all characterize Mongol verse. The first is the alliteration of the initial syllables of two or more consecutive lines. The second is parallelism, most often to be observed between couplets or quatrains. The second group of lines will in this case imitate the first, though with variations, in its ideas and its sequence of words. The effect may be reinforced by the artistic exploitation of the phenomenon of 'vowel harmony'. Vowels in the Mongol language belong either to the 'back' series or the 'front' series, with the vowel *i* being common to both. A word may contain vowels of only one series. The feeling of similarity and contrast is heightened by the use in one group of lines of words of one vowel series, and in the second of words of the other series. It happens in Mongol that pairs of words whose meanings contrast sometimes belong to opposite vowel series, as for example '*baruun*', 'west' (back), and '*züün*', 'east' (front). This facilitates artistic antithesis as displayed for example in the first two quatrains of 'Prince Sumiya'. Parallelism and the use of alliteration are the poetic basis, too, of such seeming contradictions as Sumiya's mention of his 'brown' horse in the sixth quatrain and his 'black-grey' horse in the eighth.

Mongol oral literature takes many forms, not all of which can be represented here. Thus the popular prose tale falls outside our scope, as do proverbs, riddles, tongue-twisters, and chants to accompany games. Popular verse merges imperceptibly, by way of poetry of circumstance, into folk ritual. The most important poetical genres are:

1.   *Popular religious verse*

The folk religion of the Mongols is often called shamanism, though it seems as if this term has been applied too indiscriminately. With social and ideological change, beginning with the introduction of lamaism and continuing in a different way under communism, the old rituals and incantations have fallen out of use. Many texts have, however, been recorded in writing. Apart from true shamanist invocations there are texts of fire-worship, worship of the Eternal Blue Sky, the cult of the White Old Man (the lord of the flocks), the cult of Geser Khan (the hero of the most celebrated Tibeto-Mongolian epic), the worship of Genghis Khan and his family, the cult of mountains, the cult of mounted divinities, hunting rituals, and spells.

2.   *Ceremonial poetry*

Poems of circumstance played a large part in Mongol ceremonies, particularly in wedding ceremonies, and to some extent still do so. Acts of public and private life, such as the making of a new piece of felt, the completion of a new tent for a young married couple, or the reception of the winning horse in a race, would be accompanied by recited verse, and were thereby raised, as it were, to the level of ritual. The commonest forms are the *irugel* or benediction, and the *magtagal* or eulogy. Eulogies of mountains are especially popular, but have no religious connotation, like the older mountain cults. The bard may improvise his poem, but within limits, so that familiar epithets and runs of lines are regularly encountered. Both benedictions and eulogies are still being composed. The poetic curse and the imprecation are rarer forms.

3.   *Epic*

For a short example of a Mongol epic and some description of epic as a genre of Mongol poetry, see *Zong Belegt Baatar* and its introductory note in the section of longer poems.

4.   *Dramatic verse*

The narrow confines of the Mongol tent favoured the development of the short, sung ballad-opera known as the 'conversation song'. In this, one performer might take all the parts, altering his voice and manner as appropriate, and would also accompany himself, or more than one performer might take part. The players would remain seated, and indicate action and emotion simply by gesture or change of expression. The text of 'Prince Sumiya' is typical of this genre, but much shorter poems, which occur also as simple folk songs, can also apparently be performed as conversation songs. A version of 'Siilenboor' has been published arranged in this way.

5.   *Folk songs*

The folk song covers a very wide range of subjects. There are love songs, songs about horses, nature songs, satirical songs, songs concerning historical persons, and so on. The historical song is allusive rather than narrative, as in 'Toroi Bandi', a song about a famous robber, which is quoted here in a very brief version. Folk songs published nowadays in printed editions are often accompanied by their traditional melodies. The 'long song', in which a single word or syllable may be drawn out over a long and florid melodic passage, is characteristic of Mongol sung verse. Its nature is not apparent from the printed word alone.

6.   *The 'word'*

The 'word' (*uge*) is essentially an improvisation upon a theme, in which the subject – person, beast, or thing – comments upon the fate which has overtaken it. The 'word' gives the impression of a sophisticated art form rather than of folk poetry, but is included here as being traditionally an improvised composition.

The great day of the bard, who might have been the favourite of a princely court or of a lamasery, or simply a wandering minstrel, is now over. However, there are still singers capable of performing epics and ceremonial verse, and of singing conversation songs. The composition of book epics is still a living art among the bards of Inner Mongolia. Ceremonial verse is still being performed. Skill as a singer was often passed on within the family, and is nowadays encouraged in amateur groups.

C. R. Bawden

Benediction for the felt

Seeing its corners, it is square,
Looking at its colour, it is white,
What may this be?
A sea-white piece of felt,
Pressed and made by seventy men.

Seeing it bound in a roll,
It seems like a bundle of jewels.
Looking at everyone assembled,
It looks like a general meeting.
What may this be?
It is the stiff white felt
Which forms the roof and walls of seventy tents.

Seeing it bound up reverently,
It seems like lapis lazuli.
Looking at everyone come together,
It looks like a cheerful sports-meeting.
What may this be?
It is the fresh white felt
Which forms the roof and walls of a hundred tents.

Passing winter in peace and plenty
On the south side of the lofty Khangai,
Spending spring with full family
In the broad Gobi,
Spending summer calm in mind
On the summit of the broad plateau,
Passing autumn in merriment
On the fair grassy plains,
Neatly and quickly they shear
At the right and proper time,
With steel-bladed shears,
The thick curly wool
From the richly fleeced sheep,
Reared with care and love
On the warm plateau
Amid the lush grass.

All have arrived in order,
All, in proper number.
Ladies, daughters-in-law,
Sitting along the back,
Younger sisters,
Sitting in rows,
Cleanly shearing
The fluffy white wool,
Beating it till it bubbles like foam,
Spreading it level like cotton padding,
Spreading the wool of the two-year-old sheep
A span thick,
Spreading the yearling's wool
A finger thick,
Sprinkling and mixing rain-water with it,
Pulling it behind a swift horse,
The precious white felt,
In a fine neat roll,
Like a jewel which cannot be abraded,
Like iron which cannot be broken,
The silk-fine felt,
White as a shell,
Whiter than snow, stronger than bone,
Put this way and that
On the pure white roofs,
The floss-white felt
Covering a thousand tents.

May all you who use it
Live in peace and joy
In the midst of the fair plain,
In your round, white palaces.

I offer up this sincere wish.

Eulogy to the bow and arrow

Taking between them
A specially straight willow tree
From among the many trees of the forest,
Measuring off two cubits,
Planing with gouge and plane,
Smoothing with scraper and file,
They have made the swift white arrow.

Judging as auspicious
The feathers of the vulture
Which hovers under the blue sky
That looks so blue,
And flutters to land,
They cut and examined them,
Sliced them in half,
And with the cunning of a skilful man,
Took the longest.
They hunted and shot
The gaping fish
With the golden eye,
Which crosses the Outer Sea and dives,
Which troubles the surface of the Ganges and dives.
They skinned and flayed it,
Boiled and rendered it,
Made speckled glue,
And stuck the feathers.
They carved the steel and iron
Beaten by a smith from Nepal,
Hammered by a hero-smith,
And gave it a broad white arrow-head.

They lined the bow on the inside with horn grown from the
        skull,
They backed it with sinews grown in the hollow of the knee.
They cut and flayed
The hide of a bull,
Dressed and kneaded it,

Twisted and laid it, and made a bow-string,
And said: May a fine man,
Skilled in shooting,
Gentle in making friends,
Heroic in war,
Gracious in generosity,
Heroic in wrestling,
Pull it till it bends.
And it gained the title of Yellow Bow.

Benediction for the tent

This being a fair and peaceful day,
Filled with great happiness,
Replete with ten thousand blessings,
And the commonwealth well-found,
This very day
Being an eternally historic day,
When we have awaited the best of months,
And tarried for the best of days –
We are erecting our palace
Upon the lofty plateau.

Looking to east and west
To divine the characteristics of the place,
Examining the condition of the site,
With characteristics of tiger and lion,
We have erected it
In a place where it can expand and flourish
Like the flower of the lotus.

It is a sea-white palace
With its eight sides tied down
With eighty-two thongs,
With its every side
Tied across
With seventy-two thongs.

To pick out and mention
Some of the parts which compose it:

Let us anoint its walls
With the ribs made of willow
From the northern Khangai,
Fastened back and forth
With the spine-skin of an elk.

Let us anoint its roof-beams –
The roof-beams made of a tree
From the southern Khangai,
The thongs made from the tail-hair
Of foal and colt.

Let us anoint the gate
Made by splitting a tree from the Khangai,
Made by smoothing with a plane,
Enclosing and containing all the people.

Let us anoint the roof-ring,
Which has the signs of the 'Wheel-jewel',
Made by cleaving a birch tree,
Pinned with spoke and pegs,
Letting in
The light of the sun,
Spreading abroad
The light of the fire.

Let us anoint it all:
The sea-white roof,
The stiff white walls,
The double horse-hair girth,
The door, quilted in 'palate-pattern',
The smoke-flap, quilted with a design.

Let us anoint the smoke-flap rope,
Which struggles against
The winds of the firmament,
Made by twisting
The mane-hairs of an elusive horse,

Made by sewing together
The beard of a rutting camel.

Raising the broad door,
Stepping across the high threshold,
And opening the right-hand chest and looking in,
Let us anoint everything there:
From the skin of the tiger,
The bear and wolf,
The steppe-fox and steppe-cat,
To the musk-deer.

Opening the left-hand chest and looking in,
Let us anoint everything there:
From jewels of all sorts,
Cut silk,
Pressed tea,
To woven material.

Opening the rear chest,
And looking in,
Let us anoint everything there:
From silk in rolls,
Tea in baskets,
Bamboo flutes,
Fiddle and harp,
Brush and ink-stone,
Books and ledgers,
Knuckle-bones and chess-set,
Knuckle-bone shooter,
Wrestler's jacket,
Glue for joining,
Curry for the race horse,
To tie for shaggy tail.

Let us anoint the good box-bed,
With edging of Tangut wool,
With five-fold cushions,
With coverlet of brocade.

Opening the chest beneath it,
and looking in,
Let us anoint everything there:
From hand-mirror,
Spectacles,
Tooth-brush,
Brush and comb
To powder and soap.

Let us anoint everything
On the box at the head of the bed:
Sewing-thread,
Scissors for cutting,
And everything else.

Let us anoint everything:
The fine silk curtains
With a black velvet border,
The five floor-carpets,
Quilted with a trellis pattern.

Let us anoint the brazier for the fire,
With its four imperial pillars,
With its four iron legs
And its hoops of steel armour.

Let us anoint the shears,
Hammered by a smith from Nepal,
Pinned by a smith from Kashmir.

Let us anoint
The marvellous bench and rack,
Like a four-legged table,
Like a square-backed horse,
Like an erect-humped camel.
A Russian smith found the knack of it.
A Mongol smith found the wood for it.
A blacksmith arranged its dimensions.

Let us anoint everything:
From teapot for the hand,
Poker for the fire,

Jug and pot,
Bucket and pail,
To dish and tray
For food.

Let us anoint the mortar,
Made by felling a growing tree,
Hollowed out by a skilled craftsman.

Let us anoint the axe,
Its blade made of steel,
Its haft made of fir.

Let us anoint wooden bowl and porcelain crock,
Whence all drink,
Which contain everything tasty.

Let us anoint the dung-basket,
Made by bending a willow from the Tula,
Lashed together with the hide of yearling and second-year calves,
Made by bringing wood from the north,
Lashed together with the spine-skin of a gelding.

Let us anoint the dung-rake,
Made by splitting a good tree,
Made by using branches,
Lashed together with the hide of yak and ox.

Let us offer up
With loud voice
A prayer for lasting good.
May this family
Gather all its beasts together outside,
Fill its tents with scholars,
Have a full set of carpets,
And plentiful food and fruit set out,
Be merry day and night,
Give food to all
Who pass by upwards,
And drink to all
Who pass by downwards,

Be too rich in foals and colts to know them,
Be too rich in children to know them,
Make their koumiss-bag of elephant-skin,
Make their koumiss-paddle of sandalwood,
Make their ornaments of magnolia flowers,
Peg out a tethering-line sixty fathoms long,
With foals tethered to it like minnows,
May they swarm with one hundred thousand people,
May they jostle with ten thousand people,
May the Commonwealth
Be firm like an iron surround,
May we humans
Flourish like the flowers of spring.

Title of a swift horse

This truly wonderful steed,
Chosen from the herds,
Selected from the geldings,
Galloping out from the colts,
Leaping out from the stallions
Of the herdsman Damdin
Of Gurvanbulag county of Bayankhongor province,
During the Great National Games
Which are the peak of joy
For the whole independent
People's Republic of Mongolia!
Let me tell of the wonderful form of this horse,
Replete with the eighty-eight precious signs:
It has the majesty of the lion,
The marks of the Arab,
Two wild-ass ears,
The swan's pointed snout.
It has fat on its rump,
The signs of swiftness in its knee,
The signs of luck in its tail,
And speed in its fetlock.

It has a nose like a trumpet,
Black, spy-glass eyes,
A chest, broad as a valley,
Four light hooves,
A thin padded saddle-cloth,
A light child-rider,
Stirrups like sun and moon,
A fine leaf-like saddle.
It does not stumble on the round stones
And is not overtaken by the eagle.
It does not slip on the flat stones
And cannot be caught by the alien foe.
A truly swift steed!
With its glossy golden brow
It cleaves the wind of the air.
With its two flashing eyes
It pierces the distance.
It leaps over the long ridges,
It springs across the broad plains
It waves its fine bushy tail,
It tosses its fine waving mane.
It comes in first
From ten thousand steeds.
It keeps the trust
Of its master.
It gives assurance
To its young rider
Coming first by its breeding,
Galloping ahead through its training,
Reined in and proclaimed
At the door of every tent,
Praised at every feast,
First in every race,
With clear brow,
Silk rein,
Swan's wing,
Wild ass's dust –

One from Ten Thousand!

From a satirical poem about drink

Chimediin Jigmed

The minstrel (*irugelchi*) Chimediin Jigmed (1896–1965) was born in Inner Mongolia, but lived from about 1948 in the Mongolian People's Republic. Drink and its misuse are a favourite theme of Mongol minstrels. The complete poem extends to forty verses in all.

There is drink fermented
From apples and fruits,
There is drink distilled
From koumiss and milk.

Russian and Mongol,
Drink of all sorts.
If you drink too much
A drunkard you'll be.

The three-pronged hook
Stabs the fish in the deep.
The bottle of drink
Spurs the word in the breast.

The iron spike
Stabs the fish in the lake.
The flask of drink
Spurs the secret word.

Drink in small sips
Is a happy food.
Drink in great gulps
Is destructive food.

Moderate drinking
Harms no one at all.
Immoderate drinking
Gets one in a mess.

There's the normal drunkard
Who just falls asleep,
The garrulous drunkard
Who puts all to rights.

There's the angry drunkard
Picking a fight,
The savage drunkard
Fighting mad.

There's the stupid drunkard
Waving a knife,
The bumptious drunkard
Disturbing the crowds.

There's the boastful drunkard
Praising his horse,
The conceited drunkard
Proclaiming his fame.

There's the weepy drunkard
Telling his past,
The singing drunkard
Without any voice.

There's the silly drunkard
Wandering abroad,
The obstinate drunkard
Who won't get on his feet.

There's the pleading drunkard –
'Let's have one more,'
The straggling drunkard
In search of a bed.

There's the greedy drunkard
Who can't get enough,
The pleading drunkard –
'Come on, let's have one more'.

There's the crazy drunkard
Swinging a stool,
The rowdy drunkard
Wanting a brawl.

There's the amorous drunkard
After the girls,
The abusive drunkard
With ugly approach.

There's the lazy drunkard
Averse to work,
The drunkard who won't
Look after his beasts.

There's the terrible drunkard
Grinding his teeth,
The dirty drunkard
Dribbling his spit.

There's the wandering drunkard
Who'll drop in where he can,
The intrusive drunkard
On the look-out for more. . . .

I'm not trying to wean you
Away from your vice,
I'm trying to tell you
What's good and what's bad.

Drink indeed
Is a terrible thing.
Drink to excess
And trouble results.

I'm not trying to stop you
Or put you off drink.
I'm only recalling
What trouble may come.

We can drink to the health
Of our famous young men,
Or drink to the future
Of the folk one and all.

Drink is food for the feast
At the Great National Games,
Where we offer a toast
To whomever we like.

We can drink to the health
Of our finest and best,
We can drink to the future
Of the common folk too.

Drink is food for the feast
At the peaceful Great Games,
Where women and men
Can drink at their ease.

Drink then if you please,
But be lord of your drink.
Keep yourselves well in hand
And work hard for the State.

For the cultural campaign

Chimediin Jigmed

As the sunlight in the sky
Illuminates our golden earth,
So our People's Party
Illuminates Mongolia.
It teaches all the masses,
Unfolding skills and talents,
Promoting work and culture,
And enhancing life.
Our Party specially teaches
That we should quite destroy
Outdated, bad conditions
Which hinder progress now –
Those former, old conditions
Where people would oppose
This excellent instruction;
Were quite against all learning,
Primitive and rude,
Never doing cleaning,
Or washing off the dirt;
Sadly isolated,
Antisocial too,
With their hair uncombed,
And house and yard untended;
Not enrolled in school,

Taking life too easy,
Fond of drink and smoking,
Slacking off from work;
Fond of drunken brawling,
Engaged in private trade,
Handling stolen goods,
Criminals at law;
Intent on private profit,
Absentees from clubs,
Never reading papers,
And with finger-nails uncut.

Our Party has declared
A cultural campaign
To try and lead the public
To a better way of life.
They are teaching reading
To strengthen education,
And are reforming labour
To try and increase wealth.
They are teaching hygiene,
To give us better health,
And by stressing friendship,
Make us courteous and kind.
So that we can master
This fine experience,
We have earnest teachers
We can imitate.
Let us all take part,
And follow in their wake,
Lest we should neglect
But one of these fine things.

Prince Sumiya

A conversation song.

Cast:
MISS JUYAAR
LAMYAA
PRINCE SUMIYA
JUYAAR'S MAID

JUYAAR is with her maid. Shading her eyes, she keeps staring into the distance. A cloud of dust arises, and she sings:

JUYAAR: From the north-west a cloud has come up.
           I wonder if it will rain?
           The top of my right eye keeps twitching.
           Is it Sumiya coming, my friend?

           From the north-east a cloud has come up.
           I wonder if showers will fall?
           My left ear keeps ringing for nothing.
           Is dear Sumiya coming, all eager?

           Is it the dust of my ash-grey horse
           That's flying up in flurries?
           I shade my eyes and keep staring.
           Has darling Sumiya come?

           Is it the dust of my grey horse
           That's blowing up in eddies?
           I keep standing up and gazing.
           Has dearest Sumiya come?

           [In the meantime PRINCE SUMIYA arrives.]

JUYAAR: I watched till you came to my door.
           I bend my knee to greet you.
           May I ask after your lordly home?
           And did you come longing for Juyaar?

SUMIYA: I galloped with nothing to eat
           Riding my tall brown horse.
           And if you ask after my home,
           My grey-haired father is well.

JUYAAR: I gazed till you came to my gate.
Let me hold you under the arm.
Is all well with the home you return to?
Did you think of your loving Juyaar?

SUMIYA: I galloped here loosening the rein,
Riding my black-grey horse.
If you ask after the home I return to,
My lady mother is well.

I set out on my grey horse.
I dreamed I would enter your gate.
I dreamed I would sit on the heated couch
With darling Juyaar, my love.

JUYAAR: I dreamed the lotus would blossom
On the top of the western hill.
I dreamed I would talk words of joy
With Sumiya, my childhood love.

I dreamed the magnolia would flourish
On the top of the eastern hill.
I dreamed I would speak my heart's words
To Sumiya, the love of my heart.

SUMIYA: I dreamed it would be moist on the golden earth
When showers fell from the sky.
I dreamed I would share a cup of wine
With little Juyaar, my love.

I dreamed the dry earth would be moistened
When rain fell from the heavens.
I dreamed I would share a goblet of wine
With you, my old love, Juyaar.

JUYAAR: I dreamed that the parrot in the bamboo cage
Would sing with the voice of the swan.
I dreamed I would change my dress and feast
With Prince Sumiya, my own dear love.

I dreamed I would change my gown
And look gay in the candle light.
I dreamed I would share a pillow
With you, my noble Prince Sumiya.

SUMIYA: I dreamed the pink flowers of Hunan would bloom
           Too massed to tread between.
           I dreamed I would share a goblet of wine
           With you, my own love, Juyaar.

           [While they are drinking, LAMYAA arrives.]

LAMYAA: There's a black horse tied within your gates.
           To what guest does this mount belong?
           This chap sitting on your heated couch –
           Whose son is he? Where's he from?

           The ash-grey horse tethered at your door –
           Is it the mount of this wretched chap?
           That fellow leaning against your knee –
           I suppose he's some orphan's son?

JUYAAR: The cloud-grey horse tied at my door
           Is the steed of a man of rank.
           My lover who leans on my knee
           Is the son of a high-born prince.

LAMYAA: Stepping to each other and kneeling,
           You must be orphans' children, both.
           That fellow sitting there behind you
           Is a minnow's ghost from the stream.

JUYAAR: We two, stepping to each other and kneeling
           Have parents, living Buddhas reborn.
           My lover sitting there behind me
           Is the son of a man of rank.

LAMYAA: Creeping to each other and kneeling,
           You must be orphan-children, both.
           That fellow sitting by your shoulder
           Is a minnow's ghost from the river.

JUYAAR: We two, creeping to each other and kneeling,
           Are born of noble parents, both.
           This man sitting by my shoulder
           Is a Buddha's soul reborn.

LAMYAA: The ring, what about the ring?
          Pure gold it was, refined in Peking.
          If paltry Sumiya's now your love,
          Give me back my ring, dear Juyaar.

JUYAAR: When you gave me your ring, dear Lama,
          Didn't your love belong to me?
          If you're grieving for your ring,
          Call all the girls, and beg for it back!

LAMYAA: The silk, what about the silk?
          Brightly patterned silk it was.
          If paltry Sumiya's now your love,
          Give me back my silk, dear Juyaar.

JUYAAR: When you gave me the silk, dear Lama,
          Didn't your heart belong to me?
          If you're yearning for your silk,
          Kowtow your head sore, and beg for it back!

LAMYAA: The boots, what about the boots?
          Boots with thirty-two designs they were.
          If paltry Sumiya makes you lovesick,
          Give me back my boots, dear Juyaar.

JUYAAR: When you gave me the boots, dear Lama,
          Wasn't it for my pretty self?
          If you're grieving for your boots,
          Kowtow thrice in the street, and beg for them back!

LAMYAA: The crêpe, what about the crêpe?
          Adorned with a 'wheel' pattern it was.
          If paltry Sumiya's now your love,
          Give me back my crêpe, dear Juyaar.

JUYAAR: When you gave me your crêpe, dear Lama,
          Didn't your love belong to me?
          If you're yearning for your crêpe,
          Kowtow your brow sore, and beg for it back!

LAMYAA: When you came from the north-west, darling,
          You swayed and floated like the lotus.
          Now I've spent all I have upon you,
          You'll turn me out, without a stick to hold?

SUMIYA: Does the young snake, not yet a fathom long,
            Yet seek to vie with the dragon of the skies?
            Do you, you petty pedlar of a Peking priest,
            Think you can take on Sumiya alone?

            Does the young snake, not yet a finger thick,
            Yet seek to vie with the dragon of the heavens?
            Do you, you petty hawker of a Peking priest,
            Think you can do down Sumiya, the Law?

JUYAAR: Dear Lama, please go, happy, on your way,
            And tell your beads to Buddha Chenrezi.
            Do think of naughty Juyaar as you go.
            Who knows if we shall meet upon the way?

            Dear Lama, go in peace upon the road,
            And don't reform your ways.
            Remember darling Juyaar as you go.
            I'll pray that we may meet again some day.

            [She turns LAMYAA out. As she comes in again she
            espies PRINCE SUMIYA's horse, and sings, in a jealous
            manner:]

JUYAAR: Your grey horse is all sweaty.
            Have you been to the neighbour's house?
            Your gun-sling is brand new.
            Did your divorced wife sew it?

SUMIYA: If my grey horse is sweaty,
            It's from hunting stag and deer.
            And as for my new gun-sling,
            My grey-haired mother sewed it.

JUYAAR: Your black horse is all sweaty,
            Whose house have you just come from?
            You're looking at me sidelong.
            Your dear wife shewed you how?

SUMIYA: If my black horse is sweaty,
            It's from chasing the black hare.
            And if my look is sidelong,
            It's all because you're jealous.

JUYAAR: Your ash-grey horse is sweaty.
Have you been to our neighbour's?
There's a new sling on your bow-case.
Did your ex-wife sew it?

SUMIYA: If my ash-grey horse is sweaty,
I chased the yellow hare.
The new sling on my bow-case
Was granted by the Throne.

JUYAAR: Are you angry, honest friend?
I asked with good intentions.
Oh, nobly born Prince Sumiya,
Don't leave me or forsake me!

SUMIYA: Is this the voice of true love,
Or are you just being jealous?
You chased away your lama,
And now you've turned on me.

[And PRINCE SUMIYA goes off angrily. JUYAAR weeps
after him, and falls on her bed. Meanwhile the MAID
enters and asks: 'What is the matter? What's happen-
ing?']

MAID: The gentlemen forsook you
Because you were so greedy.
Now just you learn a lesson,
Or you'll finish up alone.

[She goes out. JUYAAR, left by herself, sits up weeping.
She says: 'What shall I do now?' and falls to the
ground.]

Siilenboor

The dawning sun
Shines down on the dunes.
Tomorrow they'll marry
Siilenboor from our camp.

The rising sun
Shines down past the hills.
At dawn they'll marry
Siilenboor from South Camp.

The shafted carriage is in her camp,
The golden censer on the altar.
They're making little Siilenboor
Kowtow to her new parents.

The wheeled carriage is in her yard,
The brazen censer on the altar.
They're making little Siilenboor
Bow, joss-stick and lamp in hand.

Riding my grey horse I'll go.
Bearing bow-case and bow I'll go.
I'll grab my lovely Siilenboor
From the junction of the roads.

Riding my brown horse I'll go.
Bearing my heavy gun I'll go.
I'll grab my little Siilenboor
From the way to her new home.

With a spare bay horse I'll go.
With crupper and bridle ready I'll go.
I'll grab my darling Siilenboor
As she goes to her wedding.

The speckled horse . . .

The speckled horse is bucking.
The wolf-skin rug is spread.
If you still love me truly,
Don't go till Venus shines.
        O, my dearest Siilen.

The full-grown horse is bucking.
The fox-skin rug is spread.
If you still really love me,
Don't go till break of day.
        O, my dearest Siilen.

The dark flower of the lotus
Revives beneath the rain.
My heart, downcast and grieving,
Revives when I see you.
        O, my dearest Siilen.

The yellow lotus flower
Revives beneath the wind.
My heart, depressed and longing,
Revives when I see you.
        O, my dearest Siilen.

A cigarette

If you smoke a cigarette
It gives a pleasant fragrance.
If you're constant to our love
We'll surely meet once more.

If you smoke a nice 'Three Castles'
It gives a pleasing fragrance.
If you don't play fast and loose
No harm will e'er befall you.

Now take fermented apple wine,
You'll get drunk if you taste it.
I'm quite content to sit and flirt
With you, my well-beloved.

Now take fermented wine of grapes,
You'll get drunk if you smell it.
I'm glad to keep the company
Of you, my best beloved.

The white, orphaned camel kid . . .

The white, orphaned camel kid
Howls in its hunger.
It howls because it's longing for
Its speckle-coated mother.

It howls as it nibbles at
The shoots upon the rushes.
It howls because it misses
The teats, a finger thick.

It howls as it nibbles at
The leaves upon the broom-grass.
It howls because it's thinking of
Its mother with her udder.

The kid which has a father
Runs after him and plays.
The kid without a father
Strays along behind.

The kid which has a mother
Runs after her and howls.
The kid without a mother
Strays along the banks.

I wish the fluffy hair
Were grown about my knees.
I'd like to run to mother
Along the southern hills.

I wish the fluffy hair
Were grown upon my neck.
I'd like to run to mother
Along the mountain scarp.

Where has my mother gone,
Worth quite a hundred taels,
From amongst the hundred
Camels on the ridge?

Where has my mother gone,
Worth fully fifty taels,
From amongst the fifty
Camels on the slopes?

Toroi Bandi

When Toroi Bandi was alive
I wore the best of silks.
Now that Toroi Bandi's gone
I haven't greasy cotton.

In the shadow of the tent
He would caress my hair,
Lay his head upon my box,
And kiss me on the cheek.

I'll be reborn in a true land
Where there is no more sorrow.
I'll be reborn upon this earth
Forever in the sun.

Are you glad?

This song appears to refer to the abrogation of Mongolian autonomy in 1919 and the reappearance of the Chinese in the country.

Ministers who've sold the King
For bags and bags of money,
Ministers who've sold the Town
For sacks and sacks of money,

Ministers who've sold the State
For pots and pots of money,
Ministers who've sold the earth
For scales full of money,

Ministers with red-brown robes,
Has your business pleased you?
Ministers with silken gowns,
Are you glad you've sold us?

The 'word' of an antelope caught in a trap

Sandag

The minstrel Sandag lived in the first half of the nineteenth
century.

I dwell on the misty steppe.
I belong to Manakhan, the Lord of the Beasts.
In the deep cold of winter,
In the blinding snow-storms,
I went of my own accord
To gentler, warmer pastures.
With the changing season
I went frolicking along
With my myriad companions,
To return to our old pastures.
Through the power of former deeds
I was caught in a snare.
My twenty myriad companions,
Forming a wedge, vanished from sight,
And I, bereft of my heel-tendons,
Fell behind, gazing after them.
My hundred myriad companions,
Neck and neck, vanished from sight,
And I, caught in the middle of my way,
Fell behind, to endure my pain.
My many myriad companions
Went off, straight in line,
And I, caught in the toils,
Fell behind, to await death.
To be hunted
Is the way of the world.

May I find a peaceful new birth,
Transcending the state of the wild beast.

The 'word' of a watch-dog

Sandag

He who is my master
Fondly brought me up
From my earliest years
To splendid maturity,
And put me in charge
Of all that he owns.
When a stranger approaches
I go to meet him from afar.
Furiously I threaten him
And try to drive him off.
But, restrained by my dear master,
I watch him, and let him dismount.
When it is time to depart
I pant angrily after him.
I would tear him to pieces,
But just see him off and turn back.
When it is dark night
And the ravening wolf comes,
I keep him at bay,
And chase him off.
Knowing he may cunningly come back
I bark and bark in warning.
In the long winter's night
I freeze outside.
When dawn breaks
And the morning blast blows,
Hungry and tired,
I slink into
Our own tent.
Painful blows drive me out,

And I resent it for the moment,
But bear no lasting grudge.
When we shift pastures I follow on foot.
I gnaw a meatless bone,
I eat the poorest food – but no matter.
I shall live in happiness
And grow old faithfully
With my master
Whom I was predestined to find.

The 'word' of a wolf encircled by the hunt

Sandag

I, a blue wolf,
Born on the steppes,
Had stolen and eaten someone's cattle,
And was making for a hollow,
And a place to sleep,
When the Prince of the Banner,
Leading his men in wedge formation,
Riding a good horse,
Pursued me like the whirlwind.
My mortal body is a beggar's,
My native thoughts are a thief's,
My dwelling place is a hell.
What shall I do now?
The northern mountain is far off,
The plain betwixt is vast,
How I run, crossing my heels!
How the chestnut horses catch up on me!
Thanks to the dark
My life is spared.
Thanks to my leaping
My life is maintained.
Thanks to my prowling
At dawn and dusk alike,

I get and eat
My food.

I have nothing to call my own.
What an unhappy fate!
I have no property to call my own.
What a miserable fate!

From long ago
I have been killing and eating
Young, new-born creatures.
Alas for those poor creatures!

Though I regret it now, it is too late.
It was fine, tasty food
To kill and eat.
And when I think of the future,
How great is my sin!
I, a poor slit-eyed wolf,
Born in a gully,
Am at my wits' end how to escape,
Scheme as I will.
Now may my lord spare me!

MALAY

Malay is the mother tongue of about ten million people but it is also the official and literary language over an extensive area of mainland and islands, comprising the modern states of Indonesia and Malaysia – the old Malay Peninsula and Archipelago. In this area many cultures have met and mingled over the centuries: Hinduism and the literatures of India from the early years of our era, Islam from the fourteenth and fifteenth centuries and with it the literature of Arabia and Persia, and more recently that of Western Europe. The complex character of this culture was also fed by the many local languages and groups – like Javanese or Balinese – which together make up the Malay world. Complex written literature flowed from this, largely composed in 'classical Malay' which became established as the standard form after the fifteenth-century emergence of the powerful Muslim kingdom of Malacca, dominated by Muslim literary models, but showing the influence of many other cultures too, among them that of Hinduism.

Alongside this, and partly influenced by it, runs the rich oral literature of Malay. For the mass of Malay-speakers, for the most part illiterate, this formed their main access to literature. The unwritten literature too bears the traces of many influences – not least that of the sophisticated town life of recent times – but has little of the emphasis of many *written* Malay works on slavish imitation of foreign models. There is clearly interaction between written and unwritten forms. Certain forms are primarily oral, but there are also marginal forms, like the romantic stories based on written manuscripts which were recited or sung to non-literate audiences by travelling story-tellers. Again the ritual prayers and the magicians' charms depend on oral delivery and circulation, and yet may have a written element in being sometimes written down, in charm books and so on.

There are a number of occasions when such literature can circulate. The typically Malay *pantun*s – brief and ingenious four-line verses – appear in poetic contests, with each contender trying to rejoin and outdo his opponent's wit and poetic invention; they are also bandied between lovers, between a dancer and her partner, or between the families of bride and groom at weddings or betrothals. Other verses and poems – from romances for instance – used to be sung and recited by rhapsodists to paying audiences. A number of these have appeared in written versions – like the romance of Sri Rama – but they also circulate orally and are regarded by one authority as 'literature in solution handed down orally from father to son'.[1]

Some of the metrical passages from these romances have been given here, like the famous picture of dawn in 'Sri Rama', and the description of Sri Rama's raiment. There is also a large amount of ritual poetry, attached to particular ceremonies. Some of these concern relatively mundane occasions (on the surface at least), like offerings at rice harvest or the rituals of mining or hunting. Others belong to the mystical domain of the Malay magician, who can sell special charms to entice a haughty love or produce resounding incantations to famous spirits at emotional seances. Again new topical songs are composed and sung every year by bands of strolling minstrels: during Ramadan especially they go round the houses of wealthy Muslims, singing the praises of their hosts. Every local operatic troupe too employs a versifier to compose new words to well-known tunes: verses, jokes, and songs of praise or amusement.

Through all these runs the deep Malay interest in words: the derivation of words, the witty and beautiful use of words, word suggestions and assonance. Literary composition is thought of as a kind of stringing together of beautiful words and sayings, like pearls on a necklace, for poetry is not just useful for praise or spell, but is something loved for its own sake. It affords a relief for the poet's and listeners' feelings, especially for the sense of melancholy longing:

> For a heart oppressed with sorrow some solace
> lingers yet

1. R. O. Winstedt, *Malay literature*, Kuala Lumpur, 1923, p. 38.

In the long low notes of the viol that sweeten a song
of regret.[2]

The language of unwritten Malay literature is relatively simple in
its vocabulary and construction, but the colour and poetic style are
achieved by skilful use of imagery, the feeling for balance, and the
effective exploitation of a simple series of short statements. For
instance, a story-teller can convey the many-voiced inquisitiveness
of a crowd not by abstract and general description, but by simply
repeating a series of questions:

> Has a fortress fallen?
> Has a dyke broken?
> . . . Is the roof-tree giving?
> Has the flooring crumbled?
> Is some fleet arriving?[3]

Similarly an indefinite distance is conveyed by a succession of
simple comparisons:

> As far as a cannon batters, as far as a bullet flies,
> As far as a horse can gallop, or the flight of a bird
>   can rise,
> Or the deeds of a man be witnessed by his friends'
>   unaided eyes.[4]

A feeling for balance and antithesis is also noticeable in
this poetry. This was partly the legacy of rhapsodist recitations:
the device of chanting passages twice over gave the audience the
opportunity to catch and ponder on verses that might escape too
quickly if declaimed only once, as well as giving the reciter himself
some leeway for thought. This feature of parallelism and balance,
not unlike the antiphons of the Psalms, is exploited to its fullest
extent in the balanced thesis and antithesis of the brief *pantun*
quatrains.

The imagery of Malay oral poetry is very vivid. The
emotions of love or despair or envy are expressed through the

2. From a Malay *pantun*, quoted in R. J. Wilkinson, *Malay
literature*, Kuala Lumpur, 1924, p. 43.

3. ibid., p.13.

4. ibid.

figures of fruit and flowers, plants and birds. Basil, for instance, is known as the symbol of a mistress, and so gives meaning to the *pantun*:

> Malacca fort it cannot fall!
> My love, she could not lie.
> As does the basil in yonder tray,
> In her arms would I die.[5]

Again frangipani is a flower often planted in Malay cemeteries and its mention prepares the listener for a reference to death (as in '*Ave atque vale*'), just as a spoilt young coconut is a euphemism for a maid deflowered and earrings a sign of virginity:

> I took her for a goodly fruit,
> Just ripening on the branch, I said;
> Recked not the nut a squirrel'd bored,
> That she wore earrings not a maid.[6]

Throughout Malay oral poetry, and above all in the *pantun*s, we are given vivid images of the world of nature through which human experiences and emotions are perceived and compared – the flight of the pigeon; butterflies fluttering; a creeper twining around a cavern mouth; the wind at sea; the bitterns wheeling in flight against the sky; or raindrops gleaming in the sun.

The most famous Malay form is the *pantun*, the brief quatrain so often devoted to the theme of love. Its apparent simplicity in fact involves a four-line verse, in which the first line rhymes with the third, the second with the fourth. In literal terms, the first two lines seem to have little connection in sense with the last two and the whole quatrain to fall into two separate couplets. But there is also a close and carefully constructed connection in imagery and sound association between the two balanced halves of the quatrain. As one of the leading translators, Wilkinson, puts it: 'the first line of the quatrain does not simply "rhyme" with the third; the sound of the whole of the first line must suggest the

5. Quoted in R. Winstedt, *History of classical Malay literature*, second edition, Kuala Lumpur, 1969, p. 201.

6. R. J. Wilkinson and R. O. Winstedt, *Pantun Melayu*, Singapore, 1957, p. 15.

sound of the whole of the third. The composition of the first half of a *pantun* is therefore a harder matter than it appears at first sight to be; it calls for considerable ingenuity (if it is to be well done) and it renders translation into other tongues extremely difficult'.[7]

The sound-suggestion involved is indicated in the following rendering of a Malay *pantun*:

> The *fate* of a *dove* is to *fly*,
> It *flies* to its *nest* on the *knoll*;
> The *gate* of true *love* is the *eye*,
> The *prize* of its *quest* is the *soul*.

As Wilkinson explains this, in the first two lines 'the flight of the dove is intended to typify the passage of something rhyming with "dove" to something suggested by "knoll" . . . to the trained ear of the *pantun*-lover, the words "dove" and "knoll" would almost at once suggest "love" and "soul". . . . The theory of this form of composition is that the first pair of lines should represent a poetic thought with its beauty veiled, while the second pair should give the same thought in all its unveiled beauty. The gradual self-revelation of the poet's idea, as its true significance grows upon the mind, is one of the great charms that the *pantun* possesses in the eyes of its votaries.'[8]

This sound-suggestion is taken yet farther by the meta-phorical link that is often found between first and second half, a link that is sometimes hard to convey in a foreign language. Some are relatively straightforward, like the parallel between a fort consumed by fire and a girl by desire.

> Ah! hot I see a fortress burning –
> I'd hint not say your heart's afire:
> 'Tis not that I'd suppress your yearning,
> Forbid you, lady, wed your squire.[9]

Others depend on allusions to particular places or events, or to the Malay imagery of flowers or birds. When this is added to the sound linkages between the two halves of the *pantun*,

7. Wilkinson, *Malay literature*, p. 50.
8. ibid., pp. 50–51.
9. Wilkinson and Winstedt, *Pantun Melayu*, p. 9.

the result seems to involve a kind of inevitability of phrasing which is one of the main appeals of the *pantun*.

Another characteristic of the *pantun* is its extreme brevity. The sense is compressed, and this presents difficulties to the English reader: he is forced to stop and puzzle out what is implied. So it is worth remembering that the *pantun*s are not intended to be read at all. They are sung slowly, with a long refrain after each line, and so gain in attraction by occupying the mind during the chorus, whereas too obvious and transparent a meaning would seem merely trite.

The form of the *pantun* obviously presents many problems to the translator. Ideally he has to convey the challenge to the audience's wits, the mixed concealment and revelation of the singer's thought at the start, and its final unveiling. But even though all the facets which so attract Malay audiences cannot be reproduced in English, the fascination and ingenuity of this form of verse seems to have exerted a strong appeal to translators and to have resulted in many renderings which, even in English, can charm by their combined wit, compressed meaning, and vivid imagery, an example of poetry at once 'simple, sensuous, and passionate'.

Parting

High towers the grass where once we'd meet and wander
      'Twixt yonder fields of golden grain;
Ah! years may pass, and moons may fleet how many,
      Ere we fond lovers meet again.

In the heart of the hills . . .

In the heart of the hills the rain unabated,
      Deeper the floods refilled by the rain:
And my heart that is filled with pain unallayed yet,
      Passion comes flooding and thrilling again.

Jealousy

A cigarette my girl is smoking,
      Flower-like its rings yet linger.
Ah! mignonette, forgive my joking,
      Whose ring is that upon your finger?

Unique among girls

A set of *pantun*s

Butterflies flutter and flit o'er the bay,
      Flit and alight on rocks by the sea.
Long, long, yes and today,
      Fluttering too is the heart of me.

Flit and alight on rocks by the sea,
      To Bandan the vultures fly.
Long, long, yes and today,
      On many a lass have I cast an eye.

To Bandan the vultures fly,
    In Patani their feathers fall.
On many a lass have I cast an eye,
    Never like this a lass of them all.

Entwined

Ah blessed plant! ah lucky creeper!
    Whose tendrils wind round cavern worn.
Muhammad loved but God Almighty;
    My mistress, mind you, was not born.

Red ants

Red ants in a bamboo – the passion
    That tortures my frame is like you;
But like flask of rose-water in fashion
    Is the cure my dear flame can bestow.

May I be beautiful

The light of four Suns, five Moons,
And the seven Stars be visible in my eye.
The brightness of a shooting star be upon my chin,
And that of the full moon be upon my brows.
May my lips be like unto a string of ants,
My teeth like to a herd of elephants,
My tongue like a breaking wave,
My voice like the voice of the Prophet David,
My countenance like the countenance of the Prophet Joseph,
My brightness like the brightness of the Prophet Muhammad,
By virtue of my using this charm that was coeval with my birth,
And by grace of 'There is no god but God and Muhammad is
    His Prophet'.

Music

Voices lifted high in singing,
Till the apes fell from the branches;
The flowing water stopped to listen,
The flying bird turned back to hear.

I, lord of all mortals!

Incantation for acquiring a dominant personality.

I sit beneath the throne of Allah!
Muhammad my shelter is beside me,
Jibra'il on my right, Mika'il on my left,
All the company of angels behind me
Vicegerent of Allah . . .
Only if Allah suffer harm,
Can I suffer harm,
Only if His Prophet suffer harm,
Can I suffer harm.
A hooded snake is my loin-cloth,
A musty elephant my steed,
My ear-posy the lightning,
My shadow that of a fierce tiger.
By virtue of this spell of Awang the Pre-eminent,
In seated assembly pre-eminent I,
Erect or walking or talking pre-eminent I,
I lord of all mortals,
Precious stone of the Prophet
Pearl of God.

Love charm

In the name of Allah, the Merciful, the Compassionate!
Burn, burn, sand and earth!
I burn the heart of my beloved
And my fire is the arrow of Arjuna.
If I burnt a mountain, it would fall;
If I burnt rock, it would be riven.
I am burning the heart of my beloved,
So that she is broken and hot with love
That giveth her no rest night or day,
Burning ever as this sand burns.
Let her cease to love parents and friends!
If she sleeps, awaken her!
If she awakes, cause her to rise and come,
Yielding herself unto me,
Devoid of shame and discretion!
By virtue of the poison of Arjuna's arrow,
By virtue of the invocation 'There is no God bu.
     Allah and Muhammad is His Prophet'.

Of Iron am I

Boastful invocation for immunity in battle.

In the name of God, the merciful, the compassionate!
May this nerve of stone pierce stone,
Pierce stone and split stone,
Pierce planks and go right through them,
Pierce water and dry it up,
Pierce the earth and make a hole in it,
Pierce the grass and wither it,
Pierce mountains and cause them to fall,
Pierce the heavens that they may fall . . .

Of Iron am I, and of Copper is my frame,
And my name is 'Tiger of God'.

Invitation to a spirit

The spirit is called on to descend and possess his worshipper.

Peace be unto you, Penglima Lenggang Laut!
Of no ordinary beauty
Is the Vessel of Penglima Lenggang Laut!
The Vessel that is called 'The Yellow Spirit-boat',
The Vessel that is overlaid with vermilion and ivory,
The Vessel that is gilded all over;
Whose Mast is named 'Prince Mendela',
Whose Shrouds are named 'The Shrouds that are silvered',
Whose Oars are named 'The Feet of the Centipede'
(And whose Oarsmen are twice seven in number).
Whose Side is named 'Civet-cat Fencing',
Whose Rudder is named 'The Pendulous Bees'-nest',
Whose Galleries are named 'Struggling Pythons',
Whose Pennon flaps against the deckhouse,
Whose Streamers sport in the wind,
And whose Standard waves so bravely.
Come hither, good sir; come hither, my master,
It is just the right moment to veer your vessel.
Master of the Anchor, heave up the anchor;
Master of the Foretop, spread the sails;
Master of the Helm, turn the helm;
Oarsmen, bend your oars;
Whither is our vessel yawing to?
The vessel whose starting-place is the Navel of the Seas,
And that yaws towards the Sea where the 'Pauh Janggi' grows,
Sporting among the surge and breakers,
Sporting among the surge and following the wave-ridges.
It were well to hasten, O Penglima Lenggang Laut,
Be not careless or slothful,
Linger not by inlet or river-reach,
Dally not with mistress or courtesan,
But descend and enter into your embodiment.

Tin-ore

One of the many invocations connected with mining.

Peace be with you, O Tin-Ore,
At the first it was dew that turned into water,
And water that turned into foam,
And foam that turned into rock,
And rock that turned into tin-ore;
Do you, O Tin-Ore, lying in a matrix of solid rock,
Come forth from this matrix of solid rock;
If you do not come forth
You shall be a rebel in the sight of God.
Ho, Tin-Ore, Sir 'Floating Islet',
'Flotsam-at-sea', and 'Flotsam-on-land',
Do you float up to the surface of this my tank,
Or you shall be a rebel to God.

Sri Rama's raiment

Trousers first of ancient fabric;
Not a gore to gall their wearer,
Moving each before his limbs move;
Round the waist a hundred spangles.
Round the feet a thousand spangles,
All about the body spangles,
Larger spangles down the seams:
Such the raiment of Sri Rama.
Round his waist he wrapped a waist-band,
Broad and long the flowered linen,
With the fringe some thirty cubits:
Thrice a day it changed its colour:
In the morning dew-like tissue,
Noon-day saw it turn to purple
And at eve 'twas shining yellow:
Such the raiment of Sri Rama.
Velvet coat of glowing crimson,

Thrice nay seven times the dyer
Might erase its splendid colour
Then a stranger touch it; sailed he
For three years, 't would stain his fingers:
Such the raiment of Sri Rama.
Seven-waved the *kris* he carried.
Blade and cross-piece one unjointed;
Into haft the cross-piece fitted
Screwed without the help of craftsman;
Magic grooves at base of blade
Twin in length, of deadly import;
'Mid the blade was damask fateful
Setting foes' allotted span;
And at point the sacred letters,
Symbol of the name of Allah,
Alif Lam that greet the dying:
Next the damask silver veining.
Of no common steel 't was fashioned,
Forged of fragments of the metal
Used for bolt of God's *Kaabah*;
Work of Adam, God's own prophet;
In his hand did Adam smelt it,
With his finger tip he shaped it,
Burnished it with scented water
In a furnace brought from China.
Came its deadliness from heaven;
Would you clean the blade with acid
At the river's upper reaches,
Dead the fish at mouth of river:
Such the raiment of Sri Rama.
Round his brow he wrapped a kerchief
Blazoned with the creed of Islam;
Space in centre left unpatterned,
Craftsman's purpose unaccomplished,
Left one corner uncompleted;
Were it finished world would end:
For it was no common weaving;
Work from girlhood of his mother,
Full of love-charms and enchantments:

PHYSICS-F4

(BLOCK CAPITALS ONLY)

AUTHOR (surname first)

Order No.	A/54189

TITLE   THE PENGUIN BOOK OF ORAL

POETRY

		Date Ordered
PUBLISHER ALLEN LANE	Supplier	16.08.10

	No of copies 1	Supplier
	Date of Publication 1978	CARDT

Recommended by

	Dept	Details found / ~~found~~
Reserve for		Aleph ✓ A8680005

Price UP TO £15-   ISBN

	Sub-library	Loan	Fund				
HBK							
PBK	07,	3 9 1 0	3 0 5				
	DLRC	Loan 09	Fund CONTINUOUS				
/	**DLRC**	Loan	Fund				
	DLRC	Loan	Fund				

System No											Record bought	Y	N
	0	0	0	1	5	9	5	8	3				☒

USE REVERSE FOR NOTES

Charm to win each heart at outset;
Charm to drive a village crazy;
Charm of Solomon the Prophet
Bringing sundered hearts together;
Charm of unison for lovers,
As when salt is mixed with acid
Each more pungent for the mixing;
Charms make drunk the heart with longing;
Charm the white crow gave his name to
(This so lucky, none that have it
Need fear violence in dying);
Charm that opens every barrier
E'en as Jonah oped the whale's mouth;
All were woven in the pattern:
Such the raiment of Sri Rama.

Dawn

Long had passed the hour of midnight,
Lingered yet the coming daylight;
Twice ere now had wakening infants
Risen and sunk again in slumber;
Wrapped in sleep were all the elders;
Far away were pheasants calling;
In the woods the shrill cicada
Chirped, and dew came dropping earthwards;
Now lowed oxen in the meadows;
Moaned the buffaloes imprisoned;
Cocks with voice and wings responded,
And with feebler note the *murai*.
Soon the first pale streak of morning
Rose, and upwards soared the night birds;
Pigeons cooed beneath the roof-tree;
Fitful came the quail's low murmur;
On the hearth lay last night's embers,
Foot-long brands burned down to inches:
Heralds all of day's approaching.

Storm at sea

From the *Hikayat Awang Sulong*.

Wind searching as a sieve of brass,
Laying all things flat before it,
Driving clouds in pointed wisps,
Like the trump on the day of judgement;
Wind that's palpable in form,
Tearing up the shrub in court-yard,
From muddy soil the plants up-rooting,
Tumbling buffalo in meadow,
Toppling coconut in garden;
Wind that strips the coral reef-banks,
Till they show like slabs of metal;
Tossing mullet on the deck-house,
Bringing shark to door of cabin.

Wind

Wind would tear a dead man's shroud,
Wind as sharp as edge of spade,
Wind as keen as tip of axe,
Wind that swoops like bearded shot,
Wind umbrella-like in form,
Wind that fills the sea with bones,
Wind that levels all before it.

Om

The mystic Om symbolizes the Hindu triad Visnu, Siva, and Brahma.

Om! Virgin goddess Mahadevi! Om!
Cub am I of mighty tiger!
'Ali's line through me descends!

My voice is the rumble of thunder,
Whose bolts strike a path for my seeing!
Forked lightning's the flash of my weapons!
I move not till earth rocks!
I quake not till earth quakes,
Firm set as earth's axis.

Invocation before the rice harvest

Soul of my child, Princess Splendid!
I sent you to your mother for six months, to receive you growing
    tall in the seventh month.
The time is fulfilled, and I receive you.
I told you to sail to the sea that is black, the sea that is green,
    the sea that is blue, and the sea that is purple,
To the land of Rome, to India, China, and Siam.
Now I would welcome you up into a palace hall,
To a broidered mat and carpet.
I would summon nurses and followers,
Subjects and soldiers and court dignitaries for your service;
I would assemble horses and elephants, ducks and geese, buffa-
    loes and goats and sheep with all their din.
Come, for all is ready!
I would call you hither,
Soul of my child, Princess Splendid!
Come! my crown and my garland! flower of my delight!
I welcome you up to a palace-hall,
To a broidered mat and carpet.
Soul of my child, Princess Splendid!
Come! I would welcome you!
Forget your mother and wet-nurse.
White and black and green and blue and purple! get ye aside!
Brightness of genie and devil begone!
The real brightness is the brightness of my child.

Take up the pen . . .

Take up the pen and write a text,
    On solid rock and plainly done.
From this world right unto the next,
    Our bodies twain shall be as one.

Parting at dawn: three *pantun*s

My ketch must lead into the fray;
    My schooner head the fight.
Prepare me betel! I'll away!
    The dawn-star heralds light.
       *

From up the river orange-wood
    Was fetched to rim this tray.
My nut-brown love, prepare me food;
    Arise! I cannot stay.
       *

Crushed on yon reed a fledgeling dies,
    Eating its blossom's heart.
Loosen our tangled locks and rise!
    'Tis day and we must part.

Kisses

See! yonder hill the bitterns seek;
    Their eggs in thorny shrub they'll lay.
Come! let me kiss. I'll bite your cheek;
    And feel no hunger all the way.
       *

Across the sky the bitterns go,
    Then straight away they wheel in flight.
One kiss defrays a debt you owe;
    Another give me for that bite.

The disdainful mistress

The tiny ant at night you would be seeking,
From out your hand, the torch has fallen clean,
To bed and pulling blanket round your shoulders,
You comprehend your loneliness, I ween.

You drop a pearl . . .

You drop a pearl, 'twill keep its hue
Above the sward and gleam the same
You drop a girl. For fleet as dew
Love melts before a newer flame.

Invitation

Let's paddle, dear, by yonder fort,
Pick mussels off the wall.
May we not err of layman sort,
When priests and parsons fall?

And tomorrow wend our ways

If there's no wick within the lamp,
To light it toil is thrown away;
And what reck I of loving looks,
Except as fuel for love's play.
*

From cotton coarse our thread we fashion,
From the thread our fabric's wove.
No remorse! When sped our passion,
I'm another, not your love.
*

For tonight we cook us millet,
    And tomorrow 't may be maize.
For tonight together billet,
    And tomorrow wend our ways.

Or ever God created Adam

All night from the roof of the chieftain
    The owlets cry tuwhit! tuwhoo!
Or ever God created Adam
    We were plighted, I and you!

... Till the sea runs dry

The fruit that was atop the shelf
    A youngster picked and ran away;
Never will we break our troth
    Till the sea run dry in Malacca Bay.

Regret

On the isle of Penang there is 'stablished a city,
    'Tis a stranger that keepeth her wall;
Of the days that are dead thou shalt think not, lest pity
    Shall bow low thine head while the salt tears fall.

A little cheat!

No bird, no fabled fowl it is,
    But just an errant leaf of beet.
No true Malayan maid she is,
    But just an arrant little cheat.

The lost

High-placed above me the branches quiver,
    Tall beyond vision the tree-top is tost.
The face of my love, I seek it for ever,
    Like pigeon in quest of a mate that is lost.

Ave atque vale

Lover of mine, if upland you journey,
    The frangipani, oh hand me a flower.
Lover of mine, dead ere my day's done,
    Await me in heaven, ah stand at the door.

White as paper a-sail in the air . . .

White as paper a-sail in the air
    Are the kites of the boys on the quay;
And I feel when in love with my fair,
    Like a ship that is breasting the sea.

Breakers over the sea

Big breakers roll over the sea,
    Far sprayed by this wind from the west.
A riddle come answer for me!
    What, I pray, is this love in the breast?

The meaning of love

My homestead's with lightning aflame;
    Over yours there is thunder a-roll.
Seven heavens in one mortal frame,
    That's the meaning of love in the soul.

Two young maids ...

Two young maids of beauty fair
    In gold so fine and silk so rare;
They sit yet guileless, unaware
    When fruit is ripe the civet's there.

The loves of the birds

Birds are often used symbolically in *pantun*s: the mynah high-placed, the parakeet lowly, the peacock a fine lady, and so on.

Broken the pot, there's still the jar,
    Where folk can come and wash their feet.
And when the mynah's flown afar,
    For comfort there's the parakeet.
    *
With silver needle, golden thread,
    A wench sits sewing on a stool.
A peacock would a lory wed,
    'Tis clear the peacock is a fool.

Taunt

A Malacca girl is taunting a Straits 'bittern' – a Chinese
convert to Islam.

There is a young Muslim Chinese,
    Whose neck is as long as a chimney;
If he prays to his joss, why quickly of course
    He can move a big ship – or p'raps win me.

The opium den

As red as a starling's his peepers,
    And he hails from the isle of Ceylon.
On their beds round a lamp lounge the sleepers
    And pipes are the flutes that they play on.

A bully

With his tusk-like fierce moustaches and double-pointed beard,
He struts about the village, a warrior to be feared;
But when his country calls him to earn his meed of fame,
He finds that private business asserts a prior claim.

Sanctimony

He wears a beard to let us see that he is pure within,
His very walk suggests he feels the sinfulness of sin,
To true teetotal principles his soul is quite awake
But his poor forgetful body swallows spirits by mistake.

A battle of similes

A contrast is made and reiterated through a whole series of similes between the 'worthless' poet and the glittering far-off beloved.

In sunlight raindrops look like dew,
    To one afield his rice to dry.
Like rings of glittering fire-flies you,
    Or sun at daybreak in the sky.
        *

Drop after drop down pours the rain;
    A boatman crouches 'neath his thatch.
I'm like a cricket on a plain,
    That grovels in some dusty patch.
        *

To pick yon fruit the Chinese try;
    One fruit has fallen on the beach.
You're like an insect in the sky,
    Which from the earth one cannot reach.
        *

Up from the bay to pier I must,
    To sport beneath the shady trees.
I'm no more than a grain of dust,
    That's shaken off by passing breeze.
        *

I know a man can make a blade,
    Fit for a prince of S'tul to own.
I'm grainless husk of worthless grade,
    That floats when on the water thrown.
        *

There is a jinn with features blue,
    That lights on earth mankind to fret.
Like to a piece of incense you,
    That being burnt is sweeter yet.
        *

'In Allah's name' – it doth behove,
    A poet so his verse to start.
I'm like a rag that's coarsely wove,
    And gets no buyers in the mart.

*

If up the hill your feet have got,
     Then by yon tree I beg you stay.
As silk that with gold thread is shot,
     You glitter like the light of day.
    *

To net a fish Che' Akub's tried;
     A sorry sort his cast-net catches.
I'm cloth with indigo that's dyed,
     And age reveals the ugly patches.
    *

Cloth dark from such a dye will grow,
     The wear for those in huts who dwell.
But like a flowered cloth you show,
     That when 'tis washed will sweeter smell.

'O that my love were in my arms'

If of a beetle you'd make game,
     Then bind one in a loop of thread.
If you would keep a lover tame,
     Then wind your arms about his head.
    *

A woodpecker her eggs has laid;
     In yonder cavern is her nest.
I'm very weary. Come, dear maid!
     Let us upon one pillow rest.
    *

Their eggs where do the plovers keep?
     Above yon fall in chasm nests.
Where would your lover go to sleep?
     Upon your bosom 'tween your breasts.

Open the door

A tree I know where a love-bird's lighted,
    A woodpecker straight to the spot will fly.
Ah me, my love your word it is plighted,
    So ope me the door when I tap by and by.

The lover's prayer

If it's rice-grain, say it's rice-grain,
    Sifting straw is little gain.
If you love me, say you love me,
    Do not let me wait in vain.

Sick unto death of love

Doves flit by in their flocks of thousands,
    Room for one in my court to land.
I long to die at the beck of her finger,
    Find my tomb in the palm of her hand.

Remember thou me

Plashes the tree-trunk lost in the river,
    Dies the bird on her way over sea.
When water is splashing thy corse for sepulture,
    E'en on death's journey remember thou me.

Song of a sick child

The ends of the Hibiscus burgeon,
Thicker grow the fragrant blossoms!
Give no more thought to me, granny.
Only the calyx of the fruit is left,
Only the print of my hands, granny,
Only the print of my feet,
It is only left me to sing, granny.
My heart longs for the hills, granny.
Hear the song I sing in the hut.
I will arise and go, granny. Wrap me my rice.
I will go to the forest and snare birds.
But see! My snares catch no birds, granny.
Your child is not strong enough to climb, granny,
And the basket I bear, its cords are broken.

SOMALI

The Somali live in the 'Horn' of Africa over a large tract of country in the Somali peninsula. They number around three to four million, of which the largest portion now live in the Somali Republic, which became an independent sovereign state in 1960. There are also many Somali in Kenya, French Somaliland, and Ethiopia, and others are scattered as traders throughout East Africa, Aden, and the Persian gulf. Their language belongs to the Cushitic group, itself usually classified as part of the Hamito-Semitic family (which also includes Arabic). As comes out in much of their poetry, the Somali are strong supporters of Islam and value their Arabian heritage and their claimed links with the lineage of the Prophet himself.

In Somali culture, interest in poetry is universal and the recitation and discussion of poetry is part of everyday life. Poets sing far into the night around the campfires in desert oases or gatherings under a shady tree, while in the town people gather in tea shops for poetry and song. Among the Somali, poetry is seen as having many effective *uses*, beyond just providing or commemorating private experiences. It is common for it to be used as a powerful weapon to win friends, revile enemies, praise traditional chiefs or modern political leaders, or broadcast public events. A number of these uses are illustrated in the selection here, ranging from the political exhortations of the Dervish leader (the 'Mad Mullah') early in the century or the recent propaganda poetry over Mogadishu radio, to complaints by an old man about excessive demands for bridewealth or a warning to a dictatorial sultan.

Poetic skill is particularly developed among the northern Somali, who are mainly pastoral nomads, roaming the semi-desert tracts of the north with their camels in search of pasture and water. Many of the poems in this section originate from this arid and inhospitable region where the nomads are involved in a continuous struggle for survival, a struggle which forms a backcloth to their many poems about love or death, clan feuds, the power of Allah, and the beauty as well as the harshness of nature. Poetry thus forms a deeply meaningful part of the life of this fiercely independent and egalitarian nomadic people. But at the same time it is not just a characteristic of some rural 'traditional' way of life, for poetry is also a living and effective force in the context of modern Somali life. Political and propaganda poetry flourishes, new songs and topical poems are continually being composed (often but not invariably in the traditional genres) and oral verse plays an essential role in the new urban theatre. Oral poetry is given an even wider circulation by travelling nomads meeting at wells or trading posts or by the drivers of trading lorries, as well as through broadcasts of oral verse – for a transistor radio is now a common part of the desert nomad's equipment.

There is no specialist category of professional poets among the Somali, but some individuals are recognized as more gifted than others, and well-known poets like Mahammed Abdille Hassan, Faarah Nuur, or Salaan Arrabey can gain nationwide prestige. The admirers of a leading poet learn his poems by heart and recite them from memory wherever they go. Because of the competition for the ear of the public and the high degree of critical appreciation by Somali audiences, most Somali poets do not try to improvise but prepare their poems beforehand over many hours or even days.

Somali poetry is a highly complex and developed art in that there are a large number of different genres recognized, all demanding a degree of skill and some involving complex technical exertions, particularly the extremely strict rules of alliteration which forms one of the most characteristic features of Somali poetry. The same alliteration must be maintained throughout a whole poem (which sometimes means a hundred lines or more): in each half line, at least one word has to begin with the chosen sound.

The Somali themselves classify their poems into various distinct genres according to both the rhythmic verbal pattern and the type of tune to which it is sung or chanted. These include various 'classical' types normally chanted solo without accompaniment. The *gabay*, of which 'Battle pledge' is an example, is the typical classical form for serious and important matters; it is chanted in a slow and majestic manner and often reaches 100 lines or more. Light poetry, by contrast, is usually sung to lively tunes and accompanied by clapping, stamping, drumming, or chorus. There is also the *balwo* (or *belwo*), a short poem, often only two lines long and almost always on the theme of love. This particular form was an innovation by a lorry driver, Abdi Deeqsi, in 1954: when his lorry broke down in a deserted place, he composed the first *balwo* song. The form is now widely popular, particularly with the young, and is often recited as a form of light entertainment both before large audiences who clap in rhythm and join in the chorus, and over the radio. A number of these short *balwo* songs are included here under the heading 'Modern love poems'. They often involve highly condensed imagery. Take the *balwo*

O Distant Lightning! Have you deceived me?

Lightning for the Somali is a powerful image of hope, for it is the herald of rain – a constant inspiration for poets of the parched north of Somalia where life and freshness and the beauty of nature depend so much on rain; but distant lightning sometimes disappoints and moves away without bringing the longed for rain: rain – likened in the evocative imagery of this one-line poem in miniature to the bitter experience of disappointment in love. Later the *balwo* developed into the longer *heello*, a sequence of short poems or stanzas linked together. In addition to these genres, there are a number of others, like the topical and political *hees*, the *daanto* (often used for marching but also adapted for the 'Prayer for rain'), as well as various dance and work poems.

Traditionally Somali material possessions are meagre and the visual and plastic arts little developed. In any case the amount of physical equipment a basically nomadic group can amass is clearly limited. But, as compensation perhaps, the Somali have developed the art of poetry to a high degree and it is not inaccurate to describe them in the words of more than one observer as 'a nation of poets'.

Battle pledge

A war chant in the classical *gabay* form. The poet's son has been killed by members of a different clan who have also refused his demand for double the usual compensation (100 camels). This is the poet's war pledge, addressed in the poem to his horse Aynabo, though really directed towards his enemy. As with many Somali poems there is alliteration throughout, partially represented by the alliteration in 'f' in the English translation.

If you, O Aynabo, my fleet and fiery horse,
Do not grow battle-worn, and slow of foot, and weak;
And if your shining flanks and finely arching neck
Do not grow gaunt and thin as the branch on the dry grey thorn;
And if your frenzied hooves do not flail through the dead,
The bodies piled as high as ever grew the grass;
And if a man among us can draw the name of peace
Forth from the deepest well where I have flung it down;
And if the strong-limbed spearmen of all the Bahawadleh[1]
Do not now fight in fury, and fight unto the death;
And if our enemy's food is not scant meat alone,
With milk gone from the land, and their camels seized as loot,[2]
And if my dead son, Ali, is not greater in their eyes
Than his craven murderers thought when they stabbed away his
      life;
And if the sky in future does not its colour change,
Filled with the dust of death, reflecting the flare of the fray;
And if all that I swear does not, as I swear it, come to pass –
Then the warrior son of my father has become a witless fool.

1. The poet's group.   2. Depriving the enemy of camels, and hence of camel milk, would be a serious blow, since meat and milk are the two main foods of the interior; people sometimes live for months on milk alone.

A denunciation

Mahammed Abdille Hassan (1864–1920)

Extract from a poem by the so-called 'Mad Mullah', leader of the Dervishes in the revolts against the British at the beginning of this century. He is widely regarded as one of the greatest Somali poets and used his poetry, among other purposes, as a powerful propaganda weapon against his enemies. Here he denounces those who have gone over to the enemy.

Listen to the call of the muezzin – it calls people to prayer;
Consider God, who created people, and the people who reject
        His commands
The prophets, and those who do not follow the saints
Those who took long, heavy spears against the elders of the Order
Those who have become children of the Christians and look on
        Europeans as their relatives
Those who of their own free will performed menial tasks for the
        infidels
Those who, though not forced to do it, followed them and
        fawned on them
Those for whom Menelik is like a father who deals with their
        affairs
Those for whom Abyssinians have become God, and who babble
        prayers to them
Those who have hunted me out of the land of my God like the
        wild game
Those who have driven me into the dusty sands of the desert . . .

To a friend going on a journey

Mahammed Abdille Hassan

Leave-taking is one of the conventional topics for a Somali poem, in which advice is given and farewells said.

Now you depart, and though your way may lead
Through airless forests thick with *hhagar* trees,
Places steeped in heat, stifling and dry,

Where breath comes hard, and no fresh breeze can reach –
Yet may God place a shield of coolest air
Between your body and the assailant sun.

And in a random scorching flame of wind
That parches the painful throat, and sears the flesh,
May God, in His compassion, let you find
The great-boughed tree that will protect and shade.

On every side of you, I now would place
Prayers from the Holy Koran, to bless your path,
That ills may not descend, nor evils harm,
And you may travel in the peace of faith.

To all the blessings I bestow on you,
Friend, yourself now say a last Amen.

Our country is divided

Faarah Nuur (died about 1930)

The British, the Ethiopians, and the Italians are squabbling,
The country is snatched and divided by whosoever is stronger,
The country is sold piece by piece without our knowledge,
And for me, all this is the teeth of the last days of the world.

The limits of submission

Faarah Nuur

The poet's clan had for long lived in submission to a stronger
group, but were driven in the end to rebel.

Over and over again to people
I show abundant kindness.

If they are not satisfied
I spread out bedding for them
And invite them to sleep.

If they are still not satisfied,
The milk of the camel whose name is Suub
I milk three times for them,
And tell them to drink it up.

If they are still not satisfied,
The homestead's ram,
And the fat he-goat I kill for them.

If they are still not satisfied,
The plate from Aden
I fill with *ghee* for them.

If they are still not satisfied,
A beautiful girl
And her bridal house I offer them.

If they are still not satisfied,
I select livestock also
And add them to the tribute.

If they are still not satisfied,
'O brother-in-law, O Sultan, O King!'
These salutations I lavish upon them.

If they are still not satisfied,
At the time of early morning prayers I prepare
The dark grey horse with black tendons,
And with the words 'Praise to the Prophet' I take
The iron-shafted spear,
And drive it through their ribs
So that their lungs spew out;
Then they are satisfied!

Poet's lament on the death of his wife

Raage Ugaas

Like the *yu'ub* wood bell tied to gelded camels that are running
    away,
Or like camels which are being separated from their young,

Or like people journeying while moving camp,
Or like a well which has broken its sides or a river which has
    overflowed its banks,
Or like an old woman whose only son was killed,
Or like the poor, dividing the scraps for their frugal meal,
Or like the bees entering their hive, or food crackling in the
    frying,
Yesterday my lamentations drove sleep from all the camps.
Have I been left bereft in my house and shelter?
Has the envy of others been miraculously fulfilled?
Have I been deprived of the fried meat and reserves for lean
    times which were so plentiful for me?
Have I today been taken from the chessboard [of life]?
Have I been borne on a saddle to a distant and desolate place?
Have I broken my shin, a bone which cannot be mended?

An elder's reproof to his wife

Abdillaahi Muuse

A stream flowing steadily over a stone does not wet its core,
But on fertile soil water brings forth fresh grass,
Termite mounds when spoken to give no response,
A fool's mind is like a house barred,
When one tells people something, they profit by it,
But you, may God change you, are made worse by advice.
There is some remedy for the fools who listen to you,
But there is no medicine for a bad wife who refuses good advice;
And I was born with nobility of mind and am not readily dis-
    turbed by trifles.
My dissatisfaction goes back even to the times that I visited you
    after our engagement.
Sometimes a fully laden vessel founders with great loss of
    property,
And certainly I received no return at all for the rifles and camels
    I gave [as bridewealth],

Again and again you wearied me, when the word 'obey' brought
     no response.
Neglect, beating, or divorce
On one of these three I am resolved: make your choice!

To a dictatorial sultan

Extract from a poem addressed to a sultan trying to ignore
his clan assembly. The sultan was subsequently deposed.

The vicissitudes of the world, O Olaad, are like the clouds of the
     seasons
Autumn weather and spring weather come after each other in
     turn
Into an encampment abandoned by one family, another family
     moves
If a man is killed, one of his relatives will marry his widow
Last night you were hungry and alone, but tonight people will
     feast you as a guest
When fortune places a man even on the mere hem of her robe,
     he quickly becomes proud and overbearing
A small milking vessel, when filled to the brim, soon overflows . .

To a faithless friend

Salaan Arrabey

Salaan Arrabey, who died in the early 1940s, was one of the
most famous and prolific of Somali poets. He is said to have been able to
turn out poems 'like the rain'. This is an extract from a poem in the *gabay*
form.

A woman in childbirth, fainting with cruel pain,
May swear this suffering never to forget,
But when her menstrual time has come again,
Birth's agony has faded from her mind.

There was a man who once knew great distress,
And lost his wealth, his power, his tribe's respect.
But now, restored to eminence, he forgets
His former anguish, and my assistance then.
Ah, friend, your memory is short as any woman's!

Lament for a dead lover

Siraad Haad

You were the fence standing between our land and the
        descendants of Ali,
(Now in your departure) you are the sky which gives no rain
        while mist shrouds the world,
The moon that shines no more,
The risen sun extinguished,
The dates on their way from Basra cut off by the seas.

A woman sings of her love

Oh, you are a kilt which a young dandy set out to choose,
Oh, you are like a costly ring for which thousands were paid,
Will I ever find your like – you who have been shown to me
        only once?
An umbrella comes apart; you are [as strong as] looped iron;
Oh, you [who are as] the gold of Nairobi, finely moulded,
You are the risen sun, and the early rays of dawn.
Will I ever find your like, you who have been shown to me only
        once?

Fortitude

Like a she-camel with a large bell
Come from the plateau and upper Haud,
My heat is great.

Birds perched together on the same tree
Call each their own cries,
Each country has its own ways,
Indeed people do not understand each other's talk.

One of my she-camels falls on the road
And I protect its meat,
At night I cannot sleep,
And in the daytime I can find no shade.

I have broken my nose on a stick,
I have broken my right hip,
I have something in my eye,
And yet I go on.

The best dance

The best dance is the dance of the eastern clans,
The best people are ourselves,
Of this I have always been sure.
The best wealth is camels,
The *duur* grass is the best fresh grazing,
The *dareemo* grass is the best hay,
Of this I have always been sure.

As camels who have become thirsty . . .
the poet's lament

Ilmi Bowndheri

Ilmi Bowndheri was an oral poet who is said to have died for love shortly before the Second World War. His tragic love is famous among all the Somali – even in Somali cafés in Aden, London, or Cardiff. In this extract he has discovered that his love Hodan has already been married to another man, and is explaining to his friends the bitterness of his grief and his deep love for Hodan. His verse is composed in the classical alliterative style but was innovatory in that it was applied to what had previously seldom made up the sole theme of a classical poem: love.

As camels who have become thirsty after they have been grazing
     in the Haud for a long time
And who are stopped in front of the well,[3] while a youth sings
     to them
And while the word '*hoobay*'[4] is chanted and voices inter-
     changed,
So I grow wild with impatience when you say 'Hodan'.
What seems to you so simple, to me brings grief and woe.
Until people tread earth into her grave, I shall not give her up.
Rapt in a deceitful trance I thought I was sleeping with her
But it was only that a jinn counterfeited the image of her sister.
I aimed to snatch her by her hand – the place beside me was
     empty.
When I discovered that I was striving but that no one was there
I woke up abruptly, having tossed from side to side.
I rumpled my bed, like a prowling lion
I attacked and pounded the bedclothes as if it were they who
     had caused my deprivation.
I lowered my face, like a hero against whom men have combined.
I was humbled like a boy from whom a herd of camels, which
     belonged to the clan, were looted.
I felt disgraced like a woman to whom the words 'I divorce you'
     had been spoken.
It is degrading to yearn for what you cannot have.
Alas, alas, what a disaster has come upon me!

3. Camels have to wait by the well until the herders draw the
water for them. During the wait the camel herders sing special songs
which the camels know well and associate with water, thus intensifying
their thirst and expectation still further.   4. '*Hoobay*' is a frequent
refrain in the watering songs and helps further to evoke the familiar
scene of thirsty camels at a well.

Modern love poems

The following group of love songs are of the *balwo* genre, characterized by condensed imagery and 'miniature' form. Because of this the poems present special difficulty to the translator. In the first group given here the translator, Margaret Laurence, has felt forced to lengthen the translations slightly in her attempt to convey the images involved, while the later translations, mainly by B. W. Andrzejewski, approximate more nearly to the length of the originals.

Many of these poems are typical of the modern love songs sung in the towns and broadcast over the radio. They are also widely appreciated in the interior of the country too, whether listened to over the radio or heard through the singing of lorry drivers, a group particularly attached to this form of verse.

Since, when you die, delight
By earth's silence will be stilled,
Then let not now the priest
Drive you from your song.
*

I long for you, as one
Whose dhow in summer winds
Is blown adrift and lost,
Longs for land, and finds –
Again the compass tells –
A grey and empty sea.
*

Woman, lovely as lightning at dawn,[5]
Speak to me even once.
*

Your body is to Age and Death betrothed,
And some day all its richness they will share:
Before your firm flesh goes to feed their lusts,
Do not deny my right to love you now.
*

The curving of your breasts
Like apples sweet and small,
Tolmoon, I will know again
When night turns dusk to dark.

5. Lightning at dawn heralds rain, hence suggests happiness and good fortune.

*

The merciful will not ignore
A man whose death draws near:
Before the earth receives my bones,
Show mercy unto me.
*

Your bright mouth and its loveliness,
Your fragrance, the look of you –
Ubah, flower-named, for these
My journey is forgotten.
*

Turn not away in scorn.
Some day a grave will prove
The frailty of that face,
And worms its grace enjoy.
Let me enjoy you now –
Turn not away in scorn.
*

All your young beauty is to me
Like a place where the new grass sways,
After the blessing of the rain,
When the sun unveils its light.
*

Do not the eyes draw one towards that which one
    likes
But which is near a precipice?[6]
*

Like a sailing ship pulled by a storm,
I set my compass towards a place empty of people.[7]

6. The poet fears disaster if he gives way to his impulses –
just as in the mountainous regions of Somalia deep ravines present con-
stant danger to grazing animals. The poem recalls the Somali proverb
'Camels see a delectable bush but do not see the precipice behind it'.

7. It was not uncommon for the many sailing ships along the
Somali coast to be blown off course by a storm – a much-feared experi-
ence to which the forsaken lover likens his own situation.

*

You are like a place with fresh grass after a
        downpour of rain
On which the sun now shines.

*

Don't pass me by with your firm body,
Old age and death will have it in the end!

*

If I say to myself 'Conceal your love!'
Who will conceal my tears?

*

She passed me by, muffled,
And people forbade me to give her my last words.[8]

*

One does not hurry past a dying man,
Before I enter the grave, spare a word for me.

*

A flash of lightning does not satisfy thirst,
What then is it to me if you just pass by?

*

The girl for whom I have withered like a stick,
Are you telling me to despair of ever attaining?

*

My heart is single and cannot be divided,
And it is fastened on a single hope; O you who
        might be the moon.

*

Until I die I shall not give up the love song,
O God, forgive me my shortcomings.

8. The poet, dying of unrequited love, is prevented both
from speaking to his love and even from seeing her face. She has covered
it up with a shawl, with only the eyes showing.

Prayer for rain

Sheikh Aqib Abdullahi Jama

This poem was recited during a bad drought in 1956, when
the local inhabitants requested Sheikh Aqib to lead them in prayers for
rain. The poem is in the traditional *daanto* genre, often used for marching
songs though with certain innovations in the system of alliteration used.
Each couplet opens with an invocation of God using the praise names
common in Muslim worship.

You who give sustenance to your creatures, O God,
Put water for us in the nipples of rain!

You who poured water into oceans, O God,
Make this land of ours fertile again!

Accepter of penance, who are wealthy, O God,
Gather water in rivers whose beds have run dry!

You who are steadfast and act justly, O God,
Provide us with what we want you to grant!

You who are glorious, truly bounteous, O God,
Our cries have undone us, grant a shower of rain!

You who are clement, truly worshipped, O God,
Milk water for beasts which are stricken with thirst!

Creator of nature who made all things, O God,
Transmute our ruin to blessing and good!

Eternal rewarder of merits, O God,
Let that rain come which people used to drink!

We have done much Remembrance,[9] O God who remember,
Loosen upon us rain from the clouds!

You who are merciful and compassionate, O God,
Milk rain from the sky for Muslims in need!

Giver of victuals at all times, O God,
Who can do what you want, bestow on us rain!

9. A special ceremony consisting of long invocations accom-
panied by clapping, stamping, etc.

You who are peace and a curtain, O God,
Provide us with what we want you to grant!

Recorder of merit, who requite us, O God,
Into scorched empty ponds pour us water of rain!

You who are truthful, creator, O God,
We accept in submission whatever you say!

You who mete out good and evil, O God,
In this land we are broken, milk the clouds from above!

The earth and the sky you constructed, O God,
We cannot get water, bring forth drops of rain!

The darkness of night you transfigure, O God,
And make daylight follow; milk the sky lavishly!

You who gave brightness to sunshine, O God,
And know its principles, give us brown water from rain!

You who are rich and ward off cares, O God,
Milk temperate rain! help us with rain everywhere!

You who open all and give sustenance, O God,
People have scattered; send forth healthy rain!

Almighty, perfecter of counsels, O God,
Pour for us rain which would make the land wet!

You who are bounteous, the protector, O God,
We cannot survive drought, send us rain from your store!

You who drive the air which sways the trees, O God,
It is you whom we praised, grant us the goodness of rain!

You who are worshipped and answer prayers, O God,
Make the rain spread over the whole of the land!

Bestower of victories, benefactor, O God,
Bring us faultless rain which makes us dwell where it falls!

You who are one and are trusted, O God,
Provider of all, give water to man!

You who spark off lightning from clouds you have loaded, O God,
It is you who have power over rain which satiates!

You who fill water-holes dug in wadis, O God,
Milk rain on this land, cream-giving rain!

Who used to relieve the strangest plights, O God,
It is to you that I have turned for help!

The Suez crisis

A broadcast poem.

O men, the beautiful world is going to be spoiled
The nations assembled in London have brought about this
      trouble
The West and East have approached each other ready for war . . .
See the pride of Nasser, the Chinese, the yelling Arabs,
Nehru negotiating with all ingenuity,
Whenever the sun sets, the Russians bring equipment;
Power has been launched on the sea.
See Eden, proud and strutting
And Dulles, inciting him to conquest yet unwilling to take part
      himself;
The French, driven by jealousy and zeal, yearning for the din of
      an explosion.
If the United Nations make no decisions with mighty pens
A great explosion will come from the Suez Canal.
The people who have done this do not know the value of their
      lives;
If planes drop the equipment entrusted to them,
If cannons, resounding, fire without ceasing,
If the hidden submarines come to face each other
It is certain that smoke will billow and boil there!
Certainly, of the two sides, one will subjugate the other, as with
      a burden saddle;
How horrible is the smoke and perdition which they pursue:
O God, the Powerful, save us from the roaring thunderbolts!

Women and men

Hassan Sheikh Mumin

A dialogue from the play *Shabeelnaagood*. Shallaayo, who has been betrayed by Shabeelnaagood (Leopard among women), condemns all men while Diiddane, represented as a man with the good of society at heart, defends them.

Plays are nowadays one of the most popular entertainments in the towns. They are a relatively recent innovation and are a development both from traditional oral poetry and drama introduced through foreign influence. The art involved remains an oral one in the sense that the playwright teaches the actors their roles orally and not from a script. Though the themes are often highly topical, most of the dialogue is conducted in the traditional metres of alliterative verse.

SHALLAAYO: Women have no share in the encampments of this
    world
And it is men who made these laws, to their own advantage.
By God, by God, men are our enemies, though we ourselves
    nurtured them.
We suckled them at our breasts, and they maimed us:
We do not share peace with them.

DIIDDANE: Man and woman are two creatures
Who grew from the same first fibre, and they share this life.
Listen, listen, O women! Men are the green grass, the comfort,
The very sustenance of women: man and woman are a she-
    camel and her baby
Who take their radiance from one another.

SHALLAAYO: Men are hateful, and the women who love them
Suffer endlessly at their hands, yet are held spellbound by them.
By God, by God, men are our enemies, though we ourselves
    nurtured them
We suckled them at our breasts, and they maimed us:
We do not share peace with them.

DIIDDANE: You can find rest in a man, with him you can
    breathe freely,
He will hew for you a rock to find the honey of wild bees, he
    will give you to drink from the waters of contentment.

Listen, listen, O women! Men are the green grass, the comfort,
The very sustenance of women: man and woman are a she-
    camel and her baby
Who take their radiance from one another.

SHALLAAYO: A man has no pity, and resentment is what he
    plants in us
And when we make our promises to him he turns away from us
    to follow his own destiny.
By God, by God, men are our enemies, though we ourselves
    nurtured them.
We suckled them at our breasts, and they maimed us:
We do not share peace with them.

DIIDDANE: You cast your spell over a man who has compassion,
You cleave to evil and there is no goodness in you.
Listen, listen, O women! Men are the green grass, the comfort,
The very sustenance of women: man and woman are a she-
    camel and her baby
Who take their radiance from one another.

Colonialism

Cabdullaahi Qarshe

Composed in 1967.

The colonialist governments
Of the whole of Africa –
When they coveted it –
The meeting[10] they arranged for this,
The city where they sent delegates,
In the exact section where they debated –
Look at Berlin,
All of you look!
A wall is splitting it –
Look and be entertained!

10. The Berlin Conference of 1884–5, seen as the starting
point of the scramble for Africa.

As soon as the colonialists invaded us,
They shackled our men's legs,
And loaded them like donkeys,
And whipped them,
They filled the trough with them,
And made the camps to overflow.

When the black men felt the pain and revolted:
The drums which they beat,
The bells which they rang,
The poems which stirred them,
And the songs which they sent to each other:
All this they remembered one afternoon,
And they drove most[11] from Africa.

O Nabsi,[12] you who never tarry,
And who never get exhausted,
And whom no one directs,
And whom no one instructs,
And who never know haste,
And yet who sometimes are not late;
O you who can be as slow as a tortoise,
And yet whom airplanes can never overtake;
From time immemorial
Our lands have not been our own –
O Elder,[13] how is it that you do not act?
Is our right[14] to be forfeited?

The point on which I end,
And on which I would terminate my discourse,
And what I mean by it,
I will reveal to you:
The birds which are flying
And gliding about above
Will some day tire
And descend to earth.[15]

11. Most colonialists.   12. Avenging fate.   13. i.e. Nabsi.
14. i.e. to Somali land outside Somalia.   15. Nabsi will come; the colonialists and their acts (i.e. the division of Somalia) cannot last for ever.

Independence

A song celebrating the unification of the British Somaliland Protectorate and ex-Italian Somalia to form the independent Somali Republic.

> Freedom and dignity have reached us,
> We have brought together the two lands.
> Glory to God!
> Say: 'It is God's victory,
> It is God's victory!
> We are victorious.'
> Beat the song, join the dance!
> Everyone, with all your might!
> And now let us finish, cease!
> It is God's victory!
> It is God's victory!

ZULU

The Zulu of South Africa are probably best known to most English readers as a once fierce and aggressive people, famed for their courage and military force, and, more recently, as one of the 'native Bantu peoples' of the modern state of South Africa with their 'homeland' in Natal. What are far less well known are their poetic accomplishments: their long and elaborate praise poems, gentle and wistful lyrics, or inspired hymns.

A large number of the traditional panegyric poems of the Zulu deal with war and military exploits. This is hardly surprising, for the Zulu were for many years typical of a pastoral and aristocratic people, in that cattle-raiding and armed skirmishes between competing groups were an accepted part of life, and honour was gained by military prowess. This aspect was also continued and exaggerated in poetic convention even when it was largely past as a common way of life. For Zulu history has seen a gradual transition from a warlike, aristocratic people roaming with their cattle to a settled and often urban society, deeply influenced by both Christianity and the stringent rule of the government of South Africa.

In Zulu eyes, their most glorious period was in the early nineteenth century when their great king and leader Shaka welded together a large number of warring groups under himself as king. Shaka was an outstanding military commander as well as political leader, and made a number of effective innovations like the use of full-time soldiers and the organization of separate named regiments. His troops campaigned far outside the boundaries of his kingdom and Shaka's glorious victories are eulogized in poem after poem. Even in times of more recent adversity his great achievements are not forgotten.

In Shaka's days we lived well . . .
He was the king that ruled over kings, Shaka.
He was a hero of heroes . . .

But all his victories could not prevent dissension, and Shaka was finally assassinated by his brother Dingane – another of the oft-remembered kings of the Zulu.

Throughout the nineteenth century there was increasing contact with European powers, first through friendly relations with English traders, later in conflicts with the British who defeated the Zulu in 1880 and deposed their last real king, Cetshwayo. From then on Zululand gradually came more and more under the control of European government, and missionary activities were intensified. By now the majority of the three million or so Zulu work in towns in South Africa or on white farms in the rural areas. But their glorious past is still remembered and commemorated in poetry, and they still sing of their famous ancestors of the past – Dingane (also spelt Dingana and Dingaan), Senzangkhona, Shaka, and many others – and often cast a backward look to the cattle and land that many Zulu consider wrongfully taken from them: 'We mourn for our country' ('Take off your hat . . .') and 'Though our ancestors are dead we still remember them' ('Those were the days . . .').

The Zulu recognize a number of different genres of poetry. But there is complete agreement about which is the most valued and most 'poetic'. These are the lengthy and effusive praise poems (*izibongo*) of which several extracts open the selection here. In these the verbal rather than the musical element is predominant (they are chanted rather than sung) and they can best be described as a kind of mixture of ode and epic.

The praise poems are built up on a series of praise names. All leading personalities had these praise epithets attached to them – for instance 'Sun-is-shining' or 'Fame-spread-abroad'. Often the praise names are extended to whole lines, so that Shaka can be called 'The Ever-ready-to-meet-any-challenge' or the nineteenth-century trader Henry Fynn 'Wild animal of the blue ocean', and these lines form the building blocks of the successive stanzas of the praise poem as a whole. The poem is thus a series of eulogies in which the character and achievements of the hero are gradually revealed. The narrative element is often minimal, and the stanzas and verses can follow each other in almost any order. Vilakazi, one of the leading poets of modern Zulu, comments that 'stanzas in primitive Zulu poetry are like lights shed on a sculptured work from different angles. These lights operate independently of one another, but yet bring into relief the whole picture which the artist presents in carving'.[1]

The poetic style of the panegyrics is highly metaphorical and allusive and marked by the copious use of parallelism (of various kinds), alliteration, and assonance. Figurative expression is extremely important. The hero of a poem, for instance, is often pictured as an animal – a lion, say, or a buffalo – or some natural phenomenon like wind, fire, or storm. The poems are semi-chanted in a specially stylized intonation, and their effectiveness is greatly enhanced by the emotional and fervent tone in which they are delivered and received by the audience. The reciter declaims rapidly and dramatically, in an atmosphere of growing excitement and ecstatic elation, shared by bard and audience.

The development of these elaborate praise poems is bound up with the aristocratic nature of traditional Zulu society. There was a hierarchy of rank dependent on birth, and expressed above all in the idea of kingship and chiefship. Competition for fame and praise was central to the way of life – and mattered even after death for, as the praise poet puts it,

> People will die and their praises remain,
> It is these that will be left to mourn for them in
> their deserted homes.

It was appropriate therefore that the composition and delivery of praise poetry should be a highly valued activity and that each warrior endeavoured to have his praises declaimed in public, while kings and chiefs saw to it that they had their own specialist praise poets. Though there are also some praise poems about animals and a few other subjects, human heroes remain the central and natural topic. This is a poetic genre which has by no means van-

1. B. W. Vilakazi, 'The conception and development of poetry in Zulu', *Bantu Studies*, 2, 1938, p. 112.

ished with the advent of urbanization, for even today oral composition is a living art. Young Zulu men who come into the towns for employment still produce praise poetry and intersperse long strings of their own praises between the verses of their guitar songs.

Though panegyrics are the most complex and valued of Zulu poetic forms, there are also a number of other recognized genres, many of them sung. In fact songs were traditionally part of almost any occasion of either work or play. In addition to war songs and the special marching songs belonging to each of the established regiments, there were also special family songs (sung on occasions like marriages or funerals), love lyrics, hymns, wedding songs, children's verse, work songs, and lullabies. As with the praise poems, many of these forms of oral poetry are still performed. The experiences of living in town, of feeling the bite of local laws, saying good-bye to a migrant relative, or experiencing the world-wide joys or sufferings of love – all these find expression in oral poetic forms whether within the intimate family circle, on the concert platform, or over the radio. Many of these songs are extremely topical, like those commenting on police or pass laws, faction fighting songs, or some of the music-hall songs like 'My money! Oh, my money!'

In one way all Zulu were traditionally poets and songs were composed by almost everyone. 'Children at their play,' writes Krige, 'boys herding the cattle, girls when working in the fields or at home, all invent songs. Almost every mother invents for her child a lullaby called *isiHlabelelo*, which she sings to it during its babyhood. Each individual has his *isiHlabelelo*, the song of his childhood, regarded as something essentially his own'.[2] But, in addition to this, there were also specialist poets whose role was to compose and perform on particular occasions. In each district one or two men were recognized as particularly skilled; before a special occasion like a marriage they would be called on to compose a suitable song, then to arrange rehearsals before the event and teach it to the young people who were going to attend. More important were the performers of panegyric poetry. There were specialist praise poets (*imbongi*) attached to the court of every

2. E. J. Krige, *The social system of the Zulus*, Pietermaritzburg, 1936, pp. 338–9.

leading personality, from the king and his royal relatives down to the headmen of the local kraals. It was the praise poet's duty to compose (or at least memorize) the praise poems of his patron and his ancestors, and declaim them in sonorous cadences on public occasions. This is an office that has now in effect vanished, and the specialist role of poet has by and large been replaced by amateur poets perhaps producing their own praise poems or, as with some of the composers of modern urban lyrics, organizing a dance band or singing as a part-time supplement to other employment.

One category that has barely been mentioned so far is that of the Zulu hymn. The adoption of Christianity by the Zulu has provided the opportunity for the expression of Zulu poetry in the new form of hymns inspired by Christianity. Or rather the personality of Isaiah Shembe has made this possible. Shembe was the great Zulu prophet who founded the independent African Church of Nazareth, and his life (about 1870 to 1935) spanned a crucial period of Zulu history. It is said that he was inspired to become a prophet and healer in a series of visions, and throughout his life he was deeply conscious that his hymns, like so many of his actions, were the result of divine inspiration. His hymns very strikingly demonstrate the interplay between oral and written modes, for, though they were published in book form in 1940, in practice they circulated primarily in oral form, by being sung and transmitted by largely illiterate congregations in the context of religious services. As comes out both in the hymns and in accounts by observers, Shembe was a magnetic and powerful figure, cast in the true prophet mould, who was regarded by his followers as a new Messiah (even a new Shaka) and who himself accepted this evaluation in his own compositions and in the praise poems dedicated to him. As part of his mission as leader of a new and flourishing church, he founded what his followers called the holy city, the new Jerusalem – Ekuphakameni, not far from Durban, a locality and symbol often referred to in Shembe's compositions. The hymns themselves represent a blend of the traditions of Christianity and Zulu paganism, and reflect the conventions of Zulu poetry and dance songs. Unlike the hymns of many of the established Christian churches, Shembe's hymns are not primarily translations or adaptations of missionary hymn books, but are very much *Zulu* compositions. As the leading scholar of the subject writes, these hymns 'live in the Zulu situation, have to do with their anxieties, their hopes, their crises. No other Zulu had in this century such a lasting influence on the Zulu people in particular than Shembe'.[3] It is evident even from the selection given here how Shembe acted as a mouthpiece and inspiration for a people who felt oppressed and outcast, not just in political activity but in religion too. As Shembe expresses it,

> We were shut out,
> But now the gates are open . . .

and

> The springtime of the earth has come . . .
> Now he has come,
> You people of Dingaan.

3. G. C. Oosthuizen, *The theology of a South African Messiah*, Leiden, 1967, p. 7.

Shaka

Extracts from a 450-line poem of praise for Shaka, the famous military leader and king of the Zulu nation in the early nineteenth century. The poem is constructed on the basis of a series of praises (and praise names) for Shaka rather than a narrative account of his exploits, but the poem does go through the names of a number of opposing chiefs whom Shaka defeated or whose cattle and other property he plundered, and thus amounts by the end to a recital of his various conquests.

The extract here begins about one third of the way through the poem.

. . . The young viper grows as it sits,
Always in a great rage,
With a shield on its knees.[4]

He who while devouring some devoured others,
And as he devoured others he devoured some more;
He who while devouring some devoured others,
And as he devoured others he devoured some more;
He who while devouring some devoured others,
And as he devoured others he devoured some more . . .

Painful stabber, they will exhort one another,
Those who are with the enemy and those who are at home.
He who is dark as the bile of a goat.

Butterfly of Phunga
With colours in circles as if they had been painted on;
He who is hazy as the shadows of the mountains,
When it is dark the evil-doers move about . . .

He is curved like the ocean
Which until dawn is rolling waves;
He is as rough as the ear of an elephant,
Like gruel made of inedible millet,
Like a pot of millipedes.

You are a wild animal! A leopard! A lion!
You are a horned viper! An elephant!
You are as big as the great mountains of Mpehlela and
        Maqhwakazi,[5]

4. i.e. always ready for a fight.   5. These hills are often linked, as the road going between them was one of the main thoroughfares of Zululand.

You black one,
You grew while others loitered.
    Snatcher of a staff!
He attacks, he rages,
He puts a shield on his knees.
    Pile of firmly planted stones;
Hawk that I saw descending from the hills of Nzwakele,
And from those of Khushwayo[6] he came clearly in sight.
    Shaka found two wild beasts
Met together between the Nsuze and the Thukela,
The animals were Thondolozi and Sihayo,
He came and threw a shield and they separated.
    He who devoured the trust cattle,[7]
Even to this day he is still responsible.
    Porcupine that stabbed the disorderly young people
Between Magaye and Nzawu.[8]
    He who bored an opening amongst the Pondos,
Even today the opening is still wide open;
He captured the dun-coloured cattle of Faku of the Pondos,
He devoured also those of Ngubowencuge in Pondoland,
He ate up those of Ncokazi in Pondoland,
He captured those of Ncasana among the Majolas,
He captured those of Macingwane at Ngonyameni;
He went on and devoured those of Bhungane in their thousands,
And then those of the Suthus who clothe their loins,
And then those of the Dlodlongwanyanas,
They who twist their hair into fringes . . .
Grass that pricks while still growing,[9] son of Mjokwane;
Long shield of the Ngunis[10] and also of the elephant,
He attacked Mancengeza son of Khali among the Mbathas,
He attacked Matiwane son of Masumpa among the Ngwanes,
He attacked Makhedama among the Langenis, the home of his
    mother.

    6. Nzwakele and Khushwayo were chiefs who submitted to
Shaka.   7. Cattle lent on trust which he appropriated.   8. Chiefs who
supported Shaka.   9. Zulu proverb meaning that one shows one's
talents while still young.   10. The Bantu people between the Drakens-
burg and the sea.

Wild beast that attacks people in the thick under-
        growth;
He devoured Sigawuzana of the Mbatha clan.

    Deep pool which is in the Mavivane river,
Which drowns a person as he is washing,
So that he disappears even as far as his head-ring.[11]

        Black walking-stick, Son of Mjokwane;
He destroyed Zwide[12] amongst the Ndwandwes,
He destroyed Nomahlanjana son of Zwide,
He destroyed Sikhunyana son of Zwide.

    Glossy greenish one like the bile of a buck;
He devoured Ndimindwane of the Mswelis of the Xulu clan,
He devoured Mdladlama of the Mbhedu clan,
He destroyed Mphezeni amongst the Nxumalos.

        Burning furnace!
        Hawk that descended from above . . .

    Young raging one of Ndaba!
He lives in a great rage,
And his shield he keeps on his knees;
He has not let them settle down, he keeps them in a state of
        excitement,
Those among the enemy and those at home.

        Mandla kaNgome![13]
He crossed over and founded the Ntontela regiment,
They said he would not found it and he founded it.

    He who attempted the ocean without crossing it,
It was crossed by swallows and white people.

        He who sets out at midday, son of Ndaba, or even
            afternoon;
Pursuer of a person and he pursues him persistently,
For he pursued Mbemba born among the Gozas,
He pursued him until he put him at Silutshana,
He found the reed-bed of young boys,
But it was only the spirits of the place.

        Axe of Senzangakhona,

11. Shaka had one rival stabbed while bathing in the river.
12. Zwide, one of Shaka's strongest opponents, was conquered in 1819.
13. Praise name probably meaning 'Mighty Power'.

Which when it was chopping worked very energetically.
> He who saw the cattle right on top of the hill,
And brought them down by means of long spears and they
> came down,
He washed his face in tears.
> Ngibi naNgwadi![14]
Little leopard that goes about preventing other little leopards at
> the fords.[15]
> Finisher off! Black Finisher off!

Senzangakhona

> The praises of Shaka's father, Senzangakhona, one of the
most famous Zulu ancestors.

Menzi[16] son of Ndaba!
> Variegation like a multi-coloured animal,
Like that of Phiko[17] at Bulawini.
Buffalo that goes overlooking the fords,
He is like Mzingeli of the Mfekana people.[18]
He whose eating-mats are beautiful, Mjokwane,[19]
Whose beautiful mats are eaten from by womenfolk.[20]
He captured a woman, the wife of Sukuzwayo,
And destroyed Sukuzwayo and his son.
He who went in darkness to the Mazolo people and returned by
> moonlight,
And the men turned to vicious critics,
He who went with criticism and returned with praises.
He whose head-dress was wet with the journey.
He who spoke and his words were resisted but presently accepted,
It was as if the darkness was coming with the rain.
> Tree with fragile trunk;

14. Another praise name.   15. i.e. he is in full control of
the country.

16. Praise name meaning 'Doer' or 'Maker'.   17. A man
famous for his dress.   18. He was always travelling, 'like Mzingeli', a
hunter.   19. Praise name meaning 'The persecuted one'.   20. He was
evidently admired by women.

He whose body was beautiful even in the great famine:
Whose face had no fault,
Whose eyes had no flaw,
Whose mouth was perfect,
Whose hands were without defect;
A chest which had no blemish,
Whose feet were faultless,
And whose limbs were perfect;
Thighs also that were perfect,
And knees which could not be criticized;
Whose teeth had no spot,
Whose ears could not be bettered,
And whose head had a noble carriage.
    Tall one of the house of Mnkabayi![21]
    Leaf amongst the thorns protecting the home,
You could hear them saying 'Keep it close, Father of Secrets',
They were not talking to you, they meant your
    mother, Mbhulazikazi,
She who had imprisoned a lion in the house.
    He-who-aims-to-return[22] of Phalo!
    Sun that came forth shining brightly,
And when it was high it spread out its rays,
Seeking to supply warmth to many bodies.
    Devourer of Maqanda and Nsele,[23]
Who devoured the ground-nuts of his brother,
He devoured the ground-nuts of Mudli, shells and all.
    Peerer over precipices,
Who peered into the cave of his brother,
Who peered into the cave of Zivalele.
    Fountain of the rocks of Nobamba[24]
At which I drank and felt faint,
I was almost eaten up by the mambas
Which lay in the thickets and climbing plants.[25]

---

21. His formidable elder sister who acted as regent during his minority. 22. A praise name. 23. Important men who were 'eaten up' by Senzangakhona. 24. Senzangakhona's chief kraal. 25. There were hidden dangers in his personality, particularly an unpredictable quick temper.

Water of the Mpembeni stream, Ndwandwe
     son of Ndaba,
Gurgling water of the Mpembeni stream,
I don't even know where it is going to,
Some runs downhill and some runs uphill,[26]
It is like Qonsa of the Zigezeni kraal.

     Stake forming the gate-post of Nomgabhi,
On which owls perched,
On which Phungashe of the Buthelezis sat,
On which Macingwane of Ngonyameni sat,
On which Dladlama of the Majolas sat.[27]

     Mother's baby, get on the back and let us be off,[28]
Those who remain do not dispute the case,
Such as Mbuzo and Nsele,
Likewise Sichusa of Dungankomo.

     He who captured Nomnyani in the south,
And seized Nonhlambase, the renowned one,
Who settled the affairs of Sinyameni,
And captured Mbengelenhle in the south.

     Tall one who is higher than a hill,
Who was equal to the mountain of Sikhume.
He who was as heavy as a rock of Zihlalo,
Which could be commanded by those who carry barbed spears,
While we of the broad-bladed spears could save ourselves by
     using a sandstone.
Our inspirer at Zwangendaba,
Who inspired me when the cattle went out to graze at midday.
Who made bitter the aloe of Mahogo,
Who made pleasant the trifle of Ngcingci;
Who chewed with his mouth without eating.
He who was black on both arms,
Who is like the aloe of the Sidubela hill.

     He who plaited a long rope, son of Jama,
Who plaited a rope and climbed up,

---

26. i.e. his unpredictability was bewildering. ('Qonsa', besides being a name, also means to go uphill.)   27. These are all chiefs who were continually harassing him.   28. This expression implies 'Discretion is the better part of valour'.

There even the ancestral spirits of Mageba could not come,
When they tried to climb they broke their little toes.[29]
    Expresser of sympathy, here is a magical stone,
Not falling on the neck it will fall on the shoulder,
It will play a trick and fall on the flank.[30]
Shaker of the head until the neck dislikes it,
Perhaps in another year the trunk will protest.[31]
He who removed me from below and I went up above,
I returned with yellow corn and threshed and cooked.[32]
By Ndaba they will be left to exhort one another,
Both those with the enemy and those at home.
Red-spotted black beast of Nobamba
That goes about causing trouble.[33]

Praises of Henry Francis Fynn

Fynn was one of the white traders based at Port Natal in the
nineteenth century. He had very close contact with the Zulu and became
a great favourite of Shaka's. He was given the Zulu name of Mbuyazi.

Mbuyazi of the Bay![34]
The long-tailed finch[35] that came from Pondoland,[36]
Traveller who was never going to go home,
Hungry one who ate the scented reed of the river,[37]
The finch that never begged, unlike the 'kaffirs',[38]
Deep-voiced speaker like rumbling thunder,
Bull-calf with the capacious paunch,
Feathers that grow and then moult,[39]

29. i.e. even the spirits of his ancestors could not come near
him in greatness.   30. i.e. he had an unpredictable nature.   31. i.e. he
was headstrong and obstinate.   32. Refers to the benefits he brought
his people.   33. i.e. he was not a nonentity, he was forceful and made
his mark.

34. Durban Bay.   35. Fynn wore a bunch of feathers in
his hat. He prized it because it had been presented to him by Shaka.
36. He was often away in Pondoland on hunting and trading expeditions.
37. An indigenous variety of sugar-cane.   38. A term of contempt for
the refugees from Shaka.   39. i.e. he used to shave off his beard.

Tamer of the intractable elephant.[40]
He who became pregnant with many children,[41]
They multiplied as river after river was crossed,
And then they became dogs and barked at him;
He who when he turned his back looked like the
    tail of an antelope;
Great swaying frame, he ran heavily but fast,
Running away from Zululand he made haste.[42]
Back with thorns on it like a mamba,
Beauty like the mouse-birds of Manteku[43]
That are yellowish on their wings.
Our white man whose ears shine in the sun;
Long snake that took a year to pass by
And eventually passed in another year.
Protector of orphans;
Pusher-aside of elephants so that they fall,
He who points with a stick and thunder and lightning
    come forth,
Everything that he points at falls and dies.
Our egret that came out of the sea;
Elder brother of Shaka whom he raised from the dead.[44]
He took refugees out of the forests and nourished them,
So that they lived and became human again.
Hurrah! Hurrah! Hurrah for the Rescuer!
Wild animal of the blue ocean.

40. i.e. the great influence which Fynn had over Shaka.
41. A reference to the large number of refugees from Zululand who found sanctuary at Port Natal.   42. After Shaka was assassinated, Fynn had to fly for his life.   43. A river in Pondoland.   44. Fynn happened to be at Shaka's kraal when an attempt was made on his life. He was wounded in the side and Fynn was able to treat him successfully.

War song

The 'Great song' of King Shaka's regiments.

He has annihilated the enemies!
Where shall he now make war?
He has vanquished all the kings!
Where shall he now make war?

Praise of a train

Go on, thou noisy one!
Go on, thou fast runner!
For long thou didst lose them,
Bring them back to their homes.

Baboon

O you hollow-cheeked offspring
Of one with similar hollow cheeks
You fellow of mine with the cheek pouches,
Slung on your high hip-bones,
The big bones of your bottom
With which you sit on the rock edge;
Your face too looks like a ridge of stone.

Old age

The body perishes, the heart stays young.
The platter wears away with serving food.
No log retains its bark when old,
No lover peaceful while the rival weeps.

I thought you loved me

Composed by a Zulu woman in her fifties who worked as a domestic servant in Durban, and also ran her own group of singers with great success.

I thought you loved me,
Yet I am wasting my time on you.
I thought we would be parted only by death,
But today you have disappointed me.
You will never be anything.
You are a disgrace, worthless and unreliable.
Bring my things. I will put them in my pillow.
You take yours and put them under your armpit.
You deceived me.

My money! O, my money!

Mavimbela

A music-hall song.

My money! O, my money!
My money, I am afraid!
I changed a pound to shillings;
I came to the canteen and ate bit by bit.
I changed a pound to shillings;
I came to the canteen and drank bit by bit.
Tell my father, tell my mother.
I am afraid.
I left my home with a good reputation.
I came to Johannesburg and disappeared in
        the mine dumps.

I loved my dear Magumede,
My darling 'Studebaker', my hope.
I loved her even when I was hungry.
My darling big fat girl, my hope.
My rival was a bald-headed man like my father.

My darling 'Studebaker', my hope.
Let us go then to Durban
Where we shall get a better woman.

Jojina, my love

O Jojina my love, I always miss you.
I think of those days when we were together.
I am thinking of that day you said:
'Death alone would part us.'
Jojina, the passing days will never return, my love.

Those were the days

For the Zulu, Shaka is the most famous of their historic
figures, standing head and shoulders above the other leaders. When he
was killed by his brothers, he prophesied that they would never rule: in
this modern song this is seen as foretelling the ascendancy of the Euro-
peans.

In Shaka's days we lived well.
In Shaka's days nothing worried us,
Because we were ruled by that old man, Shaka.
He walked erect.
He never stayed behind
When his regiments went out to fight.
He was the leader of the Zulus,
He was the king that ruled over kings, Shaka.
He was a hero of heroes.
He was killed by his brothers through jealousy.
He said when he died: 'Never will you rule Zulus!'
Though our ancestors are dead we still remember
        them.

Was it all worth while?

This twentieth-century song refers to the time when the Zulu first started to wear clothes and lost their independence to the Europeans. The exclamation at the beginning and end is really a sigh of disillusion: 'Was it all worth while?'

> Yiya wo!
> This land of the Baca . . .
> This land of ours . . .
> We were nourished on it,
> We were brought up on it.
> We have grown old upon it, we and our fathers.
>
> Listen to a story of that time . . .
> There came a European
> Wearing trousers and fine clothes.
> He said: 'Take off
> All this rubbish.'
> So we threw away our skins.
> Yiya wo!

Take off your hat . . .

The translator writes: 'The scene is any pass office, where all male Africans must go to get their Registration Certificates. There they may wait in queues for hours and sometimes for days before they are attended to. It is a regulation which rankles in their minds and so they sing about it.'

> Take off your hat.
> What is your home name?
> Who is your father?
> Who is your chief?
> Where do you pay your tax?
> What river do you drink?
>
> We mourn for our country.

Lucky lion!

This expresses the envy of the Zulu worker for the lion who can lie down and sleep all day!

It sleeps by day!
How blessed it is,
Lion.

Home

The song expresses the sense of loss a family feels when its sons go off to work in Johannesburg. Originally a Xhosa song, taken over by the Zulu.

Go, let us go my friends, go home.
Go, let us go to see our little hills.
We've long been working at the mines,
We long have left our homes for this, the place of gold.

When we get home they will be waiting there,
Our Mothers happy when we come inside,
At Maxandekeni, home, my home.

Return my brother, from the place of gold.
Reject the town.
Cherish your mother, children and your own.
They'll clap their hands for joy
When you come home,
At home where they are waiting. Come, come home.

Lament for Mafukuzela

The well-known Zulu educationalist, Dr J. L. Dube (Mafukuzela) died in 1946. He founded Ohlange Institute near Durban, a school for African children up to matriculation standard, staffed entirely by Africans.

Mafukuzela, Rain-giving clouds,
Sleep in your grave, Mafukuzela.
Be still, hero of the African people.
The earth is not enriched because you are buried,
The mountains themselves are quiet and still.
Up above, where you now are, there is no sorrow,
There are no tears.
We are bereft, famous Mafukuzela.
There is Ohlange, it speaks for itself!
There are the works of this man amongst men!
Shine for ever, Mafukuzela of fame!
You have given us light, and given us the path of truth,
Mafukuzela, son of Dube, hero of heroes!

Satan is following me . . .

A song for dancing to in the town. It is in fact a skit on a Christian hymn.

Satan is following me,
Here he is near me.
O, Calf of the elephant,
Here he is near!

Dove's song in winter

This is at once the dove's song in winter when she must choose her partner, and a girl's song to her parents.

Say father, say mother,
Why should you force me to marry an old man?
Woe is me!
But why should you treat me like this?
Woe is me!

Teasing song

Princess Magogo

A teasing song (*umgqumushelo*) sung to a bride on the eve of her wedding.

A: Hey, young bride!
   Let us go and draw water!
B: I'm not going. I'm ill.

> Little crooked-flower, *gwenxe*, *gwenxe*![45]
> Little crooked-legs, *gwenxe*, *gwenxe*!

A: Hey, young bride,
   Let us go and gather firewood!
B: I'm not going. I'm ill.

> Little crooked-flower, etc.

A: Hey, young bride,
   You are being called to the bridal bed!
B: I'm coming. I feel a bit better now!

> Little crooked-flower, etc.

Work song

Raymond Mazisi Kunene

The great fool,
That despicable White man!
He handles us severely,
That despicable White man![46]

45. An ideophone denoting 'crookedness'.
46. This refers directly to their white supervisor, who has no idea of the meaning of the Zulu words.

You are lying, O missionary . . .

Raymond Mazisi Kunene

An anti-missionary song.

You are lying, O missionary!
There is not a single believer
Who went up into the sky!

Come in

Isaiah Shembe

A hymn inviting the Zulu to come in and join the movement
and no longer feel excluded from full acceptance in a church.

Let us come in to worship Jehovah.
We were shut out,
But now the gates are open.
Let them in.
See! Here are the Zulus
Descendants of Dingana
And of Senzangakhona.

Dance hymn

Isaiah Shembe

I shall dance, I have hope
I am a Nazarite girl,
I do not fear anything,
Because I am perfect.

I am the beginning

Isaiah Shembe

Shembe apparently claims to have been prior even to Christ
('His way').

My *Nkosi*[47] you loved me
Before the mountains were strong
From long ago you anointed me
I am the beginning of your way.

I am your work of old,
Before the large stretches of land were strong;
And the fountains of water
They had not yet spouted strongly.

And the fountains and rivers
Before they had flowed strongly
Jehovah created me
Before His way.

The depth was not yet there
I was already born,
He had not yet created this heaven
And also this earth.

The sun had not shone yet
In the space of this heaven.
And the moon had not yet shone
In the space of this earth.

Let Zulu be heard

Isaiah Shembe

I shouted day and night
Why did you not hear me?
Nations go to sleep that Zulu may be audible
Before the *uMsindisi*.

47. Lord.

I was stopped by all the nations
Which are under the heaven.
Nations go to sleep that Zulu may be audible
Before the *uMsindisi*.

You maiden of Nazareth
May you cry like a rushing stream
About the disgrace that has befallen you
In the land of your people.
Nations go to sleep that Zulu may be audible
Before the *uMsindisi*.

You young men of Nazareth
You cry all like a rushing stream,
About the disgrace that has befallen you
You young men of Shaka
Before the *uMsindisi*.

The springtime of the earth . . .

Isaiah Shembe

The springtime of the earth has come
The time is here
Be afraid, you hartebeests,
You are called to Ekuphakameni.[48]

The Star of Heaven
Rose in the East
Until it entered
In the holy city.

Let your testimony echo widely,
There he is, Jehovah,
Now he has come,
You people of Dingaan.

48. The Zulu New Jerusalem.

YORUBA

The Yoruba are one of the largest of the peoples represented in this volume. They control one state in the modern federation of Nigeria, and are, and have been, one of the more powerful groups of West Africa. With their long tradition of organized kingdoms, and their successful deployment of rich agricultural and commercial resources, they have developed a complex and sophisticated culture in which living in cities and the acquaintance with foreign civilizations date back many generations. By now the Yoruba number many millions (most in the Western State of Nigeria, but also with a considerable presence elsewhere in Nigeria and West Africa) and play a lively part in national and international politics. At present the vast majority of Yoruba adhere to world religions (Islam and Christianity) and Western Nigeria can boast a well-established educational system at both school and university level, based on the medium of English. But for all this, Yoruba culture is very much alive. The flowing Yoruba robes grace both the local and the international scene, Yoruba poetry and music are performed not just in the back streets and the farms but in houses of distinguished university professors, and the Yoruba language is extensively used in oral communication even among the most westernized élite, and it provides a constant source of pleasure: this 'tonal, metaphor-saturated language', as one Yoruba scholar puts it, 'which in its ordinary prose form is never far from music in the aural impression it gives and which has produced an extensive variety of spoken art characteristic of the people'.[1] In fact the Yoruba present one of the most striking examples of a people who have both selectively adapted and exploited what is recent and foreign and at the same time retained

1. S. A. Babalola, *The content and form of Yoruba* ijala, Oxford, 1966, p. v.

obvious pride in many of the values and ways of their traditional culture.

Yoruba poetry exhibits this fascinating blend of change and continuity very clearly. A number of the poems here, for instance, relate to the older Yoruba religion, in which a pantheon of gods was worshipped, headed by the supreme god Olorun (or Olodumare), who breathes life into the figures of human beings created by the deity Obatala. There are by now relatively few full followers of these gods, overtly at least, but a few priests still continue to compose and chant hymns at traditional shrines or for town festivals, and their compositions are of course still poetry even though confined to merely a few practitioners. Then there are the Ifa oracle poems whose roots lie in the traditional religious system, but whose predictions continue to be eagerly sought, by Christian and Muslim alike, to help in the varying problems of modern life. But, as well as such poems, there are also the modern election songs, poems commenting humorously on recent events, praise poems to living personalities, or funeral chants commemorating the deaths of leading figures in Nigerian politics in the 1960s.

Yoruba poetry is differentiated into a number of types, each distinguished by its own special name, style, and, often, method of singing and group of practitioners. There are at least a dozen technical Yoruba terms distinguishing different genres of oral poetry. Several, though by no means all, of these are represented in the selection here.

First, and perhaps most important to a Yoruba, are the *oriki*, praises. Many Yoruba names are praises in themselves, for the Yoruba are highly conscious of the metaphorical sense of words and names, and the praise names of prominent people are often sung or drummed in their honour. Praise poems are often loosely constructed from a series of such praises, so that they represent a piling up of honorific names and attributes rather than a narrative account of the hero's actions. Such poems are used to honour the various deities of the old religion (for instance 'Eshu, the god of fate', 'Alajire'), as well as prominent heroes of the past or present. Each ruling house in the various kingdoms into which the Yoruba people have been divided has its own series of panegyric poems praising the successive rulers. Famous warriors of the past also have their *oriki*, one good example of the genre being the

'Praise of Ibikunle', in which we get little idea of his detailed exploits but an overwhelming impression of his force and vigour through the successive and repeated use of panegyric and descriptive names and phrases. This is a genre that is very popular today: a leading chief has his own retainers to praise himself and his visitors, and members of the élite hire singers and drummers to celebrate the praises of host and guests.

Another important category represented here are the Ifa poems. Ifa (also called Ela and Orunmila) is the deity in the traditional Yoruba pantheon who gave the power of divination to man and still acts as the intermediary between men and the gods. The practice of divination associated with Ifa is extremely complex, resting on a number of mathematical permutations which result from a series of throws made by the human diviner. The total number of different throws which can be obtained is 256, and each of these throws or figures has its own name representing the two main elements in the figure (*Iwori Wotura*, *Eji Ogbe*, *Irosun Meji*, etc.), and several poems associated with it – making up in all a huge corpus of literature, one as yet unrecorded in full. The poems are in riddling and symbolic language, giving indications and hints for the listener to interpret and apply to his own case, rather than straightforward advice or prediction: 'Ifa speaks in parables. . . .' One common (but not universal) framework for Ifa poems is the reference to precedent by which some character in the past performed the required sacrifice (as the present client is expected to do) and was satisfied – like the tiger who asked for an oracle in the far past, sacrificed, and won his 'lovely and shining skin' ('Tiger'). These Ifa poems are always sung by the *babalawo* diviners, a highly specialized profession demanding at least three years' training, with sometimes up to seven or ten years spent as apprentice to a qualified diviner.

Yoruba hunters form their own special associations and these have their own form of poetry – *ijala*, or hunters' songs, which are chanted at hunters' festivals. These poems are marked, not surprisingly, by a great interest in the animals and plants of the bush, and also at times by humour and obscenity. They are often rather long and rambling and are mainly represented here in extracts only. They give vivid and carefully observed word pictures of the various animals of the wild, which demonstrate the close relationship between hunter and prey, one of affection and sympathy as well as of hostility.

In addition there are many other types of Yoruba poems: mourning songs; children's poems; satiric songs (like 'Money! money!'); topical and political songs; and many others. One final category, however, needs a little further comment: 'drum poetry' in which the poem is delivered on a drum.

To understand this one must grasp the essentially tonal nature of Yoruba speech. Each word has its correct tone(s) – low, high, or medium – and the correct intonation is essential to convey the required sense: a number of words are distinguished by tone alone, the syllables being otherwise identical. Tone is in fact so important to the Yoruba that groups of words can often be recognized by their *tonal* combinations alone, even without their phonetic forms being heard. This means that Yoruba drums, which can be adjusted to play different notes, can be used to represent the combinations of tones of Yoruba speech. The drum player can thus beat out the tones of the actual words of a poem on his drum, and be understood by his listeners. Many Yoruba praise poems are performed in this way: and the drum, it must be stressed, is heard as actually *giving the words themselves*, through their tones, and not merely acting as an accompaniment or reminder of the poem. A number of praise poems are of this kind (or could in principle be performed equally by singer or drummer) and, strange though this form of poetry must seem to a European reader, there is no doubt that to a Yoruba listener this is a perfectly acceptable mode for the expression of verbal formulations in a poem.

Tone also may play a part in the formal style of a poem. This is an elusive and somewhat controversial area, but a number of studies have suggested a kind of tone 'rhyme' in a number of Yoruba poems which is important to the total form of the poem. This is obviously one of the many aspects which is impossible to convey in an English translation. As Ulli Beier, perhaps the most effective of translators from the Yoruba, expresses it: 'Nobody who attempts to translate Yoruba into English will doubt that "poetry is what is left out in translation". For the music inherent in this language is something no rendering, however clever, can possibly attempt . . . The translator . . . cannot render the music of Yoruba poetry, nor its perpetual play on tone patterns, vowel harmonies, and sound pictures and . . . his rhythm can only be a remote approximation of the original.'[2]

Similarly the alliteration and vowel harmony of Yoruba poetry defy translation, as do the little but effective onomatopoeic words which come into many of the poems. In addition the *learned* nature of Yoruba language brings problems for the translator when the allusions which mean so much to a Yoruba audience can only be conveyed to an English public with the help of copious and distracting notes. In fact these have been avoided here for the most part, in the belief that much of the imagery and beauty of the poems can come across even without elucidating every allusion. Indeed, to quote Beier again, 'imagery and metaphor, simile and hyperbole, repetitions and refrains are some of the elements that translation can . . . do justice to'.[3] To an English reader 'the imagery of Yoruba poerty can be staggering: God sits in the sky like a swarm of bees; death drops *to*, *to*, *to*, like indigo from a cloth that's being dyed; the god of fate hits a stone until it bleeds when he is angry; the elephant tears a man like a rag and hangs him up in a tree'[4] – or, again, the image of 'tasting the world/like the fly that interprets the wine' ('Quarrel'). In representing images such as these, the translator can still offer to an English reader something of the impressiveness and range of Yoruba poems.

2. U. Beier, *Yoruba poetry*, Cambridge, 1970, pp. 11, 16.
3. ibid., p. 14.
4. ibid., p. 22.

Obatala, the creator

He is patient.
He is silent.
Without anger he pronounces his judgement.
He is distant,
But his eye rests on the town.
He kills the initiate
And rouses him to new life.
He is playful like death
He carries the child away.
He rides the hunchback,
He spreads out his arms
The right and the left.
He stands by his children,
He lets them succeed.
He makes them laugh –
And they laugh.
You, father of laughter,
Your eye is laughing.
Immense granary of the sky.
Old man with the strength of youth,
You rest in the sky like a swarm of bees.
The rich owe their riches to you.
The poor owe their poverty to you.
You take from the rich and give to the poor.
Take then from the rich and give to me.
Obatala:
You turn blood into children
Come and create the child in my own belly.
I own but a single cloth to dye with indigo.
I own but a single headtie to dye with camwood.
But I know:
You have twenty or thirty children waiting for me.
Whom I shall bear!

Eshu, the god of fate

Eshu symbolizes fate – the uncontrollable element in human life. He is a kind of trickster god, and his praises are made up of a series of paradoxes.

Eshu turns right into wrong, wrong into right.
When he is angry, he hits a stone until it bleeds.
When he is angry, he sits on the skin of an ant.
When he is angry, he weeps tears of blood.
Eshu slept in the house –
But the house was too small for him.
Eshu slept on the veranda –
But the veranda was too small for him.
Eshu slept in a nut –
At last he could stretch himself.
Eshu walked through the ground-nut farm.
The tuft of his hair was just visible.
If it had not been for his huge size,
He would not be visible at all.
Lying down, his head hits the roof.
Standing up, he cannot look into the cooking-pot.
He throws a stone today
And kills a bird yesterday.

Oshun, the river goddess

Brass and parrot feathers
On a velvet skin.
White cowrie shells
On black buttocks.
Her eyes sparkle in the forest,
Like the sun on the river.
She is the wisdom of the forest
She is the wisdom of the river.
Where the doctor failed
She cures with fresh water.

Where medicine is impotent
She cures with cool water.
She cures the child
And does not charge the father.
She feeds the barren woman with honey
And her dry body swells up
Like a juicy palm fruit.
O, how sweet
Is the touch of child's hand!

Alajire

Alajire represents the spirit of suffering. His praises here express the idea that from suffering comes wisdom.

Alajire, we ask you to be patient,
You are very quick-tempered,
And we worship you for it.
We ask you to be moderate,
You are wildly extravagant
And we pray to you for it.
We ask you not to be jealous,
You are madly jealous,
And we love you for it.
Alajire, you have a strange kind of pity:
Will you swallow my head,
While you are licking away the tears from my face?
Alajire, you frighten me,
When you fall gently, like a tired leaf.
Do not covet the beauty
On the faces of dead children.
Alajire, I am lost in the forest,
But every wrong way I take,
Can become the right way towards your wisdom.

Praises of the king of Oyo

Oyo was one of the most powerful kingdoms of Yorubaland.

Child of death,
Father of all mothers,
King of all kings.
You carry the blackness of the forest
Like a royal gown.
You carry the blood of your enemies
Like a shining crown.
Be merciful with us,
As the silk cotton tree is merciful with the forest,
As the eagle is merciful with the birds.
The town rests in the palm of your hand,
Weightless and fragile.
Do not destroy it:
Our fate rests in your hand,
Wield it carefully
Like your beaded sceptre.
The enemies who want to destroy you,
Will destroy themselves.
When they want to roast maize,
They will set fire to their roof.
When they want to sell water –
There will be drought.
The sieve will always be master of the chaff.
The water lily will always float on the lake.
Child of death,
The hairs on your chest are as numerous
As the words of a talkative woman.
You grab the heads of your enemies.
And push their faces into boiling water.
You lock the door in front of their noses
And keep the key in your pocket.
Child of death,
Father of all mothers,
King of all kings.

Praise of Ibikunle

Ibikunle was a distinguished warrior in the nineteenth century, who became the commander-in-chief (*balogun*) of the Ibadan forces and was responsible for many of the conquests in the 1850s that resulted in Ibadan becoming the leading military power in Yoruba country. The following extract is from the 142-line *oriki* of Ibikunle. The opening lines enumerate a number of his praise names, and the poem as a whole conveys the impression of Ibikunle's power and strength.

Ibikunle! the Lord of his Quarters,
The proverbial magnificent doer
The Captain that disgraces men as would the dearth of money
The Warrior! As regular as the Muslim afternoon prayers.
A strongly witted man with incomprehension comparable to that
    of Olodumare.
The affluent with enough to spend and to spare at the brewery.
A reliable military errant,
A challenger of all men . . .
A lone elephant that rocks the jungle.
Ibikunle has given up the idea of just rocking the jungle
He says he is a lone elephant
That rocks the whole world to its foundation.
A God sent for the fulfilment of a mission.
The mission that God gave to Ibikunle, he executed same before
    his death.
A chain with the thickness of a palm tree is incapable of stopping
    an elephant.
Any creeper that aims to obstruct the elephant from crossing
    the road
Will surely follow the elephant in its trail.
Balogun! my unending respects for you![5]
I will never charge you for a liar for ever.
Alara that took you for a liar.
Obiriti! the result was the subsequent despoliation of his town.
Ikogusi that took my father's words for falsehood,
Onilel'ola! his town was thus in complete ruins.

5. These and the following lines refer to his conquests in Ekiti country and how he devastated the towns of those who underestimated him.

Ajero-Ajaka that took your words for lying,
Arowolo! his town became a completely deserted place.
Balogun! Olugbaiya! I implore thee
The smoke screen has often spread round the jungle.
Balogun! I beseech thee, Olugbaiya.
The climbing rope has often retrieved the palm tree.
The sole of the feet has always led the path,
The city has always been surrounded by the town fortification
    wall
Olugbaiya!
The nursing mother usually ties the shawl for carrying the baby
    securely round her and the baby.
Arowolo!
You outwit them all in town.
Rogi-rogbe
Master in battle field
Arowolo
Terror in the battlefield.
Rogi-rogbe!
Terror in battlement.

Dirge for Fajuyi

Omobayode Arowa

> Lieutenant-Colonel Adekunle Fajuyi, Military Governor of
Western Nigeria, was killed in one of the series of military coups of 1966.
His state funeral was held in January 1967, and was introduced by an
hour-long dirge. The following comprises brief extracts from this long
poem.

Dekunle, handsome man, hail!
And farewell!
It is good-bye, as when a stranger is seen off to the town gate
Once dead and reborn, a person [spirit] does not know the front
    of his father's house.
Good-bye!
The stump of the palm tree does not owe a debt to the wind.

Dekunle, who lies dead here, owed no personal obligation
Before he went to God
As a person walks, as on parade, so it is the soldier goes away
O child of the big cloth, which makes the loom shake violently.
Greetings! . . .
This is how people are,
That is how the end of things usually goes!
Look, the World is derisive
And the uninitiated man is happy;
The uninitiated man does not know that the World can
        mock one!
Make a display of tear-laden eyelids
And when a touraco cries – [it makes us feel like weeping]
The Soldier should have gone far
Dekunle, I call you without stopping
I call you, won't you please answer?
I call you five times, six times!
I call you seven times, eight times!
I call you sixteen times, where the Olubeje mushrooms grow
        abundantly and block the road!
I call you, won't you please answer?
It is all right then
I am [not] angry
It is all right then
I, myself, am sad
If you touch my face:
        Tears, tears, tears! . . .
Greetings!
Fajuyi it has been a long time
Fajuyi it has been a long time
Your father calls you five times, six times!
He calls you seven times, eight times!
He calls you sixteen times
Where the Olubeje mushrooms grow all over the road!
He calls you without stopping!
Your mother calls you too.
Do you hear her any more?
Your mother called you without stopping,
With tear-laden eyes,

As when the touraco cries!
It is all right then.
I am not annoyed,
There are days when things are like that!
O, child of the leopard
Distinguished prince, it has been such a long time!
Child of the leopard at home
Child of the leopard in the farm!
Child of the leopard, who wears a flower garment!
Child of the leopard, who has the Ogele dress.
Child of the leopard, clean from top to toe!
Child of the leopard, clean to the tip of his tail!
Child of the leopard, who walks freely in the palace!
Who will chain the leopard?
He is going in the sky,
      An aeroplane!
As a person walks, as on parade,
So it is the soldier goes away!

Wisdom is the finest beauty of a person . . .

An Ifa oracle poem.

Wisdom is the finest beauty of a person.
Money does not prevent you from becoming blind.
Money does not prevent you from becoming mad,
Money does not prevent you from becoming lame.
You may be ill in any part of your body,
So it is better for you to go and think again
And to select wisdom.
Come and sacrifice, that you may have rest in your body,
Inside and outside.

Oracle: *Iwori wotura*

Iwori wotura is the name of one of the throws in the Ifa
divining process.

Iwori wotura
Anybody who sees beauty and does not look at it
Will soon be poor.
Red feathers are the pride of the forest.
Young leaves are the pride of the palm tree.
Iwori wotura.
White flowers are the pride of the leaves.
A swept veranda is the pride of the landlord.
Iwori wotura.
A straight tree is the pride of the forest.
A fast deer is the pride of the bush,
Iwori wotura.
The rainbow is the pride of heaven.
A beautiful woman is the pride of her husband.
Iwori wotura.
Children are the pride of their mother.
Moon and stars are the pride of the sun.
Ifa says:
'Beauty and all sorts of good fortunes arrive.'

Tiger

From an Ifa poem. Tiger performs the due Ifa sacrifice and
gains honour.

Ifa divination was performed for Tiger,
The one with lovely and shining skin.

Could he possibly have honour?
That was the reason why Tiger performed Ifa divination.

He was told that much was the prospect of honour for him,
But he should perform sacrifice.

And he performed it.
He performed sacrifice with ten knives
And one lovely and shining cloth.

The ten knives which he used for sacrifice
Were fixed to his fingers by his Ifa priests,
And with it he does havoc to all other animals.
The lovely and shining cloth which he also used for sacrifice
Was used to cover his body
And it made him a beautiful animal.

He was dancing,
He was rejoicing;
He was praising his Ifa priests
And his Ifa priests praised Ifa.
He opened his mouth,
And the song of Ifa entered therein.
As he stretched his feet,
Dance caught them.

He said: O! Animal created to have honour.
Animal created to have honour.
It is Oosa[6] who gave honour to Tiger,
Animal created to have honour.

Death killed the rich . . .

One poem for the *Eji ogbe* throw in Ifa divination.

Death killed the rich,
Spoiled his riches,
Death killed the wealthy,
Took away his wealth.
Travellers by sea,
Travellers on lagoon;
Who does not know
That a man who has many children
Shall never die without a trace.

6. One name of the god of creation.

The time of creation has come

An Ifa peom symbolically hinting that the client will
conceive.

I am blessing two, not one.
This was prophesied to the sea lily
Which reaches down into the mud,
The origin of creation.
The time of creation has come.

Ifa

Ifa speaks in parables,
A wise man is he who understands it.
When we say understand it –
The wise man always understands it.
But when we do not understand it –
We say it is of no account.

The lying Muslims

The Muslims are still lying;
They say: 'we are fasting for God every year'.
Why do you fast for God?
Do you believe God is dead?
Do you believe he is ill?
Or perhaps sad?
Olodumare is never ill,
And he can never be sad.
We shall never hear of his death,
Unless the liars lie.

Let the dead depart in peace

A funeral song.

Slowly the muddy pool becomes a river
Slowly my mother's disease becomes death.
When wood breaks, it can be repaired.
But ivory breaks for ever.
An egg falls to reveal a messy secret.
My mother went and carried her secret along.
She has gone far –
We look for her in vain.
But when you see the Kob antelope on the way to the farm,
When you see the Kob antelope on the way to the river –
Leave your arrows in the quiver,
And let the dead depart in peace.

Election songs

The 1959 federal election campaigns in Western Nigeria were partly conducted through songs. The two main contenders were the NCNC (whose symbol was the cock) and Action Group (palm tree). Women supporters danced through the town after meetings, singing abusive songs about the other side's symbol, and replying in kind to their opponents' attacks.

NCNC: The Palm tree grows in the far bush.
Nobody allows the leper to build his house in the
town.
The palm tree grows in the far bush. . . .

ACTION GROUP: The cock is sweet with rice.
If one could get a little oil
With a little salt
And a couple of onions –
O, the cock is so sweet with rice.

Never mind how many cocks there are.
Even twenty or thirty of them will be contained
In a single chicken basket,
Made from the palm tree.

Since the NCNC was in opposition it used people's reluct-
ance to pay tax as a stick to beat the Action Group.

NCNC: You have forgotten that the election is near.
          You still show your greedy red eyes
          And make your tax assessment.
          You have forgotten that the election is near.

Kob antelope

A creature to pet and spoil
An animal with a smooth neck.
You live in the bush without getting lean.
You are plump like a newly wedded wife.
You have more brass rings[7] round your neck
Than any woman.
When you run you spread fine dust
Like a butterfly shaking its wings.
You are beautiful like carved wood.
Your eyes are gentle like a dove's.
Your neck seems long, long
To the covetous eyes of the hunter.

Salute to the elephant

Odeniyi Apolebieji

O elephant, possessor of a savings-basket full of money.
O elephant, huge as a hill, even in a crouching posture.

7. White markings on the antelope's neck.

O elephant, enfolded by honour; demon flapping fans of war.[8]

Demon who snaps tree branches into many pieces and moves on to the forest farm.

O elephant, who ignores 'I have fled to my father for refuge',

Let alone 'to my mother'.

Mountainous Animal, Huge Beast who tears a man like a garment

And hangs him up on a tree.

The sight of whom causes people to stampede towards a hill of safety.

My chant is a salute to the elephant.

Ajanaku[9] who walks with a heavy tread.

Demon who swallows palm-fruit bunches whole, even with the spiky pistil-cells.

O elephant, praise-named Laaye, massive animal blackish-grey in complexion.

O elephant, who single-handed causes a tremor in a dense tropical forest.

O elephant, who stands sturdy and alert, who walks slowly as if reluctantly.

O elephant, whom one sees and points towards with all one's fingers.

The hunter's boast at home is not repeated when he really meets the elephant.

The hunter's boast at home is not repeated before the elephant.

Ajanaku looks back with difficulty like a person suffering from a sprained neck.

The elephant has a porter's knot without having any load on his head.

The elephant's head is his burden which he balances.

O elephant praise-named Laaye, 'O death, please stop following me' –

This is part and parcel of the elephant's appellation.

If you wish to know the elephant, the elephant who is a veritable ferry-man,

8. The elephant's large flapping ears.   9. Killer-of-Ajana. According to story an elephant once killed his captor, Ajana, and thus earned this attributive name.

The elephant whom honour matches, the elephant who
      continually swings his trunk,
His upper fly-switch,
It's the elephant whose eyes are veritable water-jars.
O elephant, the vagrant *par excellence*
Whose molar teeth are as wide as palm-oil pits in Ijesaland.
O elephant, lord of the forest, respectfully called Oriiribobo.
O elephant, whose teeth are like shafts.
One tooth of his is a porter's load, O elephant fondly called
      Otiko
Who has a beast-of-burden's proper neck.
O elephant whom the hunter sometimes sees face to face.
O elephant whom the hunter at other times sees from the rear.
Beast who carries mortars and yet walks with a swaggering gait.
Primeval leper, animal treading ponderously.

Leopard

Gentle hunter
His tail plays on the ground
While he crushes the skull.

Beautiful death
Who puts on a spotted robe
When he goes to his victim.

Playful killer
Whose loving embrace
Splits the antelope's heart.

Python

Swaggering prince
Giant among snakes.
They say python has no house.

I heard it a long time ago
And I laughed and laughed and laughed.
For who owns the ground under the lemon grass?
Who owns the ground under the elephant grass?
Who owns the swamp – father of rivers?
Who owns the stagnant pool – father of waters?

Because they never walk hand in hand
People say that snakes only walk singly.
But just imagine
Suppose the viper walks in front
The green mamba follows
And the python creeps rumbling behind –
Who will be brave enough
To wait for them?

Mayor of Lagos

I am greeting you, Mayor of Lagos,
Mayor of Lagos, Olorun Nimbe,
Look after Lagos carefully.
As we pick up a yam pounder with care,
As we pick up a grinding-stone with care,
As we pick up a child with care,
So may you handle Lagos with care.

Variety: Why do we grumble?

Why do we grumble because a tree is bent,
When, in our streets, there are even men who are bent?
Why must we complain that the new moon is slanting?
Can anyone reach the skies to straighten it?
Can't we see that some cocks have combs on their heads, but no
     plumes in their tails?
And some have plumes in their tails, but no claws on their toes.

And others have claws on their toes, but no power to crow?
He who has a head has no cap to wear, and he who has a cap
      has no head to wear it on.
He who has good shoulders has no gown to wear on them, and
      he who has the gown has no good shoulders to wear
        it on.
The Owa has everything but a horse's stable.
Some great scholars of Ifa cannot tell the way to Ofa.
Others know the way to Ofa, but not one line of Ifa.
Great eaters have no food to eat, and great drinkers no wine to
      drink:
Wealth has a coat of many colours!

Money! Money!

A poem of self-mockery in which the satirist recalls the incident of an escaping lamb with mock regret 'and invites everyone to watch the silly spectacle of two elderly men (in flowing robes) chasing a lamb about the highway in the afternoon'.

Money! Money!
Shillings! Shillings!
Animasaun and I went as far as Remo[10]
Just to buy some lambs.

Money! Money!
Shillings! Shillings!
Animasaun and I went as far as Remo
Just to buy some lambs.

Muse held one lamb by the legs,
The other man held the same by the horns.
The animal bolted off, rolling us on the ground
In the afternoon, at Sabo.

Money! Money! etc.

10. A deliberately absurd comment since Remo is only twenty miles away, a distance the audience would *not* consider far to travel in the cause of effective trading.

When the lamb escaped from the park,
It went straight to the highway.
When the lamb escaped from the park,
It went straight to the highway.

Money! Money! etc.

Hunger

Hunger makes a person lie down –
He has water in his knees.
Hunger makes a person lie down
And count the rafters in his roof.
When the Muslim is not hungry he says:
We are forbidden to eat monkey.
When he is hungry he eats a baboon.
Hunger will drive the Muslim woman from the
    harem
Out into the street,
Hunger will persuade the priest
To steal from his own shrine.
'I have eaten yesterday'
Does not concern hunger.
There is no god like one's stomach:
We must sacrifice to it every day.

Women

She truly needs good character
The woman who has no relatives.
The woman who has no friends among her co-wives
She needs good character indeed.

Quarrel

Nobody will quarrel with the woodcock,
Because of his blue coat.
Nobody will quarrel with the parrot
Because of his red tail.
You old people of this world,
Don't be my enemies.
Would you kill a dog because it barks?
Would you kill a ram because he butts?
Would you kill the goat because he fucks his mother?
Forgive me, don't fight,
And let me taste the world
Like the fly that interprets the wine.

Children's poems

Hunger

Hunger is beating me.
The soapseller hawks her goods about.
But if I cannot wash my inside,
How can I wash my outside?

Song of abuse

The one who does not love me
He will become a frog
And he will jump jump jump away.
He will become a monkey with one leg
And he will hop hop hop away.

Praise of a child

A child is like a rare bird.
A child is precious like coral.
A child is precious like brass.
You cannot buy a child on the market.
Not for all the money in the world.
The child you can buy for money is a slave.
We may have twenty slaves,
We may have thirty labourers,
Only a child brings us joy,
One's child is one's child.
The buttocks of our child are not so flat
That we should tie the beads on another child's hips.
One's child is one's child.
It may have a watery head or a square head,
One's child is one's child.
It is better to leave behind a child,
Than let the slaves inherit one's house.
One must not rejoice too soon over a child.
Only the one who is buried by his child,
Is the one who has truly borne a child.
On the day of our death, our hand cannot hold a
    single cowrie.
We need a child to inherit our belongings.

IRISH

Ireland is a country in which song and popular poetry have played a large part through many centuries. The long-drawn-out struggle for political independence, the pervasive interest in religion, and the combined irony and sentimentality of the national-istic fervour for Ireland, the 'Land of Saints and Scholars' – all these are both expressed and propagated in the rich corpus of Irish oral poetry. Some Irish poems, such as the more personal love poems like 'Must I go bound?' or the performers' exhibitions of wit (as in 'A new song on the taxes'), can appeal irrespective of time or place. But for many of these Irish poems some under-standing of the circumstances of Irish history and politics is essential for their full appreciation.

The Christian religion has been important to the Irish people for centuries. Its influence has been the more profound and emotive because of the long association of Irish Catholicism and Irish nationalism. Over many years Protestantism was equated with the English conquerors, and contrasted with the Roman Catholic faith and the local Gaelic language of the 'native Irish'.

In Irish Catholicism the Virgin Mary holds a central place and there are many references to her in the poems printed here, in both Gaelic and English; a number of poems are addressed directly to her ('O Virgin' and 'Welcome O great Mary' are two). Ireland is also renowned for local devotion to various saints (St Kevin, for instance, who appears in an unflattering light in one of the poems here). St Patrick has a specially important place as the patron saint of Ireland who, they say, drove out the saints and introduced the shamrock – that symbol of the Trinity, with its threefold leaf, and of the nationalist colour, green. The religious rituals of the church also provide a focus for oral poetry, as its inspiration or occasion, and a number of the poems here are asso-ciated with Mass, above all with the moment of communion when, for the faithful, the wine and wafer become blood and body of

Christ, in words like 'A hundred thousand welcomes, thou Body of the Lord', or

> May his body make me safer
> Holy Wafer, deep my sigh,
> Cleanse me from the stains that stain me,
> Nor disdain me when I die . . .

But, despite the prevalence of deeply meaningful poems like this, the Irish are not just solemn about religion, for religion forms the subject of wit and mockery as well as of devotion. Some of the most lively Irish poems and songs draw on this theme – like 'St Kevin' or 'The ould Orange flute'.

In Ulster in the north of Ireland, by contrast, Protestantism has been a powerful, grass-roots movement, often taking up an aggressively hostile attitude to Catholicism and Irish nationalism. This is epitomized in the Orange Order, dedicated to loyalty to the British Crown and opposition to 'the rule of the Pope'. The historic date for all Orangemen is 'The twelfth day of July' 1690 when, according to accepted legend, King William defeated the forces of Rome and made Ulster safe for the true Protestant faith. The Orange movement, with its thousands of adherents among Ulstermen abroad as well as at home, has produced a large number of vigorous songs, some of them highly virulent like those on the themes of 'Kick the Pope before us' or 'No peace with Rome'; after hearing some of these, one is hardly surprised by the portrayal in 'Belfast linen' of the good Belfast Protestant who 'with his dying breath . . . solemnly cursed the Pope'. But even this conflict is used as an occasion for Irish wit and amusement, like the enjoyable attempt in 'A faction song' to 'flay an Orange villin' from Enniskillen – one of the bastions of the Orange movement – or the neat comment on Irish goings on:

> Fightin' like divils for conciliation,
> And hatin' each other, for the love of God.

The tragic results arising from religious conflict in Ireland are undeniable. But this need not blind us to its potential as a source for Irish oral poetry.

The political and social background of Irish history is also very relevant for Irish poetry. Many Irish people see their history as that of a people oppressed and exploited for centuries: their language forbidden, their religion persecuted, and their leaders exiled, imprisoned, and murdered. The various insurrections have emotive and uplifting associations that nothing in English history quite matches (perhaps the more so when they were unsuccessful), and Irish leaders like Daniel O'Connell or Parnell in the nineteenth century, or Connolly and Pierce in the twentieth, have become symbols of nationalism and pride: even the mention of their names in a song is enough to give it an emotive ring for most Irish audiences. The same goes for any reference to the various emblems of the Irish nationalist cause: the Fenians (or rebels), 'dying for Ireland', exile or imprisonment, the colour green, or the many names for Ireland (or Erin) herself – Kathleen na Houlihan, Dark Rosaleen, or the *Shan Van Vocht* (the poor old woman) in its various spellings.

These constant themes of exile, imprisonment, and death have become accepted literary conventions in Irish oral poetry, with their stock situations of the oppressed Irishman struggling vainly but gloriously against his 'Saxon foe' or 'perfidious Albion'. One recent account comments on the characteristic features of the popular political songs of Ireland:

Though they depended on current events for their subject-matter, they show an ever recurring body of themes and motifs and a fairly complex system of symbols. Stock situations are usually phrased in the same words. As for their heroes, even when they are named and stand for real people they tend to conform to types. Precision of date, place, and other circumstance does not hide the fact that they are less individuals of flesh and blood than conventional characters.[1]

But, though one has to recognize the existence of these literary stereotypes, one must remember too that their appeal is built on real and deeply felt experience. Considering the long and bitter nationalist struggle in Ireland, and the great Irish famine of the 1840s, for which most of the Irish held England responsible, one can see that these stereotypes are not just artificial conceits but

1. G.-D. Zimmermann, *Songs of Irish rebellion. Political street ballads and rebel songs 1780–1900*, Dublin, 1967, pp. 9–10.

genuine symbols. When Irishmen abroad – or at home – sing of their forsaken but still beloved Ireland, they are giving expression to ideas widely shared and profoundly meaningful for Irish singers and audiences.

To an outsider some of these exile and nationalist songs seem overdone, however evocative to an Irish audience. But the sentimentality of, say, 'The moon behind the hill' is offset by the wit and self-mockery of other songs also touching on political themes, like the 'New song on the taxes', the epigram laughingly attributing the world-famous oratory of Daniel O'Connell to his distant association with the little town of Cushendall, or the serio-comic picture of the wronged but still proud and aggressive Irish-man abroad in 'No Irish need apply'. It is also worth reiterating that, contrary to the impression sometimes received by foreigners, not *all* Irish songs are the well-known songs of political rebellion. There are also the tender love songs, the religious poems, and the ballads that tell a funny story or elaborate a witticism just for the sheer entertainment of a participating audience.

The poems are presented in two parts here: first those translated from Gaelic and secondly Irish poems composed and circulating in English. This perhaps needs a word of explanation.

Gaelic, or Irish, was the native language of Ireland which already had a long history of written as well as oral literature at the time of the English occupation; Ireland in fact had the earliest vernacular written literature in Europe. Under English rule, however, Irish became very much the language of the con-quered and was deliberately discriminated against. Nevertheless the literary tradition carried on, often orally, and many of the oral poems in Gaelic that Douglas Hyde collected in nineteenth-century Ireland come from the lowliest of surroundings. A number are noted as sung by 'a beggarman' or 'an old blind piper'; and the poet of the beautiful 'My grief on the sea', Biddy Cussrooee, was found 'living in a hut in the middle of a bog' in Co. Roscommon. This indeed is a characteristic of Irish poetry – its pervasive dis-tribution among the people of Ireland so that it really is part of a common cultural heritage, once in Irish, now largely in English, rather than just the possession of a learned and minority group.

As English spread at the expense of Irish, the compo-sition and transmission of oral poems in the English language gradually became more important and from early in the nineteenth century at least these begin to emerge as a genre in their own right. But there is much continuity and overlap with the Gaelic songs. This is partly a matter of actual language. A number of Irish phrases occur even in the English songs. There are Gaelic endearments (like *a cara, gra geal mo chroi, gradh mo croidhe mo stoirin*), anglicized Irish words (like colleen or cailin for a girl, Erin for Ireland) and the use of the Irish dialect of English which has itself been influenced by Gaelic idioms and pronunciation. But it also sometimes involved direct translation from the Irish and the existence of parallel forms in Gaelic and in English. One of the most famous Irish songs, Dark Rosaleen, began as a printed translation from the Gaelic poem *Roisin Dubh* but now circulates in English as a popular poem in its own right. Similarly some of today's singers can choose between an Irish and an English version of much the same song; and the same tunes and forms come up again and again irrespective of whether the words are English or Irish. Despite some obvious differences between the Gaelic and the English songs of Ireland, it is not easy to draw any clear-cut line between them, and they must be seen as representative of the same basic Irish tradition.

Irish popular poetry also involves great interchange between written and unwritten forms. In Ireland it is particularly difficult to differentiate any 'purely oral' forms, for songs go in and out of the oral tradition, perhaps first written, then kept alive through oral circulation, or perhaps taken down in writing from an oral rendition and then used as a basis for oral variation in propaganda or entertainment. Unlike, say, the Eskimo or the Zulu of an earlier period, Ireland has long had an established tradition of written literature – allied for many centuries with an illiterate majority – and it is hardly surprising to find long-lasting interaction between oral and written modes.

Because of this it has been difficult to decide which poems warrant inclusion here as 'oral poetry'. Some readers may feel I have cast the net rather too widely. I have taken into account not just composition and mode of first publication, but also the means of circulation and transmission. Thus many nineteenth-century political songs appeared as street ballads in broadsheet form (though even these were sometimes based on earlier oral forms), and then became popular and were sung in various versions. Again, the songs of the well-known composer and entertainer Percy French have certainly appeared in printed form, but owed their inception and continued transmission to their performance as oral pieces, whereas Padraic Colum's gentle and beautiful lullaby, 'O men from the fields', probably started as a written poem but has circulated so widely in an oral form in Herbert Hughes's setting that I have given in to the temptation to include it here. Similarly with songs that have been taken up by commercial interests and now circulate through records and the broadcast media: the mass media may not appeal to the purist, but such circulation does not really make the songs either less Irish or less oral. In any case even the purist will note that many circulate by word of mouth too, for the tradition of oral performance is still strikingly important in Ireland, and the oral circulation of songs – at work, at home, at rallies or services, and in the pubs – is probably still as important for their literary existence as is their appearance in printed publications.

Translations from Gaelic

O Virgin

Glorious Virgin, heavenly vision,
Thou my riches, store, provision,
My star through the years
    When troubles rend me,
On the Mountain of Tears
    O thou defend me.

In the Garden of Paradise, hymn and story
    Are praising the Lady within the walls,
O Mary's Son from thy city of glory
    Protect my soul when the danger falls.

Let not the hunters pursue me farther,
Wash my hands from the stains that gather,
Moisten my cheeks with love for the father,
And when I die may I say the *pater*,
                   Virgin Mary.

Hell

Hell whose rains and cold appal,
Hell whose drink is bitter gall,
Crossless churchless town of fear,
Hell, for thee I shall not steer.
But as Christ shall wish, so be it all.

Had I for my voyage food,
I should steer for heaven's good,
Ah! my crop had better thriven
Had I sown and ploughed for heaven.

A hundred thousand welcomes

A poem used as a prayer during Mass after the Confession in
Innis Maan in Aran.

A hundred thousand welcomes, thou Body of the Lord,
Thou Son of her the Virgin, the brightest, most adored,
      Thy death in such fashion
      On the tree of the Passion
Hath saved Eve's race and put sin to death.

I am a poor sinner to thee appealing,
      Reward me not as my sins may be;
O Jesus Christ I deserve Thy anger,
      But turn again and show grace to me.

Jesus who bought us
Jesus who taught us
Jesus of the united prayer,
Do not forget us
Now nor in the hour of death.

O crucified Jesus do not leave us,
Thou pouredst Thy blood for us, O forgive us,
May the Grace of the Spirit for ever be with us,
And whatever we ask may the Son of God give us.

Thoughts of God

Under my thoughts may I God-thoughts find.
Half of my sins escape my mind:
For what I said, or did not say,
Pardon me Jesus Christ, I pray,
At the throne of confession I stand this day.

O Jesus sorely suffering
      Rent by Thy Passion's pain,
An iron-torn offering,
      Slain as among the slain,

Scoffed at, despised, neglected,
        Tortured by cruel men,
Trembling to be rejected
        I turn to Thee again.

I place myself . . .

I place myself at the edge of Thy grace,
On the floor of Thy House myself I place,
To the Catholic Temple I bow to pray,
And banish the sin of my heart away,
I lower my knee to my King this day.

I lower my knee unto God most high
To the blessèd Three of the Trinity.
From the armies of pain may They bring me whole,
And the blessed Trinity take my soul.

O Jesus sore-suffering,
        Martyr of pain,
Thou wast offered, an offering,
        Slain with the slain,
Despised and rejected,
        A mock among men,
May my soul be protected
        From sin and from stain.

Each sin I have sinned
        From the day of my fall,
May the One Son of Mary
        Forgive me them all!
May the child who was tortured,
        God-man without stain,
Guide us safe through the torments
        And shoutings of pain.

Welcome O great Mary

Alice O'Gallagher

Recorded in America from a woman originally from Co. Donegal.

Welcome thou of high estate,
    And when troubles seize us
Bring us through our dangers great,
    Mother dear of Jesus.

Star of the morning, shield of the poor,
Friend of the soul, our open door.

Eve's fall made flowers to fall from men,
Thou bringest these upon earth again.

Thou hast reared the Lamb who has saved the race.
Be with us when Death comes face to face.

Bring us the peace of the Lord tonight
For the fetters that bind us bind us tight.

Heavenly Mother O! grant this night
Thy food to the poor, to the blind thy sight.

Throne of wisdom enthroned on meekness,
Mirror of good, make strong our weakness.

Save us, when thy Son shall come,
From deadly retribution.

Star of the morning all fair within
Save from the blot and the spot of sin.

May the Father, the Son, and the Spirit all Three
Beneath thy protection praisèd be.

A fragrant prayer ...

Biddy Crummy

A morning prayer to be said when one is awakened by the chirping of the birds.

A fragrant prayer upon the air
    My child taught me,
Awaken there, the morn is fair,
    The birds sing free.
Now dawns the day, awake and pray
    And bend the knee,
The Lamb who lay beneath the clay
    Was slain for thee.

When your eyes . . .

When your eyes shall be closing, your mouth be opening,
    And your senses be slipping away,
When your heart shall grow cold and your limbs be old,
    God comfort your soul that day.

O holy Michael, to thee I'm calling,
    And John the Baptist – to him I pray –
And to every saint that is high in heaven,
    To save my soul that day.

The Virgin shall come, and her white arms spreading,
    'Repent of your sins', herself shall say,
In the court of heaven, your only comfort
    Must come from her that day.

Thanksgiving after Communion

May His Body make me safer,
    Holy Wafer, deep my sigh,
Cleanse me from the stains that stain me,
    Nor disdain me when I die.
Lord who enterest my members
    Like the embers Thou dost shine,
Take my soul from out my bosom,
    Cleanse from stain and make it Thine.

Great Creator, Lord of Graces,
　　Thou whose face is as the sun,
Grand artificer of heaven,
　　Make my will and Thine be one.
O Creator, show me mercy,
　　Thou whose face is as the sun,
And the body where thou lodgest
　　Take to Thee when all is done.

See! the Trinity is hidden
　　In the flesh, we know not how,
Foul the sheath the soul is sheathed in,
　　Cleanse, Oh cleanse its foulness Thou.
Michael, angel high of angels,
　　Hear the prayer we make thee now,
Be our strength and bush of shelter,
　　When our hands forsake the plough.

A low prayer, a high prayer . . .

A low prayer, a high prayer, I send through space,
Arrange them Thyself, O Thou King of Grace.

O King of the world . . .

O King of the world,
　　Who lightest the sun's bright ray,
Who movest the rains that ripen
　　The fruit on the spray.
I look unto thee; my transgressions
　　Before Thee I lay,
O keep me from falling deeper
　　And deeper away.

The merry jovial beggar

Peter Casey

The poet was a beggarman from Co. Galway.

I have no more a golden store – this sets the world a-scorning.
Yet I be happy every night and merry every morning.
Each day my bread I ask of God, He sends me not away,
So I shall always merry be, till I be laid in clay.

I thank Him when I wake me up each morn, as well I may,
He brought me safely through the night and lets me see the day.
I hear each morning precious Mass, a blessed means of grace,
And Jesus Christ I still adore within His sacred place.

Upon the roads I pray my prayer, my thanks to God I pour,
Good prayers I have upon my tongue to say at every door.
No fear have I the night to pass, exposed to winter's rigour,
For every house will welcome me, the merry jovial beggar.

I ask no bed, no sheet, no quilt – a wisp of straw lay down
And I shall sleep as sound and deep as kings on beds of down.
I dream of Heaven, the glorious home where angels walk in white,
My guardian angel at my side will watch me through the night.

I seek no gold to have or hold, for riches wear not well,
And countless thousands seeking it have cast themselves to hell,
For gold must melt like snow in Lent, before the breath of spring,
But the soul that courts it, it must die, a low unlovely thing.

How well for the birds . . .

How well for the birds that can rise in their flight
And settle together on the one bough at night,
It is not so with me and the boy of my heart,
Each morning the sun finds us rising apart.

How well for the flowers when my sweetheart goes walking,
How well for the house when he sits in it talking,
How well for the woman with whom he'll be sleeping,
Her morning star and her star of evening.

As white as the sloebush in spring is my darling,
As bright as the seabirds from wave to wave swarming,
As the sun fills the ocean all day with its gleaming,
Rising and setting he fills all my dreaming.

Ringleted youth of my love . . .

Ringleted youth of my love,
    With thy locks bound loosely behind thee,
You passed by the road above,
    But you never came in to find me;
Where were the harm for you
    If you came for a little to see me,
Your kiss is a wakening dew
    Were I ever so ill or so dreamy.

If I had golden store
    I would make a nice little boreen
To lead straight up to his door,
    The door of the house of my storeen;
Hoping to God not to miss
    The sound of his footfall in it,
I have waited so long for his kiss
    That for days I have slept not a minute.

I thought, O my love! you were so –
    As the moon is, or sun on a fountain,
And I thought after that you were snow,
    The cold snow on top of the mountain;
And I thought after that, you were more
    Like God's lamp shining to find me,
Or the bright star of knowledge before,
    And the star of knowledge behind me.

You promised me high-heeled shoes,
  And satin and silk, my storeen,
And to follow me, never to lose,
  Though the ocean were round us roaring;
Like a bush in a gap in a wall
  I am now left lonely without thee,
And this house I grow dead of, is all
  That I see around or about me.

My grief on the sea . . .

Biddy Cussrooee

My grief on the sea,
  How the waves of it roll!
For they heave between me
  And the love of my soul!

Abandoned, forsaken,
  To grief and to care,
Will the sea ever waken
  Relief from despair?

My grief, and my trouble!
  Would he and I were
In the province of Leinster,
  Or county of Clare.

Were I and my darling –
  Oh, heart-bitter wound! –
On board of the ship
  For America bound.

On a green bed of rushes
  All last night I lay,
And I flung it abroad
  With the heat of the day.

And my love came behind me –
  He came from the South;
His breast to my bosom,
  His mouth to my mouth.

From a beggarman's song

Would God that I and my darling
  Were a thousand long leagues to the west,
In some island smothered with branches
  Where all birds turn to their rest;
A place where the phoenix has nested,
  Where eagle and cuckoo live gay –
'Tis there I'd put spells upon Phoebus
  To take sunlight forever away.

From a lament for Una

Tomas Costello

Young Una, you were a rose in a garden,
You were a gold candlestick on the queen's table,
You were talk and music going before me along the road,
My ruin of a sad morning that I was not married to you.

Composed in English

No place so grand

Oh! Dublin sure there is no doubtin'
  Is the finest city upon the say;
'Tis there you'll hear O'Connell spoutin',
  And Lady Morgan makin' tay.

For it is the capital of the finest nation,
    That ever grew on a fruitful sod;
Fightin' like divils for conciliation,
    And hatin' each other, for the love of God.

The wearing of the green

Dion Boucicault

O Paddy dear, and did you hear the news that's going around;
The shamrock is forbid by law to grow on Irish ground;
St Patrick's day no more we'll keep, his colours can't be seen,
For there's a bloody law against the wearing of the green.
I met with Napper Tandy, and he took me by the hand,
And he said: 'How's poor old Ireland, and how does she stand?'
She's the most distressful country that ever yet was seen,
They are hanging men and women for the wearing of the green.

O! if the colour we must wear is England's cruel red,
Sure Ireland's sons will ne'er forget the blood that they have shed.
You may take the shamrock from your hat and cast it on the sod,
But 'twill take root and flourish there, though under foot 'tis trod.
When law can stop the blades of grass from growing as they grow,
And when the leaves in Summer-time their verdure dare not show,
Then I will change the colour that I wear in my caubeen,
But till that day, please God, I'll stick to wearing of the green.

But if at last our colour should be torn from Ireland's heart,
Her sons with shame and sorrow from the dear old isle will part:
I've heard whisper of a country that lies beyond the sea,
Where rich and poor stand equal in the light of freedom's day.
O Erin, must we leave you, driven by a tyrant's hand?
Must we ask a mother's blessing from a strange and distant land?
Where the cruel cross of England shall nevermore be seen,
And where, please God, we'll live and die still wearing of the green.

Famine song

The memory of the Irish potato ('praties') famine of the 1840s goes deep in Ireland: it resulted, directly or indirectly, in one million dead and nearly a million emigrants overseas.

O the praties are so small
    Over here, over here,
O the praties are so small
That we dig them in the Fall,
And we eat them skin and all,
    Full of fear, full of fear.

O I wish we all were geese[2]
    Night and morn, night and morn,
O I wish we all were geese,
For they live and die in peace,
Till the day of their decease,
    Eatin' corn, eatin' corn.

O we're down into the dust,
    Over here, over here,
O we're down into the dust,
But the Lord in whom we trust
Will yet give us crumb for crust
    Over here, over here.

The moon behind the hill

I watched last night the rising moon, upon a foreign strand,
Till memories came like flowers in June, of home and fatherland
I dreamt I was a child once more, beside the rippling rill,
When first I saw in days of yore, the moon behind the hill.

It brought me back the visions grand, that purpled boyhood's
    dreams.

2. Explained as the geese which had to be fattened up for the landlords to eat.

Its youthful loves, its happy land, as bright as morning beams,
It brought me back the spreading lea the steeple and the mill
Until my eyes could scarcely see, the moon behind the hill.

It brought me back a mother's love, until in accents wild,
I prayed her from her home above to guard her lonely child,
It brought me once across the wave, to live in memory still,
It brought me back my Mary's grave, the moon behind the hill.

No Irish need apply

A song reflecting the discrimination against Irish immigrant workers in America in the nineteenth century.

I'm a decent boy just landed
From the town of Ballyfad;
I want a situation, yes,
And want it very bad.
I have seen employment advertised,
'It's just the thing,' says I,
But the dirty spalpeen ended with
'No Irish Need Apply'.

'Whoa,' says I, 'that's an insult,
But to get the place I'll try,'
So I went to see the blackguard
With his 'No Irish Need Apply'.
Some do count it a misfortune
To be christened Pat or Dan,
But to me it is an honour
To be born an Irishman.

I started out to find the house,
I got it mighty soon;
There I found the old chap seated,
He was reading the *Tribune*.
I told him what I came for,
When he in a rage did fly,
'No!' he says, 'You are a Paddy,
And no Irish need apply.'

Then I gets my dander rising
And I'd like to black his eye
To tell an Irish gentleman
'No Irish Need Apply'.
Some do count it a misfortune
To be christened Pat or Dan,
But to me it is an honour
To be born an Irishman.

I couldn't stand it longer
So a hold of him I took,
And gave him such a welting
As he'd get at Donnybrook.
He hollered 'Milia murther,'
And to get away did try,
And swore he'd never write again
'No Irish Need Apply'.

Well, he made a big apology,
I told him then good-bye,
Saying, 'When next you want a beating,
Write "No Irish Need Apply".'
Some do count it a misfortune
To be christened Pat or Dan,
But to me it is an honour
To be born an Irishman.

I once lov'd a boy . . .

Old Street Ballad. The words popular in Dublin about 1800.

I once lov'd a boy, and a bonny, bonny boy
Who'd come and go at my request;
I lov'd him so well, and so very very well,
That I built him a bow'r in my breast.

I once lov'd a boy, and a bonny, bonny boy,
And a boy that I thought was my own;
But he loves another girl better far than me,
And has taken his flight and is gone.

The girl that has taken my own bonny boy,
Let her make of him all that she can;
For whether he loves me or loves me not,
I'll walk with my love now and then.

I once lov'd a boy, and a bonny, bonny boy,
Who'd come and go at my request;
I lov'd him so well, and so very, very well,
That I built him a bow'r in my breast.

I know where I'm going . . .

I know where I'm going,
And I know who's going with me,
I know who I love,
But the dear knows who I'll marry.

I have stockings of silk,
And shoes of bright green leather,
Combs to buckle my hair,
And a ring for every finger.

Feather beds are soft,
And painted rooms are bonny.
But I would leave them all,
To go with my love Johnny.

Some say he's black.
But I say he's bonny,
The fairest of them all
My handsome winsome Johnny.

I know where I'm going,
And I know who's going with me,
I know who I love,
But the dear knows who I'll marry.

Ballinderry

Oh! 'tis pretty to be in Ballinderry,
'Tis pretty to be in Aghalee;
But prettier far in Little Ram's Island
Sitting in under the ivy tree:
      Och anee!   Och anee!

It's often I've roamed in Little Ram's Island
Side by side wi' Philemy Hyland;
An' often he'd court me, and I'd be coy,
Tho' at heart I loved him, my handsome boy:
      Och anee!   Och anee!

'I'm goin',' he said, 'from Ballinderry,
Out an' across the stormy sea;
So if in your heart you love me, Mary,
Open your arms at last to me.'
      Och anee!   Och anee!

I open'd my arms, ah! well he knew me –
I open'd my arms an' took him to me,
An' there in the gloom of the groaning mast
We kissed our first and we kissed our last;
      Och anee!   Och anee!

'Tis pretty to be in Ballinderry,
But now it's sad as sad can be;
For the ship that sailed wi' Philemy Hyland
Is sunk forever beneath the sea:
      Och anee!   Och anee!

An' it's, oh, that I were a weepin' willow,
An' it's, oh, that I were a lonesome billow
To cry all over the cruel sea:
'Oh, Philemy Hyland, come back to me:
      Och anee!   Och anee!'

Must I go bound?

Must I go bound and you go free,
Must I love the lad that wouldn't love me,
Was e'er I taught so poor a wit
As to love a lad would break my heart?

I put my hand out to the bush
To pluck the fairest flower,
I pricked my finger to the bone,
But ah, I left the rose behind.

So must I go bound and you go free,
So must I love the lad that couldn't love me,
I was taught so poor a wit,
And I love the lad would break my heart.

The green autumn stubble

When stubble lands were greening you came among the stooks
And grace was in your feet then, and love was in your looks,
In your cheeks the rose grew redder, and your hair in clusters lay,
And I would we lived together, or together slipped away.

I had a dream on Wednesday that bitter was the frost,
And I saw my love lamenting at dawn that I was lost;
Methought I came beside her and held her tenderly,
And all Erin I defied then to part my love and me.

My curse on him is spoken who keeps my love from me,
And swears that to our courting he never will agree;
For though skies should send the deluge, or the snowy North its
    flakes,
We two could live as pleasant as the swans upon the lakes.

The seagull's heart is merry when the fish is in his beak,
And the eel within Lock Erne can swim from creek to creek,
And I spoke tripping Gaelic, and merry songs I've sung,
But now my wits are crazy, and leaden is my tongue.

St Kevin

At Glendalough lived a young saint,
In the odour of sanctity dwelling,
An old-fashioned odour, which now
We seldom or never are smelling;
He lived in a hole in the wall
A life of ferocious austerity,
He suffered from bile and from gall,
And on women he looked with asperity.

There was a young woman one day,
Stravagin along by the lake, sir;
She looked hard at St Kevin, they say,
But St Kevin no notice did take, sir.
When she found looking hard wouldn't do,
She looked soft – in the old sheep's eye fashion;
But with all her sheep's eyes, she could not
In St Kevin see signs of soft passion.

'You're a great hand at fishing,' says Kate
' 'Tis yourself that knows well how to hook them;
But, when you have landed them nate,
Sure you want a young woman to cook them.'
Says the saint, 'I am sayrious inclined,
I intend taking orders for life, dear.'
'Only marry,' says Kate, 'and you'll find
You'll get orders enough from your wife, dear.'

'You shall never be flesh of my flesh,'
Says the saint, with an anchorite groan, sir;
'I see that myself,' answered Kate,
'I can only be bone of your bone, sir.
And even your bones are so scarce,'
Said Miss Kate, at her answers so glib, sir,
'That I think you would not be the worse
Of a little additional rib, sir.'

The saint, in a rage, seized the lass –
He gave her one twirl round his head, sir,
And, before Doctor Arnott's invention,
Prescribed her a watery bed, sir.
Oh! – cruel St Kevin! – for shame!
When a lady her heart came to barter,
You should not have been Knight of the Bath,
But have bowed to the order of Garter.

In memoriam

Padraig de Brun

Composed on the night of 8 December 1922.

Rory and Liam are dead and gone,
  Star of the morning, Mary, come.
Slain at the Eight of December's dawn,
  Mary Immaculate, guide them home.

Rory and Liam and Dick and Joe,
  Star of the morning, Mary, come.
Red is their hearts' blood, their souls like snow,
  Mary Immaculate, guide them home.

Their slayers have rung no passing bell,
  Star of the morning, Mary, come.
But the rifles' crack is their funeral knell;
  Mary Immaculate, guide them home.

Their eyes are steady in face of death,
  Star of the morning, Mary, come.
For their minds are rapt by the vision of faith,
  Mary Immaculate, guide them home.

For Winter will pass and Spring be born,
  Star of the morning, Mary, come.
And freedom will waken the land at morn,
  Mary Immaculate, guide them home.

And what is death but an envoy sped,
      Star of the morning, Mary, come.
With a call from the Heaven of Ireland's dead?
      Mary Immaculate, guide them home.

Why reckon the pangs that have sufficed,
      Star of the morning, Mary, come.
To bring free souls to their Captain, Christ?
      Mary Immaculate, guide them home.

Rory and Liam are dead and gone,
      Star of the morning, Mary, come.
They have found the lights that go out at dawn,
      Mary Immaculate, guide them home.

Rory and Liam and Dick and Joe,
      Star of the morning, Mary, come.
Our starlight fades, but the road they know,
      Mary Immaculate, guide them home.

A new song on the taxes

All you young men an' maidens come an' listen to my song,
It is something short and comical, it won't detain you long.
Go where you will by day or night, the town or country through,
The people cry and wonder what with us they mean to do.

    No wonder people grumble at the taxes more and more,
    There never was such taxes in Ireland before.

They're going to tax the farmers, and their horses, carts and
    ploughs,
They're going to tax the billygoats, the donkeys, pigs and cows:
They're going to tax the mutton, and they're going to tax the
    beef,
And they're going to tax the women if they do not try to read.

    No wonder people grumble, etc.

They will tax the ladies' chignons and their boas, veils and mats,
They're going to tax the mouse traps and the mousies, cats and
    rats;

They'll tax the ladies' flouncey gowns, their high-heeled boots
    and stays,
And before the sun begins to shine they'll tax the bugs and fleas.

    No wonder people grumble, etc.

They're going to tax the brandy, ale and whiskey, rum and wine,
They'll tax the tea and sugar, the tobacco, snuff and pipes;
They're going to tax the fish that swim and all the birds that fly,
An' they're going to tax the women who go drinking on the sly.

    No wonder people grumble, etc.

They're going to tax all bachelors as heavy as they can,
And they'll double tax the maidens who are over forty-one;
They'll tax the ground we walk on and the clothes that keep us
    warm,
And they're going to tax the childer on the night before they're
    born.

    No wonder people grumble, etc.

They're going to tax the crutches and they'll tax the wooden legs,
They're going to tax the bacon, bread and butter, cheese and eggs;
They're going to tax old pensioners as heavy as they can,
And they'll double tax young girls that go looking for a man.

    No wonder people grumble, etc.

They'll tax the ladies all that paint and those that walk with men,
They're going to tax the ducks and geese, and turkeys, cocks and
    hens;
They're going to tax the farmers' boys that work along the
    ditches,
And they'll double tax old drunken wives that try to wear the
    breeches.

    No wonder people grumble, etc.

They're going to tax the corn fields, potato gardens too,
They're going to tax the cabbage plants, the jackdaws and the
    crows;
They'll double tax the hobble skirts and table up some laws,
But the devil says he'll tax them if he gets them in his claws.

    No wonder people grumble, etc.

'Are ye right there, Michael?'

A Lay of the Wild West Clare

Percy French

Composed after an encounter with the slow and erratic service of the West Clare Railway.

You may talk of Columbus's sailing
    Across the Atlantical sea
But he never tried to go railing
    From Ennis as far as Kilkee.
You run for the train in the mornin',
    The excursion train starting at eight,
You're there when the clock gives the warnin',
    And there for an hour you'll wait.

SPOKEN   And as you're waiting in the train,
    You'll hear the guard sing this refrain:

'Are ye right there, Michael? are ye right?
Do you think that we'll be there before the night?
Ye've been so long in startin',
That ye couldn't say for sartin' –
Still ye might now, Michael, so ye might!'

They find out where the engine's been hiding,
And it drags you to sweet Corofin;
Sez the guard, 'Back her down on the siding,
    There's the goods from Kilrush comin' in.'
Perhaps it comes in in two hours,
    Perhaps it breaks down on the way:
'If it does,' sez the guard, 'be the powers,
    We're here for the rest of the day!'

SPOKEN   And while you sit and curse your luck,
    The train backs down into a truck!

'Are ye right there, Michael, are ye right?
Have ye got the parcel there for Mrs White?
Ye haven't! Oh, begorra!
Say it's comin' down tomorra –
And it might now, Michael, so it might!'

At Lahinch the sea shines like a jewel,
    With joy you are ready to shout,
When the stoker cries out, 'There's no fuel,
    And the fire's taytotally out.
But hand up that bit of a log there –
    I'll soon have ye out of the fix;
There's a fine clamp of turf in the bog there';
    And the rest go a-gatherin' sticks.

SPOKEN   And while you're breakin' bits of trees,
    You hear some wise remarks like these:

'Are ye right there, Michael, are ye right?
Do you think you can get the fire to light?'
'Oh, an hour you'll require,
For the turf it might be drier –'
'Well it might now, Michael, so it might!'

Kilkee! Oh, you never get near it!
    You're in luck if the train brings you back,
For the permanent way is so queer, it
    Spends most of its time off the track.
Uphill the ould engin' is climbin',
    While passengers push with a will;
You're in luck when you reach Ennistymon
    For all the way home is downhill.

SPOKEN   And as you're wobbling through the dark,
    You hear the guard make this remark:

'Are ye right there, Michael, are ye right?
Do ye think that we'll be home before it's light?'
' 'Tis all dependin' whether
The ould engin' howlds together –'
'And it might now, Michael, so it might!'

Lisnagade

Ye Protestants of Ulster, I pray you join with me,
Your voices raise in lofty praise and show your loyalty;
Extol the day we marched away with Orange flags so fine.
In order to commemorate the conquest of the Boyne.

The first who fought upon that day, the Prince of Orange was,
He headed our forefathers in his most glorious cause;
Protestant rights for to maintain, and Pop'ry to degrade;
And in the memory of the same we fought at Lisnagade.

'Twas early in the morning before the rise of sun,
An information we receiv'd our foes each with his gun
In ambush lay, near the highway, intrenched in a fort,
For to disgrace our Orange flag, but it chanc'd they broke their
    oath.

We had not march'd a mile or so, when the white flag we espy'd,
With a branch of podereens on which they much rely'd
And this inscription underneath – *Hail Mary! unto thee* –
Deliver us from these Orange dogs and then we will be free.

At half an hour past two o'clock, a firing did commence,
With clouds of smoke and shower of ball, the Heaven was
    condens'd;
They call'd unto their wooden gods, to whom they us'd to pray
But my lady Mary fell asleep and the cowards ran away.

The ould Orange flute

Nugent Bohem

In the County Tyrone, near the town of Dungannon,
    Where many a ruction myself had a han' in,
Bob Williamson lived, a weaver by trade,
    And all of us thought him a stout Orange blade.

On the twelfth of July, as it yearly did come,
    Bob played on the flute to the sound of the drum –
You may talk of your harp, your piano, or lute,
    But nothing could sound like the ould Orange flute.

But the treacherous scoundrel he took us all in,
    For he married a Papish called Bridget McGinn;
Turned Papish himself, and forsook the old cause
    That gave us our freedom, religion, and laws.
Now, the boys in the townland made some noise upon it,
    And Bob had to fly to the province of Connacht.
He flew with his wife and fixings to boot,
    And along with the others the ould Orange flute.

At Chapel on Sundays to atone for past deeds,
    He'd say Pater and Aves, and counted his beads,
Till, after some time, at the priest's own desire,
    He went with that old flute to play in the choir.
He went with the ould flute to play in the loft,
    But the instrument shivered and sighed and then coughed
When he blew it and fingered it, it made a strange noise,
    For the flute would play only the 'Protestant Boys'.

Bob jumped up and started and got in a flutter,
    And he put the ould flute in the bless'd holy water;
He thought that it might now make some other sound.
    When he blew it again it played 'Croppies, Lie Down!'
And all he did whistle, and finger, and blow,
    To play Papish music he found it 'no go'.
'Kick the Pope', 'The Boyne Water', and such like 'twould
            sound,
    But one Papish squeak in it couldn't be found.

At a council of priests that was held the next day,
    They decided to banish the ould flute away;
As they couldn't knock heresy out of its head,
    They bought Bob another to play in its stead.
So the ould flute was doomed and its fate was pathetic,
    It was fastened and burned at the stake as heretic.
While the flames roared around it, they heard a strange noise,
    'Twas the ould flute still whistlin' the 'Protestant Boys'.

Cushendall

Cushendall is a small town in Co. Antrim, and Daniel O'Connell was the famed nineteenth-century orator and political leader.

Our tarin' Dan O'Connell, sure he was a mighty man,
The glorious Duke of Wellington was nothing to 'Ould Dan',
The reason why his eloquence could his Saxon foes appal,
Was because Dan's mother's cousin's aunt was born in
     Cushendall.

From a faction song

Och! What will we do for linen?
     Says the *Shan Van Voght*.
Och! What will we do for linen?
     Says the *Shan Van Voght*.
Och! We'll go to Enniskillen,
And we'll flay an Orange villin,
And we'll wear his skin for linen,
     Says the *Shan Van Voght*.

Belfast linen

A linen workers' ballad.

In a mean abode on the Shankill Road
Lived a man by the name of Bloat,
He had a wife, the plague of his life, who continually got his
     goat
Till one day at dawn, with his nightshirt on,
He cut her bloody throat.

With a razor gash, he settled her hash,
Oh, never was death so quick.

Though the drip, drip, drip on the pillowslip of her lifeblood
    made him sick.
And the pool of gore, on the bedroom floor,
Grew clotted and cold and thick.

Yet still he was glad he had done what he had,
When she lay there stiff and still.
Till a sudden awe of the angry law filled his heart with an icy
    chill.
So to end the fun, so well begun,
He resolved himself to kill.

He plucked the sheet from his wife's cold feet
And he twisted it into a rope.
And he hanged himself from the pantry shelf, 'twas an easy
    death, let's hope.
And in the jaws of death, with his dying breath,
He solemnly cursed the Pope.

Now the strangest turn to this whole concern
Is only just beginning.
He went to Hell, though his wife got well, she's still alive and
    sinning,
For the razor blade was German made,
But the sheet was Belfast linen.

The dream

Unemployment has been continuously higher in Northern
Ireland than in the rest of the United Kingdom. Unemployment means
what has been described as the 'humiliating half-life' of signing on at the
Employment Exchange, the 'Labour Bureau (Borue)'.

Last night I had a dream bad 'cess to my dreaming I thought I
    was standing at the 'Labour Borue'.
But when I got inside the clerk said he was sorry for keeping me
    standing so long in the queue.

'Just take a seat for I'm sure you're tired,
Sit down and rest and I'll sign up for you,
And if you're feeling hungry just call the attendant,' I shouted,
     'Good heavens! is this the Borue?'

Then the manager says, 'Will you have a small brandy, we've
     got Whisky, Rum, we've got Porter and Gin,
And if you're feeling thirsty, I'll bring you a shandy, sit down
     by the fire while your drink's coming in.'
He then brought me cigars, cigarettes, and tobacco.
'Just have a smoke and I'll light up for you.'
He then asked the attendant to turn on the wireless, I shouted,
     'Good heavens! is this the Borue?'

There were no forms to fill in and I got quite excited, no
     supervisors, just do as you please,
I sang and I danced and I felt quite delighted when they told
     me they had shot all the ould referees.
Says the clerk 'Here's your money, do you want notes or silver?
If you have not got enough just ask for some more.'
He then shook my hand and he bid me good morning, says he,
     'There's a taxi for you at the door.'

But when I arrived home sure the wife she embraced me, a
     thing she hasn't done for the past twenty years.
Says I, 'Here's your money I know you don't need it.' – 'Just
     keep it yourself,' as she smiled through her tears.
But oh, in the morning I heard the wife calling,
'Have you had a nightmare? I just heard you scream,
For all you are good for is eating and drinking.' I shouted,
     'Good heavens! is this the Borue?'

Lullaby. O men from the fields . . .

Padraic Colum

O men from the fields
    Come gently within,
Tread softly, softly,
    O men coming in.
For mo mhurnin's going
    From me and from you
Where Mary will fold him
    With mantle of blue.

From reek of the smoke
    And cold of the floor,
And peering of things
    Across the half-door.
O men from the fields,
    Soft, softly come through;
Mary puts round him
    Her mantle of blue.

PUEBLO

The Pueblo are a group of American Indian ('Red Indian') peoples living in the semi-desert regions of New Mexico and Arizona.

Though a number of different languages are involved – of which Zuni, Tewa, and Hopi are represented here – the Pueblo as a whole are commonly regarded as comprising a single cultural unit. They pursue more or less the same type of life, and share many common presuppositions and social institutions; they are thus often written about in general terms.

The Pueblo depend basically on an agricultural mode of livelihood, in constant struggle with drought and sandstorm. It is scarcely surprising that one of the main themes of both their poetry and their religion is rain. They continually face the threat of drought, and for them water truly means life. This comes out constantly in the ceremonies involving rain (many with songs attached to them), in their belief in rain gods, prayers for rain, and poetic reflections on the beauty of the clouds bringing rain, the snow which adds to the water supply, or the water bird singing in the fields (as in 'Song of the sky loom', 'Rains for the harvest', 'Song of the blue-corn dance', and many others).

The main traditional crops of the Pueblo are beans, squash, and corn. Among these corn holds a central place. Corn is far more than merely a means of sustenance, for, as comes out in a number of poems, it also has deep symbolic and emotional connotations for the Pueblo. Poem after poem mentions the corn, and the ceremonies to do with planting and harvesting are centred mainly round corn – 'the bread of life' – and rain, its prerequisite. The annual 'corn dances' are central events in the Pueblo year, and in Pueblo symbolism corn is the constant image for growth, as are corn maidens and corn mothers for life. An old Zuni priest summed up the needs of his people:

Five things alone are necessary to the sustenance and comfort of the 'dark ones' [Indians] among the children of earth:

> The sun, who is the Father of all
> The earth, who is the Mother of men
> The water, who is the Grandfather
> The fire, who is the Grandmother
> Our brothers and sisters, the corn, and seeds of
> growing things.[1]

The Pueblo have for centuries lived in permanent villages, built of stone and adobe. Within each of these the community is usually divided into two moieties – often known as the Summer People and the Winter People – and much of the ceremonial life of the village, including their dances, takes place according to this binary division. A number of Pueblo songs belong to just one or just the other of these two moieties. Besides the moieties, there are also a large number of separate religious societies and curing societies, while the cult of the *Kachinas* (or spirits) is universal in all Pueblo villages.

The Pueblo can scarcely be represented as comprising the untouched and unchanging culture of certain romanticist theories. Like most American Indian groups they have had long contact with European explorers and conquerers. Indeed from their conquest by the Spanish in the sixteenth century to their increasing involvement in the urban labour market in this century, they have interacted with other groups and their poems celebrate the activities of trading or warfare as well as settled agriculture or traditional religion. Pueblo devotion to their own culture has by no means been destroyed by contacts with others, however. Indeed their cultural persistence has been noted by many analysts. The village remains the local focus of life, with the dance and ceremonial plaza marking a kind of centre of the world, the 'navel of navels' as the Tewa have it. Even moving a short way from his village can bring homesickness, as comes out in several Tewa poems (see 'I wonder how my home is'), and foreign influences,

1. F. H. Cushing, *Zuni breadstuff*, New York, Museum of the American Indian Heye Foundation, 1920, p. 19.

including that of the Roman Catholic church, have by no means undermined Pueblo interest in their local culture and religion. As Fred Eggan has put it recently (of the Tewa): 'They became nominal Catholics, but they took their own religion underground and have maintained it to the present day, guarding their ceremonies and their inner life against the outside world.'[2] Their poems express absorption in Pueblo religious values and practices, in the beauty of the growing corn, the blossoming clouds, and the prayers for rain. Most of the poems given here were in fact recorded some time ago, but even now Pueblo culture has certainly not vanished and books are still written about Pueblo thought and customs – only now by native Pueblo scholars rather than by outsiders.

The poems have a number of detailed differences in style and content, as is shown in the three sub-groups represented here – Tewa, Zuni, and (briefly only) Hopi – but also a great deal in common. In Pueblo religious and social life great stress is laid on repetition and parallelism: each of the cardinal points of the compass, for instance, 'the four world-points', must be invoked in turn; each of the various colours of different kinds of cloud or sacred mountain, with particular emphasis on the number four and its multiples. This kind of parallelism is found in the poetry too. This may make some of the poems slightly tedious to the foreign reader – or at least lacking in content – and yet one cannot altogether deny that the inevitability and piling up of clause after parallel clause can sometimes have its own effectiveness (as in the 'Corn-grinding song' opening 'This way from the North . . .', or 'The cloud-flower lullaby').

Besides ceremonial poetry, there are many light-hearted and charming songs, common to all the Pueblo groups, often sung by the girls while grinding their corn by day, or by the men at night. Many of the love songs too are very touching and simple, sometimes in the form of colloquies between youth and girl, sometimes in straightforward lyrical form. In the Tewa love songs particularly, much use is made of colour imagery and of endearing diminutives – 'little heart', 'little breath'. Certain themes recur in the poems frequently; the comparison between a flower

2. In A. Ortiz, *The Tewa world*, Chicago, 1969, p. xi.

and a maiden; the picture of girls and butterflies playing in the cornfields; and the constant preoccupation with the corn growing in the fields and with rain, water, rainbows, thunder, and the rain-bearing clouds.

The Pueblo have not developed specialist poets or critics in their oral literature. Nevertheless their poems are neither merely unconsidered improvisations nor all rote-remembered traditional formulas. Even the ceremonial poetry may be deliberately and carefully composed – as with the Hopi poet Koianimptiwa's 'Yellow butterflies', which was specially composed for a coming ceremonial dance in May, for the 'Corn-planting time'. Similarly with the Tewa: though some ceremonies have more or less unchanging songs, others, like the Turtle and Squash ceremonies, have new songs composed for them each year. And, though there were no professional poets, some individuals were recognized as possessing the gift of poetry more than others: as Koianimptiwa said, 'Not all men can make songs'.

The Pueblo songs do not involve the deep intellectual searching of, say, Eskimo poems or the sustained and complex symbolism of Arnhem Land Aboriginal poetry, or, again, the sophisticated cosmopolitanism of Malay literature. But the impression we receive in these poems of clear light and bright colours, and of the imagery of cloud and rain, storm and thunder, has a charm and meaning all its own.

> . . . Now hear the corn plants murmur,
> 'We are growing everywhere!'
> Hi, yai! The world, how fair!

Rains for the harvest

Over there in your fields you have
Musk-melon flowers in the morning
Over there in your fields you have
Corn-tassel flowers in the morning.

In your fields now the water bird sings
And here in your village the fogs
And the black clouds come massing.
They come here to see! They come here to see!
Mbe'e a-ha we-o-'e.

Song of the sky loom

The small desert rains are compared to a loom hung from the sky. This also refers to the symbolic decoration on the white cotton mantle used on ceremonial occasions.

O our Mother the Earth, O our Father the Sky,
Your children are we, and with tired backs
We bring you the gifts that you love.
Then weave for us a garment of brightness;
May the warp be the white light of morning,
May the weft be the red light of evening,
May the fringes be the falling rain,
May the border be the standing rainbow.
Thus weave for us a garment of brightness
That we may walk fittingly where birds sing,
That we may walk fittingly where grass is green,
O our Mother the Earth, O our Father the Sky!

Rain magic song

Ready we stand in San Juan town,
O, our Corn Maidens and our Corn Youths!
O, our Corn Mothers and our Corn Fathers!

Now we bring you misty water
And throw it different ways,
To the north, the west, the south, the east
To heaven above and the drinking earth below!

Then likewise throw you misty water
Towards San Juan!
O, many that you are, pour water
Over our Corn Maidens' ears!
On our Wheat Maidens
Thence throw you misty water,
All round about us here!

On Green Earth Woman's back
Now thrives our flesh and breath,
Now grows our strength of arm and leg,
Now takes form our children's food.

The willows by the water side

My little breath, under the willows by the water side
        we used to sit
And there the yellow cottonwood bird came and sang.
That I remember and therefore I weep.
Under the growing corn we used to sit,
And there the leaf bird came and sang.
That I remember and therefore I weep.
There on the meadow of yellow flowers we used to walk
O, my little breath! O, my little heart!
There on the meadow of blue flowers we used to walk.
Alas! how long ago that we two walked in that pleasant way.
Then everything was happy, but, alas! how long ago.
There on the meadow of crimson flowers we used to walk.
O, my little breath, now I go there alone in sorrow.

Shadows

That somebody, my own special one,
Even his shadow and his voice are loved.
His foot fall even! But what can I do?
That other one, O how I hate his shadow!
His shirt is fine and white, his hat is grey,
His leggings and his shoes are beaded bright,
His neckerchief is gay and yellow – but
For all his clothes, his face, his face is black!

Lost love

At Su K'wa K'e there used to bloom a flower –
That flower, that flower, where'er I see it now
Alas, so far away, why then I weep;
That flower, that flower, where'er I see it now,
For yellow, fresh and full-blown once it bloomed.

Regret and refusal

The boy had left home to go and marry a Mexican woman,
and live in Truchas. Now he comes back to his first love.

BOY: All round about the door of your house
The red and full-blown flowers grow
And there are striped ones of yellow
And there are striped ones of white!

About your door how gay it used to be,
My little pony, even he had flowers,
Alas, alas, and woe is me!

GIRL: Once at my house how yellow, fresh
And full-blown was the flower you had!
How green and fresh and full-blown
Was the flower that once you had!

BOY: My woman also she has many flowers
         Yonder in Truchas, yonder in Seha.

GIRL: So now he comes back to his sweetheart.
         So now you remember me and come back!
         Yes, yonder you thought again of your sweetheart
         For they sang you a song of corn grinding,
         Those young men there, on Saturday afternoon.

BOY: Alone with myself and seeing you never
         What can I do, alas what will avail?
         Because you leave me now, you leave me,
         But ever when I think of you I weep.

GIRL: My foolish one, you cannot hold me now:
         No man will I remember. It is done.

I wonder how my home is

In San Juan I wonder how my home is.
Surrounded by green cottonwoods my home is,
Now I remember all and now I sing!
Now I remember how I used to live
And how I used to walk amid my corn
And through my fields. Alas! What can I do?

Disillusion

Long ago how fine was everything!
Fat mutton was all I ate,
Coffee and sugar were all I ate,
But now all I eat is the whip!

Scalp dance song

Next after comes Coyote, Stretched-out-in Dew,[3]
Next after braves of yesterday or the day before!
To Blue Earth town of the Navahos we go
And arriving we shall kill. So that is why
Coyote, Stretched-out-in Dew, sits straight and ready.
Wi-ya-he-na, a-nde-a-a. The next scalp!

Navaho youths! Your fault alone it is
That now you die fallen along your house.
Your fault alone it is that now you die
Fallen along your house with earth-streaked thighs,
That now your mouths are stopped and streaked with earth.
Ho-o-wi-na, a-ye-a-a. The next scalp!

Dead on the war path

This very day, a little while ago, you lived
But now you are neither man nor woman,
Breathless you are, for the Navahos killed you!
Then remember us not, for here and now
We bring you your food. Then take and keep
Your earth-walled place: once! twice!
Three times! four times! Then leave us now!

Songs in the turtle dance at Santa Clara

Long ago in the north
Lies the road of emergence,
Yonder our ancestors live,
Yonder we take our being.

3. The coyote's special name in his role of devourer of slain
enemies.

Yet now we come southwards
For cloud flowers blossom here
Here the lightning flashes,
Rain water here is falling!

A ha haya, ehe he,
A ha haya, ehe he!
Fog clouds and cloud flowers
On various mountains lie,
Cloud flowers are blooming now
Te he kwa, te he kwa!

From the north the lightning
Now makes flashes
The thunder rumbles now,
Rain water now is falling!
Aha we ahe, aha we ahe,
Aha a a a, e e he e heye!

The cloud-flower lullaby

In the north the cloud flower blossoms,
And now the lightning flashes,
And now the thunder clashes
And now the rain comes down!
A-a-aha, a-a-aha, my little one.

In the west the cloud flower blossoms
And now the lightning flashes,
And now the thunder clashes
And now the rain comes down!
A-a-aha, a-a-aha, my little one.

In the south the cloud flower blossoms,
And now the lightning flashes,
And now the thunder clashes
And now the rain comes down!
A-a-aha, a-a-aha, my little one.

In the east the cloud flower blossoms,
And now the lightning flashes,
And now the thunder clashes
And now the rain comes down!
A-a-aha, a-a-aha, my little one.

Corn-blossom maidens

Masahongva

Corn-blossom maidens
Here in the fields,
Patches of beans in flower,
Fields all abloom,
Water shining after rain,
Blue clouds looming above.

Now behold!
Through bright clusters of flowers
Yellow butterflies
Are chasing at play,
And through the blossoming beans
Blue butterflies
Are chasing at play.

Yellow butterflies

Koianimptiwa

This was specially composed for a coming dance at 'Corn-planting time' in May. Just as the Hopi paint their faces for a ceremonial dance, so have the butterflies painted themselves with pollen for their flight over the corn blossoms. 'The butterflies must go through many flowers' say the Hopi 'to make themselves so pretty.'

Yellow butterflies,
Over the blossoming virgin corn,
With pollen-painted faces
Chase one another in brilliant throng.

Blue butterflies,
Over the blossoming virgin beans,
    With pollen-painted faces
Chase one another in brilliant streams.

    Over the blossoming corn,
    Over the virgin corn
Wild bees hum:
    Over the blossoming beans,
    Over the virgin beans,
Wild bees hum.

Over your field of growing corn
    All day shall hang the thunder cloud;
Over your field of growing corn
    All day shall come the rushing rain

Butterfly maidens

Lahpu

Said Lahpu of his song: 'This is the first song that I ever made. I had been a long time away, and so my heart was happy as I came through the fields. I saw the Hopi girls playing among the corn plants, chasing one another and laughing and singing, and – I liked it; it was pretty, and I was happy, so I made this song about it.'

Rain all over the cornfields,
Pretty butterfly maidens
Chasing one another when the rain is done,
    Hither, thither, so.
How they frolic 'mid the corn,
    Laughing, laughing, thus:
    A-ha, ha-ha,
    O-ah, e-lo!
How they frolic 'mid the corn,
    Singing, singing, thus:
    O-o, o-ho,
    O-he, e-lo!

Flute song

Masaveimah and Kavanghongevah

The flute ceremony is a prayer for rain and spring water, associated with the 'flute societies' in every Hopi village. This song belongs to the Grey Flute Society.

Hail, fathers, hail!
Chieftains of the Grey Flute, hail!
At the four world-points
Ye call, ye summon clouds.
From the four world-points upstarting,
Shall the rain hither come.

Hither thunder, rain-thunder here,
Hither the rain-thunder will come;
Hither rain, moving-rain –
Onward now, over all the fields,
        Moving-rain.
And the wet earth, 'mid the corn,
Everywhere, far and near,
It will shine – water-shine.

Now from the east ...

Masahongva

A *hevebe* (or cloud) song.

Now from the east
The white dawn hath arisen.

Now from the east
The yellow dawn hath arisen.

Please ye, please ye,
Now awake!
Arouse yourselves;
Look ye here,
O, look on us!

Lift your water-jars and o'er us
    Pour ye, pour:
    Pour ye, pour ye,
    Cold, cold!
    Cold, cold!

Hevebeta, come, O, come!
    Pour down, pour down,
    Pour down, pour down!

Come we, white dawnlight-youths,
Come we, yellow dawnlight-youths.

Bringing joy to ye,
E'en as joyful, we,

Here where dwell the maids –
Dwell the shower maidens,
    Cold, cold!
    Cold, cold!

The rainbow

    In this corn-grinding song the rainbow is imagined as the
Rainbow Youth, and he is described as 'brightly decked and painted'.
The swallow is the summoner of rain: he 'sings for rain!'

Yonder, yonder see the fair rainbow,
See the rainbow brightly decked and painted!
Now the swallow bringeth glad news to your corn,
Singing, 'Hitherward, hitherward, hitherward, rain,
    Hither come!'
Singing, 'Hitherward, hitherward, hitherward, white cloud,
    Hither come!'
Now hear the corn plants murmur,
'We are growing everywhere!'
Hi, yai! The world, how fair!

Song of the blue-corn dance

Beautiful, lo, the summer clouds,
Beautiful, lo, the summer clouds!
Blossoming clouds in the sky,
Like unto shimmering flowers,
Blossoming clouds in the sky,
Onward, lo, they come,
Hither, hither bound!

The earthquake

From a Zuni legend.

There was an earthquake
At Where-the-pine-tree-stands.

The rocks fell;
The people had fear.

The Priests assembled,
The Chiefs, the Head Ones;
They took council.

> Call a fleet runner,
> Let a messenger be sent forth to Hopi;
> Call Tecaminka, Echo,
> The God who dwells South of Itiwana.

Where the earth is cracked
They have placed bundles of feathers,
They have made mats of reeds: *la'kine*.
The daylight people
Do not know how to shut up the earth:

> O Earth Mother,
> Do not open up,
> Nor let wild animals,
> Nor floods
> Destroy thy children:

> Thy valuable children,
> Thy valuable children.

The taboo woman

She is *teck'wi*,
    Taboo.

Do not go near her,
    My Brother.
She is *teck'wi*.

She may not eat the purple-flowered herb.

The holy men of Zuni,
The Darkness Priests,
These guard her.

Kolowisi,
Guardian of the Sacred Springs,
Who punishes trespassers,
He will guard her.

Do not go near her,
    My Brother,
She is *teck'wi*:
    Taboo.

The songs

I heard the songs:
    The Thunder songs,
    The Dancing songs,
    The Fire-making songs,
    The Dawn songs,
    The Flute songs
    At the grinding of the corn . . .

I heard the songs
    Chanted under a turquoise sky
    In the mountains north of Zuni:

I heard the cry of an ancient people:
>We who die
>Await the morning: Tekahanan'e.
>>Tekahanan'e.

In the mountains north of Zuni
>I heard their cry . . .

Our earth mother

Three Zuni prayers.

That our earth mother may wrap herself
In a fourfold robe of white meal;
That she may be covered with frost flowers;
That yonder on all the mossy mountains,
The forests may huddle together with the cold;
That their arms may be broken by the snow,
In order that the land may be thus,
I have made my prayer sticks into living beings.

When our earth mother is replete with living waters,
When spring comes,
The source of our flesh,
All the different kinds of corn,
We shall lay to rest in the ground.
With their earth mother's living waters,
They will be made into new beings.
Coming out standing into the daylight
Of their sun father,
Calling for rain,
To all sides they will stretch out their hands.
Then from wherever the rain-makers stay quietly
They will send forth their misty breath;
Their massed clouds filled with water will come out to sit down
>with us;
Far from their homes,

With outstretched hands of water they will embrace the corn,
Stepping down to caress them with their fresh waters,
With their fine rain caressing the earth,
With their heavy rain caressing the earth,
And yonder, wherever the roads of the rain-makers come forth,
Torrents will rush forth,
Silt will rush forth,
Mountains will be washed out,
Logs will be washed down,
Yonder all the mossy mountains
Will drip with water.
The clay-lined hollows of our earth mother
Will overflow with water,
From all the lakes
Will rise the cries of the children of the rain-makers,
In all the lakes
There will be joyous dancing –
Desiring that it should be thus,
I send forth my prayers.

That our earth mother
May wear a fourfold green robe,
Full of moss,
Full of flowers,
Full of pollen,
That the land may be thus
I have made you into living beings.

Corn-grinding song

This way from the North
Comes the cloud,
Very blue,
And inside the cloud is the blue corn.
How beautiful the cloud
Bringing corn of blue colour!

This way from the West
Comes the cloud
Very yellow,
And inside the cloud is the yellow corn.
How beautiful the cloud
Bringing corn of yellow colour!

This way from the South
Comes the cloud
Very red,
And inside the cloud is the red corn.
How beautiful the cloud
Bringing corn of red colour!

This way from the East
Comes the cloud,
Very white,
And inside the cloud is the white corn.
How beautiful the cloud
Bringing corn of white colour!

How beautiful the clouds
From the North and the West
From the South and the East
Bringing corn of all colours!

The sunrise call

Rise! arise! arise!
Rise! arise, arise!
Wake ye! arise, life is greeting thee.
Wake ye, arise, ever watchful be.
Mother Life-god, she is calling thee!
Mother Life-god, she is calling thee!
Mother Life-god, she is greeting thee.
All arise, arise, arise!
Rise! arise, arise!

Mighty Sun-god! give thy light to us,
Let it guide us, let it aid us.
See it rise! See it rise!
How the heart glows, how the soul delights,
In the music of the sunlight.
Watch it rise! Watch it rise!
Wake ye, arise, life is greeting thee.
Wake ye, arise, ever watchful be.
Mother Life-god, she is calling thee!
Mother Life-god she is greeting thee.
All arise, arise, arise!
Rise! arise, arise!

Sunset song

Good night to thee, Fair Goddess,
We thank thee for thy blessing.
Good night to thee, Fair Goddess,
We thank thee for this day.
In glory we behold thee
At early dawn again.
We thank thee for thy blessing,
To be with us this day.
This day,
We thank thee for this day.

Uru-tu-sendo's song

Yonder comes the dawn,
The universe grows green,
The road to the Underworld
Is open! Yet now we live,
Upward going, upward going!

ESKIMO

The Eskimos form one of the most remarkable and specialized cultures of the world. They circle nearly half the globe along the Arctic coast of North America, Greenland, and a short stretch of the Siberian shore near the Bering Straits. Throughout this vast area their culture and even language are amazingly uniform: despite differences of dialect, Rasmussen was able to communicate with all the Eskimos he met in his famous trek across Eskimo territory in 1921. Their language is apparently peculiar to themselves: certainly no affinities to any other language group have been conclusively proved.

The poems printed here were for the most part collected in the first quarter of the present century, and for this reason the conditions described in these introductory notes mainly refer to that period. By now many Eskimos – who number in all around 50,000 – have entered the wage labour market. However, as late as the 1960s there were still many who kept to the traditional mode of life, remote from modern western civilization, and it is unlikely that their rich heritage of poetry has vanished.

The Eskimos have to survive in an environment which, one would have thought, is hostile in the extreme to human life, at least without the advantages of a highly developed material technology. The temperature is often below freezing, the winter days provide at best only a few hours of daylight in which to seek food, and there are no trees to provide shelter or fuel – or indeed wood for making implements. Yet the Eskimos have somehow developed a way of life that enables them to cope with their environment and to create a culture which is more than a mere battle for physical survival. They imbue their experiences and even their perception of themselves and of nature around them with poetic comment and reflection. Their struggles with their harsh environment seem to provide an opportunity, rather than an obstacle, for the development of poetry of a strikingly personal and meditative nature.

The main Eskimo activities are seasonally determined

and need to be understood in outline for an appreciation of many of these poems. There are local variations, but one common traditional pattern is for the winter to be spent in settlements along the coast in pursuit of the seal, the main winter resource. At this season the solitary hunter waits hour after hour standing over the breathing holes in the ice, waiting for the seal to appear at last and fall victim to the hunter's harpoon. Sometimes his long wait is successful, but, if not, starvation or at best hunger may not be far away – an experience alluded to in a number of the poems. In the spring, as the ice floes break up and thaw, fishing becomes possible from skin-covered canoes, or kayaks, and the walrus and other sea mammals are preyed upon. By land polar bears and the heavy and slow-moving musk oxen can be pursued and brought down by the effective hunter. As summer approaches, the Eskimos move in-land to seek the herds of caribou which are feeding on the summer growth of mosses and lichen, a time when life is a little easier: 'Glorious it is to see the caribou . . .' The diet is now supple-mented by berries and roots gathered by the women, and abundant fish in rivers and lakes.

This seasonal pattern of activities is reflected clearly in Eskimo poetry. There are poems describing the fears and triumphs of hunting, as well as the deep bitterness and nostalgia felt by the ageing hunter who can no longer provide for himself or his family by the strength of his arm. There are canoe songs, berry-picking songs, and poems that spring from the solitary experience by the seal blow holes in winter or trout streams in summer.

Eskimo poetry is more than just a reflection of their physical existence. In their poems they express their wonder and excitement at the world around them, the idea that despite its trials life is 'glorious'. They have to face suffering and hunger, but they also hear 'The song of the sea, And the great sighing of the new formed ice'. The experiences of hunting or fishing are not just endured but are used in the imagery of a poem to reflect on the meaning of life or the problems of artistic creativity – a topic of deep interest to the Eskimo. Besides the various religious and cere-monial songs, men and women all have their own personal poems which they are inspired to compose, ranging from the deeply felt ecstasy of the shaman or the mother's almost unbearable lament, 'I should be ashamed' to the ironic and detached 'Old man's song' or the simultaneous resignation and happiness of the rejected wife's 'I am but a little woman'. Poetry for them is a constant experience, not a specialized activity set aside for some professional group or occasion. In at least one Eskimo dialect the same words mean both to 'make a poem' and 'to breathe'.

The solitariness of much of Eskimo activity may be connected with what is perhaps the most striking feature of all in Eskimo poetry: the preoccupation with finding oneself, the doubting, mistrustful, self-ironic, and yet determined struggle to understand and create experience through the words of a poem. In this way many poems are remarkably self-reflective and intro-spective. One of the greatest of the Eskimo poets included here, Orpingalik, called his songs 'comrades in solitude' and used to say that 'his songs were his breath', so necessary were they to him, to such an extent they were part and parcel of himself: 'All my being is song, and I sing as I draw breath.'

Orpingalik's description of the nature of poetry and poetic composition will seem very familiar to most western readers, with its stress on the emotional element in poetry and the power of unconscious forces.

Songs are thoughts, sung out with the breath when people are moved by great forces and ordinary speech no longer suffices.

Man is moved just like the ice floe sailing here and there out in the current. His thoughts are driven by a flowing force when he feels joy, when he feels fear, when he feels sorrow. Thoughts can wash over him like a flood, making his breath come in gasps and his heart throb. Something like an abatement in the weather will keep him thawed up. And then it will happen that we, who always think we are small, will feel still smaller. And we will fear to use words. When the words we want to use shoot up of themselves – we get a new song.[1]

Another Eskimo – this time from Alaska – conveyed much the same idea when he spoke of poems being born in 'stillness' and 'waiting': 'They take shape in the minds of men and rise up like

1. K. Rasmussen, *The Netsilik Eskimos*, Copenhagen, 1931, p. 321.

bubbles from the depths of the sea, bubbles that seek the air to burst in the light.'[2]

This romantic theory of poetry is apparently of great significance in Eskimo culture, and is in evidence in a number of poems here. But it is clear too that – just as in our own culture – it is not a full description of the facts of poetic composition: Eskimo poets do not *just* wait for inspiration to take hold of them, they also work hard at their poems. As Rasmussen writes: 'Great pains are taken to put the words together nicely and skilfully so that there is melody in them, while at the same time they are pertinent in expression. A man who wants to compose a song may long walk to and fro in some solitary place, arranging his words while humming a melody which he also has to make up himself.'[3] The Eskimo poet is also bound to some extent by the local artistic conventions. The emphasis on repetition throughout a poem is one striking feature, either as a refrain in the songs or used in a subtle way to mark parallelisms of language and sense. There is also frequently a use of assonance and occasionally of rhyme. In addition there are established poetic genres which the poet is likely to find himself observing.

Some of these genres have already been mentioned. There are hunting, canoeing, and berry-picking poems, all normally sung, often with a refrain. Some of the other poems are recited, without music, perhaps particularly some of the more personal songs. One interesting group are the famous Eskimo poems and songs of derision. These are sometimes exchanged between two friends without necessarily impairing their friendship – as in the case of Utahania's 'Accusation'. They also appear as song duels and competitions which function among the Eskimos as a way of resolving disputes. In this sense they have been classified as one of the quasi-legal sanctions by which Eskimos maintained law and order without any of the mechanisms of organized legal administration or state power – a remarkable tribute to the power of poetry among the Eskimos.

Another important group of poems are the religious poems. Some, like 'Spirit song', are sung in chorus, but others are the personal poems of individual shamans (or religious experts).

2. D. Freuchen (ed.), *Peter Freuchen's book of the Eskimos*, London, 1962, pp. 280–81.   3. Rasmussen, op. cit., p. 320.

Religious leadership makes almost the only exception to the lack of specialization and hierarchy. Shamans are said to be inspired – an experience vividly conveyed in 'Song of joy' – and to speak in special shamanistic language in the process of ecstatic possession. During this experience they commune with attendant spirits who have their 'own' poems. They also act as a blend of doctor, prosecutor, and psychiatrist in order to diagnose and then cure sufferers from various disorders attributed to some sin on the patient's part. The shamanistic experience of possession and inspiration, allied to the resources of special imagery and symbolism in the shaman's language, makes it not surprising that some of the most gifted Eskimo poets (Aua and Orpingalik, for instance) were shamans – even though every Eskimo aspired to some degree of poetic creativity.

Poetry pervades Eskimo life. Men and women sing constantly while travelling or working; children make up songs among themselves; solitary hunters ponder the words of a song; a woman composes an impromptu song to welcome a guest; a successful hunter boasts of his prowess as he returns home. Songs are an essential part too of festivals during the season of plenty, and in the song duels. The harsh struggle for survival among the Eskimos seems not so much to have squeezed out the time for poetry or blunted their artistic sensitivity, as to have provided its opportunity and stimulus. The hard facts of too little food may have forced the Eskimo at times to infanticide or senilicide – but an Eskimo poet can still produce a haunting and deeply emotional poem like 'Song of a dead man'. Even the self-belittling and ironic tone of some of their poems and the evocation of the puniness of man struggling against the forces of nature (their poems about hunger and the impotence of man) only make their poetry seem all the more profound and moving.

Most of the translations we have are relatively literal and Eskimo poetry seems, in any case, to have none of the easy grace or immediate attractiveness of, say, the Gond love lyrics or Hawaiian nature poems. But their searching, ironic, and even (in a sense) laboured nature, perhaps more deeply and intensely personal than any other of the poems in this volume, must surely give the lie to the once accepted idea that non-literate and non-technologically developed peoples with little division of labour are incapable of individual expression or reflective detachment.

Solitary song

Only the air-spirits know
What lies beyond the hills,
Yet I urge my team farther on
Drive on and on,
On and on!

The sun and the moon and fear of loneliness

There is fear in
Turning the mind away,
Longing for loneliness,
Amid the joyous
People's throng.
      Iyaiya – ya – ya.

There is joy in
Feeling the warmth
Come to the great world
And seeing the sun
Follow its old footprints
In the summer night.
      Iyaiya – ya – ya.

There is fear in
Feeling the cold
Come to the great world
And seeing the moon
– Now new moon, now full moon –
Follow its old footprints
In the winter night.
      Iyaiya – ya – ya.

Where does it all go?
I long for the east!
And yet, no more shall I see my uncle,
To whom my mind would fain be revealed.

Song of caribou, musk oxen, women, and men who would be manly

Glorious it is to see
The caribou flocking down from the forests
And beginning
Their wandering to the north.
Timidly they watch
For the pitfalls of man.
Glorious it is to see
The great herds from the forests
Spreading out over plains of white.
Glorious to see.
     Yayai – ya – yiya.

Glorious it is to see
Early summer's short-haired caribou
Beginning to wander.
Glorious to see them trot
To and fro
Across the promontories,
Seeking a crossing place.
     Yai – ya – yiya.

Glorious it is
To see the great musk oxen
Gathering in herds.
The little dogs they watch for
When they gather in herds.
Glorious to see.
     Yai – ya – yiya.

Glorious it is
To see young women
Gathering in little groups
And paying visits in the houses –
Then all at once the men
Do so want to be manly,
While the girls simply
Think of some little lie.
     Yayai – ya – yiya.

Glorious it is
To see long-haired winter caribou
Returning to the forests.
Fearfully they watch
For the little people,
While the herd follows the ebb-mark of the sea
With a storm of clattering hooves.
Glorious it is
When wandering time is come.
      Yayai – ya – yiya.

Hunger

Fear was about me . . .
In my little house
Remaining was intolerable.

Hungry and starving
I staggered on over land,
For ever stumbling forwards.

At 'the little musk-ox lake'
The trout made fun of me.
I got no bite.

Onward then I toiled
To 'the young man's broad' –
I had caught salmon there once.

I did so wish to see
Swimming caribou or fish in a lake.
That joy was my one wish.

My thought ended in nothing.
It was like a line
That all runs out.

Would I ever, I wondered
Have firm ground to stand on?
Magic words I mumbled all the way.

Hymn to the air spirit

Here I stand,
Humble, with outstretched arms,
For the spirit of the air
Lets glorious food sink down to me.

Here I stand
Surrounded with great joy.
For a caribou bull with high antlers
Recklessly exposed his flanks to me.
– Oh, how I had to crouch
In my hide.

But, scarcely had I
Hastily glimpsed his flanks
When my arrow pierced them
From shoulder to shoulder.

And then, when you, lovely caribou
Let the water go
Out over the ground
As you tumbled down,
Well, then I felt surrounded with great joy.

Here I stand,
Humble, with outstretched arms.
For the spirit of the air
Lets glorious food sink down to me.
Here I stand
Surrounded with great joy.
And this time it was an old dog seal
Starting to blow through his breathing hole.
I, little man,
Stood upright above it,
And with excitement became
Quite long of body,
Until I drove my harpoon in the beast
And tethered it to
My harpoon line!

Dead man's song, dreamed by one who is alive

Paulinaoq

A poem said to be by the dead man Aijuk, dreamed by
Paulinaoq.

I am filled with joy
When the day peacefully dawns
Up over the heavens,
      ayi, yai ya.

I am filled with joy
When the sun slowly rises
Up over the heavens,
      ayi, yai ya.

But else I choke with fear
At greedy maggot throngs;
They eat their way in
At the hollow of my collarbone
And in my eyes,
      ayi, yai ya.

Here I lie, recollecting
How stifled with fear I was
When they buried me
In a snow hut out on the lake,
      ayi, yai ya.

A block of snow was pushed to,
Incomprehensible it was
How my soul should make its way
And fly to the game land up there,
      ayi, yai ya.

That door-block worried me,
And ever greater grew my fear
When the fresh-water ice split in the cold,
And the frost-crack thunderously grew
Up over the heavens,
      ayi, yai ya.

Glorious was life
In winter.
But did winter bring me joy?
No! Ever was I so anxious
For sole-skins and skins for *kamiks*,
Would there be enough for us all?
Yes, I was ever anxious,
     ayi, yai ya.

Glorious was life
In summer.
But did summer bring me joy?
No! Ever was I so anxious
For skins and rugs for the platform,
Yes, I was ever anxious,
     ayi, yai ya.

Glorious was life
When standing at one's fishing hole
On the ice.
But did standing at the fishing hole bring me joy?
No! Ever was I so anxious
For my tiny little fish-hook
If it should not get a bite,
     ayi, yai ya.

Glorious was life
When dancing in the dance-house.
But did dancing in the dance-house bring me joy?
No! Ever was I so anxious,
That I could not recall
The song I was to sing.
Yes, I was ever anxious,
     ayi, yai ya.

Glorious was life . . .
Now I am filled with joy
For every time a dawn
Makes white the sky of night,
For every time the sun goes up
Over the heavens,
     ayi, yai, ya.

Men's impotence

Perhaps – well
It may not matter!
Perhaps – well.
I sing merely of him,
'The boiling one',
Who sat, fearful, his mouth fast closed,
Among women.

Perhaps – well
It may not matter!
Perhaps – well.

I sing merely of him,
'Caribou Stomach',
Who sat, fearful, his mouth fast closed,
Among women.
His two eyes ill-boding,
Bent like a horn
To be cut into leisters!

Perhaps – well
It may not matter!
Perhaps – well.
I sing merely of him,
'The Axe',
Who sat, fearful, his mouth fast closed,
Far, far away from man,
In solitude.

Perhaps – well
It may not matter!
Perhaps – well.
My tongue merely joins words
Into a little song.
A little mouth,
Curling downwards at the corners,
Like a bent twig
For a kayak rib.

Morning prayer

Aua

I rise up from rest,
Moving swiftly as the raven's wing
I rise up to meet the day –
Wa-wa.

My face is turned from the dark of night
My gaze towards the dawn,
Towards the whitening dawn.

The mother's song

It is so still in the house,
There is a calm in the house;
The snowstorm wails out there,
And the dogs are rolled up with snouts under the
     tail.
My little boy is sleeping on the ledge,
On his back he lies, breathing through his open
     mouth.
His little stomach is bulging round –
Is it strange if I start to cry with joy?

Personal song

Arnatkoak

A good and therefore respected hunter likes to belittle him-
self in song, realizing that this will double the effect among the audience.

It is a time of hunger,
But I don't feel like hunting,
I don't care for the advice of the old people,
I only care for dreaming, wishing, nothing else.

I only care for gossip;
I am fond of young caribou, the age they start getting their
    antlers;
Nobody is like me,
I am too lazy, simply too lazy,
I just can't bring myself to go and get some meat.

I should be ashamed

Uvlunuaq

The son of Uvlunuaq and her husband Orpingalik (the
poet and shaman) had killed a man and as a result had to flee from
justice and live as an outlaw in the remote hills for fear of being arrested
by the Mounted Police. When his mother heard the news, she sat for
many days in silent and tearless grief inside her tent. Then she sang this
song.

Eyaya-eya.
I recognize
A bit of a song,
And take it to me
Like a fellow-human.
Eyaya-eya.

I should be ashamed
Of the child
I once carried proudly
In the *amaut*,
When I heard of his flight
From the dwellings of people.
Eyaya-eya.

They who think so,
Right are they.
Eyaya-eya.

Right are they.
Eyaya-eya.
I am ashamed,
But only because
He didn't have a mother
Who was blameless as the blue sky,
Wise and without folly.
Now, people's tongues will instruct him,
And gossip complete the education,
Eyaya-eya.

This have I –
His mother – deserved,
I who brought forth a child
That should not become the refuge of my old age.
Eyaya-eya.

I should be ashamed!
Instead I envy those
Who have crowds of friends behind them,
Waving on the ice,
When after festive leave-taking their journey begins.
Eyaya-eya.

I remember one spring
We broke camp at 'The Squinting Eye'.
The weather was mild.
Our footsteps
Sank gently creaking
Down in sun-thawed snow –
I was then like a tame animal,
Happy in the company of people.

But when message came
Of the killing and the flight,
Earth became like a mountain with pointed peak,
And I stood on the awl-like pinnacle
And faltered,
And fell!

I am but a little woman . . .

Kivkarjuk

Kivkarjuk was inspired by the spirit to sing this song, and so stepped forward from the chorus to sing it on her own at the festival held in the tent of the man who had rejected her as his first wife.

I am but a little woman
Very willing to toil,
Very willing and happy
To work and slave . . .
And in my eagerness
To be of use,
I pluck the furry buds of willow
Buds like beard of wolf.

I love to go walking far and far away,
And my soles are worn through
As I pluck the buds of willow,
That are furry like the great wolf's beard . . .

Bear hunting

Aua

I spied a bear
On the drifting floe
Like a harmless dog
It came running and wagging its tail towards me
But all so eager to eat me up
That it swung round snarling
When I leaped aside.
And now came a game of catch-me-who-can
That lasted from morning till late in the day.
But at last it was wearied
And could play no more,
So I thrust my spear into its side.

Walrus hunting

Aua

I could not sleep
For the sea was so smooth
Near at hand.
So I rowed out
And up came a walrus
Close by my kayak.
It was too near to throw,
So I thrust my harpoon into its side
And the bladder-float danced across the waves.
But in a moment it was up again,
Setting its flippers angrily
Like elbows on the surface of the water
And trying to rip up the bladder.
All in vain it wasted strength,
For the skin of an unborn lemming
Was sewn inside as an amulet to guard.
Then snorting viciously it sought to gather strength,
But I rowed up
And ended the struggle.
Hear that, O men from strange creeks and fiords
That were always so ready to praise yourselves;
Now you can fill your lungs with song
Of another man's bold hunting.

Musk oxen

Igjugarjuk

Yai – yai – yai
Ya – ayai – ya
I ran with all speed
And met them on the plain,
The great musk ox with brilliant black hair –
Hayai – ya – haya.

It was the first time I had seen them,
Grazing on the flowers of the plain,
Far from the hill where I stood,
And ignorantly I thought
They were but small and slight . . .

But they grew up out of the earth
As I came within shot,
Great black giant beasts
Far from our dwellings
In the regions of happy summer hunting.

The gull

Nakasuk

The gull, it is said,
The one who cleaves the air with its wings
The one that is usually above you
Gull, you up there
Steer down towards me
Come to me
Your wings
Are red
Up there – in the coolness.

The ageing hunter

Avane

Lo, alas, I look and seek
All impatient, eagerly,
For the caribou in the hills;
Am I old and worthless now,
Since I hunt in vain?
I who once could stand and shoot

Swiftly without aiming
Striking down with sudden arrow
Bulls with spreading horn:
Saw the great beast fall and lie
With muzzle deep in mire.

The song of the trout fisher

Ikinilik

A somewhat free rendering based on Rasmussen's
discussions of the original text with its composer.

Oft do I return
To my little song.
And patiently I hum it
Above fishing hole
In the ice.
This simple little song
I can keep on humming,
I, who else too quickly
Tire when fishing
Up the stream.

Cold blows the wind
Where I stand on the ice,
I am not long in giving up!
When I get home
With a catch that does not suffice,
I usually say
It was the fish
That failed
Up the stream.

And yet, glorious is it
To roam
The river's snow-soft ice
As long as my legs care.
Alas! My life has now glided

Far from the wide views of the peaks
Deep down into the vale of age –
Up the stream.

If I go hunting the land beasts,
Or if I try to fish,
Quickly I fall to my knees,
Stricken with faintness.

Never again shall I feel
The wildness of strength,
When on an errand I go in over land
From my house and those I provide for –
Up the stream.

A worn-out man, that's all.
A fisher, who ever without luck
Makes holes in river or lake ice
Where no trout will bite.

But life itself is still
So full of goading excitement!
I alone,
I have only my song,
Though it too is slipping from me.

For I am merely
Quite an ordinary hunter,
Who never inherited song
From the twittering birds of the sky.

Remembering

Akjartoq

I draw a deep breath,
But my breath comes heavily
As I call forth the song . . .

There are ill rumours abroad,
Of some who starve in the far places,
And can find no meat.

I call forth the song
From above,
Hayaya – haya.

And now I forget
How hard it was to breathe,
Remembering old times,
When I had strength
To cut and flay great beasts.
Three great beasts could I cut up
While the sun slowly went his way
Across the sky.

My breath

Orpingalik

The title here is the poet's: 'this is what I call this song' said Orpingalik, 'for it is just as necessary for me to sing it as it is to breathe'. The poem was composed at a time when Orpingalik was slowly recovering from a severe illness. He reflects on his present helplessness and reminisces about the past. Most of all he remembers the seal he caught while his neighbours still slept; there was famine in the village but even though he himself was weakened with hunger he had still done his duty as a hunter.

I will sing a song,
A song that is strong.
        Unaya – unaya.
Sick I have lain since autumn.
Helpless I lay, as were I
My own child.

Sad, I would that my woman
Were away to another house
To a husband
Who can be her refuge,

Safe and secure as winter ice.
    Unaya – unaya.

Sad, I would that my woman
Were gone to a better protector
Now that I lack strength
To rise from my couch.
    Unaya – unaya.

Dost thou know thyself?
So little thou knowest of thyself.
Feeble I lie here on my bench
And only my memories are strong!
    Unaya – unaya.

Beasts of the hunt! Big game!
Oft the fleeing quarry I chased!
Let me live it again and remember,
Forgetting my weakness.
    Unaya – unaya.

Let me recall the great white
Polar bear,
High up its back body,
Snout in the snow, it came!
He really believed
He alone was a male
And ran towards me.
    Unava – unava.

It threw me down
Again and again,
Then breathless departed
And lay down to rest,
Hid by a mound on a floe.
Heedless it was, and unknowing
That I was to be its fate.
Deluding itself
That he alone was a male,
And unthinking
That I too was a man!
    Unaya – unaya.

I shall ne'er forget that great blubber-beast,
A fiord seal,
I killed from the sea ice
Early, long before dawn,
While my companions at home
Still lay like the dead,
Faint from failure and hunger,
Sleeping.
With meat and with swelling blubber
I returned so quickly
As if merely running over ice
To view a breathing hole there.
And yet it was
An old and cunning male seal.
But before he had even breathed
My harpoon head was fast
Mortally deep in his neck.

That was the manner of me then.
Now I lie feeble on my bench
Unable even a little blubber to get
For my wife's stone lamp.
The time, the time will not pass,
While dawn gives place to dawn
And spring is upon the village.
        Unaya – unaya.

But how long shall I lie here?
How long?
And how long must she go a-begging
For fat for her lamp,
For skins for clothing
And meat for a meal?
A helpless thing – a defenceless woman.
        Unaya – unaya.

Knowest thou thyself?
So little thou knowest of thyself!
While dawn gives place to dawn,
And spring is upon the village.
        Unaya – unaya.

It is hard to catch trout

Piuvkaq

The poet compares the difficulties of fishing with those of poetic composition.

> Ayaiyaja
> This why, I wonder
> My song-to-be that I wish to use
> My song-to-be that I wish to put together
> I wonder why it will not come to me?
> At Sioraq it was, at a fishing hole in the ice,
> A little trout I could feel on the line
> And then it was gone,
> I stood jigging
> But why is that so difficult, I wonder?
> When summer came and the waters opened
> Then it was that catching became so hard;
> To go hunting I am not good at!

The joy of a singer

Piuvkaq

> A wonderful occupation
> Making songs!
> But all too often they
> Are failures.
>
> A wonderful fate
> Getting wishes fulfilled!
> But all too often they
> Slip past.
>
> A wonderful occupation
> Hunting caribou!
> But all too rarely we
> Excel at it
> So that we stand
> Like a bright flame
> Over the plain.

Great grief came over me

Aleqaajik

Aleqaajik is picking berries high up on the slope above the settlement where she can look down on the kayaks on the sea below. Suddenly she is overcome by grief.

Great grief came over me –
Great grief came over me,
While on the fell above us I was picking berries.
Great grief came over me
My sun quickly rose over it.
Great sorrow came over me.
The sea out there off our settlement
Was beautifully quiet –
And the great, dear paddlers
Were leaving out there –

Great grief came over me
While I was picking berries on the fell.

Accusation

Utahania

Utahania is impeaching Kanaijuaq for quarrelling with his wife and trying to abandon her out in the wilds. His wife got the better of him and finally deserted him, taking her son with her. (Kanaijuaq later retorted with another song accusing Utahania in his turn of improper behaviour at home, but the exchange seemed to make no difference to their friendship.)

Something was whispered
Of man and wife
Who could not agree.
And what was it all about?
A wife who in rightful anger
Tore her husband's furs across,
Took their canoe
And rowed away with her son.

Ay – ay, all who listen,
What do you think of him,
Poor sort of man?
Is he to be envied,
Who is great in his anger
But faint in strength,
Blubbering helplessly
Properly chastised?
Though it was he who foolishly proud
Started the quarrel with stupid words.

Mocking song against Qaqortingneq

Piuvkaq

Eager to breathe out,
I have made ready
This little bit of a song
Down along the wide road of song . . .
Mocking in exclamation,
Shapely of form,
Cutting in meaning,
Out westwards, out westwards.

Here am I,
Yes, it is I,
Fresh and alert,
Ready to answer!

Winter night, dark night
While the others slept
Came a sound that struck me
In my ear, in my ear,
Out westwards, out westwards.

People say
That my kinsman
He whose name
Is 'Tight belt'

Cried aloud
And behaved like mad
On the firm winter ice
Fabled pettishly of food theft
At a time
When all were starving.

Here am I,
Yes, it is I,
Fresh and alert,
Ready to answer!

When in bitter winter need
Our lives we tried to save
A little meat from your store,
That was all!

Shall a hunter
Greedy be?
Out westwards, out westwards.

Out you came
Knife in hand
Jealous of meat,
Angry man!

Innocently uncomprehending
All your absurd noise.
Not a thought had I of murder!
And forgetting in my folly –
Ay, it may really be –
That a mean mind can be darkened!

But here I have now come
To punish you with mockery.

It is I who plait together
Bits of songs to answer you.
Loudly must the voice resound
To deafen noise and clamour!

I would rather fight a fist fight,
All too oft words fade away,
Words melt away
Like hills in fog.

Take your accusation back!

Kittaararter

The translator writes: 'This song is remarkable in the picture it gives of the degree of culture of a young Eskimo . . . his desire "to know all things and all sort of people".'

That song there I borrow,
That song I strike up.
Let us sing it a little,
Let us strike it up a little!
What a pity it is that you make accusation [against
      me]!
Would that you would change your mind!
Cease, turn back with it!
Almost touching your object, turn back with it!
While you have immediately begun to be afraid,
While you have immediately begun to be inconstant.
I did not know fear,
I was not a coward,
When I grew up to my life's work,
When I thirsted after life –
When I weighed and investigated,
That I might know bad people,
That I might know all things.

Song of joy

Uvavnuk

The personal song of the shaman Uvavnuk, which she sang quite suddenly the first time she was possessed, and continued to sing as her own particular song, repeating it incessantly 'so that all in the house felt the same intoxication of delight'.

The great sea
Has sent me adrift,
It moves me as the weed in a great river,

Earth and the great weather
Move me,
Have carried me away
And move my inward parts with joy.

Spirit song

I will visit
Unknown woman,
Search out hidden things
Behind the man.
Let the boot-thong hang loose –
Seek thou under man
And under woman!
Smooth out the wrinkled cheeks,
Smooth wrinkles out.

I walked on the ice of the sea,
Seal were blowing at the blow holes –
Wondering I heard
The song of the sea
And the great sighing of the new-formed ice.
Go, then, go!
Strength of soul brings health
To the place of feasting.

Darkened in the soul

Napa

A song about a woman who had been bewitched and 'made dark internally'; a shaman has been summoned to investigate her condition.

What on earth! I fear and tremble!
I fear and tremble on account of myself
That he will begin to look at me again.

Does he begin to make it out, he down there.
A great terrible darkness,
A great terrible blackness,
Dreadful.

Invocation

Nakasuk

To be said in the morning when rising.

Land earth-root
Great land earth-root
Here is these
Song-texts' master
The world's pillars
They pale,
They turn white.

Song of Sukkaartik, the assistant spirit

Ajukutooq

This spirit is supposed to be an inland dweller; he sings of
having been on a trip to the coast and thinks longingly of all the sea
animals he saw there but did not catch.

Let us sing of it ever and long,
When, for a moment, I got out to the sea-side
And, at the edge of the land, in direction out over
        the sea
That I, fancy, should again really catch sight of it!

Although, in spite of that,
From out there I shouldn't get anything,
Should make no find of spoil,
Should bear home no spoil on my back,
Not even a common seal as before
And a bone-seal.

Although without prospect of spoil,
Without prospect of getting anything from out there,
I was not to make any find of spoil,
I was not to bear home any spoil on my back,
Not even a common seal as before
And a crested seal.

Although without prospect of spoil,
Without prospect of getting anything from out there
I was not to make any find of spoil,
I was not to bear home any spoil on my back,
Not even a common seal as before
And a white whale.

Although without prospect of spoil,
Without prospect of getting anything from out there
I was not to make any find of spoil.
I was not to bear home any spoil on my back,
Not even a walrus as before.

I sang of these things,
Because they are so nice to think about.

The old man's song

I have grown old,
I have lived much,
Many things I understand,
But four riddles I cannot solve.
Ha-ya-ya-ya.

The sun's origin,
The moon's nature,
The minds of women,
And why people have so many lice.
Ha-ya-ya-ya.

HAWAIIAN

Hawaii – 'the cluster of islands floating on the sea' (as it is called in one poem) – is an archipelago of islands[1] situated in the remote north-eastern region of the Pacific. The Hawaiians themselves – those whose poems are translated here – are Polynesians who believe they first came to Hawaii from the mythical land of Kahiki in the far distant past. By now the Hawaiian islands contain representatives of many races and since the nineteenth century have been much influenced by Christian missionaries. Most of the poems given here date from the nineteenth century and many of them revolve round the religious beliefs and practices of tradition.

The Hawaiians share the same basic Polynesian tradition as the Maori. They too are seafarers who look back on the great sea voyages of their ancestors who brought them from their legendary home to settle in their present islands. They also share in the aristocratic organization of the Polynesians, with their strong respect for birth and rank. Each of the larger islands was held as a kingdom under a ruling family, and ambitious chiefs used to try from time to time to control the whole group (never with success until Kamehameha I, who was able to employ European military equipment). Though they are at the other end of the Pacific Ocean from the Maori, separated from them by about 4,000 miles of sea, some of the religious traditions are strikingly alike: there is a similar interest in the process of creation and the Hawaiian god *Kane* is recognizably the equivalent of the Maori *Tane*.

The most striking characteristic of Hawaiian poetry is its remarkable feeling for the world of nature. The creation chant ('Kumulipo') enumerates in meticulous detail the creation of the various corals, fish, oysters, molluscs, turtles, and so on and so on;

1. The seven main islands are: Kauai, Niihau, Oahu, Molokai, Maui, Lanai, and Hawaii itself.

while even in the religious songs and the stories of legendary
voyages the weather and landscapes and localities involved are
constantly dwelt on. In the love poetry the images are almost
entirely drawn from nature: landscapes, the phases of the sea,
storms and rain squalls or the fragrant smell of trees. The idea that
non-literate peoples have no real 'nature poetry' becomes laughable
in face of Hawaiian poetry, when it is more likely that the reader
will feel that the Hawaiian passion for nature is, if anything, over-
done. It is full of local references – and the whole literary expression
is pervaded by the deep love of Hawaiians for their verdant
islands

> . . . Hawaii-with-the-green-back,
> A land that was found in the ocean,
> That was thrown up from the sea.

Lyric and figurative rather than narrative expression
seems to be characteristic of Hawaiian verse. A few poems, how-
ever, relate personal events (like 'Sure a poor man' or Ka-'ehu's
tragic evocation of the experience of becoming a leper). Others are
embedded in stories, interspersed with prose narrative (like 'A
stormy day' or 'The ocean is like a wreath'), and the composer of
the poem is then said to be the character who declaims or sings it in
the story. One of the longest and most complex tales is that of Pele,
the legendary heroine and goddess who set out from the mythical
land of 'Kahiki' and, after many adventures, came and settled in
Hawaii. There are often references to 'Kahiki', which becomes the
symbol of anything that is mysterious and far off. There are also
many specifically religious poems. A number of these are connected
with the rituals of the *hula*, a kind of religious service in which, as
Emerson wrote, 'poetry, music, pantomime, and the dance' are
blended into a form of dramatic art.[2] The goddess Laka is the
patron of the *hula*, and she is singled out for particular praise in
many of their songs. Otherwise the major gods of the Hawaiian
pantheon are Kane, god of light and life and the father of all
creatures, Ku, the god of war, Kanaloa (or Loa), lord of death,
and Lono, the god of harvest and of peace. Besides these there are

2. N. B. Emerson, *Unwritten literature of Hawaii*, Washing-
ton, 1909, pp. 11–12.

a number of lesser gods – like Kuula, god of fishermen, and Pele, the volcano goddess.

Besides praise of the gods, there are also many poetic eulogies to chiefs and kings as befitted the aristocratic flavour of Hawaiian life. Each king or chief had his own poet and genealogist – his 'master-of-song' – and court patronage provided a sought-after audience and source of largess to competing composers or *hula* groups. Some of the praises (or name chants) are in veiled and symbolic language, but the patron and purpose of each was known, and it belonged to the chief or family to whom it was addressed. Similarly with the genealogies and formal poetic chants about the heroic ancestors – these all formed part of the social assets of the family.

In the poetic style of Hawaii, repetition and parallelism are of great importance. This is obvious particularly in the 'Kumu-lipo', with its constant parallelisms of paired creatures and linked genealogies. Perhaps even more significant is the constant use of indirect and allusive expression. This runs through everyday speech too, but is brought to a particularly high pitch in poetry. Allusion and double meaning are extremely common, and in some poems the 'inner meaning' (*kaona*) was so veiled that only those who owned the poem understood it – though in other cases it would be obvious to anyone acquainted with the figurative speech of Hawaiian poetry.

This will be clear from a number of the poems repro-duced and commented on here. The outward or literal meaning – which may in itself already manifest poetic coherence and beauty – may be quite other from the figurative meaning. 'The Kona Sea', for instance, is ostensibly about the sea to the west of Hawaii, but the hidden meaning is of abuse and detraction; the same basic point applies to 'Love by the water-reeds', symbolically about love, and to many of the 'nature' poems in Hawaiian. This aspect is of course in a sense common to most poetic expression, but it is particularly marked in Hawaiian poetry, and clearly raises great difficulties in translation. Emerson, one of the main translators of Hawaiian lyrics, sometimes despaired of being able to convey the sense, even with the help of quite lengthy commentaries.

But, even in the cases where much of the inner mean-ing eludes us, there is still much to delight the foreign reader in the wonderful Hawaiian descriptions of nature, perhaps best of all the poetic comments on the many phases of the sea in which the Hawaiian islands are embedded:

> . . . masculine sea, feminine sea, mad sea,
> Delirious sea . . .
> . . . up-rearing billows that come hither from Kahiki.

Born was the island

Born was the island –
It budded, it leafed, it grew, it was green.
The island blossomed on tip, 'twas Hawaii
This Hawaii was an island.
Unstable was the land, tremulous was Hawaii,
Waving freely in the air;
Waved the earth.
From Akea 'twas fastened together
Quiet by the roots was the island and the land,
It was fast in the air by the right hand of Akea
Fast was Hawaii, by itself –
Hawaii appeared an island.

Old creation chant

O Kane, O Ku-ka-Pao,
With great Lono, dwelling on the water,
Brought forth are heaven and earth.
Quickened, increasing, moving,
Raised up into Continents.

The great ocean of Kane,
The ocean with the dotted seas,
The ocean with the large fishes,
And the small fishes,
The sharks, and *niuhi*,
The whales,
And the large *hihimanu* of Kane.
The rows of stars of Kane,
The stars in the firmament,
The stars that have been fastened up,
Fast, fast, on the surface of the heaven of Kane
And the wandering stars,
The sacred stars of Kane;

The moving stars of Kane.
Innumerable are the stars.
The large stars,
The small stars,
The red stars of Kane, O infinite space!
The great moon of Kane,
The great sun of Kane,
Moving, floating,
Set moving about in the great space of Kane.
The great earth of Kane,
The rain-encircled earth of Kane,
The earth that Kane set in motion.
Moving are the stars, moving is the moon,
Moving is the great earth of Kane . . .

The Kumulipo: A creation chant

Keaulumoku

The Kumulipo is a genealogical prayer chant of about 2,000 lines in all, said to have been composed by Keaulumoku in 1700. It was first printed at the end of the last century from a manuscript held by King Kalakaua.

The poem is divided into sixteen sections or *wa*, a term which also means an interval in time or space. The first seven *wa* fall in the Period of Dark, the others in the Period of Light. The earlier sections enumerate the various species created in each period, presented in long lists of pairs bound together by word associations. The later parts (over half of the entire poem) list genealogies. By these the royal family who owned the poem is linked, through the process of creation, to the primary gods, the deified chiefs in the family line, and the various other life-forms whose creation is depicted with such meticulous care in the poem. The words 'Man for the narrow stream, woman for the broad stream . . .' followed by a couplet then a three-line refrain (the 'Refrain of Generation') recur throughout the creation sections and bring out the underlying theme of procreation.

Four sections are reproduced here: the first, fourth (part only), seventh, and eighth.

Birth of sea and land life

At the time when the earth became hot
At the time when the heavens turned about
At the time when the sun was darkened
To cause the moon to shine
The time of the rise of the Pleiades
The slime, this was the source of the earth
The source of the darkness that made darkness
The source of the night that made night
The intense darkness, the deep darkness
Darkness of the sun, darkness of the night
Nothing but night.

The night gave birth
Born was Kumulipo in the night, a male
Born was Po'ele in the night, a female
Born was the coral polyp, born was the coral, came forth
Born was the grub that digs and heaps up the earth, came forth
Born was his child an earthworm, came forth
Born was the starfish, his child the small starfish came forth
Born was the sea cucumber, his child the small sea cucumber
    came forth
Born was the sea urchin, the sea urchin tribe
Born was the short-spiked sea urchin, came forth
Born was the smooth sea urchin, his child the long-spiked came
    forth
Born was the ring-shaped sea urchin, his child the thin-spiked
    came forth
Born was the barnacle, his child the pearl oyster came forth
Born was the mother-of-pearl, his child the oyster came forth
Born was the mussel, his child the hermit crab came forth
Born was the big limpet, his child the small limpet came forth
Born was the cowry, his child the small cowry came forth
Born was the *naka* shellfish, the rock oyster his child came forth
Born was the *drupa* shellfish, his child the bitter white shellfish
    came forth
Born was the conch shell, his child the small conch shell came
    forth

Born was the *nerita* shellfish, the sand-burrowing shellfish his
      child came forth
Born was the fresh-water shellfish, his child the small fresh-water
      shellfish came forth
Born was man for the narrow stream, the woman for the broad
      stream
Born was the *Ekaha* moss living in the sea
Guarded by the *Ekahakaha* fern living on land

Darkness slips into light
Earth and water are the food of the plant
The god enters, man can not enter

Man for the narrow stream, woman for the broad stream
Born was the tough seagrass living in the sea
Guarded by the tough landgrass living on land

Darkness slips into light, etc.

Man for the narrow stream, woman for the broad stream
Born was the *'A'ala* moss living in the sea
Guarded by the *'Ala'ala* mint living on land

Darkness slips into light, etc.

Man for the narrow stream, woman for the broad stream
Born was the *Manauea* moss living in the sea
Guarded by the *Manauea* taro plant living on land

Darkness slips into light, etc.

Man for the narrow stream, woman for the broad stream
Born was the *Ko'ele* seaweed living in the sea
Guarded by the long-jointed sugar-cane, the *ko 'ele'ele*, living on
      land

Darkness slips into light, etc.

Man for the narrow stream, woman for the broad stream
Born was the *Puaki* seaweed living in the sea
Guarded by the *Akiaki* rush living on land

Darkness slips into light, etc.

Man for the narrow stream, woman for the broad stream
Born was the *Kakalamoa* living in the sea
Guarded by the *moamoa* plant living on land

Darkness slips into light, etc.

Man for the narrow stream, woman for the broad stream
Born was the *Kele* seaweed living in the sea
Guarded by the *Ekele* plant living on land

Darkness slips into light, etc.

Man for the narrow stream, woman for the broad stream
Born was the *Kala* seaweed living in the sea
Guarded by the *'Akala* vine living on land

Darkness slips into light, etc.

Man for the narrow stream, woman for the broad stream
Born was the *Lipu'upu'u* living in the sea
Guarded by the *Lipu'u* living on land

Darkness slips into light, etc.

Man for the narrow stream, woman for the broad stream
Born was the Long-one living at sea
Guarded by the Long-torch living on land

Darkness slips into light, etc.

Man for the narrow stream, woman for the broad stream
Born was the *Ne* seaweed living in the sea
Guarded by the *Neneleau* living on land

Darkness slips into light, etc.

Man for the narrow stream, woman for the broad stream
Born was the hairy seaweed living in the sea
Guarded by the hairy *pandanus* vine living on land
Darkness slips into light
Earth and water are the food of the plant
The god enters, man can not enter

The man with the water gourd, he is a god
Water that causes the withered vine to flourish
Causes the plant top to develop freely
Multiplying in the passing time

The long night slips along
Fruitful, very fruitful
Spreading here, spreading there
Spreading this way, spreading that way
Propping up earth, holding up the sky
The time passes, this night of Kumulipo
    Still it is night

The crawlers

Plant the *'ahi'a* and cause it to propagate
The dusky black *'ape* plant
The sea creeps up to the land
Creeps backward, creeps forward
Producing the family of crawlers
Crawling behind, crawling in front
Advancing the front, settling down at the back
The front of my cherished one
He is dark, splendid,
Popanopano is born as a male
Popanopano, the male
Po-lalo-wehi, the female
Gave birth to those who produce eggs
Produce and multiply in the passing night
Here they are laid
Here they roll about
The children roll about, play in the sand
Child of the night of black darkness is born
The night gives birth
The night gives birth to prolific ones
The night is swollen with plump creatures
The night gives birth to rough-backed turtles
The night produces horn-billed turtles
The night gives birth to dark-red turtles
The night is pregnant with the small lobster
The night gives birth to sluggish-moving geckos
Slippery is the night with sleek-skinned geckos

The night gives birth to clinging creatures
The night proclaims rough ones
The night gives birth to deliberate creatures
The night shrinks from the ineffective
The night gives birth to sharp-nosed creatures
Hollowed is the night for great fat ones
The night gives birth to mud dwellers
The night lingers for track leavers
Born is the male for the narrow stream, the female for the broad
     stream
Born is the turtle living in the sea
Guarded by the *Maile* seedling living on land . . .
With a dancing motion they go creeping and crawling
The tail swinging its length
Sullenly, sullenly
They go poking about the dunghill
Filth is their food, they devour it
Eat and rest, eat and belch it up
Eating like common people
Distressful is their eating
They move about and become heated
Act as if exhausted
They stagger as they go
Go in the land of crawlers
The family of crawlers born in the night
     Still it is night

The dog child

Fear falls upon me on the mountain top
Fear of the passing night
Fear of the night approaching
Fear of the pregnant night
Fear of the breach of the law
Dread of the place of offering and the narrow trail
Dread of the food and the waste part remaining
Dread of the receding night

Awe of the night approaching
Awe of the dog child of the Night-creeping-away
A dog child of the Night-creeping-hither
A dark-red dog, a brindled dog
A hairless dog of the hairless ones
A dog as an offering for the oven
Palatable is the sacrifice for supplication
Pitiful in the cold without covering
Pitiful in the heat without a garment
He goes naked on the way to Malama
[Where] the night ends for the children [of night]
From the growth and the parching
From the cutting off and the quiet
The driving *Hula* wind his companion
Younger brother of the naked ones, the *'Olohe*
Out from the slime come rootlets
Out from the slime comes young growth
Out from the slime come branching leaves
Out from the slime comes outgrowth
Born in the time when men came from afar
    Still it is night

The dawn of day

Well formed is the child, well formed now
Child in the time when men multiplied
Child in the time when men came from afar
Born were men by the hundreds
Born was man for the narrow stream
Born was woman for the broad stream
Born the night of the gods
Men stood together
Men slept together
They two slept together in the time long ago
Wave after wave of men moving in company
Ruddy the forehead of the god
Dark that of man

White-bearded the chin
Tranquil was the time when men multiplied
Calm like the time when men came from afar
It was called Calmness [*La'ila'i*] then
Born was La'ila'i a woman
Born was Ki'i a man
Born was Kane a god
Born was Kanaloa the hot-striking octopus
      It was day
The wombs gave birth
Ocean-edge
The-damp-forest, latter of the two
The first chief of the dim past dwelling in cold uplands, their
      younger
The man of long life and hundreds upon hundreds of chiefs
Scoop out, scoop out,
Hollow out, hollow out, keep hollowing
Hollow out, hollow out, 'the woman sat sideways'
La'ila'i, a woman in the time when men came from afar
La'ila'i, a woman in the time when men multiplied
Lived as a woman of the time when men multiplied
Born was Groping-one, a girl
Born was Dim-sighted, a girl
Born was Beautiful called Clothed-in-leaves
Naked was another name
'She lived in the land of Lua
At that place called 'pit of the *'Olohe*'
Naked was man born in the day
Naked the woman born in the upland
She lived here with man
Born was Creeping-*ti*-plant to man
Born was Expected-day, a female
Born was Midnight, born First-light
Opening-wide was their youngest
These were those who gave birth
The little ones, the older ones
Ever increasing in number
Man spread abroad, man was here now
      It was Day

The water of Kane

In Hawaiian poetry the water of Kane has something of the mystery and romance about it that is attached to the Holy Grail in English literature.

A query, a question,
I put to you:
Where is the water of Kane?
At the Eastern Gate
Where the Sun comes in at Haehae;[3]
There is the water of Kane.

A question I ask of you:
Where is the water of Kane?
Out there with the floating Sun,[4]
Where cloud-forms rest on Ocean's breast.[5]
Uplifting their forms at Nihoa,
This side the base of Lehua;
There is the water of Kane.

One question I put to you:
Where is the water of Kane?
Yonder on mountain peak,
On the ridges steep,
In the valleys deep,
Where the rivers sweep;
There is the water of Kane.

This question I ask of you:
Where, pray, is the water of Kane?
Yonder, at sea, on the ocean,
In the driving rain,
In the heavenly bow,

3. The Eastern gate in the solid walls which support the heavenly dome, through which the sun enters in the morning.   4. When the sun is setting in the sea it appears to float on the surface of the ocean. The Hawaiian proper name for this 'Floating of the Sun' is turned into a sort of personification of the locality where it takes place. 5. Another instance of name-giving, referring to the bright clouds which seem to rest on the horizon, especially in the west.

In the piled-up mist-wraith,
In the blood-red rainfall,
In the ghost-pale cloud-form;
There is the water of Kane.

One question I put to you:
Where, where is the water of Kane?
Up on high is the water of Kane,
In the heavenly blue,
In the black piled cloud,
In the black-black cloud,
In the black-mottled sacred cloud of the gods;
There is the water of Kane.

One question I ask of you:
Where flows the water of Kane?
Deep in the ground, in the gushing spring,
In the ducts of Kane and Loa,[6]
A well-spring of water, to quaff,
A water of magic power –
The water of life!
Life! O give us this life!

Altar prayers

O goddess Laka!
O wildwood bouquet, O Laka!
O Laka, queen of the voice!
O Laka, giver of gifts!
O Laka, giver of bounty!
O Laka, giver of all things!

This my wish, my burning desire,
That in the season of slumber
Thy spirit my soul may inspire

6. According to story Kane brought out a stream of pure
water to quench the thirst of his travelling companion, Kanaloa.

Altar-dweller,
Heaven-guest,
Soul-awakener,
Bird from covert calling,
Where forest champions stand.
There roamed I too with Laka,
Of Lea and Loa a wilderness-child;
On ridge, in forest boon companion she
To the heart that throbbed in me.
O Laka, O Laka,
Hark to my call!
You approach, it is well;
You possess me, I am blest!

Ending

The ending in one version of the cycle of Pele and Hiiaka.

Awake, O rain, O sun, O night,
O mists creeping inland,
O mists creeping seaward,
O masculine sea, feminine sea, mad sea,
Delirious sea, surrounding sea of Iku.
The islands are surrounded by the sea,
The frothy sea of small billows, of low-lying billows,
Of up-rearing billows that come hither from Kahiki.[7]

Prayer of the fishing net

PRIEST: O deep-blue sea, O god Uli!
O blue of the wild, tossing sea!
Net of heaven, O Uli.
Green are the leaves of God's harvest fields.
The net fills the heavens – Shake it!

7. The mythical land of origin.

PEOPLE: Shake down the god's food!
Scatter it O heaven!
A season of plenty this.
Earth yield thy plenty!
This is a season of food.
Life to the land!
Life from Kane,
Kane the god of life.
Life from Kanaloa!
The wonder-working god.
Life to the people!
Hail Kane of the water of life! Hail!
Life to the king of the Makahiki!
Amama. It is free.

PRIEST: Free through whom?

PEOPLE: Free through Kane.

O Kane, O Lono of the blue sea . . .

O Kane, O Lono of the blue sea,
The white sea, the rough sea,
The sea with swamping breakers,
The sea, O Ku, that reaches to Tahiti,
O Ku of the ocean at Tahiti,
The sacred ocean,
Sea of the bleached skull.
Take of the sea-foam
That is the brine wherewithal to consecrate,
Consecrate the *ohia*, *ohia* of Kuamu,
Of the woodland deities, Kua-wao Kua-wa, and Kua-lana,
That the *kaei* god may make his circuit
About the pavement guarded by the *aha ula* obedient only to
         royalty.
The *ohia*, god-image of *ohia*,
God-image that shall fly to the conquest of the whole land.
That shall overthrow all enemies.

Oh Kane, here is your life-giving brine,
To be mixed with food to be drunk, to be sopped up.
Long life to the king! Long life to the *kahunas*.
Long life to all true worshippers in the temple!
It is lifted, there is freedom!
The load is removed! Freedom!
Freedom through Kane, the life-giving one!

O thirsty wind

Whence art thou, thirsty wind,
That gently kissest the sea,
Then, wed to the ocean breeze,
Playest fan with the bread-fruit tree?
Here sprawl Hala-lii's canes.
There stands bird-haunted Lehua.

The rain

'Twas in Koolau I met with the rain:
It comes with lifting and tossing of dust,
Advancing in columns, dashing along.
The rain, it sighs in the forest;
The rain, it beats and whelms, like the surf;
It smites, it smites now the land.
Pasty the earth from the stamping rain:
Full run the streams, a rushing flood;
The mountain walls leap with the rain.
See the water chafing its bounds like a dog,
A raging dog, gnawing its way to pass out.

The Kona Sea

A poem overtly about the sea which borders the west coast of Hawaii but concealing a hidden meaning of envy and abuse.

Leaf of *lehua* and *noni*-tint, the Kona Sea,
Iridescent saffron and red,
Changeable watered red, peculiar to Kona;
Red are the uplands Alaea;
Ah, 'tis the flame-red stained robes of women
Much tossed by caress or desire.
The weed-tangled water-way shines like a rope of
        pearls,
Dew-pearls that droop the coco leaf,
The hair of the trees, their long locks –
Lo, they wilt in the heat of Kailua the deep.
A mat spread out narrow and grey,
A coign of land by the sea where the fisher drops
        hook,
Now looms the mount Kilohana –
Ah, ye wood-shaded heights, everlasting your fame!
Your tabu is gone! your holy of holies invaded!
Broke down by a stranger!

Praise song for King Kalakaua

The places in the poem are all cliffs and precipices near the great volcano of Kilauea.

Ka-la-kaua, a great name,
A flower not wilted by the sun;
It blooms on the mountains,
In the forests of Mauna-kea;
It burns in Ki-lau-e-a,
Illumines the cliff Wahine-kapu,
The heights of Uwe-kahuna,
The sacred *pali* of Ka-au-e-a.

Shine forth, king of bird-hunters,
Resplendent in plumage of *mamo*,
Bright flower of Hawaii:
Ka-la-kaua, the illustrious!

Invocation for a storm

Ye fog that creeps there in the uplands,
Ye fog that creeps there in the lowlands,
Ye ugly seas, ye raving seas,
Ye seas that rise and stand.
Ye rains arise, ye winds arise,
Arise! Arise!!

A stormy day

The pointed clouds have become fixed in the heaven,
The pointed clouds grow quiet like one in pains before child-
    birth,
Ere it comes raining heavily, without ceasing.
The umbilicus of the rain is in the heaven,
The streams will yet be swollen by the rain,
The roar of thunder, the shock of the earthquake,
The flashing of the lightning in the heaven.
The light rain, the heavy rain,
The prolonged rain, the short rain.
The rain in the winter comes slanting,
Taking the breath away, pressing down the hair,
Parting the hair in the middle.
One sleeps doubled up, one sleeps with the face up.
When anger rises, the hand acts tardily.
Trouble has overcome thee, stubborn master.
See, ye sailing masters, it has come;
Trouble will overtake you in mid ocean,
You have gone out to sea and have become castaways,
You are spoken of as castaways.

You will cut out hooks from the teeth of sharks,
And fasten them to the fish-line, the fish will bite,
The *paka* eel, the *ulua*,
For Kaulua is the month.
Take good care of the favourite son,
Else he will be washed away by the sea of Kaulua.
Let the canoe therefore come ashore,
There is food ashore, there is *kapa*, there is *malo*,
Live out the stormy days and continue on your way when it
          becomes calm,
Then you can sail away, my master.
This is a stormy day; yesterday was the calm day.

The ocean is like a wreath

Kuapakaa

Gently! Gently! Gently!
Hasten this way, hasten that way,
The ocean is like a wreath around your neck.
The heaven is cloudless,
The earth is in distress,
The month is Kalo-pau.
Up comes *lepe*, down sits *lepe*.
The *iwa*[8] bird is in the sky, it is a windy day.
The rain falls, the water runs.
The shrimps are coming up, the sea-caves are exposed.
Where the sea is foamy, there the *moi*[9] dwell;
Where the sea is rough, the mullet spawn.
When the sea is at low tide, the squids are speared,
The *ina*[10] are gathered, the *wana*[10] are hooked up.
The turtles come up to breathe on a windy day.
Where the sea is not clear, there the *manini*[11] live;

8. Man-of-war bird.   9. A fine fish.   10. Sea-eggs.
11. Surgeon-fish.

Where the shoals are rocky, the *uoa* turn over;
Where the sea is blue, the sharks dwell;
Where the feeding ground is deep, the *kahala*[12] grows thin;
Where the *kukui*-nut is spat on, the sea is smooth,
The *uhu* are caught;
Caught by those in front, by Mumu, by Wawa.
As it falls down, the rain leaves holes,
The wind doubles over,
The beach at Kaunakahakai is marshy,
The scent of Kawela is strong,
The sound is deafening,
As you paddle to destruction at the point of Lehua,
Ualapue, Kaluaaha, Molokai.

Song

Kaiama

Kaiama is pictured looking from the shore as the woman he
loves departs in a canoe. He sees the boat, paddled by a throng of men,
vanishing in the twilight and it seems to him like a hazy mountain
thicket floating on the waves and concealing in it some rare flower.

Misty and dim, a bush in the wilds of Kapa'a,
The paddlers bend to their work, as the flower-laden
Shrub inclines to the earth in Maile-huna;
They sway like reeds in the breeze to crack their bones –
Such the sight as I look at this tossing grove,
The rhythmic dip and swing on to Wailua.
My call to the witch shall fly with the breeze,
Shall be heard at Pua-ke'i, e-he, e-he!
The flower-stalk Laukona beguiles man to love,
Can bring back the taste of joys once our own,
Make real again the hours that are flown.
Turn hither, mine own, let's drench us with love –
Just for one night!

12. Amber-fish.

A skilful spearman!

He could hit a blade of grass with his spear,
He could hit a flea with a spear,
He could hit an ant with his spear.

Anklet song

Each stage in putting on the costume for the *hula* dance has
special songs.

Fragrant the grasses of high Kane-hoa.
Bind on the anklets, bind!
Bind with finger deft as the wind
That cools the air of this bower.
Lehua bloom pales at my flower,
O sweetheart of mine,
Bud that I'd pluck and wear in my wreath,
If thou wert but a flower!

The rainbow stands red . . . A tiring song

When the *hula* girls have finished dressing in the tiring
room, they come out in front of the waiting assembly who greet them with
applause.

The rainbow stands red o'er the ocean;
Mist crawls from the sea and covers the land;
Far as Kahiki flashes the lightning;
A reverberant roar,
A shout of applause
From the four hundred.
I appeal to thee, Laka!

Laieikawai's lament after her husband's death

O you who come to me – alas!
Here I am,
My heart is trembling,
There is a rushing at my heart for love.
Because the man is gone – my close companion!
He has departed.

He has departed, my *lehua* blossom, spicy *kookoolau*,
With his soft pantings,
Tremulous, thick gaspings,
Proud flower of my heart,
Here – alas!

Behold me desolate –
The first faint fear branches and grows – I cannot bear it!
My heart is darkened
With love.
Alas, my husband!

Cold and Heat

O my comrade, it is cold,
Cold as the snow on the mountain top,
The cold lies at the soles of my feet,
It presses upon my heart,
The cold wakens me
In my night of sleep.

The heat, ah! the heat,
The heat of my love stifles me.
Its quivering touch scorches my heart,
The sick old heat of the winter,
The fiery heat of summer,
The dripping heat of the summer season,
The heat compels me to go,
I must go.

The beloved's image

Rising fondly before me,
The recollection of the *lehua* blossom of Puna,
Brought hither on the tip of the wind,
By the light keen wind of the fiery pit.
Wakeful – sleepless with heart longing,
With desire – O!

Love by the water-reeds

The scene is on one of the little bird islands, where the *iwa* bird flies heavily to its nest, symbolizing the man's flight in his canoe carrying off the girl he loves. The screaming sea-birds warning him off the island represent the cries of the girl's relatives. The whole poem speaks figuratively of the beauty of the girl and the passion of love through the images of the island, the storm, and the birds and trees.

The *iwa* flies heavy to nest in the brush,
Its haunt on windy Ke-ula.
The watch-bird, that fends off the rain from Le-hu-a –
Bird sacred to Ku-hai, the shark-god –
Shrieks, 'Light not on terrace of Lei-no-ai,
Lest Unu-lau fiercely assail you.'
Storm sweeps the cliffs of the islet;
A covert they seek neath the hills,
In the sheltered lee of the gale,
The cove at the base of Le-hu-a.
The shady groves there enchant them,
The scarlet plumes of *lehua*.
Love-dalliance now by the water-reeds,
Till cooled and appeased by the rain-mist.
Pour on, thou rain, the two heads press the pillow:
Lo, prince and princess stir in their sleep!

Fathomless is my love

Kalola

The cloud-piles o'er Kona's sea whet my joy.
Clouds that drop rain in fair weather.
The clustered dew-pearls shake to the ground;
The boys drone out the *na-u* to the West,
Eager for Sol to sink to his rest.
This my day for a plunge in the sea –
The Sun will be warming other shores –
Happy the tribes of that land of calm!
Fathomless, deep is my love
To thee, my passion, my mate.

Resemblance

When the rain drums loud on the leaf,
It makes me think of my love;
It whispers into my ear,
Your love, your love – she is near.

Thou art the end of my longing,
The crown of evening's delight,
When I hear the cock blithe crowing,
In the middle watch of the night.

This way is the path for thee and me,
A welcome warm at the end.
I waited long for thy coming,
And found thee in waft of the breeze.

Thou art the end of my longing, etc.

Love is a shark

Alas! I am seized by the shark, great shark!
Lala-kea with triple-banked teeth.
The stratum of Lono is gone,
Torn up by the monster shark,
Niuhi with fiery eyes,
That flamed in the deep blue sea.
Alas! and alas!
When flowers the *wili-wili* tree,
That is the time when the shark-god bites.
Alas! I am seized by the huge shark!
O blue sea, O dark sea,
Foam-mottled sea of Kane!
What pleasure I took in my dancing!
Alas! now consumed by the monster shark!

My sweetheart in the rippling hills of sand . . .

Princess Likelike (?)

My sweetheart in the rippling hills of sand
With the sea rustling the pebbles,
There, the memory is impassioned
In the forest where we delighted.

The gentle rustle of the sea
Softly in the pleasant centre
Where I looked
We delighted in the forest.

The wind came first
The Puʻu-lena wind passed by.
You've lost your chance, O friend:
She and I delighted in the forest.

Here, please listen,
Here, your lover is here.
He came last night.
We delighted in the forest.

Albatross

Lele-io-Hoku

While we are at peace
Peacefully soars the albatross
And a sweetheart makes love,
Makes love with warm heart.

I thought it was so,
Quiet taking over, unsurpassed,
Never before to see such mist
Drooping over calmed water.

To woo in the coolness,
To sway in the purple mist
And hazy view.
To throb here, throb there, throb so.

So that's your way
Superior but bubbling
Sweet clever acts
Like Wai-'ale'ale.

Puna's fragrant glades

Princess Lili'u-o-ka-lani

Puna is associated with fragrance especially of *pandanus*, and
fragrance is associated alike with noble birth and love-making.

In Puna's fragrant glades
And ever-present perfume
Passion
Is ever in the thoughts.

Puna's fragrant glades
Are drenched with perfume
In a tracery of love
Where you and I suffice.

Entranced with beauty
The *lehua* blossoms.
I come quietly to find
A flower to place upon my heart.

The glory of Hanalei is its heavy rain . . .

Alfred Alohikea

Alfred Alohikea, a popular Kauai musician and politician, composed this song in the 1920s in honour of Hanalei valley. He drew on traditional materials, such as bright green seaweed growing on the shore, the streams of Molokama tumbling down the valley and Mamalahoa, the mountain peak. Most of Alohikea's political speeches consisted of songs.

A well-known expression of grief is 'Hanalei is burdened beneath great rain'. Two places associated with rain are Hilo and Hanalei.

The glory of Hanalei is its heavy rain,
Slippery seaweed of Manu'akepa.
There I felt
Tingling cool sensation of the skin.
Greetings, O sand and rose flowers
Drenched by sea-spray.
Never have I seen such splendour.
The glory of Hanalei is its heavy rain.

Majestic streams of Molokama
Mist-covered.
You are the mist of the land
That Hanalei cherishes.
Behold the beauty of Mamalahoa
Drenched by the dew.
She and I are two,
Three with the rustle of sea-spray.

Hilo, Hanakahi, rain rustling *lehua* . . .

This song names various places on the island of Hawaii and things for which they were noted: rain, *pandanus*, wind, and sea. The listing is more or less in clockwise direction. Hanakahi was a famous chief of Hilo and a symbol of peace. Hilo-Hanakahi is a section of Hilo towards Ke-au-kaha.

Hilo, Hanakahi, rain rustling *lehua*.
Puna, fragrant bowers, bowers fragrant with *hala*.
Ka'u, the wind, the dirt scattering wind.
Kona, the sea, the streaked sea.
Ka-wai-hae, the sea, the whispering sea.
Wai-mea, the rain, the Kipu'upu'u rain.
Kohala, the wind, the Apa'apa'a wind.
Hamakua, the cliff, the tropic birds flying cliffs.
Tell the refrain, rain rustling *lehua*.

The sea! O the sea!

The sea! O the sea!
The sea is breaking,
Breaking on Kanaloa.
At the cliffs is the grave of the sea.
Passed is the quietness of the sea:
It is breaking double,
It is breaking triple.
It is a sea carried on the back of Pele.
The sea turned around and smote the earth.
The sea is rising, rising to Kilauea,
Raising up the hand of Pele.
The sea of Pele is growing larger –
The sea nestled on the breast of Pele.
The voice of the sea is tumultuous at Papalauahi;
The sea is rising to the height of Akanikolea;
The sea is spreading to the *ki* at Wahinekapu.
It is the sea of Pele the goddess!
Thy compassion be on us!

I'm going to California

Bina Mossman

In this *hula*, the man off to California asks his fiancée what he should bring her. The clothes she wants suggest post-First-World-War styles.

> I'm going to California
> When I come back, we'll be married.
> What do you want?
> She answered:
> A hat with a crooked brim,
> High-heeled shoes,
> A fringed shawl,
> A scalloped petticoat,
> And a short skirt.

Sure a poor man

The song is modelled on the subject matter and stanzaic structure, with prominent refrain, of American work ballads and marching songs, especially those in the form of autobiographical narrative mixed with social protest. It is sung to the tune of 'When Johnny comes marching home'.

> I went to a foreign land to work for money,
>   Wasted money.
> Then I went to harpoon whales,
>   Worthless whales.
> My ship soon belonged to a senator,
> My ship soon belonged to a senator.
> I came home a poor man,
> I came home a poor man.
>
> In Ke-kaha I worked as a pedlar,
>   A pedlar was I.
> The dust blew up, the sun scorched,
>   The sun did scorch and burn.
> The tax collector took all my gain,
> The tax collector took all my gain.

I came home a poor man,
I came home a poor man.

I laboured on a sugar plantation,
        Growing sugar-cane.
My back ached, my sweat poured,
        All for nothing.
I fell in debt to the plantation store,
I fell in debt to the plantation store.
And remained a poor man,
And remained a poor man.

I decided to quit working for money,
        Money to lose.
Far better work day by day,
        Grow my own daily food.
No more labouring so others get rich,
No more labouring so others get rich.
Just go on being a poor man,
Just go on being a poor man.

Piano at evening

Palea

The composer, a Hawaiian poet and chanter named Palea
(b. 1852), was a native of Ka'u, island of Hawaii. He was already a young
man when he went down to a village and heard a piano for the first time.
After he arrived home he immediately composed this chant, which soon
became popular throughout the Ka'u region. At one moment he recalls
the occasion when he and his wife ('I remember when my dear and I')
saw a mirror for the first time aboard the sailing vessel *Nautilus*.

O Piano I heard at evening,
Where are you?

Your music haunts me far into the night
Like the voice of landshells
Trilling sweetly
Near the break of day.

I remember when my dear and I
Visited aboard the *Nautilus*
And saw our first looking glass.

I remember the upland of Ma'eli'eli
Where the mists creeping in and out
Threaded their way between the old
Houses of thatch.

Again I chant my refrain
Of long ago and a piano singing
Far into the night.

The leper

Ka-'ehu

Ka-'ehu, a native of Kaua'i, was a composer, chanter, and
hula master who was active during the reigns of Ka-mehameha V,
Luna-lilo, and Ka-la-kaua. He was noted especially for his speed of
invention, being able to compose words, set them to a chant tune, and
then perform them in an hour or so. He was markedly original, particu-
larly in his use of vivid figurative language, as well as productive. He
frequently drew the subject matter of his poetry from his observations of
everyday life in Hawaii, as when he describes in one chant, for example,
belt-operated machinery in motion at the Honolulu Iron Works, or when,
in another, he celebrates the inter-island steamer, *Kilauea*, valiantly
battling the rough waters of a channel passage with a storm coming on.
This chant is autobiographical. Ka-'ehu became a leper and died at the
Ka-laupapa settlement on Moloka'i. It is his last known composition.

What will become of Hawaii?
What will leprosy do to our land –
Disease of the despised, dreaded alike
By white or brown or darker-skinned?

Strange when a man's neighbours
Become less than acquaintances.
Seeing me they drew away.
They moved to sit elsewhere, whispering,
And a friend pointed a finger:
'He is a leper.'

I bowed my head.
I knew it was true.
In my heart I hugged my shame.

Word reached the medical authorities.
The doctors sent the military to fetch us.
We were caught like chickens, like cattle herded
Along roadway and country lane.
Then they paraded us before the Board of Health
But there was no health in that Board for such as we.
Examining doctors eyed us, squinted this way and that.
More fingers pointed Diamond Head way:
'You go to Kala-wao!'

Again the militia took over.
Soldiers escorted us to the wharf for farewell.
Prisoners, we were marched aboard,
Victims of leprosy, branded for exile.
Abandoned, cut off from family and dear ones,
We were left alone with our grief, with our love.
Rain of tears streamed from leper eyes.
Leper cheeks glistened with raindrops in the sun.
Never again would we look upon this land of ours,
This lovely harbour town.

Quickly the sails were hoisted.
Ropes dangled from the foremast,
Tails of wild animals writhing,
Whipping in the channel breeze.
The *John Bull*[13] drew anchor.
In the stern the rudder turned.
So sailed we forth to dim Moloka'i Island,
Enshrouded in fog.

So ends my song and this refrain.
What will leprosy do to my people?
What will become of our land?

13. The Hawaiian name for the *Warwick*, an inter-island
sailing ship used frequently during later decades of the nineteenth
century for transporting lepers to Moloka'i. Finding the English word
Warwick unfamiliar and unpronounceable, Hawaiians preferred an easier
and still appropriate name.

Behold

Mary Kawena Pukui

'The chant is traditional in theme and structure. It is organized around four words, four indispensable terms in speaking Hawaiian, the directional words *luna* (above); *lalo* (below); *mauka* (inland, mountainward); *makai* (towards the sea). Schoolchildren in Hawaii sometimes learn this perfect chant in kindergarten, in the original; and it is taught in park recreational programmes. In compact form, with its generous, simple, strong rhythms and gestures, the chant demonstrates the Polynesian sense of the kinship of man and nature, the continuity of life in space, the magic of language, and the power of the poet's creations to triumph over time.'[14]

Above, above
All birds in air

Below, below
All earth's flowers

Inland, inland
All forest trees

Seaward, seaward
All ocean fish

Sing out and say
Again the refrain

Behold this lovely world

Prayer on making a canoe

Grant a canoe that shall be swift as a fish!
To sail in stormy seas,
When the storm tosses on all sides!

14. Note from M. K. Pukui and A. L. Korn, *The Echo of Our Song*, Honolulu, 1973, p. 107.

MAORI

The Maori of New Zealand belong to the far-flung Polynesian peoples who live in the islands scattered over thousands of miles of the Pacific with the sea as their thoroughfare. The ocean provides a link as well as a barrier, and the basic similarities in culture between Polynesian groups, apparently over many centuries, bear witness to their continuing contacts as well as their common origin.

The Polynesians are famous as great navigators over the Pacific and some of these voyages are celebrated in song. No one knows exactly when the Maori first reached New Zealand – perhaps they came in several waves of canoe voyages, one suggested date for the final migration being the fourteenth century – but, whenever it was, they still speak and sing of their first mythical home, Hawaiki. One song here celebrates the first arrival in New Zealand (Te Aotearoa, or Land of the Long White Cloud) of a group of voyagers after travelling hundreds of miles over the sea from Hawaiki – 'I arrive where an unknown earth is under my feet . . .' ('Landfall'). In another, the 'Whispering ghosts of the west' are asked to depart from this new land and leave them in peace.

Among the Maori of New Zealand, poets were traditionally held in great honour. They were, in a sense, priests and were believed to have access to inner mysteries withheld from other peoples. The traditional Maori 'school of learning' was, among other things, a means for training poets in the sacred lore pertaining to their craft. A youth of high birth could enter this school after passing the prerequisite tests, and if he was proficient proceed through the various grades of learning. In the lower grades the 'inferior' forms of knowledge were preserved – for instance the 'historical' records of legendary voyages – but in the highest grades the initiate had access to the sacred and hidden learning which was *tapu* (or taboo – forbidden) to others. By the twentieth century the formal institution of this school had disappeared, and poets like

Sir Apirana Ngata or even the late-nineteenth-century poetess
Puhiwane seem to have practised without its aid. But the aura of
mystery seems basic to the Maori idea of poetry, and with a few
exceptions a certain air of solemnity pervades much of their verse.[1]

One important theme in Maori poetry is that of crea-
tion. This topic was obviously one that preoccupied the Maori
priest-poets, for many different variations on this have been re-
corded including 'The six periods of creation', 'Chant to Io', 'The
creation of man', and many others not included here.

The religious interest comes out both in the creation
chants and in a number of other sacred songs (*karakia*). Here one
needs to know a little about the various Maori gods. There is
Tane, the god of light and of forests; Tangaroa, the god of sea and
fish; Ruaumoko, the earthquake god; and a host of minor spirits
and sprites. The most mysterious and controversial is Io. Io was in
some respect the mysterious Supreme Being, kept as a secret from
outsiders, and traditionally known only to those who attained the
highest grades of esoteric learning. The exact nature of the indi-
genous belief in Io, and its independence or otherwise of Christi-
anity, is a matter of controversy, at the heart of which lies the
'Chant to Io' quoted in the selection here. The question has been
raised of whether the expression and content have been influenced
by the first chapter of Genesis – it would be scarcely surprising if
this were the case, for Christian missionaries have been active in
New Zealand for generations. But synthesis or not of indigenous
and Christian beliefs, it is at least clear that the poem is very much
Maori in expression and form: 'the product of a Polynesian mind'
as Alpers puts it, and an example of 'what the Maori was able to
make of Judaeo–Christian influence'.[2] It can stand here as an
example of one of the most beautiful of Maori poems.

Among other forms of Maori poetry, laments (*waiata*

1. This impression may also *partly* result from the some-
what biblical language ('thee' and 'thou' are common) into which Maori
poetry has traditionally been translated. But it is noticeable that even a
recent translator like the poet Barry Mitcalfe has adopted a relatively
solemn style as the appropriate one for translations of Maori verse.

2. A. Alpers, *Legends of the South Seas*, London, 1970, p.
369.

tangi) and love songs (*waiata aroha*) seem to be the most common. Poems with the title 'lament' or 'dirge' occur in such profusion – even concerning events which are not on the face of it mournful at all – that one wonders how far it was a favourite title of early collectors rather than of the poets themselves. But the mood of solemnity that runs through many of these poems makes this description not so inapt as might appear – and in some cases (like the impressive 'Lament for Taramoana') highly appropriate. As in Hawaiian poetry, a number of songs were originally inset in stories, for instance 'O beautiful calm . . .' and 'Oh, how my love with a whirling power. . . .'

The action songs (or *haka taparahi*) are also very popular. They have undergone a marked revival in this century and many new and adapted ones have been performed in public. They have been used for such formal occasions as the presentation of medals to soldiers in the Second World War (often posthumously) or the visit of the Queen to New Zealand, as well as for more personal concerns (as in 'Government' or 'We object'). Many of these new *hakas* for public performance were composed or arranged by the leading Maori poet, Sir Apirana Ngata. Together with other leaders of the Young Maori Party he effectively blended traditional and new elements to evolve a new form of Maori poety.

One of the striking characteristics of Maori poetry is the interest in natural phenomena. While descriptions of nature are perhaps not elaborated quite as much as in some Hawaiian poetry, there are constant references both to the names of places – obviously a matter of deep meaning – and to the stars, the sky, dawn, lightning, the waves of the sea, 'the voyage through life'. Poems often have a double meaning – an inner sense as well as the overt one. Similarly in the 'Canoe-hauling chant' or 'Ruaumoko – the earthquake god', the mythological references are used to apply and add symbolic meaning to something in fact much nearer home.

Oral expression through poetry clearly played an important role in traditional Maori culture. The scholar Elsdon Best details a number of occasions for sung poems:

If a woman was accused of indolence, or some other fault by her husband, she would in many cases retaliate or ease her mind, by composing and singing a song pertaining to the subject. In the event of a person being insulted or slighted in any way he was likely to act in a similar way. Songs were composed for the purpose of greeting visitors, of imparting information, of asking for assistance in war, and many other purposes of an unusual nature from our point of view. Singing entered largely into the social and ceremonial life of the people, and in making a speech the Maori breaks readily into song.[3]

The question may well be raised as to whether this picture is by now outdated. After all a large proportion of the poems given here were recorded in the nineteenth century and are, for the most part, presumably no longer current. By now too Maori culture has more and more blended with New Zealand culture in general and has for long involved education through the written word. But that this has not meant the end of Maori traditional poetry is made clear not only by some of the recent examples quoted here but by the explicit comment on this by Barry Mitcalfe, one of the most eminent translators of Maori poetry.

The tradition of Maori songs is not dead. There have been changes in form, but the social, cultural, and even the religious purposes of song have not changed as much as one might imagine. There are hundreds of Maori Clubs in New Zealand where the main – or often the only – activity is Maori action song, in its various forms. Each year there are several competitions (like the Welsh Eisteddfodau), generally sponsored by religious or political organizations. Examples are the Church of England Hui Topa and the Waikato King's Birthday celebration, in which as many as twenty teams from all over the island compete for three days or more.[4]

3. E. Best, *The Maori as he was*, Wellington, 1952, p. 158.
4. B. Mitcalfe, *Poetry of the Maori*, Hamilton and Auckland, 1961, p. 76.

The six periods of creation

The first period: the epoch of thought –
          From the conception the increase,
          From the increase the swelling,
          From the swelling the thought,
          From the thought the remembrance,
          From the remembrance the consciousness, the desire.

The second period: that of night or darkness –
          The word became fruitful;
          It dwelt with the feeble glimmering;
          It brought forth night:
          The great night, the long night,
          The lowest night, the loftiest night,
          The thick night, to be felt,
          The night to be touched, the night unseen.
          The night following on,
          The night ending in death.

The third period: that of light –
          From the nothing the begetting,
          From the nothing the increase,
          From the nothing the abundance,
          The power of increasing, the living breath;
          It dwelt with the empty space,
          It produced the atmosphere which is above us.

The fourth period: the creation of the moon and sun –
          The atmosphere which floats above the earth,
          The great firmament above us, the spread out space
                    dwelt with the early dawn,
          Then the moon sprung forth;
          The atmosphere above dwelt with the glowing sky,
          Forthwith was produced the sun,
          They were thrown up above as the chief eyes of
                    Heaven:
          Then the Heavens became light,
          The early dawn, the early day,
          The mid-day. The blaze of day from the sky.

The fifth period: the creation of land –
   The sky which floats above the earth,
   Dwelt with Hawaiki,[5]
   And produced Taporapora.
   Tauware nikau and Kukupara,
   Wawauatea and Wiwhi te rangi ora.[6]

The sixth period: the formation of gods and men –
   Ru and from Ru Ou hoko,
   From Ou hoko Ruatupu,
   Rua tawito, from Rua tawito,
   Rua kaipo, from Rua kaipo,
   Ngae, Ngae nui, Ngae roa,
   Ngae pea, ngae tuturi, ngae pepeke,
   Pepeke, ko Tatiti, ko Rua tapu, ko toe,
   Ko Rauru ko Tama rakei ora, ko, &c.[7]

The creation

   By an old Nga-ti-rua-nui priest.

Grew in Hades,[8]
Conceived in Hades,
Increased the conception in Hades,
Rooted in Hades,
Going on until light appeared;

Burst forth water,
Burst forth the earth,
Sprung forth God,
Sprung forth man,
From God, or the Spirit, was the causing to spring forth;

   5. The islands of Hawaiki, being then the only land known,
is put for *papa*, the earth.   6. The names of lands or islands, supposed
to have been first created.   7. Probably a list of ancestors tracing the
descent of the chief who furnished it from the god Ru.
   8. Or Darkness.

The felling,
The falling,
The settling down,
The making permanent,
The bending,
The opening,
The conceiving,
The sweetening,
The manna,[9]
The resin,[10]
The fruit,
The causing the conception to grow,
The causing it to increase,
The principle of life,[11]
The clear light,
The Deity;

The Heaven which stands above,
Dwelt with the earth spread out,
And forth came Tane, causing to hear,
Tu, Tangaroa,
Ru, Ouhoko,
Tao. Thence came
Religion.
The world made light;

The nothing clashing, the void,
The nothing contending,
The nothing increasing,
The nothing abounding,
The nothing; finished the nothing;

The following after the nothing;
The nothingness;
The nothing springing forth;
The nothing sacred,
The nothing religious,
The proceeding forth,
The form of worship, the world made light;

9. Sugar.   10. Thickening.   11. Seed.

The nothing giving way,
The no hail,
Dark-coloured hail,
Hail darting forth,
Hail destroying,
Hail melting,
Flowing beyond the dry places;

The nothing, increasing,
The nothing, abounding,
The nothing, the finishing.
The finishing, the nothing,
The going on from the nothing,
The power, the nothing,
The pursuing the nothing;

Meru the Releaser from Hades,
Meru the Breaker of the bonds of Hades,
Who alone can cause the feet to retrace the path
        to the world above,
The ancient world,
That death may not cleave to us.

Chant to Io

Tiwai Paraone

Io dwelt within the breathing-space of immensity,
The universe was in darkness, with water everywhere.
There was no glimmer of dawn, no clearness, no light.
And he began by saying these words,
That he might cease remaining inactive:
'Darkness, become a light-possessing darkness.'
And at once a light appeared.
He then repeated these self-same words in this manner,
That he might cease remaining inactive:
'Light, become a darkness-possessing light.'
And again an intense darkness supervened.

Then a third time He spake, saying:
'Let there be one darkness above.
'Let there be one darkness below,
'Let there be a darkness unto Tupua,
'Let there be a darkness unto Tawhito,
'A dominion of light,
'A bright light.'
And now a great light prevailed.
Io then looked to the waters which compassed him about
And spake a fourth time, saying:
'Ye waters of Tai kama, be ye separate.
'Heaven, be formed.'
Then the sky became suspended.
'Bring forth thou Te Tupua horo nuku.'
And at once the moving earth lay stretched abroad.

The creation of man

This chant records Tane's search and his discovery of man.

Seeking, earnestly seeking in the gloom.
Searching – yes, on the coast-line –
On the bounds of light of day.
Looking into night.
Night had conceived
The seed of night.
The heart, the foundation of night,
Had stood forth self-existing
Even in the gloom.
It grows in gloom –
The sap and succulent parts,
The life pulsating,
And the cup of life.
The shadows screen
The faintest gleam of light.
The procreating power,
The ecstasy of life first known,

And joy of issuing forth
From silence into sound.
Thus the progeny
Of the Great-extending
Filled the heavens' expanse;
The chorus of life
Rose and swelled
Into ecstasy,
Then rested in
Bliss of calm and quiet.

Ruaumoko – the earthquake god

Mohi Turei

Besides the surface meaning about the earthquake god there
is also an underlying sexual symbolism throughout the poem.

Hark to the rumble of the earthquake god!
Au! Au! Aue ha!
It is Ruaumoko who trembles and stirs!
Au! Au! Aue ha!
A ha ha!
It is the wand of Tungawerewere A! ha! ha!
The sacred rod given by Tutaua to Uenuku.
It struck the monster Rangitopeka
And smashed the head of Rangitopeka
Cleaving the twin peaks of Hikurangi
From where the carved rock emerges
It is divine, yet it is of man.
Yet it is divine
Behold! It is the dark mystery of the womb!
Where the dogs gnash their teeth.
A ha ha!
In my ecstasy I see the sky inflamed
I gasp for breath
'Tis like a shag soaring on high
Hei ha!

As the rod drives deep
Thus it remains
Now it is the bell-bird singing
Even though I am quiescent as in death
I soar amongst the stars.

Landfall

Said to have been chanted by a leader on arrival in the new
land (New Zealand) Te Aotearoa – The Long White Cloud – after voy-
aging hundreds of miles over the sea from the old home of 'Hawaiki'.

I arrive where an unknown earth is under my feet,
I arrive where a new sky is above me,
I arrive at this land
A resting place for me.
O spirit of the earth! The stranger humbly offers his
        heart as food for thee.

Whispering ghosts of the west . . .

Whispering ghosts of the west,
Who brought you here
To our land?
Stand up and depart!
Whispering ghosts of the west,
Who brought you here
To our land?
Stand up and depart!

Song of longing

A wife is left behind in the ancient homeland of Hawaiki while her first husband has voyaged far across the sea searching for new lands.

Just as eventide draws near,
My old affection comes
For him I loved.
Though severed far from me,
And now at Hawa-iki,
I hear his voice
Far distant, and,
Though far beyond
The distant mountain peak,
Its echoes speak
From vale to vale.

Disturb me not . . .

Sung by an old man who was laughed at by youths for his grey hairs.

Disturb me not, O buoyant youths!
I of myself must travel on,
And go the road that you must tread,
And wait your coming there.
Yes, close to you the weeds of Tura wait;
Grey hairs and death not distant are.
My days of youth and power are past,
And darkness hath embraced my eyes.
Leave me now, enfeebled, here to lie,
And let me gaze on what ye soon must be.

Give me my infant now

Te-whaka-io-roa

Where are the hands and feet
That Tiki made? Gone with the gods.
Yes, O my children's mother!
Speak, and let me know
That I shall soon an infant see,
And priests shall stand before
The Ahu-rewa altar, where,
With incantations, they shall chant
To bones of those of ancient days,
And taunt the earthquake god.
Yes, yes, my children's mother,
Give me my infant now,
That, dandling it upon my knees,
My joy may be complete –
That I no more may feel
A want and ache not yet appeased.

A sentinel's song

Rarawa Kerehoma

This is said to have been the watch-cry of Te Okenga,
chief of Te Kerekere, which he sang to discourage his enemies' attack.

Shine on me, moon
Shine on me.
Spears stand against the darkness.
I don't fool you
You don't fool me.
Stay, keep your distance –
You are at the place where
The sky blocks the plain.
Let them come. The blue heron
Is awake and on guard.

Love dirge

This was composed by a wife for her husband and family who had been killed by a war-party and had been spoken evil of by her people.

Shine, O sun! tenderly on my skin.
But hearken: far off in the sky
There peals a sound like sea-dashed surf.
'Tis I alone am closed by net of death,
And followed by the January fly.
Oh! where is now the ocean-kelp,
That I may pour my tears on it,
Because of depth of pain I feel.
I long had hoped that death,
In days gone by, had ceased to come on me;
But you could see. Like rope let down,
So are the words of slandering tongue;
They go to depth of weariness and woe,
And, like the acts of ancient days,
Reverberate and strike the sound of evils past.
Nor dare they tell in open day
To my beloved my negligence or want
Of care or kindly act. I, like a
Fish out of water, am dangling in the sun.

Dirge sung at death

See the headlands yonder stand
At Taka-pu;
But nearer still than they
Is my beloved.
Yes, all have passed behind,
Have fled and gone,
With all the evil loudly spoken,
But yet with me still
Shall ever rest my own beloved.

Song of despair

Rangiaho

Rangiaho's husband had taken a second wife and turned away from her. In despair Rangiaho, according to one version at least, committed suicide.

I weep for my loved one
Give me a sharp stone
Let the salt blood run
From these barren breasts
This once-sweet flesh.

Turn away, hard-hearted one, lest
You see these two hands pressed
Against my heart, see it quiver
Like a leaf, like the breath
Of his last caress.

This red blood from the heart
Is for the mountains, torn apart,
Te Tara below and Tauhara above
Each cold, remote
As the man I loved.

Let the mist come
Blot them out, swallow the sun.
Let the bitter wind blow
From the west, bringing snow
From the mountains of Maniapoto.

Come, Hoki of the evil omen
He cannot hide; there is no horizon.
I shall leap the cliff of death,
This blood, my breath –
One thrust, and I am there.

Too many nights I have yearned
For one who would not return.

The mist over Pukehina

Look where the mist
Hangs over Pukehina.
There is the path
By which went my love.

Turn back again hither
That may be poured out
Tears from my eyes.

It was not I who first spoke of love.
You it was who made advances to me
When I was but a little thing.

Therefore was my heart made wild,
This is my farewell of love to thee.

Lament for Taramoana

Makere

O my son,
Only your name remains;
Now you are gone, alone.
Love has no power to restore the heart,
So slow to live, so swift to die.
Your bones lie like a necklace
At the throat of the sky,
Your blood soaks into the wood,
But you have flown –
You will greet your ancestors,
The great await thee,
Hine-a-wai will meet thee,
Will spread soft mats,
Sprinkle strange scents,
And young girls will dance.
Go my son,
And may this poor song
Go with thee;

Words tell only of my inadequacy.
There lives not a man on this earth
Who can avenge thy death;
Some have mouths to speak, but lack
Hands to act, others have no ears,
Will not hear breath or hint of war.
Only the gods beneath
Will give thee death for a death,
Only the weeds of the earth
Will give thee birth,
I go to the ridge of Okawa
I will pluck out his liver
That will show these men
What I mean when I speak of revenge.
I will destroy the house of speech
And drink at the source of rage.

Where is the man that could kill you?
Where is the hand that defiled you?
No! The gods of the sky
Willed you to die,
Tore out your heart and lungs,
Splintered bones and splattered brains
Like vomit, ribs picked clean
And blood oozing through the stones
Of the feast.
Let your foul cousins taste
The sweetness of their ancestress
In thy breast. Maire-i-rangi
Will lie like a stone in their belly.

The heron has flown,
The canoe is gone
The river is no haven,
The root is drawn from the earth,
But in Otahu, the place of birth,
You cannot die, there is no death.
You dart like the shag beneath
The dark waters of the stream,
Dive like the gannet to a death

In the deep where small fish gleam.
O my fish, rise from the depths.
No! That cannot be,
Death has swallowed thee.

O my friends,
Is this the way the fight ends,
Cast from the world of light,
Knowing neither sorrow nor delight?
Yet night cannot last forever,
The *taro* has too many roots to sever,
The *taniwha* has a hundred parts,
It is a shoal of red-eyed mullet darting
Over the deep where he lies sleeping.
There is only one stone that will sharpen
The broken axe to a keener edge!
Go the dark way of death,
Treachery knows the path!
The Black Whale is cast high
On Hikumutu to die!
The cloak is swept aside.
The last of Rakei, dead,
The image of Rongomai, destroyed.

Are the gods of the skies
To be scattered like scraps from the fires?
Then shall Venuku eat men
Till none remain.

Lament

Matangi Hauroa

I lie in darkness, as the dead shades gather,
Feeling you here, at my side –
I turn to greet you, reach out to grasp
A world of nothing, no one, nowhere.
You passed like a shadow in the night –
Lie still, my aching heart.

Let the sharp blades gouge me.
Let the children see.
Take it, Whiro, blood, strength, spirit –
I walk the path of our fathers,
They speak well of the way you died,
Your courage cries to the empty skies.

You were caught in Whanganui's coils.
Remember, watch the son of Tuwhakairihau;
Beware, there are other sons of Rakamaomao there;
Motai's hundred sons lie in wait.
Walk their beaches, scorn them –
Your body lies here.

Your name will live
In this place
And perhaps in this poor house of proverbs here.

O beautiful calm . . .

Tu-kehu and Wetea

In the story two young chiefs were taken prisoner and about to be killed. Before death they asked for a chance to utter their love and farewell to their home and people. This and the following poem are the songs they are said to have chanted together.

O beautiful calm,
Placid and fair
Out on the sea.
No dewdrop or rain
Beclouded the sky
When Hau-hoa-te-puni
Began his long voyage.
Bewildered I was
Not to follow him then
And sing a love song
As thou, Ahu-rei,
Him far away paddled

Past rock-jutting point
At the distant Ko-hi.
I then might have seen
Whakaari foretell
My future, my doom,
And beguile me in thought,
As storm follows calm;
We doomed are to part,
Thou from my presence
Art dragged to the post
That holds the great net
Of Tara-mai-nuku.
I cannot now see,
Mine eyes are grown dim
With mist of my tears
I cannot now see
The mountain; the peak,
Of great Moe-hau;
But take me away,
Away far and place me
Where surge of the ocean
Can never more move me
From the kelp and its hold-fast
On rocks firmly anchored.

Oh, how my love with a whirling power . . .

Tu-kehu and Wetea

This is the second song by the two captured chiefs, sung
while their executioner waited with his spear ready. When they had
finished, they were both killed.

Oh, how my love
With a whirling power
Makes blank my mind;
But could I know
That thou hast gone

Back home from yonder
Bank of lonely river,
While I am doomed to feel
The pain and anguish
Of Mata-ora's instrument,
I then might seek
Some priest whose power
Might sever from this heart
The love I now
Am doomed to feel.
Had Tuki-rau but left
Some token of his power
To drive intruders
Far away, I might
Have felt no dread
Of northern hosts;
But oh! how sad
I feel to hear
Discordant sounds from thee!
As apprehensive here I sit
While tears bedim mine eyes
I mourn for house, and tribe, and home.

A mourning-song for Rangiaho

Te Heuheu Herea

Sung by Te Heuheu Herea for Rangiaho, his wife.

Many women call on me to sleep with them
But I'll have none so worthless and so wanton
There is not one like Rangiaho, so soft to feel
Like a small, black eel.
I would hold her again –
Even the wood in which she lies;
But like the slender flax stem
She slides from the first to the second heaven
The mother of my children

Gone
Blown by the wind
Like the spume of a wave
Into the eye of the void.

Hitler, frothy-mouth

This song is reminiscent of the traditional *kaioraora* (cursing song). It was used during the Second World War for a VC investiture ceremony and became widely known and sung.

Hitler, frothy-mouth, wooden-head,
He's the man who wanted to fight,
Beaten here, beaten there, all over Russia,
You can wipe him and his works.

Raise it, raise it on high,
Raise the blade of my club over his head –
Let him have it, bash the jaw of
That cowardly slave called Hitler.
Mussolini has had news of how
The Maori Battalion will soon take Rome
Up! Up to the heights! There's no escape,
He's so scared his buttocks quake.

Canoe-hauling chant

Apirana Ngata

A version of an ancient canoe-hauling chant, adapted for the *Ngarimu hui* (medal presentation) ceremony. The young Victoria Cross winner is symbolized as the *kai kakariki*, or canoe leader, commanding and inspiring the crews of five of the canoes during the Great Migration. The translation is Ngata's own.

The Rising
Let me proceed by this way!
Sidling along!

Perhaps I shall meet there
Some ancient,
Lolling his tongue at me!
It is heeling over! It has capsized!
New Zealand has heeled over! Aue!

The Body of the Taparahi
The thunder crashes, the lightning flashes
Illuminating the heavens.
While the shock strikes earth.
Which trembles and quakes, ha!
So nature bears witness that Porourangi
Has pierced the great Fish of Maui
Which lies beneath us! A ha ha!
So 'tis your belly upturned and laid bare
So that your people may mount
And spear you!
A ha ha!
Arise then my son and take your stand
To direct and urge on your canoes, Horouta,
Takitimu, Mataatua, Tainui, Te Arawa,
The great fleet drawn up here!
Striking, sweeping, paddling!
Now on the other side paddling!
Down dips the blade of the paddle
Sweeping behind, flashing before!
The speeding canoe sings in the wind.
Vibrant, it chants to the breeze
Behold the first light of dawn
Is reflected from the crest of Hikurangi!
A ha ha! Dipping close to this side!
Now changing and plunging to that side!
Urging and urging the canoe on!
Now faster and faster!
Is it not like the foam from your mouth,
Thrown out, expelled with force!
So it speeds, so it speeds –
So my canoe rushes swiftly on!
For it is the canoe of war!

It is the master of the seas!
Cleaving the ocean waves,
Parting the wild rushing seas!

Fishing song

According to the legend this was composed by the *turehu*,
or fairies. In the old days, it is said, the Maori did not know how to fish
with nets. One night a chief, Kahukura, hid on the beach at Rangiawhia
and watched in amazement as the *turehu* fished with their nets and sang
their fishing songs. He managed to steal one of their nets and memorize
this song.

Pull in the net!
Do your work with a will
Rehua is the guiding spirit
The creature of the mist
Who will ensure
The abundance of our catch . . .
So therefore, haul the net in!

Drag in the net! Drink up also
The water is there, pure and sweet,
How good it is!
We are indeed quenched!
Go and pour out our refreshment,
As we haul the nets inshore!

Yes, pull and haul!
The harvest writhes and squirms
Our catch is good
There is the frost fish!
The upturned bellies of sharks
A quicksilver band!
Twisting this way and that
Yea, haul in the nets!

A song of sickness

Hine Tangikuku

Neap-tide and the ebbing days slide
From my side as I stand
Here beyond the land
I loved. The open doors
Of Mihimarino call me no more.

Sing cicada, for soon you will die,
And so must I;
The bitterns cry doleful death,
The parrot chokes on his last breath.

The morning star swims in the sky
To this shore, where I
Lie washed in a sea of pain,
Writhing like one insane.
Fever-drunk, drifting
Like pollen in a dream, sifting
Like seed, I am not what I seem.

I see myself, twisted sinew,
Wasted flesh; the body I once knew
Has no substance, unsustained,
Is itself the sustenance of pain.
I am dead weed cast upon the shore.

Government!

Tuta Nihoniho

Nihoniho was a famous chief who was engaged in litigation
in the late nineteenth century over rights to land. The judgment went
against him and as he left the courtroom in anger he composed this half-
bitter, half-quizzical denunciation of the white government and their
complicated laws.

The Rising

The darkness presses all around!
The House which enacts the laws ensnares me
The Maori is plaited in its bonds! Brought low!
Its rates and its taxes gnaw at my vitals
Alas! It cannot be shaken!
The land will be engulfed
Hei!
Submerged beneath these laws!
Hei!
From the members of the House has come this treacherous act
The Governor has aided and abetted them.
The laws are confused
Even the tobacco leaf falls victim to them!

The Taparahi Proper

The loss of our land
Bears on us like the hand of death!
Alas! Heard continually
Are the sinister discussions, clinging fast
As does the warrior's headband before the enemy!
Alas! I am seared and burned
By the sacrifice of blood
It goes to the heart of the land
I am indeed sorely distressed.
A ha ha!
We are raised aloft by promises
Even as we are put aside!
It is so
Was it not your promise to teach the Maori?
And wean him from his primitive ways?
Yet you come as marauders
To devour our land
No insult can express my contempt!
Alas!
How can the bow of our canoe
Forge past the headlands of New Zealand?

Obstructed as it is by the laws
Of the government
Alas! They cannot be shaken!

We object . . .

The Tuhoe group object to the Land Commissioners about
their attitude to the piece of land named Te Whaiti.

We are croaking as does the frog
Croak, croak!
Tuhoe are croaking at Te Whaiti
Croak, croak!
Look up and look down!
Gaze at the special power flying yonder!
Listen to the pen of the Commissioner
As it goes 'hihi', scratch, scratch.

Lullaby

Nohomaiterangi

O my son, born on a winter's morn,
The way is long and you are alone,
Your ancestors watch you from afar,
Will you be the next bright star?
O my son, born into war,
Grow swiftly, that you might wear
Their mantle, if you dare.
Greet them without fear,
You will be remembered there.
Kaka feather on your spear,
Feather of an albatross in your hair –
Land, sea and air
Here in the hollow of my hand –
Take them, lest they disappear.

Lament for Apirana Ngata

Arnold Reedy

This *waiata tangi* was improvised and performed at the
Maori funeral ceremonies for Sir Apirana Ngata. It is influenced by
Ringatu chant which is in turn influenced by the style of the Christian
chanted psalms in Maori. The lament became a widely known popular
song.

> Stop there, old one, within your haven
> The earth quivers with your spirit
> We look towards Hikurangi, there inland,
> The fabled mountain of our ancestor, Porourangi
> Barely clothed in Rangitawaea's cloak,
> Our tears flow towards you,
> Our sadness is the sadness of all mankind
> Misery of a crushed people.
> You are gone, steersman of the canoe
> Of Porourangi. Oh that we might greet
> You still with the calls of your people
> So your name might be on every man's lips.
> Man is in pain, in a state of shock,
> But you have gone, old one, into the night – alas.

Seaweed, seaweed

Hannah Tatana

The original composer is unknown, but this song has now
become widely known through the performances and recordings of
Hannah Tatana.

> Seaweed, seaweed, drifting, drifting
> Drifting endlessly on the sea
> Moved by currents
> Far below.

Your image flutters like a fantail
On the edge of consciousness
It fills me
With sadness.

The dew still sparkles on the hills
But the spirit curls and sleeps
Huddled up
Within me.

The breeze is blowing . . .

The breeze is blowing
Towards the open sea at Turanga,
You are far away, my dear
My love goes out to you from here.

My love falls like the rain
On the open sea at Turanga,
I am left behind here
Living with my love for you.

AUSTRALIAN ABORIGINES
OF ARNHEM LAND

The Australian Aborigines have long been famous for their elaborate myths and symbolism. With the Aborigines of Arnhem Land this is expressed primarily through their songs, rather than in prose or spoken verse, and singing is one of the most highly developed of their arts. In this area there are a great number of long song-cycles which, with their complex symbolism and style, make nonsense of the older idea that, because Aboriginal material technology was relatively undeveloped, their artistic and intellectual life was correspondingly simple and meagre.

Like other Australian Aboriginal groups, the Arnhem Landers were traditionally hunters and gatherers: far from having a highly developed material technology, they did not even rely on agriculture or domesticated animals for their food, but foraged from the natural supplies around them. On the coastal areas of Arnhem Land, indigenous food and natural resources are both abundant and varied: in the sea, dugong, turtle, fish, shellfish; on land, birds, animals, vegetables, fruit, and nuts. But the constant supply of these rich natural resources on which the Arnhem Landers rely is conditional on the rhythm of the seasons and also, in Arnhem Land belief, on the mythical beings of the 'Eternal Dreaming'. The great rituals of the indigenous religion and the long song-cycles are centred round these Ancestral Beings, and the rituals are considered essential to ensure a continued supply of animal and vegetable food.

The song-cycles have around a dozen to 200 or 300 parts, each of which is in a sense a complete song (rather than merely a verse of a longer poem) but at the same time gains its effect and meaning from forming part of a larger whole. The basic action which links together the cycle is often located in the pre-human era in the 'Dream time', and the central characters are spirit beings often in human shape, sometimes important creator figures, like the Djanggawul. There are also subsidiary figures, and all the most important things in the natural world appear too – everything that 'has a name' in the sense of being mentioned in song.

The possession of these cycles, including the right to sing them, is divided up according to a fairly complex system. The people of this area divide the human and natural world into two separate moieties called *dua* and *jiridja*. Every person or being belongs to just *one* of these (with various rules about marriage and social affiliation that follow from membership), and this division cuts across the kinship links which play so important a part in Aboriginal society. Each of the moieties has different series of songs associated with it. The Djanggawal are *dua* for instance, whereas the Moon-Bone cycle belongs to the *jiridja* moiety. Within this moiety frame the population is divided among a number of named dialect units (*mada*) and named clans (*mala*), some related more closely than others; each person belongs to a *mada-mala* pair, and the songs are specifically associated with these. The songs are connected with the series of mythologically based totems associated with each clan and linguistic unit, for the beings in the song-cycles – like the Djanggawul Sisters and Brother or the Wauwalak Sisters – are depicted as wandering over the territory in the Dream time and creating the animals and birds and other natural phenomena which then became the totems. Some of these spirit beings are local only, and associated just with one or two dialect units; but the major figures, who travelled through great areas in the myths, are known widely and claimed by a number of units, each with its own perspective on the myth.

The song-cycles therefore are closely associated with the complex social organization in Arnhem Land, with some overlapping between those of different socially distinct units. There is also the added complication that there are 'outside' (public) and 'inside' (secret) versions of the main cycles.

The imagery in the songs ties up with these links between social groups. On the surface the imagery is appealing and colourful enough just in its obvious meaning. All the creatures and plants and places that are locally important are mentioned, and we are given a series of pictures of the natural world in the songs: the morning star moving along, shining on the sea as the paddlers look back at it from their canoe; the 'spray and sea splash' as the whale moves; the rays of the rising sun, reflected in the sea; the parakeet's feathers gleaming red; or the constantly reiterated picture of the red sky at sunset. But to this one also has to add the overtones for the group who possess the song. Many of the places mentioned are sacred, some of them secret-sacred, and all of them are traditionally owned by particular groups. The natural creatures mentioned come in not just for the poetic attraction of their description but because they were created in the Dream time and now have religious as well as social significance. The various creatures too are identified as either *dua* or *jiridja*, and the interaction of the two symbolically refers to complex social and ritual links.

This comes out in the Djanggawul song-cycle, from which a fairly large selection is given here (twenty-seven songs out of 188 or so in the complete cycle). In this selection we are given colourful descriptions of a journey over the sea, with the various sea animals and plants, and the storms and weather encountered there; travels through the land and the different creatures there; and the constantly recurring motif of a bird crying out in the red sunset and drying its feathers in the warmth of the setting sun. There is also the basic story – which is not always explicit in the songs (particularly in the abridged selection here) – that the Djanggawul came over the sea to the mainland coast where the Arnhem Landers now live; they came on the path of the rising sun and finally disappeared westwards into the sunset. But there is more to the cycle than this. The Djanggawul are important creative figures who travelled over wide areas in the songs, created the beings of the natural world today and are associated with phenomena of wide (not just local) interest – the sun, the morning star, clouds – and they are referred to in many songs. But in the cycle here they are particularly associated with the *dua* moiety and its special *nara* ritual. The various objects they bring with them are central to a complex of symbols. The string that is often mentioned, and which may sound mundane enough, is not only traditionally one of the most valuable items of wealth but also plays a prominent role in the *nara* ritual. It is a length of twine with orange-coloured birds' feathers worked into it (*jiridja* moiety members use white feathers) and is also referred to in the songs as a cluster of living birds.

Another song-cycle from which a few extracts are

given is that belonging to the Wonguri linguistic unit, the Sandfly clan – the song-cycle of the Moon-Bone. Moon was an ancestral man, in the song, who lived near the clay-pan of the Moonlight at the Place of the Dugong by Arnhem Bay. After his death he went down into the sea, and his bones became a nautilus shell; but ever since then Moon repeats his death, casting away his bone, and being reborn. Again the beings and places in the songs carry strong local overtones and symbolism, too detailed to note here.

The events in these song-cycles are not presented in straightforward narrative style (the audience, after all, can be assumed to know the basic story) but rather unfold in a leisurely and discursive way. Particular creatures or actions are dwelt on at length, often returned to again and again. Repetition is extremely important, both direct repetition of separate songs and the same set of images and actions presented again and yet again in slightly differing combinations. The song about the parakeets calling out and drying their feathers in the red of the setting sun, from the Djanggawul cycle, is a good example of this. It may seem overdone in this small selection to give so many cases of what might seem at first just the 'same' song, but the repetition and development of this deeply meaningful complex of images is so important (and even to the outsider so effective) that it would give a very false impression of the poetic essence of the cycle to eliminate this re-iteration (of course not *all* of these songs could be included).

The language of the songs is not in general archaic or highly specialized. Most is quite ordinary interspersed with special 'inside' and 'singing' words and enhanced by symbolic allusion and repetition. The rhythm and tunes are conventional (varying in different song-cycles) and the words are abbreviated, lengthened, or elaborated so as to fit the poetic constraints imposed by the tune. Song-cycles of this mythic type are not the only kinds of oral poems by the Arnhem Landers. They also sing some topical songs on everyday events, and love songs (none unfortunately available for publication here[1]), some of them grouped in song-cycles. There are also a number of mourning songs (or emotional-stress songs), mainly sung by women, which commemorate not

[1]. A selection by R. M. Berndt is to be published shortly by Nelson.

just a death but an illness or the departure (or arrival) of a relative. A number of these are given here.

There are various occasions for these songs. Sometimes they are primarily for entertainment, even though the symbolic overtones are always present – for example, open public singing in an ordinary camp situation, often accompanied by stylized gestures. But the more weighty and formal version is performed in a secret-sacred context restricted to fully initiated men who can follow the complex interpretations, the intermeshing of symbols, and references to secret rituals. In a cycle the songs are usually sung straight through, and then repeated *ad lib*. This means that it is unusual for any cycle to be completed in one evening – and certainly not with any of the long cycles. There are also more leisured occasions where the singer interprets and discusses the meanings of the songs with a group of men from his own clan and linguistic unit. In such circumstances, younger men are taught the words of the songs, particularly the 'inside' words or special singing words which function as alternates in song, and also the sacred words which occur in religious cycles.

The mourning or 'stress' songs are sung at times of particular emotional crisis. Catherine Berndt sums up the many occasions for these:

The illness, injury, death or remembered death, the departure for or return from a journey of a husband, potential husband, or close relative; the initiation of a son, close relative, or member of the same clan or linguistic group; the first menstruation of a daughter or close relative; the sight of some object, creature, or scene associated with local mythology, such as a pregnant shark captured, belonging to the great *dua* moiety shark cycle . . . or the quiet sea, connected with a large *jiritja* song cycle: any or all of these may evoke real or conventionalized sentiments which find expression in song.[2]

On all these occasions women are traditionally expected to sing wailing songs, and at the same time cut their heads in token of their grief: a woman who fails to do this on an appropriate occasion

2. 'Expressions of grief among Aboriginal women', *Oceania* 20, 1950, p. 307.

is likely to be severely criticized. Though both the form of song and the ceremonial actions are dictated by convention, it will be obvious from some of the songs here that this does not preclude the songs also being used for a vehicle of real and bitterly felt personal emotion ('The blowflies buzz', for instance) expressed particularly through the interjections.

The arrangement and sequence of words in these mourning songs are according to the conventions of the particular clan of the singer. But individual women interpret these in their own way. Particularly when under the stress of some powerful emotion, they emphasize one aspect rather than another and take some liberties with the traditional form. It is customary to include interjections in these songs. But a singer who is merely formally mourning is likely to use few or none of these while a woman experiencing acute sorrow often elaborates them, sometimes into lengthy monologues. The songs are thus traditional in form and content and yet give scope for the expression of individual experience and emotion by the singer.

The same point applies to the song-cycles generally. Basically they are traditional in form. Each clan-linguistic constellation has its own tune and rhythm for its series of songs.

The tune itself and the presence of others who share the complex of words, music, and associated meanings and who are sensitive to any marked divergence from the normal range serve as a check on too loose a treatment of the words. The more proficient a songman is, the more detail he presents in his rendering; nevertheless variation is limited and too much innovation frowned upon. But personal interpretation is significant in this area of knowledge, especially where . . . symbolic meanings have to be explained. . . . There is thus a certain amount of variation and even of personal interpretation in ritual singing as well as in women's mourning chants.[3]

Nevertheless the local theory is that all sacred songs are basically traditional, 'handed down from the Dreaming or mythical era'.[4]

3. R. M. Berndt, 'The Wuradilagu song-cycle of North-eastern Arnhem Land' from M. Jacobs (ed.), *The anthropologist looks at myth*, Austin, 1966, p. 198.   4. ibid.

The translations given here are all by C. H. and R. M. Berndt, either jointly or separately. Their general principle is to follow a fairly literal translation of the words (though sometimes a rather more free poetic translation is given). Obviously many words have no real equivalent in English: 'The different words referring to sounds of various kinds, for instance, are not easy to transcribe: and "noise" is a poor, although often necessary substitute.' The translators concentrate on conveying the surface images and make no attempt to reproduce the original rhythm or metre; the division into lines, however, represents pauses made by the singers themselves. But, as the translators continually point out, a vast amount is inevitably lost in translation – perhaps even more in these songs than with some others. One loses not just the 'considerable technical skill, in the choice and arrangement of words, the use of metre and stress in the total patterning, the matching of words',[5] but the complicated system of symbols and allusions. A full appreciation of these is obviously only possible by working with the originals, interlinear translations, and copious notes. But, though this ideal remains unattainable for most of us, some real approach to appreciating the beauty and imagery of these rich and unusual songs is still possible through the Berndts' sympathetic translations.

The Djanggawul song-cycle

The basic story of the cycle concerns the journeys and actions of the three Djanggawul spirit beings: the Elder Sister (Bildjiwuraroiju), the Younger Sister (Miralaidj) and the Brother (usually just called Djanggawul). In company with another being named Bralbral they leave Bralgu, the mythical land of the Eternal Beings, which lies far out to sea, out of sight of the land, and paddle towards the mainland on the path of the rising run. Then they travel through various places in Arnhem Land, bringing people and natural life to the whole area.

The cycle is closely associated with the special ritual (*nara*) of the *dua* moiety, and the ritual overtones are thus significant for understanding the importance of the songs. The various

5. R. M. and C. H. Berndt, *The world of the first Australians*, Sidney, 1964, p. 311.

objects the Djanggawul carry with them play a part not only in the songs but in the ritual too. First there is the sacred conical mat (*ngainmara*) which is also identified with the whale, and with the uterus of each Sister, containing the people who later emerge. There are also *rangga*, special poles which are regarded as particularly sacred, now used only on the ritual ground by initiates. There are several kinds of *rangga* mentioned in the poems: the *mauwulan*, used as a walking stick by the Djanggawul and plunged into the ground to make wells; and the *djuda*, which makes trees grow when the Djanggawul plunge it into the ground. They also bring with them a spirit bag (another symbol of the uterus) with fringe and feathered pendants, and the special feathered string made with red feathers from the breast of the parakeet, the feathers symbolizing the rays of the sun and the red sunset sky.

All these objects – mundane though they may seem – have symbolic and ritual significance for the singer and his audience. The basic theme, as R. M. Berndt puts it,

is fertility, manifested in the perpetually pregnant Women, the Two Sisters, in the growth of trees and foliage, in the creation of running springs, and in the abiding and life-giving warmth of the sun's rays. . . . These material objects, then, such as the sacred *rangga*, bag and mat, are focal points, or symbols, through which we may grasp the significance of the concept as a whole. The mat is a uterus symbol; so is the whale, although used in this sense only incidentally. Here is the source of all life, for it was from the Uteri of the Sisters that the first people sprang.[6]

Through all this runs the theme of sexual symbolism. The *rangga*, the sacred poles, are explicitly associated with the penis and sexual intercourse, and the conical mat (*ngainmara*) is likened not only to a whale and a well, but also to the vagina and the uterus of the Sisters from which all life flowed.

The continual interweaving of these various symbols is what gives the cycle its poetic unity and beauty. There are constant references to the mat (and the whale); the *rangga* poles (among them the *mauwulan* walking-stick and *djuda* or tree pole); the red parakeet and the sacred string from its feathers laid out to

6. R. M. Berndt, *Djanggawul*, London, 1952, pp. 5–6.

dry; also the ebb and flow of the sea waves and tides through which the Djanggawul first paddle and the fresh water springing up as they travel onwards; and the warmth and light of the sun, so closely associated with the Djanggawul themselves. The symbols are interlinked and elaborated as the cycle proceeds, each repetition building yet further on the last.

Obviously only a selection of the complete cycle can be included (the whole comprises around 188 songs, usually presented in ten parts). The songs given here do not necessarily include all the episodes which in a full analysis might be considered important – for example, how the men stole the sacred objects from the sisters. (For this the analyst would have to turn to the full translation in R. M. Berndt, *Djanggawul*, Routledge & Kegan Paul, London, 1952.) But even in this selection it is possible to glimpse something of the artistry and complex symbolism of this Aboriginal poetry, and their image of the earth as fertilized 'in much the same way as man – through symbolic coitus, the plunging *mauwulan*, the piercing *djuda* roots, the flooding well, and the spreading incoming tide'.[7]

Songs from the Djanggawul cycle

From Part I. The Djanggawul leave Bralgu and paddle
across the sea in their bark canoe, carrying their sacred objects. At first
they are in twilight, guided only by the rays of the Morning Star, but at
last as they near land the sun rises, warming them and illuminating the
sacred sites. As they travel they see the various creatures of the sea, and
the waves and foam surge around them. Finally they reach the shore of
Arnhem Land, at Port Bradshaw.

Song 1

Although I leave Bralgu, I am close to it. I, Djanggawul, am
    paddling . . .
Paddling with all the paddles, with their flattened tapering ends.
Close I am coming, with Bildjiwuraroiju,
Coming along from Bralgu. We splash the water as we paddle,
    paddling wearily,
With Miralaidj, undulating our buttocks as we paddle.
We paddle along through the roaring tide, paddle a long way.
I am paddling along fast, through the rough sea . . .
Beside me is foam from our paddling, and large waves follow us.
With Bralbral, we move our wrists as we paddle, making noise
    as we go through the sea . . .
We, Djanggawul, are paddling along, lifting our paddles, slowly
    going along . . .
All the way we have paddled. I rest my paddles now, as we glide.
On the sea's surface the light from the Morning Star shines as
    we move,
Shining on the calmness of the sea.
Looking back I see its shine, an arc of light from the Morning
    Star. The shine falls on our paddles, lighting our way.
We look back to the Morning Star and see its shine, looking
    back as we paddle.
Star moving along, shining! We saw its disc quite close,
Skimming the sea's surface, and mounting again above Bralgu.
Close to us it rises above the expanse of sea; we look back, seeing
    its shine.
Morning Star, sent by the dancing Spirit People, those people of
    the rain, calling out as they dance there with out-
    stretched arms.

They send it for us, that we may travel along its shining path
    from Bralgu.
Close, its 'feathered ball' appears above Dangdangmi! Close is
    the Morning Star, on the end of its string and pole!
Close is the Morning Star, stretching from its pole, extending
    out from its string . . .
Shining from Bralgu, as we paddle through the sea.
Bubbles rise to the sea's surface; our canoe is carried on the
    crest of waves. Ah, *waridj*[8] Bralbral!
Sound made by our splashing paddles, and the sea's roar as we
    rise to the crest of a wave!
We make our paddles sound, with the noise of the sea, sound
    that is heard far away at Bralgu.
We, the Djanggawul, make sound with our paddling, make spray
    as we paddle fast . . .
The salty smell! The roaring sea, and its foam! Its wide expanse
    behind us!
We paddle, with Bildjiwuraroiju, following the waves along,
Pushing our way through the waves that block us
Sound from our sacred *ngainmara* mat! Noise as the waters
    surge around it!
Sound, as the sacred poles are moved about with the rolling of
    the canoe!

Song 4

I, Djanggawul, am leaving Bralgu, paddling away from there,
    paddling fast.
The sweep of the paddle of Miralaidj, out in the deep sea, far
    from the mainland!
Paddling fast as we smell the Baijini from far away.
Sound within the water, as we pull on our paddles! Bildji-
    wuraroiju paddling . . .
Coming close to the mainland, splashing as we skim through the
    open sea . . .
See the shine of the Morning Star, as we look back, shining from
    Bralgu.

      8. Kinsman.

Sound of our narrow paddle . . . paddling along.

Spray falls across the canoe, coming strongly in from the heavy
　　sea.

Close up! Paddling against the strong high tide; waves spread
　　　out as we go, waves from our paddling:

Waves that roar as they spread – coming from us, from our
　　canoe.

Spraying like rain, churning to foam. The smell of the sea!

We paddle fast through the sea, for we hear the distant sound
　　　of the Baijini,

Sound and sea smell from them, from far away, spreading across
　　the sea's expanse . . .

Carefully we must go, for the sea is rough, Miralaidj. Let us rest
　　　on our paddles, Bralbral. (They are speaking to one
　　　another.)

Sound of the sea from the Djanggawul's paddling!

Song 6

What is that which blocks us? The whale!

As we paddle, we see its gaping mouth. What is that?

Spray and sea splash as it moves.

We paddle gently, for we see the open mouth of the whale.

What is this swimming? Our *ngainmara* mat, swimming under
　　　the water!

Water swirling! We hear the noise of the water, and of its spray.

We saw it out at sea, a long way from Bralgu – spray from the
　　　swimming whale.

Water rises and swirls, with noise caused by the whale: spray
　　　and foam from the whale . . .

As we paddle, we see it swimming. Bralbral calls to the Djang-
　　gawul,

It is our mat, our basket! Let us take some. The others we leave
　　　in the sea!

Waves rise from the large *ngainmara* mats that they leave be-
　　　hind, swirling waters spraying from them!

Water comes in from them, coming to us: foaming, spraying and
　　　roaring, out on the sea!

Song 7

Splashing, a fish swishes its tail as it rises, close to the whale's
    'whiskers'.
A splashing catfish, turning over on to its belly . . .
From Bralgu, from the mouth of the whale . . .
It splashes, its spike protrudes as it swims before the gaping
        mouth of the whale,
Splashing and chasing it. 'I (says the whale) am splashing. I
        chase this fish, under the water.'
Touching the fish with its 'whiskers'. The catfish splashes . . .
Splashes before the open mouth of the whale,
Spraying, dragging its spike through the sea . . .
And the noise of the sea, being churned up . . .!
Waves rising and splashing, caused by fish . . .
Noise of the water and foam from that fish . . .
Waves spreading out, spraying and splashing, caused by the
        fish . . .

Song 8

What is that? A sea egg!
We must paddle with care, with the spade paddle, dragging it
        through the sea as we rest.
Oh *waridj* Bralbral! Oh *waridj* Miralaidj! It is a stranger to us,
        from Bralgu.
Sea eggs forming in lines, with their spiny 'hands',
Drift with the waves in the calm sea, spread with the moving
    waves,
Drift on the surface, glistening in the shine of the Star.
The continuous lap of the sea, and its waves! Lines of sea eggs
        spreading across the sea!
Strangers! At the fringe of the shine of the Star from Bralgu,
        they spread out in the rising waves . . . The sound of
           the sea . . .!
Paddling, the Djanggawul see these eggs, as they move their
        shoulders . . .

Their heads are grey.[9] They have paddled far, and the salt water
    has whitened their hair.
They are tired from paddling.
They pause as they see the eggs . . .
Drifting in the calm sea, their lines spreading, their short 'hands'
    moving:
Sea eggs we see as we paddle. Gently we drag our paddles along,
    as we rest them.
We paddle through the shine from the Morning Star, from
    Bralgu, slowly along as we see these eggs.

Song 10

What is that blocking us, *waridj* Bralbral? Carefully we must
    paddle.
Resting on paddles, dragging them, we see that stranger from
    Bralgu,
Stranger drift-wood, revealed in the shine of the Star . . .
Carefully moving our arms, we see it drifting by . . .
Making sounds as it drifts, splashing and making waves,
This stranger from Bralgu: drift-wood, drifting and splashing . . .
Pushed by the waves, and making a noise, drifting, and sending
    out foam . . .
Spray from the sea! Spray from away at Bralgu . . .
Foam all over the sea, stretching out from Port Bradshaw . . .
'I leave the foam on my body,'[10] says the drift-wood. Foam
    stretching from Walbinboi Island!
We see it close as we paddle. Drag our paddles, *waridj* Bralbral,
    waridj Djanggawul.
Foam and spray spread all over the sea, stretching out from Port
    Bradshaw . . .
See our heads! Grey from paddling, from salt and foam!

       9. From the sea water and foam. These leave patterned
markings all over their bodies, later used for clan designs.
       10. Foam accumulates on the drift-wood, making patterns
like totemic designs.

The Djanggawul are tired . . . See Bildjiwuraroiju paddling
    carefully, Bralbral undulating his buttocks.
It [the wood] is a stranger from Bralgu, from the source of the
    Star's shine.

Song 11

What is that crying? Careful! We must rest from paddling,
    waridj Bralbral.
We hear a sound. What is that now? A plover, *waridj*, hovering
    above the drifting timber.
It has seen our canoe, and circles about it.
It cries as it circles about the drift-wood, goes soaring cloud-
    wards,
Cries as it swoops about the drift-wood. *Waridj*, it circles round
    and round our canoe.
Paddle carefully, Djanggawul, rest on our oars.
Its screeching cry sounds over the waters from Bralgu, mingling
    with the roar of the sea, spreading across it.
Sound as it skims the sea's surface, sound from its splashing;
    and foam!
The birds and clouds leave that cry for us, *waridj* Bralbral. It is
    a message for us . . .
Its cry echoes back from the clouds, as it circles around and cries
    through its beak:
Screeching that comes through its beak, up from its throat,
    reaching up to the sky.
Its eye is keen; it sees our canoe, and all within it, and sees the
    drifting wood.
Up and down goes its cry. The bird flies with hanging claws.
    Its eyes are closed, but the eye of its anus is open.
See, a message for us, *waridj* Bralbral!
The noise of its cry, as it circles! Foam covers the sea! It cries
    as it circles, away out from Port Bradshaw.

Song 12

We paddle fast, *waridj*, moving our arms. Bralbral, we paddle
fast.

We have come far from the island of Bralgu. What is that
shining, *waridj* Miralaidj?

The Morning Star shines on us, as we paddle along. See the
Star shining!

Lift up the paddle carefully, *waridj*! Bralbral paddles, moving
his buttocks.

Now we are paddling fast, moving our shoulders, lifting the
narrow paddle:

Swaying our hips as we paddle. We have left Bralgu behind us,
waridj Djanggawul.

We follow that Baijini[11] sound, smelling the mainland, and
paddling fast.

We must rest on the paddles, *waridj*. Going along, we hear the
sound of the Baijini talking.

We paddle in on the morning tide, in through the breakers . . .

Our water is rushing onwards; from somewhere it must be
ebbing.

Sound of the surf: waves from our paddling: splashing – foam
from the surf!

Waves arise from our paddling, *waridj* Bralbral . . .

We are paddling fast along, sweeping our paddles . . .

Tired from paddling, with head grey from the foam . . . O
Bildjiwuraroiju!

We are paddling fast, we are close to land, to Port Bradshaw.

Song 18

What is that blocking us, *waridj* Djanggawul? Carefully rest our
paddles, *waridj* Bralbral.

It is a bird, that cries as it swoops along, circling about our
canoe, *waridj* Miralaidj.

11. Earlier visitors to Arnhem Land.

It stretches its neck as it cries, gliding with outstretched wings,
 waridj, giving us strength for paddling.
Our seagull dives to the water, sending out spray with its beak
 as it skims the surface . . .
That bird, *waridj*, goes flying up and down, shaking itself dry:
Carefully we paddle, dragging the paddles along, as we hear that
 bird.
The female gull, with its beak, cries out as it sees the dark rain
 clouds rising.
The seagull cries out at the time of the wet season: it thinks of
 nesting.
Gliding along, it thinks of its home at Bremer Island.
Diving, it skims the water, sending out spray. Its eyes can see in
 the night. It shakes itself dry.
We paddle fast as we smell the sea, smell where the Baijini are.
The seagull splashes the water, making a noise, giving us power
 to go quickly.
We move our wrists fast, swaying our hips as we paddle.
We are moving fast, *waridj*: hear the swish of our paddles.
Our heads are grey from the foam . . . we are tired from
 paddling.

Song 21

What do we see, *waridj*, as we look back?
Paddling, we see the shine of the Morning Star.
Yes, *waridj* Bralbral, paddling we see it close to us. The
 Morning Star sends out its rays as it rises near us:
It skims the water, shining across the sea, the Bralgu Star, its
 rays shining near us.
It skims the sea, from Bralgu, shining upon us, on the end of its
 string, attached to a young sapling.
Another Star, *waridj*, a feathered ball held by the Spirits . . .
 Close is the Morning Star . . .
It shines near, as we turn to see it. O Morning Star, O pole and
 strings . . .

The Star and its rays rise gradually for us, *waridj* Miralaidj; we
     rest our paddles, dragging them through the sea.
See the shine from the disc of the Star, close to us, *waridj*.
The Bralgu Spirits are dancing, sending the Star . . .
Rain people, the stamping sound of their dancing . . .! Dust
     rises, *waridj*, from under their dancing feet . . .!
There from the fresh water place, from the Spirit country.
The shine falls on us, from Bralgu, covering us with its shine . . .
     Close, it shines across to the mainland, to Port Bradshaw.
The morning Star shines, bringing the dawn . . . putting an end
     to the night . . .
Close to us, ending the darkness, bringing the dawn . . .
It pierces the darkness, that Star, sent by the Spirits. The sound
     of their dancing!
The morning Star shines from Bralgu, shines like the *mauwulan*
     pole . . .
It rises from the sandhills at Bralgu, where the Spirits dance,
     waridj, for us.
We move fast with the narrow paddle; we hasten, moving our
     wrists, as the tide roars in.
For the daylight is on us, the dawn, before the cry of the
     morning pigeon. The Star still shines for us, *waridj*
     Djanggawul.
Our hips and buttocks are swaying. Let us go carefully, because
     of the water,
It is rising for us, and roaring, with foam and spray of the surf.
We push the water along with our canoe, our paddles swishing.
Waves come up, with the rising tide. Spray comes from our
     swishing paddles. From us the tide is flowing.
Is that the mainland we are approaching from Bralgu?
Is that the mainland, Port Bradshaw, we are approaching . . .?
The smell of the sea! *Waridj*, we paddle fast, quickly moving
     our wrists.
We lift up the narrow paddles – *waridj* Bralbral, our paddles . . .
We lift up the big paddles, moving fast, swishing the paddles . . .
Our paddles! We drag them along, the flat and the narrow
     paddles . . .

Song 22

What is that, *waridj*, in front of us? We rest, dragging our
     paddles.
There ahead of us, *waridj* Bralbral.
That is the morning pigeon. Darkness goes, with its cry!
We saw darkness only towards the west . . .
Bird that 'twists' its tongue as its whistles! Daylight comes with
     its cry.
We saw the calmness of dawn (no sound but the pigeon's cry).
It ruffles itself, *waridj*, crying, and shaking its feathers. Its cry
     goes out to its nestlings.
The small clear cry of that pigeon and of its nestlings . . .
Talking fast from their nest . . . The pigeon flies down from the
     smooth inside of the nest. Their cries reach us, 'twisting'
     their tongues . . .
We saw the Morning Star ending the darkness. Then, the cry of
     the pigeon! Cries like the speech of different linguistic
     groups, like the Madarlpa dialect!
The bird talks fast, a sound like the Dalwongu dialect . . .
If flew across from its nest in the 'arm-band' bushes . . .
It teaches that cry to its young: the nestlings ruffle themselves.
Teaching that cry! It calls from the limbs near its nest. They are
     'twisting' their tongues . . .
We saw it, flying down, as the darkness was clearing, 'twisting'
     its tongue and whistling.

Song 24a

What is that, *waridj* Bralbral? We rest our paddles at the cry,
     and drag them along.
We look round to see the cry. It comes from Bralgu. It's close
     to us!
It is coming up, moving along. The sun, with its *mauwulan
     rangga* emblem!
As it rises, its rays warm the Djanggawul's backs. It comes
     rising, close to them.

The sun, with rays emerging before its disc! Close, it shines on
    the water, warming our backs, *waridj* Djanggawul.
Close it is rising, from the sand, from the sea into the sky.
Hot sun, burning our backs, its rays leading back to Bralgu!
Rising sun, reflected in the sea! Sun for us, with its heat!
Rays of the sun emerging, *waridj*, leaving its home beneath the
    water!
Sun coming up close, with spreading rays!
For us, *waridj*, it leaves its home under the sea.
Its rays touch us like hands; their reflections shine in the water.
We go fast. Paddling along we see the rays touching us, so that
    the sweat comes out.
The sun comes up for us, leaving its home; the glare is hurting
    our eyes.
It comes closer, rising above the sea, burning our backs.
The smell of the sea! It leaves its home in the water, and warms
    us . . .
We paddle fast, to Port Bradshaw, to the Place of the Sun, to
    where the Baijini are.
Reflections shine in the sea. The rays warm us, on our way to
    Port Bradshaw.
We lift up our paddles, *waridj*, we go fast but carefully, moving
    our arms and our buttocks.
The sun reaches us, with its rays. Its red glow, *waridj*, for us,
    from the sacred parakeet feathers!
We rest our paddles. It is for us! We paddle fast, *waridj*, and
    carefully.
Our buttocks are moving. It is for us, *waridj* Djanggawul! We
    paddle fast!
Our hips sway as we paddle along, lifting the paddles,
On our way to the Place of the Sun, at Port Bradshaw.
The sun's rays touch us, warming our backs . . .
Rays like the parakeet-feathered string of our *rangga*! Feathered
    string like our child! Red glow of the sun.
Rays warming our backs, like feathered string! Like feathered
    rangga!
That sun rises above us, burning our backs, going to the Place
    of the Sun.

It burns our backs, and it shines on the water at Lilildjang.
Its warm rays touch us, stretching to Arnhem Bay . . .
It leaves its home in the water, and rises, burning.
Warm rays touching our backs, touching our *rangga*! Shining,
    and making the mainland clear to see!
For us it shines on the sacred sandhills at Port Bradshaw . . .
Stretching out its rays, warming our backs, illuminating the
    water-holes at Arnhem Bay . . .
That sun, sending out its rays to Elcho Island,
Burning our backs, from the red ochre there . . . at Elcho
    Island . . .
That sun sends out its rays to shine on the sea, *waridj*, on the
    mainland near Milingimbi . . .
Warming our backs as it reaches west to the wide Barara
    country.

Song 27

Let us rest on our paddles, *waridj*, for I (Bralbral) am tired.
Stop paddling, *waridj*.
What is happening there, *waridj*? (Bralbral says) My body aches
    with tiredness.
Tired, because you are worrying (about the mat containing the
    rangga).
I am worrying (says the Djanggawul Brother) about the *rangga*.
    (Why didn't we open the mat?)
I am just tired! That was why, *waridj*, we threw away the sacred
    rangga and mat.
We are coming close to the mainland: our journey, our paddling
    is done.
We land on the beach at Port Bradshaw.
That is our country! We plant our *mauwulan* here.
We have arrived, oh *waridj*!

From Parts II to V. The Djanggawul walk around in the land near Port Bradshaw, 'making the country' and plunging in the *mauwulan* sacred pole to make wells. Then they continue their journey towards and around Arnhem Bay.

Song 30

We walk along, making the country, with the aid of the
    mauwulan rangga.
We put the point of the *rangga* into the ground and sing all the
    way along, swaying our hips.
Oh, *waridj* Miralaidj, our heads are lolling in weariness! Our
    bodies ache, after our long journey from Bralgu!
We are making country, Bildjiwuraroiju, the large sandhill at
    the Place of the Mauwulan!
We Djanggawul, walking along, see clouds coming up in the
    distance . . .
See those spreading white clouds, that rise above Wobilinga
    Island,
See them rising over Bilari Hill. Clouds coming up for us,
    waridj!
We plunge the *mauwulan* point into the ground, making it good.
We shall put it in at our sandhill, for us, *waridj* Bralbral!
We are clapping our sticks and singing, to make ourselves
    strong, swaying our hips as we walk.
We saw the clouds, there, above Ganjumingalei,
Saw those clouds coming up, behind Port Bradshaw;
Rising for us, rising to guide us, *waridj*.
Ourselves we are making the country, making it around Port
    Bradshaw: the Place of the Sun, the Place of the Mauwulan
    Rangga!
For these are the places which we saw first of all!
There are clouds coming, from the country at Arnhem Bay!
Clouds we saw, making us feel good as we walk, swaying our
    hips, oh *waridj* Djanggawul.

Song 33

What is this crying, *waridj* Djanggawul? *Waridj*, it is a parakeet,
Calling softly from the sacred tree, its red breast feathers
      glistening in the sun.
It grasps the *rangga* tree, watching them, cocking its head from
      side to side as if it were weary.
It ruffles its breast feathers, making them dry. Trilling and
      calling, with head moving, grasping the sacred tree!
Softly, it calls the invocations of the sacred tree.
There, on the tree, it saw the sun's rays and the glowing sunset
      sky,
Saw the rays of the sun setting, in the west beyond Milingimbi.
Drying its red feathers in the glow of the sun, it clasps and
      scratches the tree with its claws . . .
It watched the sinking sun, saw the last rays shining at Arnhem
      Bay,
Saw the red glow spreading over Arnhem Bay, multi-coloured
      rays of the sunset!
Shining into the sacred shade, lighting it up, away towards
      Arnhem Bay!
Calling softly, it watched the sun setting at Bulibuli,
Looked at the sun, and spoke: 'I am drying myself, my red
      breast feathers, my *rangga* feathers – my children!'

Song 51

We are going along, *waridj*, near Bulibuli . . .
Yes, indeed, I listen to your word, for I always follow you . . .
We walk along with the aid of the *mauwulan*, making country,
      inserting the *mauwulan* point, our hips swaying.
Carefully, *waridj* Djanggawul, we put in the *mauwulan*, drag it
      along.
We are walking with grey hair, stained by the splashing foam,
      from the Spirit Country, from Bralgu.
Stained with salt and foam from the sea, splashing at the Place
      of the Sun, the Place of the Mauwulan.

Our bodies are shadowed by clouds as we walk, at Buginja:
With hips swaying, our bodies shadowed, as the clouds come
  rising and spreading for us, *waridj* Miralaidj!
Step by step we walk along, making country, inserting the
  mauwulan point.
Hips swaying, we walk along, dragging our *rangga*, and plunging
  it into the ground, making the country . . .
We reach Bulibuli. We are tired, *waridj*, but we sing as we go
  along!

Song 57

What is that for us, *waridj*? It is a duck, crying out!
Yes, *waridj* Djanggawul. I thought it was a stranger, for it is
  flying fast, with flapping wings!
It is ours, this duck, flying to the *munji* berry bushes . . .
We shall sing about it, *waridj* Bralbral, as we go along . . .
For we saw them, those ducks, flying fast as we walked along,
  females and males by themselves.
They leave tracks behind, everywhere! Their feathers are stained
  with foam, from the open sea, from Bralgu!
The heads of these birds are grey . . .
We sing about them as we go along, *waridj* Miralaidj;
Yes indeed, *waridj* Bralbral, we leave them behind. They are
  flying wearily with foam marks upon them!
They scratched the ground with their claws as they took to the
  air, flying at Banbaldji.
Our ducks are flying fast, craning their necks in flight.
Ducks, crying out! We look at them, and leave them to go their
  way.

Song 67

Oh! What is this! A small black mangrove bird, *waridj*.
Yes, it is a mangrove bird! I thought I heard a strange sound, as
  it cried among the mangroves.

Yes, it saw the daylight coming, the stars fading . . .
This is the mangrove bird: it heard the water rising and roaring,
    with foam splashing:
Crying at the water swirling within the well at Wagulwagul,
    splashing against the mat, the fish trap!
So the bird looked back, and saw the daylight spreading from
    Bralgu, driving away the night:
Saw the daylight coming, the darkness clearing away . . .
Looking back, it saw the Morning Star sinking.
Its long-drawn cry echoed up to the clouds – to the woman
    clouds, to the large spreading, pregnant clouds . . .
Sound drifting upwards into the message clouds, clouds massing
    together.
Its long cry comes from the *djuda* trees, the poles of the fish
    trap: scratching the trunk as it sits clasping the tree . . .
Tired, it cries as the water comes rising up:
The long-drawn cry merges with the roar of the water . . .
The long-drawn cry, as the water rises, tossing: it grows tired,
    from the splashing spray, the rising well water.
With a long cry it clasps the *djuda*, watching the water at
    Wagulwagul, rising against the mat.

Song 84

What is that crying, *waridj*? The *lindaridj* parakeet, with red
    breast feathers, is calling!
Crying, for it saw the red sunset, the warm rays of the sinking
    sun . . .
Saw the hot sun, and the glowing reflections of sunset, in the
    west beyond Milingimbi.
Saw the sun's rays, as it clasped the sacred *djuda*, among the
    small twigs: red breast feathers reflecting the glow of
    sunset!
Cocking its head from side to side and crying softly, clasping
    the *djuda* – like feathered pendants!
Drying itself, ruffling its breast feathers!
'Myself' (says the parakeet) 'I have baby nestling feathers!'

Saw them reflecting the rays of the red sunset in the west
 beyond Milingimbi:
The bright, glowing haze of the sinking sun!
It saw the red glow at Jiganjindu, at Marabai; shining over at
 Bulbulmara, at Arnhem Bay.
Parakeets calling softly, clasping the *djuda*, just as the feathered
 pendants cling to the *rangga* . . .
The *djuda* roots well planted, the *djuda* standing: parakeets
 clasping it, calling softly . . .
They see the well water rising and bubbling, splashing and
 murmuring . . .
Soft cry of the parakeets, cocking their heads from side to side,
 gently twittering!
Drying their red breast feathers, like feathered pendants, like
 nestlings . . .
They cry into the rays of the sun, watching the sun sinking:
Their gentle cries fade away, as the last rays shine into the
 mouth of the shade, into the mat:
Crying, as the rays disappear from the inner peak of the mat,
 from its transverse fibre!

   From Parts VI to X. The Djanggawul continue their
journey, and more people are gradually removed from the Sisters'
wombs (symbolically the mat). The sacred feathered strings taken from
the parakeet's breast down are spread out, leading to the various places
associated with the Djanggawul.

Song 92

We turn over this mat, carefully, with its peak uppermost . . .
Go, turn it over so it becomes conical!
Yes indeed, *waridj*, carefully we put the mat within the mouth
 of the shade . . .
Come, we see the clan of people, the *rangga*! Carefully part the
 fringe of the mat, with its transverse fibre . . .
Go, put them along! Go, pull them out, putting your hand
 within the mouth!
Yes, pull out another, and another – one by one!

Pull them out! We see the clansfolk in the mouth of the mat:
Just pull them out one by one. Grasp it and straighten it,
    pulling it hard so it comes out head first from this
    mat . . .
Yes, yes indeed, *waridj* Miralaidj. I just asked you, for you are
    my great leader . . .
Here we are putting the sacred *rangga* people from that mat:
    drying them carefully, *waridj*.
One has been caught on the transverse fibre of the mat! Put
    your hand through, grasp and straighten the feathered
    string!
Now that is done! Yes, finished *waridj*, indeed!
Come, let us take them from within this other mat, where we
    see another clan of people:
Come! Quickly, put your hand within the mouth of the mat,
    within the sacred shade . . .
We come from far away, from Bralgu, the Place of the Spirits,
    far across the sea: from the Place of the Mauwulan, from
    the Place of the Sun, from the shine of the Morning Star!
There, where the foam splashes and stains!
We plant the *djuda* roots in the warm rays of the sun, invoking
    the sacred *bugali*.
Carefully, put in the *djuda*, calling the invocations . . .
Carefully, let them sit there, as we invoke the sacred names . . .
They stand with shining feathers, quietly, in sacred tabu-ness;
Drying there in the hot rays of the sun, the glaring heat.
It looks down on them, and sweat comes from them in the rising
    heat:
Red breast feathers splashed and stained with foam from the sea
    beyond the Place of the Mauwulan.
Thus we lay them out carefully, reverently,
They see the water rising at Dulabang.
The roots are standing within the well, covered up by its waters:
    for they are very sacred.
There, take hold of two of them within the well!
We put in the *djuda* roots, the *rangga* standing erect!
They see the water at Ngubarei:
Water rising and bubbling, splashing and roaring, spreading out
    like the tide . . .

Song 135

There, *waridj* Djanggawul, put in the *djuda* roots, the *rangga*,
    making a well!
We call the sacred invocations . . .
Carefully drag along the mud and grass in the well, straightening
    them up, *waridj* Djanggawul.
They stand with shining feathers, quietly and solemnly, standing
    up in the ground . . .
They see the well water at Bulbulmara, rising and bubbling,
    splashing and foaming . . .
Pushing along the silt, flowing, with waves splashing together:
Waves, and rough water splashing, spraying up like the rising
    tide . . .
For they come from within the transverse fibre of the mat, from
    the mouth, the fringe of the mat, from its inner peak:
    covered up so no one may see, like younger siblings . . .
They are splashed with foam that stained them from far away on
    the deep sea, from the Spirit Country, the Place of the
    Sun, the Place of the Mauwulan . . .
From the sound of the Baijini talking, the smell of the sea . . .

Song 144

What is that crying? It is a parakeet nestling, perched on the
    sacred *djuda* tree.
Clasping the tree, cocking its head from side to side, crying
    softly:
It saw the rays of the sun sinking beyond Milingimbi:
Crying, it saw the warm red sunset, the red reflections in the
    clouds . . .
Saw the glare of the sun's glow, crying softly . . .
Perched on the *djuda* tree, clasping the limbs with its claws,
    moving down the branches . . .
It saw the red sun sinking, the spreading sunset.
Saw the sun going down in the west, beyond Milingimbi . . .
Looking at the sun, playing there in its rays like the *djuda* roots,
    at Maluwa . . .

Crying softly, looking at the peak of the mat, and the *djuda*:
Drying its breast feathers, its babies, in the warm rays of the
    sun . . .
Birds quietly, solemnly, watching the sinking sun:
They look at the mouth of the sacred basket, hanging there . . .
Always clasping the limbs of the *djuda* tree, moving their claws.
We hear them within the mouth of the mat!
Crying out, the parakeets vanish within the mat, going deep
    within it so no one may see them . . .
They are covered up, like younger siblings, taboo, covered up for
    sleep . . .
The sacred pendants, the feathered strings . . .

The next two songs are sung during the dancing in the *nara*
ritual in which the Djanggawul re-enact their canoe voyage from Bralgu,
reiterating the symbolism of the well and the feathered pendants.

Song 166

Go, roar like the water!
Sister, we call out the sacred names for the water, roaring loudly!
Go, call out, roaring like the water from far away, from Bralgu,
    out at sea near the Spirit Country . . .
From the wide sea beyond Port Bradshaw, waves splashing to-
    gether out at sea, near Bralgu . . .
Roaring and surging, foam rising and waves splashing together . . .
Carefully, roar like the sea, putting in the *djuda rangga* . . .
Put the *djuda* roots into the well, calling the invocations . . .
We put them into the well, making the well, at Djumbulwara, at
    Marabai, at Bulbulmara, Jiganjindu, Gwoijaring, Dambala!
Carefully, led by the leader, putting the *djuda* into the mud,
    dragging the mud . . .
Quietly they shine, covered up, for they are sacred . . .

Song 172

Go, roar again like the sea, carefully inserting the *djuda*:
Dance like the water, far away at Bralgu!
Gently paddle along, resting the paddles, dragging them through
   the sea . . .
Go, put in the *djuda*, and the *rangga* from within the peak of the
   mat . . .
Carefully roar like the sea from far away, at the shine of the
   Morning Star, away near the Spirit Country . . .
The leader holding the sacred mat, dancing within the shade,
   calling the invocations . . .
Carefully straighten the pendants, the feathered strings, covered
   up like younger siblings, so no one may see, in sacred
   taboo-ness . . .

Song 174

What is that crying? It is a nestling, crying softly, as it saw the
   sun.
It is perched on the sacred *djuda* tree, clasping the *rangga* tree
   with its claws . . .
From the tree it looked at the rays of the sun, in the west
   beyond Milingimbi:
Saw the warm rays of the sun, the shining sun!
Drying itself, ruffling its feathers, its nestlings. 'Myself (says the
   bird), I am drying my red breast feathers, my babies!'
Parakeets, perched in a row on that *djuda* limb . . .
Crying softly, cocking their heads from side to side . . .
They saw the rays of the sun, and felt its heat . . .
Crying softly, they saw the mouth of the sacred basket . . .
Saw the sun, as they sat quietly, and solemnly:
Crying, they fly deep down within it, covered up like younger
   siblings, so no one may see.
'Myself (says the bird), I have red breast feathers, my nest-
   lings . . .'
It is done: they are asleep.

Song *182*

Go, take another mat and put it within, carefully turning over
    its mouth . . .
Go, undo it: carefully part its fringe, then put in your hand . . .
Come, carefully pull them out, shining, from the transverse fibre
    of the mat . . .
It is done. Yes, pull out another basket.
It is done? Yes, come, put them upon the flattened part of the
    mat,
Carefully dry them, in the warm rays of the sun.
Here is another basket. Have you grasped it?
Yes, come, pull it out, into the transverse fibre of the mat.
Go, grasp another basket. You have it? Yes, let us pull it out!
Go, pull out two more baskets and put them within . . .
Let the hot sun dry them, for they are splashed with foam . . .
Splashed with foam from far away on the wide sea, near the
    Spirit Country . . .

Snails

As sung by Liagarang

From the Wuradilagu song-cycle (a *jiridja* moiety cycle),
made up of a series of clan songs.

Sound of snails – crying,
Sound drifting through the brush, sound of crying.
Slime of snails, dragging themselves
Along the low-lying plain, crying;
Snails with their slime, crying.
Sound drifting through the bush: dragging themselves along,
    crying,
Snails, their sound blowing overhead from among the bushes.

Yellow cloud

As sung by Liagarang

Also from the Wuradilagu song-cycle.

Yellow cloud rising up from that fighting, from the people
   playing and throwing spears.
Wide cloud, shaking itself, sun shining along the top, great
   cloud bending down,
With black girdle. Yellow cloud with black girdle, rising up,
   bending downwards.
Wide cloud joining others, shaking itself: yellow cloud with
   black girdle
Hitting together, its cloud hands extended.
Yellow cloud with black girdle, rising up in the sea, touching the
   open sea.
Standing above the sea,
Rising, bending downwards; yellow cloud with the black girdle,
Standing above Blue Mud Bay; its tips toward Guninalju,
   Ngigaboi, Wondralna.
Wide cloud with hands extended, and black girdle.

The blowflies buzz

Djalparmiwi

   The singer is so distressed by her daughter's death that she
wants to blame someone for it. She is already jealous of her younger co-
wife Jandin, and seizes the opportunity to upbraid her husband Banga-
lawi for paying her too much attention and neglecting his sick daughter.

Ah, the blowfly is whining there, its maggots are eating the flesh.
The blowflies buzz, their feet stray over the corpse . . .
The buzzing goes on and on . . .
Who is it, eating there, whose flesh are they eating? . . .
Ah my daughter, come back here to me!
Ah, our daughter was taken ill –
You didn't sing for her, as a father should!

You are foolish and silly, you sing only to please the ears of
    women!
You like to lie close to a young girl, a virgin, and give her a
    child!
You will not stay in one place;
Here and there, all over the place, you go among the camps,
You go walking hither and thither, looking for sweethearts.
Ah, before it was here that you used to stay.
You should be ashamed to do that before all these strangers!
Presently I will take up a knife and cut you!
(Bangalawi says: 'This is all that I do: I get food to eat, and
    tobacco to smoke!')
No, you go to sit down beside some woman,
You sit close, close beside her . . .
Ah, my lost, sick child – ah, the blowflies!
Soon I will hit that woman of yours, that Jandin! She is rubbish,
    that woman of yours, her face is ugly, she smells like an
    evil spirit! Presently, when she is pregnant, I won't look
    after her! You, Bangalawi, you, her husband, you indeed,
    all by yourself, you can help her in childbirth!

All you others, eat

Djurberaui

        The singer is wailing over the illness of her husband's
daughter, Ganal.

Ah my daughter, my grandchild!
Ah, the snake with its tongue flickering, at Dagalbauwei . . .
Ah my daughter, ah, the mound of the snake!
Ah my grandchild! My grandchild!
At Bumbiwalwal'jun, and far away, the snake scatters its young,
At Waidja and Dirmalanan, Ganal and Noiwul . . .
My daughter, my grandchild! My daughter is sick and hungry!
All you others, you eat till your bellies burst!
You used to be jealous before, when your husband called her.
All you lot are alive still – ah, my daughter, my grandchild!

Ah, your father has cried and cried, while mucus flowed into his
     mouth!
My daughter, my husband! My daughter, sick and hungry!
Ah my daughter, my husband!
Presently your child will grow, and you won't be looking after
     him, because you will be dead! Presently other children
     will hit him, other women will not look after him
     properly . . .!
Ah, my daughter, my grandchild!

Sail at the mast head . . .

The sail at the mast head dips from side to side,
As the boat comes up from the south . . .
The sail unfurled at the mast head flaps in the wind,
It stands upright and flaps, as the boat goes on.
The wind tosses the sail, up on the mast.
And the mast head moves, dipping from side to side.
The sail on the mast flaps, dancing, and 'talks' in the wind . . .

Three songs from the Moon-Bone cycle

In the *jiridja* cycle of the Moon-Bone the Moon lived with
his sister Dugong in the ancient Dream time. They collected Lily and
Lotus Roots, symbolically associated with the Evening Star. The Moon
eventually travelled out to sea, cast his bone into the water, and after
three days climbed up into the sky. Now every month he repeats this: he
throws his bone into the sea, where it becomes the nautilus shell, and is
born again. In the last song the Evening Star is revealed as a Lotus
Bloom and a Lily Root, and the string attached to it is the stalk of these
plants.

The birds

The birds saw the people walking along.
Crying, the white cockatoos flew over the clay pan of the Moon-
     light;

From the place of the Dugong they flew, looking for lily-root
    food; pushing the foliage down and eating the soft roots.
Crying, the birds flew down and along the clay pan, at that
    place of the Dugong . . .
Crying, flying down there along the clay pan . . .
At the place of the Dugong, of the Tree-Limbs-Rubbing-
    Together, and of the Evening Star.
Where the lily-root clay pan is . . .
Where the cockatoos play, at that place of the Dugong . . .
Flapping their wings they flew down, crying, 'We saw the
    people!'
There they are always living, those clans of the white cockatoo . . .
And there is the Shag woman, and there her clan:
Birds, trampling the lily foliage, eating the soft round roots!

New Moon

Now the New Moon is hanging, having cast away his bone:
Gradually he grows larger, taking on new bone and flesh.
Over there, far away, he has shed his bone: he shines on the
    place of the Lotus Root, and the place of the Dugong,
On the place of the Evening Star, of the Dugong's Tail, of the
    Moonlight clay pan . . .
His old bone gone, now the New Moon grows larger;
Gradually growing, his new bone growing as well.
Over there, the horns of the old receding Moon bent down,
    sank into the place of the Dugong:
His horns were pointing towards the place of the Dugong.
Now the New Moon swells to fullness, his bone grown larger.
He looks on the water, hanging above it, at the place of the
    Lotus.
There he comes into sight, hanging above the sea, growing
    larger and older . . .
There far away he has come back, hanging over the clans near
    Milingimbi . . .
Hanging there in the sky, above those clans . . .

'Now I'm becoming a big moon, slowly regaining my round-
    ness . . .'[12]
In the far distance the horns of the Moon bend down, above
    Milingimbi,
Hanging a long way off, above Milingimbi Creek . . .
Slowly the Moon-Bone is growing, hanging there far away.
The bone is shining, the horns of the Moon bend down.
First the sickle Moon on the old Moon's shadow; slowly he
    grows,
And shining he hangs there at the place of the Evening Star . . .
Then far away he goes sinking down, to lose his bone in the sea;
Diving towards the water, he sinks down out of sight.
The old Moon dies to grow new again, to rise up out of the sea.

The Evening Star

Up and up soars the Evening Star, hanging there in the sky.
Men watch it, at the place of the Dugong and of the Clouds, and
    of the Evening Star,
A long way off, at the place of Mist, of Lilies and of the Du-
    gong.
The Lotus, the Evening Star, hangs there on its long stalk, held
    by the Spirits.
It shines on that place of the Shade, on the Dugong place, and
    on to the Moonlight clay pan . . .
The Evening Star is shining, back towards Milingimbi, and over
    the 'Wulamba people . . .
Hanging there in the distance, towards the place of the Dugong,
The place of the Eggs, of the Tree-Limbs-Rubbing-Together,
    and of the Moonlight clay pan . . .
Shining on its short stalk, the Evening Star, always there at the
    clay pan, at the place of the Dugong . . .
There, far away, the long string hangs at the place of the
    Evening Star, the place of Lilies.

12. The Moon speaks about himself.

Away there at Milingimbi . . . at the place of the Full Moon,
Hanging above the head of that *'Wonguri* tribesman:
The Evening Star goes down across the camp, among the white
    gum trees . . .
Far away, in those places near Milingimbi . . .
Goes down among the *'Nurulwulu* people, towards the camp and
    the gum trees,
At the place of the Crocodiles, and of the Evening Star, away
    towards Milingimbi . . .
The Evening Star is going down, the Lotus Flower on its
    stalk . . .
Going down among all those western clans . . .
It brushes the heads of the uncircumcised people . . .
Sinking down in the sky, that Evening Star, the Lotus . . .
Shining on to the foreheads of all those headmen . . .
On to the heads of all those Sandfly people . . .
It sinks there into the place of the white gum trees, at Milin-
    gimbi.

ENGLISH

English is one of the most widely spoken languages in the world, and the selection of oral poems in English presented here can only cover a small fraction of what might have been included. This section is therefore perhaps even less 'representative' of the particular language and culture involved than are others in this book. This inevitably means that readers will find many of their own favourite poems (and types of poems) missing, and that many English-speaking areas of the world simply do not appear in any direct way. The selection has in fact been drawn just from Britain and America. The limitations have been unavoidable, however, since it seemed fair on the one hand not to allow this section to overshadow others in length, while, on the other, making a point of including *some* selection of English oral poems to parallel those from other cultures.

It is sometimes supposed that 'oral poetry' occurs only in non-literate and 'primitive' contexts, or perhaps in centuries in the distant past – far away and long ago. But, as is illustrated in this section, this is just not so. At least in the wide sense of 'oral poetry' adopted in this book, there is plenty of English oral poetry now in circulation, from Negro spirituals and miners' songs to pop songs and well-known Christian hymns.

Collectors of English oral poetry (often under the title of 'folk songs' or 'popular verse') have often gone out of their way to select the 'traditional', often the forms supposedly descended from the past through 'folk transmission' from distant ages. It is partly to balance this tendency, as well as to make the point that oral poetry is not merely a remnant of the past, that I have concentrated here on poetry in circulation this century. Some of the poems may have been *composed* earlier (in fact some certainly were, while others are more recently composed), but the emphasis is on the oral *circulation* and *performance* during this century.

The poems are of many different types, sometimes overlapping. One of the most memorable categories is that of Negro spirituals, shading into the blues songs and the popular songs that are part of mass-acclaimed entertainment throughout the English-speaking world today. Another large category – and one that has already been fairly well publicized in collections by Greenway, Lloyd, and others, as well as in explicitly left-wing publications – are the songs of 'protest' and 'oppression'. Among these the prison songs are particularly striking, many of them heart-rending and yet signifying the humanity and artistry that find expression even in what might seem to the outsider the unlikeliest of contexts. There are also the tramp songs and those of what are often regarded as the 'working-class' occupational groups – songs of miners, railworkers, weavers, and so on – as well as the lyrics of those who, like Woody Guthrie, were regarded as in some sense their spokesmen. In fact it is common for all occupational or otherwise separate groups to have their own songs – poems special to themselves which help to mark out and consolidate their separate identity: those of soldiers, Mormons, lumbermen in the northern woods, prisoners, tramps, cowboys, even children – not to mention the many other groups that could not be represented here.

Most of the poems just mentioned, in common with most oral poetry in English, are said to occur among minority or marginal groups who are somehow separated from 'high culture' and apart from establishment and 'mainstream' forms. There is of course some truth in this view. The sung verses of Negroes, prisoners, colliers, schoolchildren, or remote woodsmen have tended – with just a few exceptions – not to have reached the world of schoolbooks or university education, but to have remained very much a *performed* rather than a written art. For one reason or another the social convention in our culture has been that such forms are often not regarded as part of the established and formally taught 'high culture'.

But it would be misleading to argue from this that oral art is *confined* to marginal and minority groups in English culture. On the contrary. The songs, for instance, propagated by the mass media of radio and television, supplemented by gramophone records and tapes, have every right to be regarded as a type of oral poetry; and, even if many are favoured more by some age groups than others, they can scarcely be seen as circulating merely among minority or underground audiences. The quality of the words may vary, admittedly, but it is hard to deny some of these lyrics, like the Beatles' 'Eleanor Rigby' for example, the title of true poetry. Again much of the 'left-wing' and 'protest' verse has been as popular among intellectuals as 'workers', and the relatively recent pheno-menon of 'jazz poetry', like Dannie Abse's 'Song of a Hebrew', has been practised by a number of recognized poets as yet another instance of orally performed and oriented poetry. There is every reason too to regard many well-known hymns – frequently sung as much from memory as from the printed text – as a continuing manifestation of oral poetry in contemporary society. All in all it seems as appropriate to look for instances of oral poetry in 'estab-lishment' and intellectual circles as among the marginal, localized or underground groups which used to be seen as the obvious collecting ground for enthusiasts.

As far as the overall cultural background of these poems goes, it is impossible to make any quick generalizations. There is a great deal of variation, as indeed could only be expected from poems drawn from as wide and complex an area as Britain and America. This is far from a closed and unchanging area too, as far as songs are concerned, for there has obviously been long and fruitful interaction with, for instance, Irish and African forms. One recurrent theme that is striking, however, is that of Christianity. Though references to this are by no means universal, the Christian (and biblical) tradition is clearly one that has frequently offered both inspiration and a literary frame of reference to oral poets composing in English, from earlier Negro spirituals to popular songs today.

One of the main properties the poems share is their musical setting: they are almost all sung or musically accompanied in some way. Sometimes the tune has a specific connection with particular words, but in many cases there are either several recog-nized tunes for the words, as with 'O God of Bethel', or else – a very common practice – the tune is taken over or adapted from somewhere else: 'The peeler's lament' goes to the tune of 'The wearing of the green', Woody Guthrie's 'Jesus Christ' to 'Jessie James', and Joe Hill's 'The preacher and the slave' to the tune of the popular Salvation Army gospel hymn 'In the sweet bye and bye'.

Another feature these poems share with much oral poetry is their textual variability. There is often no one 'correct' text, but a number of varying and equally authentic versions. 'O God of Bethel', for instance, has appeared in several different forms, and even recent compositions like 'Jesus Christ' or 'The preacher and the slave' are known and sung in several versions.

It is obvious that in the circumstances of English culture today, there is bound to be constant interaction between oral media and the written word (one striking instance is the near-quotation from Elizabeth Barrett Browning in part of 'The peeler's lament', but the interaction also comes out in a more general way in many of the other examples). The poems thus hardly conform to the stereotype of 'pure' oral poetry. Nevertheless they most certainly are oral in the sense of being essentially orally performed and (often) orally circulated. In these poems too there is much that, by its vigour, insight, or pathos, can bear comparison both with the other poems in this collection and with the written verse of our 'standard' English text books.

Chain gang blues

Many days of sorrow, many nights of woe,
Many days of sorrow, many nights of woe,
And a ball and chain, everywhere I go.

Chains on my feet, padlocks on my hands,
Chains on my feet and padlocks on my hands,
It's all on account of stealing a woman's man.

It was early this mornin' that I had my trial,
It was early this mornin' that I had my trial,
Ninety days on the county road, and the judge didn't even smile.

Jeff Buckner

Frank Beddo

'I saw Jeff Buckner lynched in Texas when I was about eight years old. I wrote this song to express my grief and my feeling of helplessness. . . . It is to be sung very slowly and mournfully.'

They hanged Jeff Buckner from a sycamore tree,
And I was there, and I was there.
He went to his death so silently,
And I was there, but I never said a word.

They put him in a wagon with a rope around his neck,
And I was there, and I was there.
They pulled away the wagon and his neck it did break,
And I was there, but I never said a word.

Jeff Buckner's face was as black as coal,
And I was there, and I was there.
But white as snow alongside of my soul,
For I was there, but I never said a word.

They nailed King Jesus to an iron-bolted tree,
And I was there, and you were there.
And meek as a lamb to the slaughter went he,
And we were there, but we never said a word.

I's gonna shine . . .

I's gonna shine
Whiter dan snow,
When I gits to heaven
An' dey meets me at de do'.

Oh, shine, I will shine,
How dey shine, glory shine,
When I gits to heaven
An' dey meets me at de do'.

Shine, God a'-mighty shine,
All de sinners shine in de row;
But I'll be de out-shinedest
When dey meets me at de do'.

Oh, shine, de brudders shine,
Dey sisters shine ever mo',
When we all gits to heaven
An' dey meets us at de do'.

Dey got each and de udder's man

See two passenger trains, Lawd,
Runnin' side by side.
See two womens, see two womens,
Stan' an' talk so long.
Bet yo' life dey got
Each and de udder's man.

Judgement day

My Lord, what a morning when de stars begin to fall,
You'll see de worl' on fire,
You'll see de moon a bleedin' an'
De moon will turn to blood,

Den you'll see de elements a meltin',
You'll see de stars a fallin',
O yes, de stars in de elements a fallin',
An' de moon drips way in blood,
When God goin' call dem chilluns from de distant lan',
Den you see de coffins bustin',
Den you see de bones a creepin',
Den you see po' sinner risin',
Den you hear de tombstones crackin',
An' you see de graves a bustin'.
Hell an' seas gwine give up their daid,
Den you see de forked lightnin',
Den yo hear de rollin' thunder,
Earth shall reel an' totter,
Hell shall be uncapped,
De dragon be loosed –
Don't you hear them sinners cryin'?

I work all day long for you . . .

I work all day long for you, until the sun go down,
I work all day long for you, baby, from sun-up until the sun go
    down,
An' you take all my money and drink it up and come home and
    want to fuss and clown.

I worked for you so many times, when I really was too sick to
    go,
I worked for you, baby, when your man was slipping in my
    back-door,
I can see for myself so tell your back-door man I won't be your
    fool no more.

I worked for you, baby, when snow was above my knees,
I worked for you, baby, when ice and snow was on the ground,
Trying to make you happy, an' you chasing every man in town.

It hurts to love a person that don't belong to you,
It hurts to love a person that don't belong to you,

'Cause when they found out that you really love them and they
    don't care what they do,

They'll take your heart and they'll use it like a football on a
    football ground,
They'll take your heart and they'll use it like a football on a
    football ground,
And when they gits to playing with your heart and they starts
    blackin' your heart around.

If you see my mother . . .

Mack Maze

A work song sung by Negro prisoners in Texas to accompany group work like cotton-picking or sugar-cane-cutting, and recorded in 1964. The collector writes: 'This is another of those songs that are too anguished to come through on a printed page. The words are simple, the tune sometimes becomes no more than a moan, then the moan becomes words again.'

If you see my mother, partner, tell her pray for me,
I got life on the river, yeah, never will go free, never will go free.

They 'cuse me a murder,
Never harmed a man, never harmed a man.

I say wake up ol' dead man,
Help me carry my row, help me carry my row.

Well the row so grassy,
I can hardly go, I can hardly go.

The peeler's lament

A cowboy song. Note the interaction here between oral and written forms with the (slightly modified) quotation from one of Elizabeth Barrett Browning's *Sonnets from the Portuguese*.

She had no business doin' it, but she come out o' the East,
The fust time I scanned her face, her eyes were all my feast;

And when I come to tell her 'Mornin',' a lump clim' up my throat
That made me feel like a maverick, or more like our camp goat.

I loved the gal, nor dared to tell, couldn't strike love's talkin'
    trail,
Till one fine day with trappin's on I blurted out my tale;
I landed on her with my rope, and choked her into submission.
With 'bout the ease and grace the devil uses when he's fishin'.

And here's what I slipped in her hand – remember, my fine
    buck –
'If you's no objections, lady, to the parson you'll be tuck.'
Whoop! She just stuck out her hand and says to me, 'Old Pard,
You're the lad for me, I'm sure, and you have played the right
    card.

'I always have wished for the cowboy's daring,
And a hell-roarin' life I have forever been craving.'
So I lifted her into the right stirrup astride,
And we doubled that horse to parson's warm side!

But, hell, she didn't last longer – that gal –
Than the dry hot winds came and the sandstorms fell;
She wrote them out East to wire her the money,
And now, for all I know, she is some financier's honey.

But – 'I love her with the passion put to use
    In my old griefs, and with my childhood's faith.'
And – 'I love her with the love I seem to lose
    With my lost saints – yes, with the breath,
    Smiles, tears of all my life; and if God choose,
    I shall but love her better after death.'

There is no need of tellin' any punchin'-dog 'Beware!'
For the best thing you could tell him is just to get his share;
'Cause the only thing will cure him is a bit of calico,
And when he gets his needin's he will be a wiser beau.

There's no use a-lyin', for I'm glad I saw that gal,
And if she's doin' any stunts, she still will be my pal;
'Cause this is no place for her, I know that very well,
For the devil, after prospectin' round, called it a damn poor
    place for hell.

Bow down your head and cry

A cowboy ballad of north-west Texas.

I went down to the river, poor boy,
To see the ships go by;
My sweetheart stood on the deck of one,
She waved to me good-bye.

Bow down your head and cry, poor boy,
Bow down your head and cry;
Stop thinking of the girl you love,
Bow down your head and cry.

I followed her for months and months
And offered her my hand;
She was just about to have me, when
She ran off with a gambling man.

Bow down your head and cry, poor boy, etc.

He came at me with a jackknife,
I went at him with lead,
And when the fight was over,
He lay beside me dead.

Bow down your head and cry, poor boy, etc.

They took me to the jail-house,
The days and days rolled by;
The jury found me guilty,
And the judge says, 'You must die.'

Bow down your head and cry, poor boy, etc.

'Oh, do you bring me silver, poor boy,
Or do you bring me gold?'
'I bring you neither,' said the man,
'I bring you a hangman's fold.'

Bow down your head and cry, poor boy, etc.

'Oh, do you bring my pardon, poor boy,
To turn me a-loose?'
'I bring you nothing,' said the man,
'Except a hangman's noose.'

Bow down your head and cry, poor boy, etc.

> And yet they call this justice!
> And justice let it be!
> I only killed the man that was
> Just fixing to kill me.

Bow down your head and cry, poor boy, etc.

> I went down to the river,
> To see the ships go by;
> My sweetheart stood on the deck of one
> She waved to me good-bye.

Bow down your hear and cry, poor boy, etc.

The preacher and the slave

Joe Hill

Long-haired preachers come out every night,
Try to tell you what's wrong and what's right;
But when asked about something to eat,
They will answer in voices so sweet:

> You will eat, bye and bye,
> In that glorious land in the sky;
> Work and pray, live on hay,
> You'll get pie in the sky when you die.

And the Starvation Army they play,
And they sing and they clap and they pray,
Till they get all your coin in the drum,
Then they'll tell you when you're on the bum:

> You will eat, bye and bye, etc.

Holy Rollers and Jumpers come out,
And they holler, they jump and they shout,
'Give your money to Jesus,' they say,
'He will cure all diseases today.'

> You will eat, bye and bye, etc.

If you fight hard for children and wife,
Try hard and get something in life,
You're a sinner and bad man they tell,
When you die you will sure go to hell;

    You will eat, bye and bye, etc.

Working men of all countries unite,
Side by side for our freedom we'll fight;
When the world and its wealth we have gained,
To the grafters we'll sing this refrain:

    You will eat, bye and bye,
    When you've learned how to cook and to fry;
    Chop some wood, 'twill do you good,
    And you'll eat in the sweet bye and bye.

Two hoboes

Railroad look so pretty,
Box car on the track.
Here come two hoboes,
Grip sack on their back.

    Oh, babes,
    Oh, no-home babes.

One is my brother,
'Nother my brother-in-law,
Hike all the way from N'Orleans
Back to Arkansas.

    Oh, babes, etc.

Back where you ought to be
Instead of being at home;
Instead of being at home, babes,
You're on the road like me.

    Oh, babes, etc.

Clothes are all torn to pieces,
Shoes are all worn out,
Rolling 'round an unfriendly world,
Always roaming about.

Oh, babes, etc.

Where you gwine, you hoboes?
Where you gwine to stay?
Chain gang link is waiting –
Can't make your getaway.

Oh, babes, etc.

They can't do that

An American tramp song.

When you've just been jugged by an upright judge
    For fifteen years or so
For a job that was done by another gun,
    And you not in on the dough –
You tell your friend as you leave the court
    How they framed you and left you flat,
And doesn't it make you sore as hell
    When he says, 'They can't do that!'

They slam you in a lousy, musty cell
    In the dirty county jail,
And your lawyer comes and shakes you down
    For the last jit of your kale;
Then they throw your frail out in the street,
    And sell the furniture in the flat –
And then some bird in the old bull pen
    Says, ' 'Bo, they can't do that!'

Then you start your stretch in the stinking stir,
    With numbers on your back,
And jump and dodge to the yell of a screw,
    As you walk the narrow track;

Just kick because you get the slum
        While the cream goes to some rat,
And some poor simp with the brains of a louse
        Will pipe, 'They can't do that!'

When your time on earth is over,
        And you start your stretch in hell,
You can hope they'll peg each and every egg
        That ever made that yell;
And as they stand on the red-hot coals
        And fry in their own thick fat,
You can hope to stand by the Devil's side,
        And yell, 'They can't do that!'

Down in the valley . . .

A prison song from Harlan, Kentucky.

Down in the valley,
Valley so low,
Hang your head over,
Hear the train blow.

        Hear the train blow, love,
        Hear the train blow,
        Hang your head over,
        Hear the train blow.

If you don't love me,
Love whom you please,
But throw your arms round me,
Give my heart ease.

Step right up to me,
Before it's too late.
Throw your arms round me,
Feel my heart break.

I'll write you a letter,
Only three lines:
'Answer my question,
Will you be mine?'

Go build me a castle,
Forty feet high,
So I can see you,
As you pass by.

Roses of sunshine,
Violets of dew,
Angels of heaven
Know I love you.

Bird in a cage, love,
Bird in a cage,
Dying for freedom,
But forever a slave.

Write me a letter,
Write it out plain,
And send it me care of
The Barbourville Jail.

>Barbourville Jail, love,
>Barbourville Jail,
>And send it me care of
>The Barbourville Jail.

Drill man blues

George Sizemore

I used to be a drill man,
>Down at Old Parlee;
Drilling through slate and sand rock,
>Till it got the best of me.

Rock dust has almost killed me,
 It's turned me out in the rain;
For dust has settled on my lungs,
 And causes me constant pain.

I can hear my hammer roarin',
 As I lay down for my sleep;
For drilling is the job I love,
 And this I will repeat.

It's killed two fellow workers,
 Here at Old Parlee;
And now I've eaten so much dust, Lord,
 That it's killin' me.

I'm thinkin' of poor drill men,
 Away down in the mines,
Who from eating dust will end up
 With a fate just like mine.

The Donibristle Moss Moran disaster

As sung by J. Ferguson of Markinch, Fife

In the accident at Donibristle, Fife, in August 1901 fourteen miners in all were entombed.

On the twenty-sixth of August, our fatal moss gave way,
Although we tried our level best, its course we couldn't stay,
Ten precious lives there were at stake. 'Who'll save them?' was
 the cry,
'We'll bring them to the surface or along with them we'll die.'

 There was Rattery and McDonald, Hynd and Paterson,
 Too well they knew the danger and the risk they had to run.
 They never stopped to count the cost. 'We'll save them,'
  was the cry,
  'We'll bring them to the surface, or along with them we'll
  die.'

They stepped upon the cage, they were ready for the fray.
They all meant business as they belled themselves away.
Soon they reached the bottom, far from the light of day,
And went to search the workings and Tom Rattery led the way.

They lost their lives, God help them. Ah yes, it was a fact,
Someone put in a stopping and they never did get back.
Was that not another blunder? My God, it was a sin.
To put a stopping where they did, it closed our heroes in.

We never shall forget them, though they have lost their lives,
So let us pay attention to their children and their wives.
It simply is our duty now, and let us all beware.
Their fathers died a noble death and left them in our care.

> There was Rattery and McDonald, Hynd and Paterson,
> Too well they knew the danger and the risk they had to run.
> They never stopped to count the cost. 'We'll save them,'
>   was the cry,
> 'We'll bring them to the surface, or along with them we'll
>   die.'

I'll have a collier for my sweetheart

William Oliver, Widnes

My mother said I must not have a collier,
For if I do he'll surely break my heart.
But I don't care what my mother tells me,
I'll have a collier for my sweetheart.

Collier lads get gold and silver,
Factory lads get nowt but brass.
Who'd be bothered with a naughter bobber,
When there's plenty collier lads?

If you'll leave your collier sweetheart,
I'll buy thee a guinea gold ring.
I'll buy thee a silver cradle,
For to rock thy baby in.

I don't want your silks and satin,
Nor your guinea golden ring.
I don't want a silver cradle
For to rock my baby in.

My mother said that I could be a lady,
If from my collier lad I'd quickly part;
I'd sooner walk the bottom of the ocean
Than I'd give up my collier sweetheart.

Robens' promised land

George Purdom

Composed in 1963 on the gradual transfer of miners away from the so-called 'Novia Scotia' pit in County Durham to South Wales and Nottingham coalfields.

Ye brave bold men of 'Cotia,
The time is drawing near.
You'll have to change your language, lads,
You'll have to change your beer.
But leave your picks behind you,
You'll ne'er need them again,
And off you go to Nottingham,
Join Robens' merry men.

Ye brave bold men of 'Cotia,
The time is drawing thus.
You'll have to change your banner, lads,
And join the exodus.
But leave your cares behind you,
Your future has been planned,
And off you go to Nottingham,
To Robens' Promised Land.

Ye brave bold men of 'Cotia,
To you I say farewell.
And somebody will some day
The 'Cotia story tell.

But leave your cares behind you,
The death-knell has been tolled.
'Cotia was a colliery.
Her men were true and bold.

The Lake of the Caogama

As sung by Lennox Gavan

A Canadian lumbermen's song, recorded in 1964.

Oh, now we're leaving home, me boys; to Ottawa we're goin',
Expecting to get hired, and yet we do not know.
We met with old Tom Patterson, saying, 'Ain't you goin' awa?'
'I'm going up the Gatineau River round the lake of the
    Caogama.'[1]

Oh, now we're leaving Ottawa in sorrow, grief, and woe;
We're going to a place, to a place we do not know.
We've fifty miles to travel and hard biscuits for to chaw –
May the devil take old Patterson and the lake of the Caogama!

Oh, now we're in the shanty, no comfort can we find.
We're thinking of our own dear girls, the ones we left behind,
And dreamed that night they visit us, and their merry face we
    saw
Until we woke broken-hearted round the lake of Caogama.

Oh, we'll all be down in April – that's if we are alive,
If Paddy doesn't keep us on the cursed creeks to drive.
There's big lakes and small lakes and lakes you never saw,
But the darndest lake among them is the lake of the Caogama.

1. Pronounced Kegama.

Have courage, my boy, to say no!

L. M. Hilton

A Mormon song. Mormons were strictly forbidden to take alcohol, along with tea, coffee, and tobacco.

You've started today on life's journey
Alone on the highway of life,
You'll meet with a thousand temptations,
Each city with evil is rife,
The world is a stage of excitement
No matter wherever you go.
But if you are tempted in weakness,
Have courage, my boy, to say no.

Have courage, my boy, to say no,
Have courage, my boy, to say no,
Have courage, my boy, have courage, my boy,
Have courage, my boy, to say no!

The bright ruby wine may be offered,
No matter how tempting it be.
From poison that stings like a viper
Have courage, my boy, to flee.
The vile gambling dens are before you,
The lights how they dance to and fro,
But if you are tempted to enter,
Have courage, my boy, to say no.

Have courage, my boy, to say no, etc.

In courage alone lies your safety
When you the lone journey begin,
But trust in your Heavenly Father
Will keep you unspotted from sin.
Temptations will keep on increasing
Like streams from a rivulet flow,
But if you are true to your manhood,
Have courage, my boy, to say no.

To the pines . . .

A banjo song.

To the pines, to the pines,
Where the sun never shines,
Goin' to shiver when the cold winds blow.

My husband was
A railroad man
Killed a mile and a half down the road.

His head was found
In the driver's wheels;
But his body they never saw.

'Twas transportation
Brought me here;
Takes money for to carry me home.

The long steel rails
That have no end
Have caused me for to roam.

They've caused me to weep,
They've caused me to mourn,
They've caused me to leave my home.

Through the pines, through the pines,
Where the sun never shines,
Goin' to shiver when the cold winds blow.

Ballad of the D-Day Dodgers

An ironic Second World War ballad, arising from a rumour
in Italy that Lady Astor had referred to the men of the CMF as D-Day
dodgers. To the tune of 'Lili Marleen'.

We're the D-Day Dodgers, out in Italy –
Always on the vino, always on the spree.
        8th Army scroungers and their tanks
        We live in Rome – among the Yanks.
We are the D-Day Dodgers, way out in Italy.

We landed at Salerno, a holiday with pay;
The Jerries brought the bands out to greet us on the way . . .
    Showed us the sights and gave us tea,
    We all sang songs – the beer was free,
To welcome D-Day Dodgers to sunny Italy.

Naples and Cassino were taken in our stride,
We didn't go to fight there – we went there for the ride.
    Anzio and Sangro were just names,
    We only went to look for dames –
The artful D-Day Dodgers, way out in Italy.

On the way to Florence we had a lovely time.
We ran a bus to Rimini right through the Gothic line.
    Soon to Bologna we will go
    And after that we'll cross the Po.
We'll stick to D-Day dodging, way out in Italy.

Once we heard a rumour that we were going home,
Back to dear old Blighty – never more to roam.
    Then someone said: 'In France you'll fight!'
    We said: 'No fear – we'll just sit tight!'
(The windy D-Day Dodgers, way out in Italy.)

We hope the Second Army will soon get home on leave;
After six months' service it's time for their reprieve.
    But we can carry on out here
    Another two or three more years –
Contented D-Day Dodgers to stay in Italy.

Dear Lady Astor, you think you know a lot,
Standing on a platform and talking tommy-rot.
    You, England's sweetheart and its pride,
    We think your mouth's too bleeding wide.
That's from your D-Day Dodgers – in far off Italy.

Look around the mountains, in the mud and rain –
You'll find the scattered crosses – (there's some which have no
    name).
    Heartbreak and toil and suffering gone,
    The boys beneath them slumber on.
Those are the D-Day Dodgers who'll stay in Italy.

Plane wreck at Los Gatos

Woody Guthrie

Here, as in 'Pastures of plenty', Guthrie shows his feeling for the migrant labourers. This poem is about the death of twenty-eight Mexican migrant deportees in a crash near Coalinga, California, 1948.

The crops are all in and the peaches are rottening
The oranges are piled in their creosote dumps;
You're flying them back to the Mexico border
To pay all their money to wade back again.

　　　Good-bye to my Juan, Good-bye Rosalita;
Adios muy amigo, Jesus and Marie,
You won't have a name when you ride the big airplane
　　　All they will call you will be deportees.

My father's own father he waded that river;
They took all the money he made in his life;
My brothers and sisters come working the fruit trees
And they rode the truck till they took down and died.

　　　Good-bye to my Juan, Good-bye Rosalita, etc.

Some of us are illegal and some are not wanted,
Our work contract's out and we have to move on;
Six hundred miles to that Mexico border,
They chase us like outlaws, like rustlers, like thieves.

　　　Good-bye to my Juan, Good-bye Rosalita, etc.

We died in your hills, we died in your deserts,
We died in your valleys and died on your plains;
We died neath your trees and we died in your bushes,
Both sides of this river we died just the same.

　　　Good-bye to my Juan, Good-bye Rosalita, etc.

The sky plane caught fire over Los Gatos Canyon,
A fireball of lightning and shook all our hills.
Who are all these friends all scattered like dry leaves?
The radio says they are just deportees.

　　　Good-bye to my Juan, Good-bye Rosalita, etc.

Is this the best way we can grow our big orchards?
Is this the best way we can grow our good fruit?
To fall like dry leaves to rot on my top soil
And be called by no name except deportees?

Good-bye to my Juan, Good-bye Rosalita, etc.

Pastures of plenty

Woody Guthrie

It's a mighty hard road that my poor hands have hoed,
My poor feet have travelled a hot dusty road,
Out of your dust bowl and westward we roll,
Through deserts so hot and your mountains so cold.

I've wandered all over your green growing land,
Wherever your crops are I've lent you my hand,
On the edge of your cities you'll see me and then,
I come with the dust and I'm gone with the wind.

California, Arizona, I've worked on your crops,
Then north up to Oregon to gather your hops,
Dig beets from your ground, I cut grapes from your vines,
To set on your tables that light sparklin' wine.

Green Pastures of plenty from dry desert ground,
From the Grand Coulee dam where the water runs down,
Ev'ry State of this Union us migrants have been,
We come with the dust and we're gone with the wind.

It's always we ramble that river and I,
All along your green valleys I'll work till I die,
I'll travel this road until death sets me free,
'Cause my Pastures of plenty must always be free.

It's a mighty hard road that my poor hands have hoed,
My poor feet have travelled this hot dusty road,
On the edge of your cities you'll see me and then,
I come with the dust and I'm gone with the wind.

Jesus Christ

Woody Guthrie

Jesus Christ was a man that travelled through the land,
A carpenter true and brave;
He said to the Rich, 'Give your goods to the poor,'
So they laid Jesus Christ in his grave.

>   Yes, Jesus was a man, a carpenter by hand,
>   A carpenter true and brave;
>   And a dirty little coward called Judas Iscariot
>   Has laid Jesus Christ in His grave.

The people of the land took Jesus by the hand,
They followed him far and wide;
'I come not to bring you peace but a sword,'
So they killed Jesus Christ on the sly.

>   Yes, Jesus was a man, a carpenter by hand, etc.

He went to the sick and he went to the poor,
He went to the hungry and the lame;
He said that the poor would win this world,
So they laid Jesus Christ in his grave.

>   Yes, Jesus was a man, a carpenter by hand, etc.

One day Jesus stopped at a rich man's door,
'What must I do to be saved?'
'You must sell your goods and give it to the poor.'
So they laid Jesus Christ in his grave.

>   Yes, Jesus was a man, a carpenter by hand, etc.

They nailed him there to die on a cross in the sky,
In the lightning and thunder and rain;
And Judas Iscariot he committed suicide
When they laid Jesus Christ in his grave.

>   Yes, Jesus was a man, a carpenter by hand, etc.

When the love of the poor shall turn into hate,
When the patience of the workers gives away,
' 'Twould be better for you rich if you'd never been born,
For you laid Jesus Christ in his grave.'

Yes, Jesus was a man, a carpenter by hand, etc.

This song was written in New York City,
Of rich men, preachers and slaves;
If Jesus was to preach like he preached in Galilee,
They would lay Jesus Christ in his grave.

Yes, Jesus was a man, a carpenter by hand, etc.

O God of Bethel . . .

Philip Doddridge and John Logan

Though composed in the eighteenth century, this is still a popular and much-sung hymn today.

O God of Bethel, by whose hand
Thy people still are fed;
Who through this earthly pilgrimage
Hast all our fathers led:

Our vows, our prayers, we now present
Before Thy throne of grace;
God of our fathers, be the God
Of their succeeding race.

Through each perplexing path of life
Our wandering footsteps guide;
Give us each day our daily bread,
And raiment fit provide.

O spread Thy covering wings around,
Till all our wanderings cease,
And at our Father's loved abode
Our souls arrive in peace.

Children's poems

1952

A counting-out and ball-bouncing rhyme.

Down in the jungle
Living in a tent,
Better than a pre-fab –
        No rent!

Salome

A camp-fire song and skipping rhyme.

Salome was a dancer
She danced the hootchie-cootch,
She shook her shimmy shoulder
And she showed a bit too much.
Stop! said King Herod,
You can't do that there 'ere.
Salome said, Baloney!
And kicked the chandelier.

School dinners

If you stay to school dinners
Better throw them aside,
A lot of kids didn't,
A lot of kids died.
The meat is of iron,
The spuds are of steel,
If that don't get you
Then the afters will.

Song of a Hebrew

Dannie Abse

A jazz poem.

Working is another way of praying.
You plant in Israel the soul of a tree.
You plant in the desert the spirit of gardens.

Praying is another way of singing.
You plant in the tree the soul of lemons.
You plant in the gardens the spirit of roses.

Singing is another way of loving.
You plant in the lemons the spirit of your son.
You plant in the roses the soul of your daughter.

Loving is another way of living.
You plant in your daughter the spirit of Israel.
You plant in your son the soul of the desert.

I'm through with you

The time has come for us to part,
I ain't goin' to cry, it won't break my heart,
'Cause I'm through with you and I hope you don't feel hurt.

You're like an old horseshoe that's had its day,
You're like an old shoe I must throw away,
I'm through with you and I hope you don't feel hurt.

You ain't got no money, you're down and broke,
You're just an old has-been like a worn-out joke,
So I'm through with you and I hope you don't feel hurt.

For no one

John Lennon and Paul McCartney

The day breaks, your mind aches,
You find that all her words of kindness linger on,
When she no longer needs you.

She wakes up, she makes up,
She takes her time and doesn't feel she has to hurry,
She no longer needs you.

> And in her eyes you see nothing,
> No sign of love behind the tears cried for no one,
> A love that should have lasted years.

You want her, you need her,
And yet you don't believe her
When she says her love is dead,
You think she needs you.

> And in her eyes you see nothing, etc.

You stay home, she goes out,
She says that long ago she knew someone but now,
He's gone, she doesn't need him.

The day breaks, your mind aches,
There will be times when all the things she said will fill your
    head,
You won't forget her.

> And in her eyes you see nothing, etc.

Eleanor Rigby

John Lennon and Paul McCartney

Ah, look at all the lonely people.
Ah, look at all the lonely people.
Eleanor Rigby picks up the rice in the church where a wedding
    has been,
Lives in a dream.
Waits at the window, wearing the face that she keeps in a jar by
    the door,
Who is it for?
    All the lonely people, where do they all come from?
    All the lonely people, where do they all belong?

Father McKenzie, writing the words of a sermon that no one
    will hear,
No one comes near.
Look at him working, darning his socks in the night when
    there's nobody there,
What does he care?
    All the lonely people, where do they all come from?
    All the lonely people, where do they all belong?

Ah, look at all the lonely people.
Ah, look at all the lonely people.
Eleanor Rigby died in the church and was buried along with her
    name.
Nobody came,
Father McKenzie, wiping the dirt from his hands as he walks
    from the grave.
No one was saved.
    All the lonely people, where do they all come from?
    All the lonely people, where do they all belong?

EPIC AND NARRATIVE POETRY

New coasts and Poseidon's son

from *The Odyssey*

Homer

The text of Homer's *Odyssey* was probably written down in Greece in the sixth century BC and since that date has come down to us through the written form. However, despite the continuing controversy about everything to do with Homer, it is now fairly generally agreed that a period of oral performance and composition preceded the recording of the epic, and that in some sense at least *The Odyssey* can be classified as 'oral poetry'. In particular the recurring formulaic terms and phrases (like the repeated 'Dawn with finger-tips of rose') can be interpreted as conventional forms appropriate for the exigencies of oral composition when the poet must both keep to the demands of the metre and avoid pauses in his continuous delivery-cum-composition of the poem. (It is fairly clear both from the length and from comparative evidence from elsewhere that word-for-word memorization was probably not involved.) Indeed it is from the analysis of the Homeric style as compared with a similar formulaic style in twentieth-century Yugoslav oral epic that the influential 'oral-formulaic' theory has developed which sees this kind of reliance on formulae as typical of oral poetry. This formulaic aspect may not emerge fully in the piece translated here, but it is clear from analyses of the *Odyssey* as a whole that a high proportion of the lines here have at least some formulaic element and appear elsewhere in the poem.

The poem has always been attributed to Homer, about whose exact identity (or even existence as one poet at all) there has long been bitter argument. In fact nothing is known about him at all with real certainty, though Greek legend had it that he was blind.

The Odyssey consists of twenty-four 'books' (or chapters) in all, of which one (the ninth) is translated in full here. It is written in Greek, in hexameter lines, and tells the story of the wanderings of Odysseus, a Greek king who is on his way back

from the siege of Troy to his own island kingdom of Ithaka, where
his wife Penelope is waiting for him. But he meets many disasters
on the way, loses all his companions, encounters many fantastic
beings and takes part in numerous adventures. One of his landings
is in the land of the Phaiacians, ruled over by King Alkinoos.
There he is asked to recount his adventures and in this way the
poet is able to add to the basically third-person narrative of the
poem several long sections in the first person, in which Odysseus
narrates his own adventures. In the section here he describes his
first adventures and his encounter with the monstrous Kyklops (or
Cyclops), Poseidon's son. The title has been given by the translator.

Now this was the reply Odysseus made:

'Alkinoos, king and admiration of men,
how beautiful this is, to hear a minstrel
gifted as yours: a god he might be, singing!
There is no boon in life more sweet, I say,
than when a summer joy holds all the realm,
and banqueters sit listening to a harper
in a great hall, by rows of tables heaped
with bread and roast meat, while a steward goes
to dip up wine and brim your cups again.
Here is the flower of life, it seems to me!
But now you wish to know my cause for sorrow –
and thereby give me cause for more.
                    What shall I
say first? What shall I keep until the end?
The gods have tried me in a thousand ways.
But first my name: let that be known to you,
and if I pull away from pitiless death,
friendship will bind us, though my land lies far.

I am Laertes' son, Odysseus.
                    Men hold me
formidable for guile in peace and war:
this fame has gone abroad to the sky's rim.
My home is on the peaked sea-mark of Ithaka

under Mount Neion's wind-blown robe of leaves,
in sight of other islands – Doulikhion,
Same, wooded Zakynthos – Ithaka
being most lofty in that coastal sea,
and northwest, while the rest lie east and south.
A rocky isle, but good for a boy's training;
I shall not see on earth a place more dear,
though I have been detained long by Kalypso,
loveliest among goddesses, who held me
in her smooth caves, to be her heart's delight,
as Kirke of Aiaia, the enchantress,
desired me, and detained me in her hall.
But in my heart I never gave consent.
Where shall a man find sweetness to surpass
his own home and his parents? In far lands
he shall not, though he find a house of gold.

What of my sailing, then, from Troy?
        What of those years
of rough adventure, weathered under Zeus?
The wind that carried west from Ilion
brought me to Ismaros, on the far shore,
a strongpoint on the coast of the Kikones.
I stormed that place and killed the men who fought.
Plunder we took, and we enslaved the women,
to make division, equal shares to all –
but on the spot I told them: "Back, and quickly!
Out to sea again!" My men were mutinous,
fools, on stores of wine. Sheep after sheep
they butchered by the surf, and shambling cattle,
feasting – while fugitives went inland, running
to call to arms the main force of Kikones.
This was an army, trained to fight on horseback
or, where the ground required, on foot. They came
with dawn over that terrain like the leaves
and blades of spring. So doom appeared to us,
dark word of Zeus for us, our evil days.
My men stood up and made a fight of it –
backed on the ships, with lances kept in play,

from bright morning through the blaze of noon
holding our beach, although so far outnumbered;
but when the sun passed towards unyoking time,
then the Akhaians, one by one, gave way.
Six benches were left empty in every ship
that evening when we pulled away from death.
And this new grief we bore with us to sea:
our precious lives we had, but not our friends.
No ship made sail next day until some shipmate
had raised a cry, three times, for each poor ghost
unfleshed by the Kikones on that field.

Now Zeus the lord of cloud roused in the north
a storm against the ships, and driving veils
of squall moved down like night on land and sea.
The bows went plunging at the gust; sails
cracked and lashed out strips in the big wind.
We saw death in that fury, dropped the yards,
unshipped the oars, and pulled for the nearest lee:
then two long days and nights we lay offshore
worn out and sick at heart, tasting our grief,
until a third Dawn came with ringlets shining.
Then we put up our masts, hauled sail, and rested,
letting the steersmen and the breeze take over.

I might have made it safely home, that time,
but as I came round Malea the current
took me out to sea, and from the north
a fresh gale drove me on, past Kythera.
Nine days I drifted on the teeming sea
before dangerous high winds. Upon the tenth
we came to the coastline of the Lotos Eaters,
who live upon that flower. We landed there
to take on water. All ships' companies
mustered alongside for the mid-day meal.
Then I sent out two picked men and a runner
to learn what race of men that land sustained.
They fell in, soon enough, with Lotos Eaters,
who showed no will to do us harm, only
offering the sweet Lotos to our friends –

but those who ate this honeyed plant, the Lotos,
never cared to report, nor to return:
they longed to stay forever, browsing on
that native bloom, forgetful of their homeland.
I drove them, all three wailing, to the ships,
tied them down under their rowing benches,
and called the rest: "All hands aboard;
come, clear the beach and no one taste
the Lotos, or you lose your hope of home."
Filing in to their places by the rowlocks
my oarsmen dipped their long oars in the surf,
and we moved out again on our seafaring.

In the next land we found were Kyklopes,
giants, louts, without a law to bless them.
In ignorance leaving the fruitage of the earth in mystery
to the immortal gods, they neither plough
nor sow by hand, nor till the ground, though grain –
wild wheat and barley – grows untended, and
wine-grapes, in clusters, ripen in heaven's rain.
Kyklopes have no muster and no meeting,
no consultation or old tribal ways,
but each one dwells in his own mountain cave
dealing out rough justice to wife and child,
indifferent to what the others do.
          Well, then:
across the wide bay from the mainland
there lies a desert island, not far out,
but still not close inshore. Wild goats in hundreds
breed there; and no human being comes
upon the isle to startle them – no hunter
of all who ever tracked with hounds through forests
or had rough going over mountain trails.
The isle, unplanted and untilled, a wilderness,
pastures goats alone. And this is why:
good ships like ours with cheekpaint at the bows
are far beyond the Kyklopes. No shipwright
toils among them, shaping and building up
symmetrical trim hulls to cross the sea

and visit all the seaboard towns, as men do
who go and come in commerce over water.
This isle – seagoing folk would have annexed it
and built their homesteads on it: all good land,
fertile for every crop in season: lush
well-watered meads along the shore, vines in profusion,
prairie, clear for the plough, where grain would grow
chin high by harvest time, and rich sub-soil.
The island cove is landlocked, so you need
no hawsers out astern, bow-stones or mooring:
run in and ride there till the day your crews
chafe to be under sail, and a fair wind blows.
You'll find good water flowing from a cavern
through dusky poplars into the upper bay.
Here we made harbour. Some god guided us
that night, for we could barely see our bows
in the dense fog around us, and no moonlight
filtered through the overcast. No look-out,
nobody saw the island dead ahead,
nor even the great landward rolling billow
that took us in: we found ourselves in shallows,
keels grazing shore: so furled our sails
and disembarked where the low ripples broke.
There on the beach we lay, and slept till morning.

When Dawn spread out her finger-tips of rose
we turned out marvelling, to tour the isle,
while Zeus's shy nymph daughters flushed wild goats
down from the heights – a breakfast for my men.
We ran to fetch our hunting bows and long-shanked
lances from the ships, and in three companies
we took our shots. Heaven gave us game a-plenty:
for every one of twelve ships in my squadron
nine goats fell to be shared; my lot was ten.
So there all day, until the sun went down,
we made our feast on meat galore, and wine –
wine from the ship, for our supply held out,
so many jars were filled at Ismaros
from stores of the Kikones that we plundered.

We gazed, too, at Kyklopes Land, so near,
we saw their smoke, heard bleating from their flocks.
But after sundown, in the gathering dusk,
we slept again above the wash of ripples.

When the young Dawn with finger-tips of rose
came in the east, I called my men together
and made a speech to them:
          "Old shipmates, friends,
the rest of you stand by; I'll make the crossing
in my own ship, with my own company,
and find out what the mainland natives are –
for they may be wild savages, and lawless,
or hospitable and god-fearing men."

At this I went aboard, and gave the word
to cast off by the stern. My oarsmen followed,
filing in to their benches by the rowlocks,
and all in line dipped oars in the grey sea.

As we rowed on, and nearer to the mainland,
at one end of the bay, we saw a cavern
yawning above the water, screened with laurel,
and many rams and goats about the place
inside a sheepfold – made from slabs of stone
earthfast between tall trunks of pine and rugged
towering oak trees.
          A prodigious man
slept in this cave alone, and took his flocks
to graze afield – remote from all companions,
knowing none but savage ways, a brute
so huge, he seemed no man at all of those
who eat good wheaten bread; but he seemed rather
a shaggy mountain reared in solitude.
We beached there, and I told the crew
to stand by and keep watch over the ship;
as for myself I took my twelve best fighters
and went ahead. I had a goatskin full
of that sweet liquor that Euanthes' son,
Maron, had given me. He kept Apollo's

holy grove at Ismaros; for kindness
we showed him there, and showed his wife and child.
He gave me seven shining golden talents
perfectly formed, a solid silver wine-bowl,
and then this liquor – twelve two-handled jars
of brandy, pure and fiery. Not a slave
in Maron's household knew this drink; only
he, his wife and the storeroom mistress knew;
and they would put one cupful – ruby-coloured,
honey-smooth – in twenty more of water,
but still the sweet scent hovered like a fume
over the wine-bowl. No man turned away
when cups of this came round.
        A wine-skin full
I brought along, and victuals in a bag,
for in my bones I knew some towering brute
would be upon us soon – all outward power,
a wild man, ignorant of civility.

We climbed, then, briskly to the cave. But Kyklops
had gone afield, to pasture his fat sheep,
so we looked round at everything inside:
a drying rack that sagged with cheeses, pens
crowded with lambs and kids, each in its class:
firstlings apart from middlings, and the "dewdrops",
or new born lambkins, penned apart from both.
And vessels full of whey were brimming there –
bowls of earthenware and pails for milking.
My men came pressing round me, pleading:
        "Why not
take these cheeses, get them stowed, come back,
throw open all the pens, and make a run for it?
We'll drive the kids and lambs aboard. We say
put out again on good salt water!"
How sound that was! Yet I refused. I wished
to see the caveman, what he had to offer –
no pretty sight, it turned out, for my friends.

We lit a fire, burnt an offering,
and took some cheese to eat; then sat in silence

around the embers, waiting. When he came
he had a load of dry boughs on his shoulder
to stoke his fire at supper-time. He dumped it
with a great crash into that hollow cave,
and we all scattered fast to the far wall.
Then over the broad cavern floor he ushered
the ewes he meant to milk. He left his rams
and he-goats in the yard outside, and swung
high overhead a slab of solid rock
to close the cave. Two dozen four-wheeled wagons,
with heaving wagon teams, could not have stirred
the tonnage of that rock from where he wedged it
over the door-sill. Next he took his seat
and milked his bleating ewes. A practised job
he made of it, giving each ewe her suckling;
thickened his milk, then, into curds and whey,
sieved out the curds to drip in withy baskets,
and poured the whey to stand in bowls
cooling until he drank it for his supper.
When all these chores were done, he poked the fire,
heaping on brushwood. In the glare he saw us.

"Strangers," he said, "who are you? And where from?
What brings you here by sea-ways – a fair traffic?
Or are you wandering rogues, who cast your lives
like dice, and ravage other folk by sea?"

We felt a pressure on our hearts, in dread
of that deep rumble and that mighty man.
But all the same I spoke up in reply:
"We are from Troy, Akhaians, blown off course
by shifting gales on the Great South Sea;
homeward-bound, but taking routes and ways
uncommon; so the will of Zeus would have it.
We served under Agamemnon, son of Atreus –
the whole world knows what city
he laid waste, what armies he destroyed.
It was our luck to come here; here we stand,
beholden for your help, or any gifts
you give – as custom is to honour strangers.

We would entreat you, great Sir, have a care
for the gods' courtesy; Zeus will avenge
the unoffending guest."
        He answered this
from his brute chest, unmoved:
        "You are a ninny,
or else you come from the other end of nowhere,
telling me, mind the gods! We Kyklopes
care not a whistle for your thundering Zeus
or all the gods in bliss; we have more force by far.
I would not let you go for fear of Zeus –
you or your friends – unless I had a whim to.
Tell me, where was it, now, you left your ship –
around the point, or down the shore, I wonder?"

He thought he'd find out, but I saw through this,
and answered with a ready lie:
        "My ship?
Poseidon Lord, who sets the earth a-tremble,
broke it up on the rocks at your land's end.
A wind from seaward served him, drove us there.
We are survivors, these good men and I."

Neither reply nor pity came from him,
but in one stride he clutched at my companions
and caught two in his hands like squirming puppies
to beat their brains out, spattering the floor.
Then he dismembered them and made his meal,
gaping and crunching like a mountain lion –
everything: innards, flesh, and marrow-bones.
We cried aloud, lifting our hands to Zeus,
powerless, looking on at this, appalled;
but Kyklops went on filling up his belly
with manflesh and great gulps of whey,
then lay down like a mast among his sheep.
My heart beat high now at the chance of action,
and drawing the sharp sword from my hip I went
along his flank to stab him where the midriff
holds the liver. I had touched the spot
when sudden fear stayed me: if I killed him

we perished there as well, for we could never
move his ponderous doorway slab aside.
So we were left to groan and wait for morning.

When the young Dawn with finger-tips of rose
lit up the world, the Kyklops built a fire
and milked his handsome ewes, all in due order,
putting the sucklings to the mothers. Then,
his chores being all dispatched, he caught
another brace of men to make his breakfast,
and whisked away his great door slab
to let his sheep go through – but he, behind,
reset the stone as one would cap a quiver.
There was a din of whistling as the Kyklops
rounded his flock to higher ground, then stillness.
And now I pondered how to hurt him worst,
if but Athene granted what I prayed for.
Here are the means I thought would serve my turn:

a club, or staff, lay there along the fold –
an olive tree, felled green and left to season
for Kyklops' hand. And it was like a mast
a lugger of twenty oars, broad in the beam –
a deep-sea-going craft – might carry:
so long, so big around, it seemed. Now I
chopped out a six foot section of this pole
and set it down before my men, who scraped it;
and when they had it smooth, I hewed again
to make a stake with pointed end. I held this
in the fire's heart and turned it, toughening it,
then hid it, well back in the cavern, under
one of the dung piles in profusion there.
Now came the time to toss for it: who ventured
along with me? whose hand could bear to thrust
and grind that spike in Kyklops' eye, when mild
sleep had mastered him? As luck would have it,
the men I would have chosen won the toss –
four strong men, and I made five as captain.

At evening came the shepherd with his flock,
his woolly flock. The rams as well, this time,
entered the cave; by some sheep-herding whim –
or a god's bidding – none were left outside.
He hefted his great boulder into place
and sat him down to milk the bleating ewes
in proper order, put the lambs to suck,
and swiftly ran through all his evening chores.
Then he caught two more men and feasted on them.
My moment was at hand, and I went forward
holding an ivy bowl of my dark drink,
looking up, saying:
      "Kyklops, try some wine.
Here's liquor to wash down your scraps of men.
Taste it, and see the kind of drink we carried
under our planks. I meant it for an offering
if you would help us home. But you are mad,
unbearable, a bloody monster! After this,
will any other traveller come to see you?"

He seized and drained the bowl, and it went down
so fiery and smooth he called for more:
"Give me another, thank you kindly. Tell me,
how are you called? I'll make a gift will please you.
Even Kyklopes know the wine-grapes grow
out of grassland and loam in heaven's rain,
but here's a bit of nectar and ambrosia!"

Three bowls I brought him, and he poured them down.
I saw the fuddle and flush come over him,
then I sang out in cordial tones:
      "Kyklops,
you ask my honourable name? Remember
the gift you promised me, and I shall tell you.
My name of Nohbdy: mother, father, and friends,
everyone calls me Nohbdy."
      And he said:
"Nohbdy's my meat, then, after I eat his friends.
Others come first. There's a noble gift, now."

Even as he spoke, he reeled and tumbled backward,
his great head lolling to one side; and sleep
took him like any creature. Drunk, hiccuping,
he dribbled streams of liquor and bits of men.

Now, by the gods, I drove my big hand spike
deep in the embers, charring it again,
and cheered my men along with battle talk
to keep their courage up: no quitting now.
The pike of olive, green though it had been,
reddened and glowed as if about to catch.
I drew it from the coals and my four fellows
gave me a hand, lugging it near the Kyklops
as more than natural force nerved them; straight
forward they sprinted, lifted it, and rammed it
deep in his crater eye, and I leaned on it
turning it as a shipwright turns a drill
in planking, having men below to swing
the two-handled strap that spins it in the groove.
So with our brand we bored that great eye-socket
while blood ran out around the red-hot bar.
Eyelid and lash were seared; the pierced ball
hissed broiling, and the roots popped.

          In a smithy
one sees a white-hot axehead or an adze
plunged and wrung in a cold tub, screeching steam –
the way they make soft iron hale and hard – :
just so that eye-ball hissed around the spike.
The Kyklops bellowed and the rock roared round him,
and we fell back in fear. Clawing his face
he tugged the bloody spike out of his eye,
threw it away, and his wild hand went groping;
then he set up a howl for Kyklopes
who lived in caves on windy peaks nearby.
Some heard him; and they came by divers ways
to clump around outside and call:
          "What ails you,
Polyphemos? Why do you cry so sore
in the starry night? You will not let us sleep.

Sure no man's driving off your flock? No man
has tricked you, ruined you?"

Out of the cave
the mammoth Polyphemos roared in answer:

"Nohbdy, Nohbdy's tricked me, Nohbdy's ruined me!"

To this rough shout they made a sage reply:

"Ah well, if nobody has played you foul
there in your lonely bed, we are no use in pain
given by great Zeus. Let it be your father,
Poseidon Lord, to whom you pray."

So saying
they trailed away. And I was filled with laughter
to see how like a charm the name deceived them.
Now Kyklops, wheezing as the pain came on him,
fumbled to wrench away the great doorstone
and squatted in the breach with arms thrown wide
for any silly beast or man who bolted –
hoping somehow I might be such a fool.
But I kept thinking how to win the game:
death sat there huge; how could we slip away?
I drew on all my wits, and ran through tactics,
reasoning as a man will for dear life,
until a trick came – and it pleased me well.
The Kyklops' rams were handsome, fat, with heavy
fleeces, a dark violet.

Three abreast
I tied them silently together, twining
cords of willow from the ogre's bed;
then slung a man under each middle one
to ride there safely, shielded left and right.
So three sheep could convey each man. I took
the woolliest ram, the choicest of the flock,
and hung myself under his kinky belly,
pulled up tight, with fingers twisted deep
in sheepskin ringlets for an iron grip.
So, breathing hard, we waited until morning.

When Dawn spread out her finger tips of rose
the rams began to stir, moving for pasture,
and peals of bleating echoed round the pens
where dams with udders full called for a milking.
Blinded, and sick with pain from his head wound,
the master stroked each ram, then let it pass,
but my men riding on the pectoral fleece
the giant's blind hands blundering never found.
Last of them all my ram, the leader, came,
weighted by wool and me with my meditations.

The Kyklops patted him, and then he said:

"Sweet cousin ram, why lag behind the rest
in the night cave? You never linger so,
but graze before them all, and go afar
to crop sweet grass, and take your stately way
leading along the streams, until at evening
you run to be the first one in the fold.
Why, now, so far behind? Can you be grieving
over your Master's eye? That carrion rogue
and his accurst companions burnt it out
when he had conquered all my wits with wine.
Nohbdy will not get out alive, I swear.
Oh, had you brain and voice to tell
where he may be now, dodging all my fury!
Bashed by this hand and bashed on this rock wall
his brains would strew the floor, and I should have
rest from the outrage Nohbdy worked upon me."

He sent us into the open, then. Close by,
I dropped and rolled clear of the ram's belly,
going this way and that to untie the men.
With many glances back, we rounded up
his fat, stiff-legged sheep to take aboard,
and drove them down to where the good ship lay.
We saw, as we came near, our fellows' faces
shining; then we saw them turn to grief
tallying those who had not fled from death.
I hushed them, jerking head and eyebrows up,

and in a low voice told them: "Load this herd;
move fast, and put the ship's head towards the breakers."
They all pitched in at loading, then embarked
and struck their oars into the sea. Far out,
as far off shore as shouted words would carry,
I sent a few back to the adversary:

"O Kyklops! Would you feast on my companions?
Puny, am I, in a Caveman's hands?
How do you like the beating that we gave you,
you damned cannibal? Eater of guests
under your roof! Zeus and the gods have paid you!"

The blind thing in his doubled fury broke
a hilltop in his hands and heaved it after us.
Ahead of our black prow it struck and sank
whelmed in a spuming geyser, a giant wave
that washed the ship stern foremost back to shore.
I got the longest boat-hook out and stood
fending us off, with furious nods to all
to put their backs into a racing stroke –
row, row, or perish. So the long oars bent
kicking the foam sternward, making head
until we drew away, and twice as far.
Now when I cupped my hands I heard the crew
in low voices protesting:
          "Godsake, Captain!
Why bait the beast again? Let him alone!"

"That tidal wave he made on the first throw
all but beached us."

          "All but stove us in!"
"Give him our bearing with your trumpeting,
he'll get the range and lob a boulder."

          "Aye
He'll smash our timbers and our heads together!"

I would not heed them in my glorying spirit,
but let my anger flare and yelled:
          "Kyklops,
if ever mortal man inquire

how you were put to shame and blinded, tell him
Odysseus, raider of cities, took your eye:
Laertes' son, whose home's on Ithaka!"

At this he gave a mighty sob and rumbled:
"Now comes the weird upon me, spoken of old.
A wizard, grand and wondrous, lived here – Telemos,
a son of Eurymos; great length of days
he had in wizardry among the Kyklopes,
and these things he foretold for time to come:
my great eye lost, and at Odysseus' hands.
Always I had in mind some giant, armed
in giant force, would come against me here.
But this, but you – small, pitiful and twiggy –
you put me down with wine, you blinded me.
Come back, Odysseus, and I'll treat you well,
praying the god of earthquake to befriend you –
his son I am, for he by his avowal
fathered me, and, if he will, he may
heal me of this black wound – he and no other
of all the happy gods or mortal men."

Few words I shouted in reply to him:
"If I could take your life I would and take
your time away, and hurl you down to hell!
The god of earthquake could not heal you there!"

At this he stretched his hands out in his darkness
toward the sky of stars, and prayed Poseidon:
"O hear me, lord, blue girdler of the islands,
if I am thine indeed, and thou art father:
grant that Odysseus, raider of cities, never
see his home: Laertes' son, I mean,
who kept his hall on Ithaka. Should destiny
intend that he shall see his roof again
among his family in his fatherland,
far be that day, and dark the years between.
Let him lose all companions, and return
under strange sail to bitter days at home."

In these words he prayed, and the god heard him.
Now he laid hands upon a bigger stone
and wheeled around, titanic for the cast,
to let it fly in the black-prowed vessel's track.
But it fell short, just aft the steering oar,
and whelming seas rose giant above the stone
to bear us onward towards the island.
     There,
as we ran in we saw the squadron waiting,
the trim ships drawn up side by side, and all
our troubled friends who waited, looking seaward.
We beached her, grinding keel in the soft sand,
and waded in, ourselves, on the sandy beach.
Then we unloaded all the Kyklops' flock
to make division, share and share alike,
only my fighters voted that my ram,
the prize of all, should go to me. I slew him
by the seaside and burnt his long thighbones
to Zeus beyond the stormcloud, Kronos' son,
who rules the world. But Zeus disdained my offering;
destruction for my ships he had in store
and death for those who sailed them, my companions.

Now all day long until the sun went down
we made our feast on mutton and sweet wine,
till after sunset in the gathering dark
we went to sleep above the wash of ripples.

When the young Dawn, with finger-tips of rose
touched the world, I roused the men, gave orders
to man the ships, cast off the mooring-lines;
and filing in to sit beside the rowlocks
oarsmen in line dipped oars in the grey sea.
So we moved out, sad in the vast offing,
having our precious lives, but not our friends.'

Beowulf's fight with Grendel's mother

from *Beowulf*

Beowulf is famous as the only native English heroic epic. It recounts the adventures of the hero Beowulf: how he slaughters first the monster Grendel who has been terrorizing the royal court at Heorot, then (in the extract given here) Grendel's mother. He later becomes king of the Geats and finally, in his old age, dies in battle against a dragon. The setting is a heroic world in which the Germanic forebears of the English are involved, including Scandinavian peoples like the Danes and the Geats. Compared to the Homeric epics the poem is relatively short (just over 3,000 lines in all) and at times marked by a somewhat reflective, even lyric, tone.[1] It was composed in England sometime in the eighth century, in Anglo-Saxon. The poet's name and the circumstances of the composition are unknown.

Beowulf has come down to us through the written tradition and it would be difficult to argue for its being a purely oral poem. However, many scholars have detected in it the same type of 'oral-formulaic' properties as in the Homeric poems and regarded these as indications of possible oral composition in some sense. It seems clear too, both from references in Anglo-Saxon poetry itself and from what is known of the historical circumstances of the time, that heroic poems were often chanted aloud by a bard or *scop* to the king and his court or to local chiefs surrounded by their followers. It is fair to conclude that *Beowulf* was similarly recited aloud and that it can in this sense at least be classed as a type of oral poetry.

The metre of Beowulf is marked by both stress and alliteration. Each half-line has two main stresses, however few or many syllables it contains in all. At least two of the stressed syllables must alliterate in each line. The style is also characterized by the use of special poetic compounds ('kennings'): the sea is 'whale's road' or 'swan's way', a ship is 'Foamy-neck' or 'Twisted-prow'. Both these stylistic features are retained in Michael Alexander's translation. As he writes: 'I have never seen the point of

1. For these reasons some would prefer to avoid the term 'epic'.

translating verse into anything but verse. . . . All the poetry . . . is
in the way it was said, and it is in this belief that I have borrowed
the form of the Old English verse in making these versions.' To
fully appreciate its remarkable effectiveness, one really needs to
read his translation aloud, strongly emphasizing the regular four
stresses in each full line, with a definite mid-line pause

> The *prince* had al*ready*   *pick*ed his *men*
> From the *folk*'s *flower*   the *fierc*est am*ong* them.

After these words the Weather-Geat prince[2]
dived into the Mere – he did not care
to wait for an answer – and the waves closed over
the daring man. It was a day's space almost
before he could glimpse ground at the bottom.

The grim and greedy guardian of the flood,[3]
keeping her hungry hundred-season watch,
discovered at once that one from above,
a human, had sounded the home of the monsters.
She felt for the man and fastened upon him
her terrible hooks; but no harm came thereby
to the hale body within – the harness so ringed him
that she could not drive her dire fingers
through the mesh of the mail-shirt masking his limbs.

When she came to the bottom she bore him to her lair,
the mere-wolf, pinioning the mail-clad prince.
Not all his courage could enable him
to draw his sword; but swarming through the water
throngs of sea-beasts threw themselves upon him
with ripping tusks to tear his battle-coat,
tormenting monsters. Then the man found
that he was in some enemy hall
where there was no water to weigh upon him
and the power of the flood could not pluck him away,

2. Beowulf.   3. Grendel's mother.

sheltered by its roof: a shining light he saw,
a bright fire blazing clearly.

It was then that he saw the size of this water-hag,
damned thing of the deep. He dashed out his weapon,
not stinting the stroke, and with such strength and violence
that the circled sword screamed on her head
a strident battle-song. But the stranger saw
his battle-flame refuse to bite
or hurt her at all; the edge failed
its lord in his need. It had lived through many
hand-to-hand conflicts, and carved through the helmets
of fated men. This was the first time
that this rare treasure betrayed its name.
Determined still, intent on fame,
the nephew of Hygelac renewed his courage.
Furious, the warrior flung it to the ground,
spiral-patterned, precious in its clasps,
stiff and steel-edged; his own strength would suffice him,
the might of his hands. A man must act so
when he means in a fight to frame himself
a long-lasting glory; it is not life he thinks of.

The Geat prince went for Grendel's mother,
seized her by the shoulder – he was not sorry to be fighting –
his mortal foe, and with mounting anger
the man hard in battle hurled her to the ground.
She promptly repaid this present of his
as her ruthless hands reached out for him;
and the strongest of fighting-men stumbled in his weariness,
the firmest of foot-warriors fell to the earth.
She was down on this guest of hers and had drawn her knife,
broad, burnished of edge; for her boy was to be avenged,
her only son. Overspreading his back,
the shirt of mail shielded his life then,
barred the entry to edge and point.
Edgetheow's son would have ended his venture
deep under ground there, the Geat fighter,
had not the battle-shirt then brought him aid,
his war-shirt of steel. And the wise Lord,

the holy God, gave out the victory:
the Ruler of the Heavens rightly settled it
as soon as the Geat regained his feet.

He saw among the armour there the sword to bring him victory,
a Giant-sword from former days: formidable were its edges,
a warrior's admiration. This wonder of its kind
was yet so enormous that no other man
would be equal to bearing it in battle-play,
– it was a Giant's forge that had fashioned it so well.
The Scylding champion, shaking with war-rage,
caught it by its rich hilt, and, careless of his life,
brandished its circles, and brought it down in fury
to take her full and fairly across the neck,
breaking the bones; the blade sheared
through the death-doomed flesh. She fell to the ground;
the sword was gory; he was glad at the deed.

Light glowed out and illumined the chamber
with a clearness such as the candle of heaven
sheds in the sky. He scoured the dwelling
in single-minded anger, the servant of Hygelac;
with his weapon high, and holding to it firmly,
he stalked by the wall. Nor was the steel useless yet
to that man of battle, for he meant soon enough
to settle with Grendel for those stealthy raids
– there had been many of them – he had made on the West-
        Danes;
far more often than on that first occasion
when he killed Hrothgar's hearth-companions,
slew them as they slept, and in their sleep ate up
of the folk of Denmark fifteen good men,
carrying off another of them
in foul robbery. The fierce champion
now settled this up with him: he saw where Grendel
lay at rest, limp from the fight;
his life had wasted through the wound he got
in the battle at Heorot. The body gaped open
as it now suffered the stroke after death
from the hard-swung sword; he had severed the neck.

And above, the wise men who watched with Hrothgar
the depths of the pool descried soon enough
blood rising in the broken water
and marbling the surface. Seasoned warriors,
grey-headed, experienced, they spoke together,
said it seemed unlikely that they would see once more
the prince returning triumphant to seek out
their famous master. Many were persuaded
the she-wolf of the deep had done away with him.
The ninth hour had come; the keen-hearted Scyldings
abandoned the cliff-head; the kindly gold-giver
turned his face homeward. But the foreigners sat on,
staring at the pool with sickness at heart,
hoping they would look again on their beloved captain,
believing they would not.
       The blood it had shed
made the sword dwindle into deadly icicles;
the war-tool wasted away. It was wonderful indeed
how it melted away entirely, as the ice does in the spring
when the Father unfastens the frost's grip,
unwinds the water's ropes – He who watches over
the times and the seasons; He is the true God.
The Geat champion did not choose to take
any treasures from that hall, from the heaps that he saw there,
other than that richly ornamented hilt,
and the head of Grendel. The engraved blade
had melted and burnt away: the blood was too hot,
the fiend that had died there too deadly by far.
The survivor of his enemies' onslaught in battle
now set to swimming, and struck up through the water;
both the deep reaches and the rough wave-swirl
were thoroughly cleansed, now the creature from the other-
      world
drew breath no longer in this brief world's space.

Then the seamen's Helm came swimming up
strongly to land, delighting in his sea-trove,
those mighty burdens that he bore along with him.

They went to meet him, a manly company,
thanking God, glad of their lord,
seeing him safe and sound once more.
Quickly the champion's corselet and helmet
were loosened from him. The lake's waters,
sullied with blood, slept beneath the sky.

The story of Bamsi Beyrek of the grey horse

from *The Book of Dede Korkut*

Dede Korkut

This tale is one of twelve which, together with a pro-
logue, make up the medieval Turkish *Book of Dede Korkut*. These
are the epic stories of the Oghuz or Turkomen who migrated from
the area of, roughly, the present Uzbekistan in the USSR to be-
come, eventually, the Turks of Turkey.

The twelve episodes are bound together not by a uni-
fied plot or chronology, but by similarities of style and context,
recurrent protagonists and by the attribution of overall authorship
to Dede Korkut, the minstrel who also appears in the narrative
itself. The heroic deeds of the tales are pictured as taking place in
the nomadic and aristocratic setting of the original homeland of
Central Asia – the 'heroic age of the Oghuz Turks', as the trans-
lator puts it – fraught with constant battles against warring infidels
hostile to the true faith of Islam, and dominated by a man's need
to prove himself against the enemy.

The story is in a blend of prose and poetry, most of the
narrative being in prose, most of the dialogue in verse. In one form
or another this combination is common throughout Asia as well as
parts of Europe (as instanced by the well-known *chante fable* of
Aucassin and Nicolette); it also appears in the *Ballad of the Hidden
Dragon* and other Chinese compositions. This medium is so com-
mon a framework for 'epic' and 'ballad' that an example is being
quoted at some length here which includes a substantial portion of
the prose narrative rather than mere selections from the verse
(which would inevitably mean tearing them from their context) –
even though such large chunks of prose may seem out of place in
an anthology of poetry. Overall, the verse portion of *The Book of
Dede Korkut* runs to about thirty-five per cent of the total wordage
– considerably less than in the *Ballad of the Hidden Dragon*. The
poetry normally consists of speeches or soliloquies by the various
characters, expressed in alliterative and assonant or rhyming form,
known as *soylama*, 'declamation'. These passages are often charac-
terized by formulaic phrases and repeated images like, for instance,

the comparison of success in life with a mountain's running streams, pastures, and shady trees.

Minstrel tales sung before the king and his court or in the camps of military and political leaders have apparently had a long history among the Turks. It is probable that the narratives in *The Book of Dede Korkut* had their origins in similar occasions and tales, though nothing definite is known about the original minstrel Dede Korkut to whom they are attributed – not even whether he was a real person or not. The present text is based on two manuscripts dating from the sixteenth century.

'The Story of Bamsi Beyrek of the Grey Horse', of which most of the second half is given here, opens with Beyrek's birth as the long-awaited son of Bay Bure, and describes how he is given his full name by the minstrel Dede Korkut after he has proved his courage. He woos as his wife the Lady Chichek, 'the queen of beauties'. But on his wedding night he is attacked by 700 infidels and, with his thirty-nine companions, carried off into captivity.

Prince Bay Bure's pavilion with its golden smoke-hole was invaded by mourning. His daughters and daughters-in-law laughed no more, the red henna no more adorned their white hands. Beyrek's seven sisters took off their white dresses and put on black, they lamented and wailed together, saying, 'Alas, my only brother, princely brother, who never attained his heart's desire!' News was brought to his betrothed. The Lady Chichek dressed in black and put away her white caftan, she tore at her cheeks, red as autumn apples, and she mourned, saying,

'Alas, master of my red veil!
Alas, hope of my forehead and head!
Alas, my kingly warrior, my falcon-like warrior!
Warrior at whose face I never gazed my fill!
Where have you gone leaving me alone, my soul, my warrior?
Whom I see when I open my eyes,
Whom I love with all my heart,
With whom I share one pillow,
For whose sake I would die, a sacrifice.

Alas, trusty minister of Prince Kazan!
Alas, darling of the teeming Oghuz!
My lord Beyrek!'

Sixteen years passed, during which they did not know whether Beyrek was alive or dead. One day, the girl's brother, Crazy Karchar, came to the court of Bayindir Khan, bowed the knee and said, 'May the life of the Khan's Majesty be long. If Beyrek were alive, in sixteen years either news of him would have come or he himself would have come. If any man were to bring news that he was alive I would give him richly embroidered robes and gold and silver; to any who brought news of his death I would give my sister.' Thereupon Yaltajuk son of Yalanji[1] (curse him, may he not prosper) said, 'My Sultan, I shall go and bring news of whether he is alive or dead.' Now it seems that Beyrek had given him a shirt, which he never wore but had kept. He went and dipped that shirt in blood, then brought it to Bayindir Khan. 'What is this shirt?' asked Bayindir Khan. 'My Sultan,' he replied, 'it is Beyrek's shirt; they killed Beyrek at the Black Pass, and this is the proof of it.'

Among the Oghuz nobles, lying was unknown; they believed him and wept. But Bayindir Khan said, 'What are you crying for? We do not know this shirt. Take it and show it to his betrothed; she will know it well, for she sewed it and will recognize it.' They brought it to the Lady Chichek. As soon as she saw it she knew it and said, 'That's it.' She ripped the neck of her dress, she drove her sharp nails into her white face, she tore at her cheeks, red as autumn apples, and she mourned:

'Alas for him whom I see when I open my eyes,
Whom I gave my heart and love!
Alas, master of my red wedding-veil!
Alas, hope of my forehead and my head!
Lord Beyrek!'

The news was brought to her parents, and mourning invaded their many-coloured encampment; they put off their white

---

1. Literally 'Little Toady, son of Liar'. A number of personal names in these minstrel tales are used as humorous or satirical descriptions of their bearers.

clothes and put on black. The nobles of the teeming Oghuz gave
up hope of Beyrek. Yaltajuk son of Yalanji held his betrothal feast
and appointed a day for his wedding.

Once again Beyrek's father Prince Bay Bure summoned
the merchants and said, 'Merchants, go and search in every land
and bring me news whether Beyrek is dead or alive.' The merchants
made preparation for the journey and departed, travelling on with-
out regard for day and night. Eventually they reached Parasar's
castle of Bayburt. Now that day was the infidel's feast-day. Every
one of them was eating and drinking. They brought Beyrek and
made him play his lute. Beyrek looked out from a high platform
and saw the merchants. When he saw them he asked them for
news; let us see, my Khan, how he asked.

'Caravan, coming from the broad lowlands,
Caravan, precious gift of the lord my father and my lady mother,
Caravan, on your long-hooved falcon-swift horses,
Understand my words, hear what I say, O caravan.
Among the teeming Oghuz
If I ask for news of Salur Kazan son of Ulash,
Does he yet live, O caravan?
If I ask for news of Wild Dundar son of Kiyan Seljuk,
Does he yet live, O caravan?
And Kara Budak son of Kara Gone,
Does he yet live, O caravan?
If I ask for news of my white-bearded father, my white-haired
        mother,
My seven sisters; do they yet live, O caravan?
She whom I saw when I opened my eyes,
Whom I love with all my heart,
The Lady Chichek daughter of Prince Bay Bijan;
Is she yet in her house or has she married another?
Tell me, O caravan,
And my dark head be a sacrifice for you.'

The merchants replied:

'Are you alive, are you well, dear Bamsi?
Sixteen years we have sorrowed over you, lord Bamsi.
If, among the teeming Oghuz, you ask about Prince Kazan,

He lives, Bamsi.

If you ask about Wild Dundar son of Kiyan Seljuk,

He lives, Bamsi.

If you ask about Kara Budak son of Kara Gone,

He lives, Bamsi.

Those nobles have put off their white clothes and put on black,
Bamsi.

If you ask about your white-bearded father and your white-
haired mother,

They live, Bamsi.

They have put off their white clothes and put on black for you,
Bamsi.

Your seven sisters I saw crying at the place where seven roads
meet, Bamsi.

I saw them tearing their cheeks, red as autumn apples,

I saw them bewailing their brother who had gone and never
returned.

She whom you saw when you opened your eyes,

Whom you gave your heart and loved,

Prince Bay Bijan's daughter, the Lady Chichek,

Has celebrated her betrothal and appointed the day for her
wedding.

I saw her on her way to marry Yaltajuk son of Yalanji.

Lord Beyrek, contrive to fly from Parasar's castle of Bayburt,

To reach your many-coloured marriage-tent.

If you do not, you have lost Prince Bay Bijan's daughter, the
Lady Chichek;

Be sure of this.' . . .

[On hearing this, Beyrek escapes with the help of his captor's
daughter.]

He gave thanks to God and began to walk, until he
came to the infidels' horse-pasture, thinking that he might find a
horse, take it and ride. And there he saw his own grey horse, the
sea-born, standing and cropping the grass. The grey horse recog-
nized Beyrek too when he saw him; he reared up on his hind legs
and whinnied. Then Beyrek praised him; let us see, my Khan,
how he praised him.

'Your dear forehead is like a broad open field,
Your dear eyes are like two glowing jewels,
Your dear mane is like rich brocade,
Your dear ears are like twin brothers,
Your dear back brings a man to his heart's desire.
I shall not call you "horse" but "brother" – and better than any
    brother.
"There's work to be done, comrade," I shall say – and better
    than any comrade.'

The horse raised his head, pricked up one ear and came towards Beyrek, who hugged his chest and kissed both his eyes. Then he leaped onto his back and rode towards the castle gate, where he committed his thirty-nine comrades to the infidels' care; let us see, my Khan, how he did so.

'Infidel of filthy religion!
You were for ever casting insults in my mouth; I have not had
    my fill.
You gave me stew to eat, of the black swine's flesh; I have not
    had my fill.
God has given me my freedom and I am on my way.
My thirty-nine young men I commit to your care, O infidel;
If I find one missing I shall kill ten in his place.
If I find ten missing I shall kill a hundred in their place, O
    infidel.
My thirty-nine young men I commit to your care, O infidel!'

Then he rode away. Forty infidels mounted and rode after him; they chased him but they could not catch him, and they rode back.

Beyrek came to the Oghuz land and saw a minstrel journeying. 'Whither away, minstrel?' said he. 'To the wedding, young lord,' the minstrel replied. 'Whose is the wedding?' 'Yalta-juk's, son of Yalanji.' 'And who is the girl he is marrying?' 'The betrothed of the lord Beyrek,' said the minstrel. 'Minstrel,' said Beyrek, 'give me your lute and I shall give you my horse. Keep him till I come and bring you his price and take him.' 'Lo and behold!' said the minstrel, 'I've won a horse, without cracking my voice or straining my throat or breaking my lute! I'll take him and look after him.' And he gave his lute to Beyrek, who took it and made his way to the vicinity of his father's encampment.

There he saw some shepherds lined up at the side of the road, weeping and at the same time ceaselessly piling up stones. 'Shepherds,' said he, 'if anyone finds a stone on the road he throws it away; why are you piling these stones on the road and crying?' The shepherds replied, 'You know about yourself but you know nothing of what ails us.' 'Well, what does ail you?' 'Our lord had a son,' they said, 'but for the last sixteen years no one knew whether he was alive or dead. A man called Yaltajuk son of Yalanji has brought news that he is dead, and they have decided to marry his betrothed to this man. He has to pass this way and we're going to stone him, so that she won't have to marry him but can marry a man worthy of her.' 'All honour to you,' said Beyrek, 'that will be an honest day's work!' Then he came to his father's encampment.

Now before their tents was a great tree, with a fair spring at its foot. Beyrek saw his little sister coming to get water from that spring, and she wept saying, 'My brother Beyrek, how evilly has your wedding-feast turned out!' A mighty grief at his long separation came over Beyrek; he could not endure it and his great tears flowed. He called out to her, declaiming; let us see, my Khan, what he declaimed.

'Girl, why do you cry and sob for your brother?
(I burn within, my heart is aflame.)
So your brother is gone.
Boiling oil has been poured over your heart.
You are racked with inward pain.
Why do you cry and sob for your brother?
(I burn within, my heart is aflame.)
If I might ask, whose summer-pasture is yonder black mountain?
Whose drink its cold cold rivers?
Whose mounts those stables full of falcon-swift horses?
Whose beasts of burden those camels, caravan on caravan?
Whose feast the white sheep in the folds?
Whose shade the black and sky-blue tents?
Tell me, maiden, from your own mouth;
My dark head be a sacrifice for you this day.'

The girl replied,

'Play not, minstrel; tell no tales, minstrel!
What use is that, to a wretched girl like me?
If you ask about yonder black mountain,
It was my brother Beyrek's summer-pasture.
Since my brother Beyrek left I have gone to no summer-pasture.
If you ask about its cold cold rivers,
They were my brother Beyrek's drink.
Since my brother Beyrek left I have not drunk.
If you ask about the stables full of falcon-swift horses,
They were my brother Beyrek's mounts.
Since my brother Beyrek left I have not ridden.
If you ask about the camels, caravan on caravan,
They were my brother Beyrek's beasts of burden.
Since my brother Beyrek left I have laden no beasts of burden.
If you ask about the white sheep in the folds,
They were my brother Beyrek's feast.
Since my brother Beyrek left I have not feasted.
If you ask about the black and sky-blue tents,
They were my brother Beyrek's shade.
Since my brother Beyrek left I have not migrated.'

Again she spoke,

'Minstrel,
On your way here, when you climbed yonder black mountain,
Did you not meet a man named Beyrek?
On your way here, when you crossed the swollen rivers,
Did you not meet a man named Beyrek?
On your way here, when you passed through famous cities,
Did you not meet a man named Beyrek?
If you have seen him, minstrel, tell me;
My dark head be a sacrifice for you, minstrel.'

Yet again she spoke,

'My black mountain yonder has fallen in ruins;
Minstrel, you are unaware.
My great shady tree has been cut down;
Minstrel, you are unaware.
My only brother in all the world has been taken;
Minstrel, you are unaware.

Play not, minstrel; tell no tales, minstrel.
What use is that, to a wretched girl like me, minstrel?
There is a wedding-feast along the road;
Go to the wedding-feast and sing!'

Beyrek left her and came to where his older sisters
were. He saw them sitting dressed in black, and he called out to
them, declaiming; let us see, my Khan, what he declaimed.

'Girls who rise up from your place at early morning,
Who have abandoned the white tent for the black tent,
Who have put off your white clothes and put on black clothes,
Have you any yoghurt, clotting like liver?
Have you any cakes in the black oven?
Have you any bread in the crock?
Three days have I journeyed; give me to eat.'

The girls went and brought food and filled Beyrek's
belly. Then he said, 'As charity for your brother's head and eye, if
you have a worn-out caftan I might wear to the feast; there they
will present me with caftans and I shall return yours.' They went
and found a caftan of Beyrek's and gave it to him. He took it and
put it on and it fitted him, its length his length, its waist his waist,
its arm his arm. His eldest sister noticed how like he was to
Beyrek, and her black almond eyes filled with bloody tears. She
declaimed; let us see, my Khan, what she declaimed.

'Were not your black almond eyes without lustre,
I should call you my brother Beyrek, minstrel.
Were your face not covered in black hair,
I should call you my brother Beyrek, minstrel.
Were your strong wrists not shrunken,
I should call you my brother Beyrek, minstrel.
With your proud swaggering walk,
Your lion-like stance,
Your intent gaze,
You are so like my brother Beyrek, minstrel.
You have rejoiced me, minstrel; do not cast me down!'

Again she declaimed,

'Play not, minstrel, tell no tales, minstrel.
Since my brother Beyrek left no minstrel has visited us.
None has taken our caftan from our back,
None has taken our nightcap from our head,
None has taken our curly-horned rams.'

Beyrek said to himself, 'Do you see, the girls recognized me by this caftan, and so too will the nobles of the teeming Oghuz. Let me find out who my friends and enemies are among the Oghuz.' He took off the caftan and threw it at the girls, saying, 'Confound you and Beyrek! You gave me an old caftan, you took my head and my brains.'[2] So saying, he went and found an old camel-cloth, poked a hole in it, put his head through and pretended to be mad.

He went on his way and came to the wedding-feast. He saw the bridegroom shooting arrows, with Budak son of Kara Gone, Uruz son of Prince Kazan, Yigenek the paramount noble, Sher Shemseddin son of Gaflet Koja, and Crazy Karchar, the girl's brother. Every time Budak shot, Beyrek said, 'Luck to your hand!' Every time Uruz shot, Beyrek said, 'Luck to your hand!' Every time Yigenek shot, Beyrek said, 'Luck to your hand!' Every time Sher Shemseddin shot, Beyrek said, 'Luck to your hand!' But when the bridegroom shot, he said, 'May your hand wither, may your fingers rot, pig and son of a pig! May you be a sacrifice for all true bridegrooms!' Yaltajuk son of Yalanji, infuriated, said, 'You rogue and son of a rogue, is it your place to talk to me like this? Come here, you rogue, and draw my bow or I shall cut your head off this instant.' Straightway Beyrek took the bow and drew it; it broke in half at the grip and he threw it down in front of him, saying, 'It'll do for shooting larks at close range.' Enraged that his bow was smashed, Yaltajuk son of Yalanji said, 'There's that bow of Beyrek's; fetch it.' They went and brought it. Seeing the bow, Beyrek was reminded of his comrades, and tears came to his eyes. He said,

'My strong white-gripped bow, which I bought at the price of a
        stallion,

2. He means 'you have made me act stupidly, in that I was on the point of declaring myself to you and abandoning my plan to go to the feast incognito.'

My twisted string, which I bought at the price of a bull.
In a distressful place I abandoned
My thirty-nine comrades, my two messengers.'

Then he said, 'My lords, with your leave I shall draw this bow and shoot an arrow in your honour.' Now they were aiming at the bridegroom's ring, and Beyrek's arrow struck that ring and broke it in pieces. The Oghuz nobles clapped their hands and laughed at the sight. Prince Kazan was looking on and he summoned Beyrek. The crazy minstrel came, bowed his head, placed his hand on his heart and declaimed; let us see, my Khan, what he declaimed.

'You of the white pavilion, pitched afar in the morning twilight,
You of the blue parasol made of satin,
You of the falcon-swift horses, drawn up stall on stall,
You of the many officers, who summon and give justice,
You of limitless bounty when the oil is poured,
Prop of forsaken warriors,
Hope of the wretched and the helpless,
Son-in-law of Bayindir Khan,
Chick of the long-plumed bird,
Pillar of the Turkish lands,
Lion of the Emet river,
Tiger of the Karajuk,
Master of the chestnut horse,
Father of Khan Uruz,
My Khan Kazan!
Hear my voice, pay heed to my words.
You rose in the morning twilight,
You entered the white forest,
You passed through the white poplar boughs, shaking them,
You bent down its side-poles,
You threw on its top-struts,
You called it a marriage-bower.
Princes of the right hand, seated on the right!
Princes of the left hand, seated on the left!
Ministers at the threshold!
Princes of the entourage, seated at the foot of the throne!
Good fortune on your realm!'

To which Prince Kazan replied, 'Crazy minstrel, what do you ask of me? Do you want tents and pavilions, slaves and slave-girls, gold and silver? I shall give them to you.' 'My lord,' said Beyrek, 'would you permit me to approach the banquet? I am hungry and would fill myself.' Kazan replied, 'The crazy minstrel has struck lucky. Nobles! For today my realm is to be his; let him go where he will, do what he will.' Beyrek came to the banquet and ate his fill, then kicked the cauldrons, spilt them and overturned them. He hurled some of the stewed meat to his right, some to his left. Those on the right got what went to the right, those on the left got what went to the left. The righteous wins his just deserts, the unrighteous wins disgrace. The word was brought to Prince Kazan: 'Lord, the crazy minstrel has upset all the food and now he wants to join the girls.' 'Well let him do what he likes; let him go where he wants, let him even join the girls,' said Kazan.

Beyrek upped and went in the direction of the girls. He chased away the pipers, he chased away the drummers. Some he beat, some he split the heads of. He came to the tent where the girls and the ladies were sitting, and he sat down across the threshold. Prince Kazan's wife, Burla the Tall, was furious at the sight and said, 'You crazy rogue and son of a rogue, is it your place to come upon me without ceremony?' 'Lady,' replied Beyrek, 'I have Prince Kazan's orders: none is to interfere with me.' 'Very well,' said the Lady Burla, 'since Prince Kazan has so ordered, let him sit.' Then she turned again to Beyrek and said, 'Crazy minstrel, what do you want?' 'I want the bride to get up and dance while I play the lute.' There was a lady called Kisirja Yenge, and they said to her, 'You stand up and dance, Kisirja Yenge. How will the crazy minstrel know the difference?' Kisirja Yenge stood and said, 'Crazy minstrel, I am the bride. Play your lute and I shall dance.' Beyrek knew who she was and he declaimed; let us see, my Khan, what he declaimed.

'I take my oath I have never mounted a barren mare,[3]
Never have I mounted one and ridden off on foray.
The herdsmen behind the gully watch you;
They follow your footsteps to see which valley you have taken,

3. A play on the lady's name, *kisir* meaning 'barren'.

They watch the road to see which way you come,
Great tears flow from their eyes.
Go to them.
They will give you what you want.
I have no business with you.
Let the girl who is to marry stand,
Let her wave her arms and dance,
And I shall play the lute.'

'Oh dear!' said Kisirja Yenge, 'this accursed madman speaks as if he had seen me!' and she went and sat down again, and all the great khans' wives laughed out loud behind their yashmaks.

There was another lady, called Boghazja Fatima. 'You get up and dance,' they said to her. 'And suppose that crazy nobody says the same sort of impossible things about me?' said she. 'There's no harm in saying you're the bride,' they said, and made her put on the bride's caftan. 'Play, crazy minstrel,' she said, 'and I'll dance. I'm the girl who is to be married.' Beyrek replied,

'This time I take my oath I have never mounted a pregnant
        mare,[4]
Never have I mounted one and ridden off on foray.
Behind your house was there not a little river?
Was your dog's name not Barak?
Was your name not Boghazja Fatima of the forty lovers?
Go to your place and sit,
Or I shall expose more of your shame; be sure of that.
I do not play with you.
Let the one who is to marry stand,
And I shall play the lute.
Let her wave her arms and dance.'

At that, Boghazja Fatima said, 'Oh dear! The secrets are coming out! The crazy minstrel, coming and spoiling our agreeable party, throwing all our faults in our faces, insulting us and blackening our good name in front of all these people!' She went to the girl and said, 'The things that have happened because of you! Our friends and our enemies have all laughed at us! Now, if you're going to dance, get up and dance! If you won't dance, go and dance in hell!'

4. A similar play, *boghaz* meaning 'pregnant'.

Of course the Lady Chichek was wondering what he would say to her, but they said, 'What are you wondering about? We knew you'd have this sort of adventure once Beyrek was gone.' The Lady Burla the Tall said, 'Come girl, get up and dance, make the best of it.' The Lady Chichek put on her red gown, drew her hands inside the sleeves so that they should not show, and prepared to dance, saying, 'Play, crazy minstrel, and I shall dance; I am the girl who is to be married.' Beyrek replied,

'Since I left this place the weather has been icy.
Heavily has the white snow fallen, up to the knee.
In the house of the Khan's daughter there were no more slaves
    or slave-girls,
She herself took the pitcher and went for water,
Her ten fingers were frostbitten from the wrist down.
Bring red gold and I shall make fingers for the Khan's daughter.
Bring white silver and I shall fashion fingernails for her.
Shame for a Khan's daughter not to be perfect on her wedding-
    day!'

Angered at this, the Lady Chichek said, 'Crazy minstrel, is there any flaw in me that you should cast shame on me?' She put out her hands, showing her silver-white wrists, and the gold ring which Beyrek had given her was plain to see on her finger. Beyrek recognized the ring and declaimed; let us see, my Khan, what he declaimed.

'Since Beyrek left, have you tramped to the hilltop, maiden?
Have you strained to see on all four sides, maiden?
Have you torn your black hair like reeds uprooted, maiden?
Have you shed bitter tears from your black eyes, maiden?
Have you slashed your cheeks, red as autumn apples, maiden?
Have you asked news of Beyrek from every traveller, maiden?
Have you cried for Bamsi Beyrek whom you loved, maiden?
You are marrying another; the gold ring is mine.
Give it to me, maiden!'

The girl replied,

'Since Beyrek left, often have I tramped to the hilltop,
Much have I torn my black hair, like reeds uprooted,
Much have I slashed my cheeks, red as autumn apples,

Much have I asked news of travellers,
Much have I shed bitter tears from my black eyes,
Much have I cried for my young prince, my young Khan
    Beyrek,
Who has gone and comes not again.
You are not Bamsi Beyrek my lover, my beloved;
Not yours the golden ring.
In the ring are many tokens;
Tell the tokens if you desire the ring.'

Beyrek said,

'Daughter of Khans, did I not rise up in the morning twilight?
Did I not mount my grey horse?
Did I not fell a stag before your tent?
Did you not summon me to your side?
Did we not race our horses over the plain?
Did my horse not outstrip yours?
When we shot, did I not split your arrow?
Did I not throw you when we wrestled?
Before I put the gold ring on your finger,
Did I not kiss you thrice and bite you once?
Am I not Bamsi Beyrek your lover, your beloved?'

Then the girl recognized him and knew that he was Beyrek, and
she cast herself at his feet. The ladies knew that he was Beyrek and
each went to bring the good news to one of the nobles, while the
serving-maids dressed Beyrek in robes. The girl leaped up and
mounted her horse and galloped off to bring the good news to
Beyrek's parents. When she reached them, she said,

'Your rugged black mountain had fallen; it is risen at last.
Your blood-red rivers had dried up; they are in spate at last.
Your great tree had withered; it is green at last.
Your falcon-swift mare had grown old; she has foaled at last.
Your red camel had grown old; she has brought forth at last.
Your white ewe had grown old; she has lambed at last.
Your son Beyrek, sixteen years mourned, has come home at last.
Father and mother of my husband, tell me,
What will you give me for this good news?'

Beyrek's parents replied,

'Dear daughter-in-law, may I die for your tongue!
May I be a sacrifice for your life!
If your words are a lie, may they prove true!
If he should come, alive and well,
Let yonder black mountains be your summer-pasture,
Let their cold rivers be your drink,
My slaves and slave-girls be your servants,
My falcon-swift horses be your mount,
My caravan on caravan of camels be your beasts of burden,
My white sheep in the folds be your banquet,
My gold and silver be yours to spend,
My white pavilion with its gold smoke-hole be your shade,
My dark head be a sacrifice for you, daughter-in-law!'

At that moment the nobles, having heard the news, were swarming round Beyrek, and the princes and khans escorted him to his father. Prince Kazan said, 'Good news, Prince Bay Bure! Your son has come home.' Now since his son Beyrek had gone, Prince Bay Bure's eyes had become blind with weeping. Prince Bay Bure said, 'This is how I shall know that he is my son: let him draw blood from his little finger, smear it on a towel and wipe my eyes with it. If they open, he is indeed my son Beyrek.' Beyrek did so; he wiped it across his father's eyes and they were opened. His parents cried aloud and fell on Beyrek, saying,

'Son, prop of my white pavilion with its gold smoke-hole!
Son, flower of my swan-like daughters and daughters-in-law!
Son, light of my eyes that see!
Son, strength of my hands that hold!
Darling of the teeming Oghuz, my soul, my son!'

They wept and cried together, they gave thanks to mighty God, they sacrificed horses, camels, sheep and cattle, and freed many slaves and slave-girls. . . .

Dede Korkut came and played joyful music, he told stories and declaimed, he related the adventures of the heroic fighters for the Faith, and said, 'Let this tale of the Oghuz be Beyrek's.'

I shall pray for you, my Khan: may your firm-rooted black mountains never be overthrown, may your great shady tree never be cut down, may your white-bearded father's place be paradise, may your white-haired mother's place be heaven. May He never part you from your sons and brothers, may the end of days not part you from the pure Faith. May those who say 'Amen' see His face. May He grant you increase and preserve you in strength and forgive your sins for the honour of Muhammad the Chosen of beautiful name, O my Khan!

Zong Belegt Baatar

The Mongols have a rich and living repertory of heroic epics. These are composed either entirely in verse, or in verse interspersed with prose passages which carry the narrative along. The epic is intended for oral performance, though some written versions exist. It is generally chanted or sung, either without any accompaniment, or with an accompaniment played on a stringed instrument by the bard himself. This accompaniment may vary from a simple repetition of two notes played consecutively to a variety of melodies. With few exceptions, the Mongol bards have been drawn from the common people rather than from the nobility. The contemporary bard is unlikely to be fully professional, but will usually be a member of a herding cooperative, a worker on a state farm, or the like. He will have learned his repertory from other bards.

We can illustrate this from two concrete examples. Mr Gongor, whom I met at Mankhan Cooperative in Khovd Province in western Mongolia in 1967, was then aged fifty-one, and was a shepherd in one of the brigades of the cooperative, in charge of 800 communally owned sheep. He was also a noted hunter. He not only knew epics, but had composed at least one eulogy ('Eulogy of the Cooperative Member'), together with the melody to it. He could play the horse-headed fiddle (*morin khuur*). As his own father and mother had done before him, he would sometimes perform his epics in order to lull his young children to sleep. Gongor told me that, whereas he had composed his own melodies, his father had recited without a melody. He performed one of the epics he knew, 'Prince Lord Sky' (*Ezen tengger khaan*), chanting it first, though without any accompaniment, and then reciting it. Mr Tseveenaravdan, a member of the same cooperative, and also a shepherd, was a young man of eighteen at the time, who knew, he said, about thirty tales, both long and short. He performed one of these, 'Goose Hero' (*Galuu baatar*), to an accompaniment played on the horse-headed fiddle. This performance lasted seventeen minutes, and was one of his longer pieces. Tseveenaravdan had learned his epics and other pieces from older singers, including his father, who had also made the fiddle he used.

The themes of the Mongol epic are uncomplicated narratives of heroes and ogres, warring princes, ravished wives, talking horses, death and resurrection and the like. Kalmuck and Buriat epics tend to be much longer than those of the mainly Khalkha population of the People's Republic, which often consist of one episode only. It is hardly realistic to try to say when any particular epic may have been composed, since it may well contain elements from different periods and is also, to some extent, the re-creation of the bard performing it. The ethos of the Khalkha epic seems to reflect the period of confusion and war which persisted during the fourteenth, fifteenth, and sixteenth centuries, but the use of titles which belong to the Manchu dynasty (1644–1912) and of Buddhistic phraseology point to more recent manipulation of the material. The epic is not historical in content, even when, as occasionally happens, historical personages are mentioned, but relates fantastic happenings.

There are favourite themes which occur over and over again, in particular that of the young hero who, temporarily transformed into a 'snotty-nosed youth', defeats the khan's champion in the three traditional sports of archery, horse-racing, and wrestling, and so wins the princess as his wife. Stylistically, the epic is distinguished by alliteration and parallelism, and by the frequent use of hyperbole. There are lengthy descriptions of heroes and enemies, palaces, horses, and so on, and enumerations of objects associated with them. Especially in these passages use is made of what appear to be standard runs of lines and stock epithets. One such standard type of run is almost always found, in one of its variant forms, at the beginning of an epic, where it serves to define the remote period of time in which the action is situated.

A more sophisticated genre is that of the 'book epic' which is practised more especially in those parts of Mongolia more subject to Chinese influence. A book epic is essentially the reduction to narrative form of a romance, novel, or other tale, or of an episode from one such, or nowadays even of a modern stage play, usually of Chinese origin. The narrative is much more complex than in the heroic epic. The bard may construct his work in alternating passages of prose and verse. The second of a pair of such passages often repeats, in different words, what has just been said in the first, rather than continuing the narrative. The book epic is intended for live performance, and the musical accompaniment is much more varied than with the heroic epic. A book epic may reach considerable proportions. One recently published text contains over 5,000 lines.

The short heroic epic *Zong Belegt Baatar* was published in a printed edition in Ulaanbaatar in 1948, without any commentary. A very similar text was recited to me in January 1968 by a member of the Writers' Circle in the town of Darkhan. The translation is based upon the printed text, but a few variations, affecting the first twenty lines, have been adopted from the recited version.

It is difficult to be fully consistent in the treatment of names in translating a Mongol epic. Some names have an obvious meaning. Thus the hero and the ogre in this epic are called 'Well-omened hero' and 'Cold iron-belted' respectively, and the hero's wife is called 'Girl Lapis-lazuli'. The name of the ogre's father, however, is ambiguous, and may be translated as 'Hero of the blue glass' or 'Hero of the blue plateau' according to the meaning to be given to the Mongol word *shil*, which may indeed also mean 'nape of the neck'. The names of the seas, trees, and birds are, in one form or another, traditional in Mongol epics, and, because they are subject to variation either at the wish of the bard, or to suit the alliteration, they cannot always be translated. Apart from this, some of the elements which go to make up these names are archaic, or distorted, and so frequently unintelligible.

Dewajing, *Dewaan*, and *Maidar* are Mongol forms respectively of Tibetan *bde-ba-can* (the Buddhist paradise), Sanskrit *Dipamkara* (the name of one of the Buddhas who preceded the historic Buddha), and Sanskrit *Maitreya* (the name of the Buddha who is to come).

C. R. Bawden

Once upon a time,
In the realm of Dewajing,
In the era of Dewaan,
Before our era,

In the era of Maidar,
At the beginning of a good epoch,
At the end of a bad epoch,
When the Altai was the size of a hand,
When the earth was the size of a gown,
There lived Zong Belegt Baatar,
Who ruled the eastern continent,
Whose native body was formed of steel,
Whose born body was formed of iron.
He appeared in a good time to appear,
And from that time on
There was neither drought nor famine.
He was born in a good time to be born,
And from the time when he was born
His realm flourished and prospered
In both peace and joy.
He grew up in a good time to grow up,
And from the time when he grew up
His far-flung legions surrounded him,
His numerous peoples
Flourished and shone.

Now as for the palace
Where young Baatar Belegt dwelt,
It had a door of yellow gold,
A girth-rope of live serpents,
A skirting of black silk,
Curtains of fine silk,
And a good firm base,
And was a vitriol-white palace.
In this vitriol-white palace
He had a most wise wife,
Who was equal and companion
To the sturdy hero
Whom she attended.
She had cheeks of bright red
With rays like the light.
She had clear red lips
Whose rays pierced the tent-wall.

She was called Okhin Nomin,
And had a most lovely form.
From the ground where she stepped
Grew up gay flowers.
From the ground where she walked
Spurted beams of light.
She could look at the hairs of the beasts and count them.
She could hold the hairs of a hat and count them.

As for the waters he drank,
He had the 'Hundred-thousand sea',
The 'Sugar sea',
The 'New sea',
The 'Pure-gold sea'.
Four kinds of precious sea
Like these, he possessed.
The birds which dived and frolicked
Upon these seas
Were azure Tonjid,
Duck Tonjid
Mirror Tonjid,
Peacock Tonjid,
These four kinds of bird.
The trees which grew
By the edge of the waters
Were elephant-sandal,
Buckthorn sandal,
Good sandal,
Fine sandal,
These four sorts
Of precious tree.
He had one hundred thousand grey sheep.
His hundred thousand grey sheep
Drank from the Boir-sugar sea
And grazed on the Budam-sandal mountain.
He had deer-red oxen
Filling the Tamarisk river.
His deer-red oxen
Grazed on the yellow plain of Saikh.

He had thirty times ten million camels.
His thirty times ten million camels
Drank from the sea called Pure-gold,
And grazed on the yellow plain of Shinet.
He had twenty times ten million fallow and dapple horses.
His twenty times ten million fallow and dapple horses
Drank from the sea called Hundred-thousand,
And grazed on the yellow plain of Bolzoot.
The horse he rode,
Had a body the size of a day's journey,
Ears of six spans,
Eyes the size of a hare,
A spine the size of a plain,
A fine combed mane,
A fine bushy tail.
Looked at from behind
It might have been a city.
To look at its buttocks and sinews,
It could be seen to be a horse.
Looked at from in front
It might have been a mountain pass.
To look at its lips and mouth,
It could be seen to be a horse.
The fiery brown horse
He would saddle for a war-campaign.
The frolicsome black horse
He would ride to the hunt.
This famous hero
Had enormous pastures
And many subjects.
His realm was peaceful
And bathed in joy,
And the ten thousand creatures were happy.
It was a land of matchless beauty
Where they dwelt in their multitudes
Like growing flowers,
Like flowing streams.

Zong Belegt Baatar
Who always approved what was right,
Would mount his frolicsome black horse,
On which he rode to the hunt,
And go to hunt the game
On the hills to north and south.
He would meet all his people,
Greet them and ask them
About their lives.

To the north-west
Of Baatar Belegt's land
There dwelt a malevolent ogre
Called Khuiten Tomor Bust,
Son of Khokh Shiliin Baatar.
The nails of his feet
Grew out towards the steppes,
And had turned to hooks of blue iron.
The nails of his hands
Grew towards the outside,
And had turned to hooks of steel.
He had blue-striped eyes,
And a brown-striped tongue.
He sucked people's blood
And ate children's flesh.
He had a tall cast-iron fort,
With a fence of thorny trees.
What he thought of day and night
Was how to destroy famous heroes,
Capture their golden seals,
Unite their subject peoples,
And steal their virgin pastures.
He had the foul desire
Of making them
The slaves of his slaves
And drudges at his threshold.

The ogre Khuiten Tomor Bust
Awoke from a wishful dream
In which he had taken the life

Of young Zong Belegt Baatar,
Who ruled the eastern continent,
And had captured his golden seal.
He had ravaged his people,
And plundered his goods and beasts.
He had strung together his children
And cast them beneath his feet,
And had turned to ashes
His well-peopled palace.
The savage black ogre
Kept thinking over
This happy dream of his
And saying: 'The god Khormusda has given me
A sign of good omen
That the time for me to rule the world
Is now not far off.'

He prepared his hard weapons,
Drew up his cruel troops,
Mounted his black speckled horse
Which was the size of the Khangai range,
Troubled with murderous war
The people near at hand,
And carved out a terrible and bloody path
Wherever he marched.
He turned towards the east
And went to spy upon
The fair and bright domain
Of Zong Belegt Baatar.

He climbed the grey knoll of Bolzoot,
Offered an incense offering for success,
Took out his goose-necked pipe,
And drew on his mad yellow tobacco.
He covered the western continent
With smoke from the right corner of his mouth,
And covered the eastern continent
With smoke from the left corner of his mouth,
Then saw an eagle flying
Through the choking smoke,

And was quite amazed and said:
'Has this silly bird
Got lost in the mist and fog?
Is it stupefied by my smoke?'
And the brown eagle came flying
And came up to
The big squat body
Of Khuiten Tomor Bust,
And as he watched, it turned into a hero
With the strength of ten thousand tigers,
With a stout brown body,
Long black hair,
Broad wide brow,
And full of vigour.
He said: 'Did you think my lord was a youngster?
Did you despise him as a baby?
Did you think my hosts were few?
Did you think I had no brave heroes?
Why have you come lurking,
Bearing no message?'
And with his grey-brown body,
Which showed no signs of flinching
From the hard iron sword,
He barred his way.

The ogre Khuiten Tomor Bust
Fell into a rage.
His brown-red heart
Pounded furiously.
He slapped his right thigh
And pulled off flesh the size of a tiger.
He slapped his left thigh
And pulled off flesh the size of a roe-deer.
He made the crusted earth shake.
He made the blue waters spill over.
In a coarse, harsh voice
He called out thus:
'The god Khormusda has said
It is time for me to rule the world.

Alas for your poor head!
It is vain to bar my way.
Wretched little fellow,
Clear off to your own lands!'

The bronze-willed hero
Would not heed his words, but said:
'No ogre may enter
My sacred pastures.
Careless of my life I shall protect
The hearth of my parents,
The cradle of my children,
My fair golden pastures.'
And he grappled with
The hostile black ogre.

They began a bitter combat
To decide their fates.
They wrestled over the peaks
Of the lofty Khangai mountains.
They battled right through
The fair, rich plains.
They fought leaping and tumbling
In the azure-blue sea.
They challenged each other in the mountain forest.
They fought as hard as could be.
They fought for three years.
They fought with might and main.
They fought for four years.
They wrinkled the high hills.
They levelled the lonely peaks.
They made the plains a pit.
They turned the crops into flour.
And Khuiten Tomor Bust
Felt his strength fail.
Cold sweat poured from him,
And he fled the same way as he came,
Saying: 'I had better flee this strange land,
And go back to my home,
And return to my wife and child,

While I am still in one piece,
While saddle and bridle are whole.
After I have got back home,
When it is time to return here,
I shall sharpen the weapons I wield,
And increase my warrior-troops,
And without fail defeat this wretch.'

Saying: 'Though that filthy ogre
Is running away back home,
His aim of disturbing the people
Is no doubt the same as before.
If we let the murderous ogre
Get away with his life,
He will never leave in peace
The creatures of the golden earth',
Young Zong Belegt Baatar,
Who always discovered what was right,
Put on his double silk gown
With its seventy-five buttons.
Over it he doubled his fine war-dress
And his warrior's armour.
He took his stiff yellow bow,
Made by piecing together
The horns of seventy stags,
With notches as big as a mountain pass,
With arrow heads as big as a valley.
He girded on his brown conical quiver,
Made by piecing together
The hides of seventy stags,
Drank tea for the long journey,
And ate the flesh of a sheep to sustain him.
He blew on his melodious flute,
Calling his brown horse to come.
His brown steed
Heard the sound of the melodious flute,
And saying: 'Why has the saddle creaked
While my lord's sway is unbroken?
Why has the bridle rattled,

While the people are not scattered?'
It came trotting,
From as far as it could be seen,
From the top of the rugged peak,
Whinnying and neighing.
He fitted on its head
The studded silver bridle.
He laid on it the double white saddle-cloth,
The size of a wheat-cake.
He laid on it the curved sandal-wood saddle,
The size of a mountain pass.
He pulled tight the saddle-girth and strap,
Made by a skilled man,
And tightened the fine leather crupper,
Made from the spine skin of a good ox.
Young Baatar Belegt
Took his shield and armour,
Mounted his dear horse,
And rode off to do battle with
The ogre Khuiten Tomor Bust
For the good of his whole people.

He leaped along the edge
Of the blue silver sky,
And trotted along the horizon
Of the crusted golden earth.
Following the track
Of the malevolent ogre,
He tried to enter
The tall cast-iron fort
With its fence of thorny trees.
Though he went round it many times,
No door to enter it
Could be found.
Saying: 'What is this hut,
Without entry or exit,
Sticking up here for?',
He notched an arrow to his bow,
And shot at it till it collapsed,

And he made a gaping hole
Through which a loaded camel could pass.
Young Baatar Belegt,
Flourishing his battle axe,
Galloped inside
As fast as his horse could run.
He ran straight into
Tens and hundreds of thousands of troops,
Protected with shields and armour,
Armed with battle-axes,
And dressed in hard iron,
Unyielding to the sword.
Young Belegt Baatar
Hewed to the right
And cut down most of them.
He hewed to the left
And cut them down by hundreds and thousands.
Those who attacked him
He utterly destroyed,
And he rushed at full speed
Into the black ogre's palace,
And the cruel ogre came to meet him,
With all his weapons ready.
Then the two of them wrestled,
And struggled for seven and eight days.
He suffused with blood the blue-striped face
Of the ogre Khuiten Tomor Bust,
And made his brown-striped tongue hang down.
He brandished his iron-red sword,
With which he took without tiring
The heads of ten thousand enemies,
And as he was going to cut off his head,
The ogre Khuiten Tomor Bust
Kowtowed at the soles of his feet,
Bobbed up and down like a bustard,
Bowed his head like a crane,
Bent his fat knee,
Hung his egg-head,
And cried thus

To young Belegt Baatar:
'Oh Zong Belegt Baatar,
Please let me go.
If you spare my life,
No thicker than a thread,
I will be a slave
At your threshold.
I will be the lengthening-piece
Of your short horse-catching-pole.
I will be a halter
For your tame horses,
I will be a hobble
For your wild horses.
Rule the peoples I own!
Take my women and girls!
Only leave my body
Alive in this epoch.'

Then Baatar Belegt's anger
Could not be restrained,
And for the last time he spoke
To the haughty ogre:
'Having looked at my father's divination-books,
I must kill you.
Having looked at my mother's divination books,
I cannot make it up with you.
Even if the people wish it,
I cannot spare you.
Even if the old men and women wish it,
I must get rid of you forthwith.
I just cannot leave you alive,
You who are cruel beyond measure
In making the innocent suffer.'

He cut him into pieces,
And so as not to leave on the ground
The nasty dirty corpse
Of that filthy ogre,
He burned it in the fiery flame,

And scattered in the evening wind
The nasty ashes of the corpse.

And from that time forward,
On all the suffering lands
Of the ogre Khuiten Tomor Bust,
There fell a pure rain
Which watered the thirsty land,
Revived the withered trees,
And decked the ground and earth.
The mountain-forests grew green,
And the cuckoo sang.
The sufferings of men were relieved,
And the foot of the steed was eased.

The peoples who had been conquered
By that aggressive black ogre
Found their happiness,
And rejoiced at coming into peace.
Happily they praised
Young Belegt Baatar.
They came to meet him, offering
A great scarf of rejoicing.
Having suppressed the common enemy,
And brought happiness to the world,
Young Zong Belegt Baatar,
Who always discovered what was right,
Cheered his family and tribe,
Spread abroad his fame,
And for the sake of great deeds afar
He drank his kumis and wine,
Ate his pure food,
And lived happily ever after.

Blood Marksman and Kureldei the Marksman

This Tatar poem was recorded in the nineteenth century from the Turkic-speaking Tatars inhabiting the steppes and valleys of the Upper Yenisei and Sayan Mountains in south-eastern Siberia. At this period the Tatars in the area led a pastoral and nomadic life, roaming through the undulating steppes of rich grassland and gold-dust laden rivers with their small, tough horses.

The narrative poems of this group of Tatars have attained a degree of fame among students of oral literature. H. M. and N. K. Chadwick write in their massive study of *The Growth of Literature*:[1]

The literary technique of the poems has attained to a remarkably high level . . . Their narratives are the most complicated, and their structure the most ambitious which we have found outside Sanskrit literature, to which in this respect they bear some resemblance. The scene shifts constantly, and numerous characters are swept into the course of the narrative, each bearing a fresh set of complicated circumstances in his train. The handling of the material is astonishingly competent, and the poet never fails to resolve his discords, every villain being duly punished in his own turn, every hero provided with a wife, or refurnished with his own lost possessions before the end is reached . . . They are, in a sense, stories of adventure; but we are often in doubt as to whether these adventures are actual physical realities, or whether they are merely spiritual or intellectual adventures – adventures of the mind.[2]

The poems were sung at night round the fire to an audience of hunters and herdsmen. One eye-witness described the scene:

1. H. M. and N. K. Chadwick, *The Growth of Literature*, 3 vols., Cambridge, 1932–40.
   2. ibid., vol. 3, pp. 89–90.

When the hunters, weary with the chase, sit covered in their furs round the fire, and have just refreshed themselves at their meal, and are rejoicing in the warmth of the fire, the singer takes his instrument in his hand and begins in a deep guttural voice the monotonous melody of a heroic lay. The dark night which envelops the whole scene, the magic of the firelight, the roar of the storm which howls around the hut, and accompanies the gutteral tones of the singer, all these form the necessary framework for the highly coloured shifting pictures of the songs.[3]

The basic themes of the poems were traditional, but each singer could embroider and interpret the stock themes in a way that suited his individual inspiration or the mood and interests of his audience. Thus no two performances were ever exactly alike. However, there were certain conventions which the singer was expected to follow, including the mode of delivery, the setting and atmosphere, and the use of special personal names almost all of which had concrete meanings – like the men's names Ag Ai (White Moon) or Kan Mirgan (Blood Marksman).

This translation is based on German and Russian translations made from the original Turkic in the nineteenth century. Norman Cohn, the translator, writes that they 'have reached their English form by a roundabout route. Their characteristic details have nevertheless remained untouched. It has been my chief aim that their emotional tone, their unique "atmosphere", should also be faithfully preserved.' This claim has been borne out by Turkic scholars who have examined his versions, and the power and style of his translations have been compared by Arthur Waley to the celebrated translation of Indian poetry by William Archer (in *The Blue Grove*) and of Verrier Elwin, the translator of Gond poetry.

The poem 'Blood Marksman and Kureldei the Marksman' is reprinted here in its entirety.

3. Radlov, quoted in Chadwick, op. cit., vol. 3, p. 177.

He lives in the outer land
drinks from the outer waters
at the edge of the white sea
he has built his *yurta*.[4]
All the *yurtas* shine with whiteness
the herds are like white nits in the vast spaces of the steppe.
Though the *yurta* overflows with his belongings
Kan Mirgan, the lord of all the land,
is childless:
Kan Areg, his dear wife,
has borne no heir.
A blood-red horse stands tethered to the golden post
before his *yurta*.

A golden arrow flies from the highest sky
down to the earth.
It strikes the golden post.

Kan Mirgan takes the golden arrow in his hand
he plucks it from the post.
On the arrow's base nine gods have stamped their sign.
Kan Mirgan knows the sign
reads what is carved upon the arrow:
'Tomorrow morning you must come to us.'

Kan Mirgan snaps the arrow
throws the pieces to the flames.
He cries aloud:
'I owe nothing to the gods
I have nothing here to give them!'

The warrior lies down upon his golden bed
Kan Mirgan sleeps quietly that night.
When the day breaks
when the sun rises through the blue-gleaming morning
like a glowing coal
the hoofs of a warrior's stallion
and the snorts from a stallion's nostrils
sound through all the land.

4. Nomad tent.

On the golden mountain-crest there came to birth
a warrior's stallion.
There Alten Kus was born
the greatest of all warriors:
he is a poplar with no branches
he is a camel with no hump.
Alten Kus rides on his stallion
the warrior comes to fight with Kan Mirgan.
From far off he cries:
'Is the blood-red stallion on its tether?
Is Kan Mirgan at home?'

At the sound of his voice stones on the ground are shattered
the sea-flood rises
mountains fall apart.
Kan Mirgan comes out from his *yurta*.
Running he puts a bridle on his stallion
binds a ninefold girth about its belly
takes reins of ninefold strength.
The warrior mounts his blood-red stallion
he gallops to the mountain-crest.

On the golden mountain-crest stands the greatest of all warriors.
He greets the warrior Kan Mirgan:
'Are you in good health and strength
Kan Mirgan, you valiant warrior?'
The warriors seize each other round the body
drag one another from the stallions
they wrestle limb to limb.
They wrestle nine days long and do not rest
fight on for seven days.
At the end of seven days
Kan Mirgan lifts the warrior off his feet
and throws him down.
He cuts the backbone in two pieces
the warrior's soul must leave his flesh.

The warrior's white-blue stallion gallops up the sky.
Kan Mirgan turns back
to the white *yurta* on the hill of gold.

He dismounts from his stallion
binds it to the golden post.
The warrior goes inside the *yurta*
sits down on his golden couch.
Kan Areg, his dear wife,
sets food upon the table of pure gold.
Kan Mirgan takes food
the warrior eats his fill.
He who was lean can grow fat now.

Kan Areg speaks to her husband:
'Kan Mirgan, my chosen one,
why do you struggle with the gods
why fight the gods who live up in the sky?
Kan Mirgan, greatest of warriors,
why do you fight against the gods?
Your wife has been with child six months.
In the ninth month I will feel great pain
and in the tenth month bear the child.
The nine Kudais[5] are even now
forging nine stallions to a single horse
making a brown white-muzzled stallion
giving the stallion piebald legs.
Even now the nine Kudais are forging
nine strong warriors to a single warrior
named Buidalei Mirgan.
Tomorrow morning they will send him here to fight you.
Kan Mirgan
what is there you can do?'

When Kan Mirgan stretches all his limbs
he is a boulder
when he stands upright
he towers like a mighty rock.
He is a poplar with no branches
he is a camel with no hump.

---

5. Kudai (literally 'The strong one') signifies God or the gods, sometimes pictured as singular, but also often as sevenfold or (as here) ninefold.

He lies down on his golden couch.
When he snores
the noise from the warrior's nostrils roars through all the sky.

Kan Mirgan sleeps quietly that night.
Day breaks blue-gleaming
the sun is like a glowing coal.

The day shines yellow and the pure sun soars across the sky.
The hoofs of a warrior's stallion
and the snorts from a stallion's nostrils
sound from beyond the hills.
The warrior's stallion stands on the high crest of the mountain
the horse sinks through the black soil to its knees.
At the sound of the warrior's voice
mountains fall asunder
the sea-flood rises
all the earth is shaken
the high peaks bow down to the ground.
At that sound the light of day is darkened
from the ceiling of the sky the Seven Stars fall crashing to the
    earth.

The warrior cries:
'Is the blood-red stallion on its tether?
Is Kan Mirgan in readiness?'

Kan Mirgan bounds out from his *yurta*.
Running he puts the bridle on the blood-red horse
flings a great saddle on the stallion's back
binds a ninefold girth about its belly
takes reins of ninefold strength.
The warrior mounts his blood-red stallion
he rides up to the golden peak.

The brown white-muzzled stallion with four piebald legs
gallops towards him.
Buidalei Mirgan gives greetings.
Above their horses' heads
the warriors thrust at one another with their spears
but the spears will not go in.

They try to wound each other with their swords
the sharp swords will not cut.
The warriors seize each other round the body
drag one another from the stallions
bellow like great bulls
they bend, crush, drag one another
neighing like wild foals.
They wrestle nine days long and do not rest
fight on for seven days.

Kan Mirgan begins to weaken
the warrior staggers on his feet
props himself up with both his hands.
Buidalei lifts him off his feet
hurls him against the black soil's face.
He cuts the backbone in six pieces
and stamps it underfoot.
The blood-red stallion runs to Kan Mirgan's *uluss*
runs to the *yurta* of his master
gallops to the fair Kan Areg.

Kan Areg's eyes are shining,
she has borne two children, boy and girl.
The blood-red stallion calls to the woman
calls in a man's voice, crying:
'Let me have the boy and girl!'
The stallion takes the children in its nostrils
it gallops far away.
The moon is darkened
thick fog sweeps across the steppe
no eye can see ahead.
The light hoofs beating the black earth make no sound
the sky is windless.
The stallion runs upon its way.

Buidalei Mirgan runs down to Kan Mirgan's *uluss*.
He goes inside the white *yurta*
the warrior shouts so loud
that Kan Areg falls upon the ground
the woman weeps for fear.

The warrior cries:
'Where have you hidden the two children?
Bring out the boy and girl!'

Kan Areg answers:
'When I was young I bore no children
how shall I bear them now that I am old?
Youth left me barren
and shall old age make me a mother?'

Buidalei takes Kan Areg by her plaits
drags the woman from the *yurta*.
The warrior flogs her with his plaited whip
till the tongue is dumb behind the forty teeth
till her soul must leave her flesh.

Buidalei throws the body from him.
He mounts his horse
beats the white-muzzled stallion with his whip
till strips from its flanks fly on the steppe
he flogs the horse
till the whip strikes on bare bones.
He pulls on the bit so hard
that the horse's mouth is wrenched back to its ears.

Buidalei follows the blood-red stallion on from peak to peak.
The black earth shudders
each mountain-crest bows down.
The warrior follows up the horse.

The blood-red stallion gallops on.
Only its bones are left
the flesh has long since fallen from its limbs
the red flesh is all gone
the horse is nothing but dry bones.
The stallion cries in a man's voice
laments in the words of men:
'If I could find a warrior
full of pity for the weak
who would help us
who would take these children in his care!'

The horse has already run all ways
runs on the border of the sky.

Buidalei on his brown white-muzzled stallion
follows up the horse.

There is a warrior
Ai Mirgan of the white-blue stallion
whom all men praise.

The blood-red stallion
comes to Ai Mirgan.
It cries in a man's voice
laments in the words of men
the horse forms these words with its tongue:
'Warrior
I have come to you
because men say that you are full of pity.
I have come
that you may take these orphans in your care.
Great warrior Ai Mirgan
give us what help you can!'

Ai Mirgan replies:
'I have reached middle-age
my time of flowering strength is past.
Stallion
you must not put your trust in me!
If you gallop on
if you run through forty lands
you will find a mighty warrior.
He has just received his name
Kartaga Mirgan of the black white-muzzled horse.
Blood-red stallion
gallop on to him!'

The horse runs on.
The hardest tree has bark
but the blood-red stallion has no hide:
the driest tree has bark
but the blood-red stallion is stripped bare.

Its haunches are so sharp
a bucket could hang safely from them.
Sunken-eyed
the blood-red stallion gallops to that warrior's land.

Through forty lands Buidalei follows the running stallion.
He comes to Ai Mirgan.
He hurls himself upon the warrior
strikes at him with his sword
thrusts at the old man with his spear.

The voice of Buidalei is thunder
is a roaring lion.
Ai Mirgan drops down for fear
lies there weeping on the ground.
With a sword like flashing moonlight
Buidalei kills the warrior and his horse.
He gallops on
following the blood-red stallion in its flight.
The cracking of his whip
and the snorts from his stallion's nostrils
sound through all the land.

The blood-red stallion comes to Kartaga's homeland
gallops from the golden mountain down to the *uluss*.
The horse steps half inside the *yurta*.
It speaks in a man's voice to the warrior
laments in the words of men
forms these words with its tongue:
'Men say that you are full of pity.
Warrior
help this boy
give shelter to this girl!
Kartaga Mirgan
save the pure lives of these children!'

Kartaga Mirgan is seated on his couch of gold
fitting feathers to his arrows
at work with sixty, seventy feathers.
The warrior's tongue is dumb behind his forty teeth

behind his thirty teeth the breath is silent
his voice is still.
The warrior makes no sound.
His fair wife stands beside him
in her arms a beaker of fine gold.

The blood-red stallion comes there in the morning
stands there weeping till the evening.
When evening comes the horse runs on
through forty lands.

At the foot of a blue hill a blue sea surges.
At the blue hill's foot
at the blue sea's edge
lives the great blue bull.
The blood-red stallion gallops to the blue bull's home.

Buidalei comes to the homeland of Kartaga
sees the hoof-prints of the stallion near by the *uluss*.
The warrior follows up the blood-red horse.

In the back wall of his *yurta*
Kartaga Mirgan has bored himself a hole.
He sets an arrow to his bow
aims at the warrior's horse.
The arrow strikes the stallion on the neck
springs back as from a rock
it clangs as if it hit hard iron.

Buidalei Mirgan rides on
he follows up the blood-red horse.

The horse has run through forty lands
it comes to the blue hill.
It looks down from the hill-top
sees the blue bull standing by the sea.
The dewlap of that bull hangs on the ground
its mighty horns
thrust in six places through the dappled clouds
and touch the sky.
The blood-red stallion bows down before the bull.
The stallion begs:

'Save these children, boy and girl,
save the pure lives of these children!'

The blue bull answers:
'For all my strength
I cannot save these children's lives.'

The blood-red stallion gallops on through forty lands
to the Khan-maiden's land.
Sixty Khans pay tribute to this maid.
The stallion gallops to her home.

Buidalei comes to the blue hill
sees the blue bull and rides against it.
The warrior hurls himself upon the bull
gripping it by the horns.
These two fight together
they wrestle nine days long and do not rest
fight on for seven days.
At the end of seven days
the warrior throws the bull upon the ground.
He rips the belly open
kills the bull.
Buidalei Mirgan rides on
the warrior follows up the blood-red horse.

With forty bounds
the blood-red stallion leaps across forty lands
comes to the Khan-maiden's land.
The horse steps half inside the *yurta*.
It speaks in a man's voice to the maiden
laments in the words of men
forms these words with its tongue:
'Save these children, boy and girl,
save the pure lives of these children!'

The Khan-maiden is lying on a couch of gold
she plays a harp with forty strings.

The maiden makes no sound
she gives no answer.
The blood-red stallion comes there in the morning

stands there waiting till the evening.
When evening comes it gallops on.

There is no land left to run through
the horse has galloped through all lands.
It cannot climb the mountains
they are far too high
and cannot plunge beneath the earth
the black soil is too hard.
From the stallion's eyes tears fall like drops of blood
the water from its nostrils is like hanging ice.

Beyond the forty lands lives Katai Mos of the red stallion
at his side Kezil Dyibak the Fair.
The blood-red stallion gallops to the warrior and his wife.
Buidalei follows close upon its tracks.
In forty mighty bounds
the horse has run across the forty lands.

The stallion cries to Katai Mos:
'Warrior
I have come to you
because men say that you are full of pity.
Save these children, boy and girl,
save the pure lives of these children!'

Katai Mos answers:
'Give both the children to Kezil Dyibak.
She is my wife
and she will take them in her care.'

The horse runs down from the high mountain
seeking Kezil Dyibak.
The woman runs to meet the stallion.
She takes the children in her arms
takes them with her to the *yurta*.
The woman feeds the boy and girl.

Buidalei rides on the brown white-muzzled stallion
comes to Katai Mos.
Above their horses' heads

the warriors thrust at one another with their spears
they slash with their sharp swords.
They seize each other round the body
drag one another from the stallions.
The warriors wrestle seven days
fight on nine days and do not rest.
Neither can throw the other
in the black soil's dust.

Look! the children on unsteady legs stand up
walk step by step.
The girl has plaits that hang down to her cheeks.
The five-year-old boy born of warrior stock
has himself grown strong.
He looks up to the mountain
sees the two warriors wrestling
runs to the mountain-crest.
The boy drags Katai Mos on one side
he hurls himself at Buidalei
himself begins to fight.
The warriors wrestle seven days
fight on for seven years
they wrestle limb to limb nine days
they fight nine years.
The strength of Buidalei Mirgan begins to fail.
The boy lifts the strong warrior off his feet
hurls him against the black soil's face.
He cuts the backbone in six pieces with his sword
till the soul must leave the flesh.
The boy cuts off the warrior's head.
He cries aloud:
'No warrior who comes to fight upon this ground
shall ever leave
if once he dismounts from his horse!'

The boy turns back to his home.
Katai Mos walks beside him as his father
they walk together down to the *uluss*.
They go inside the white *yurta*
sit down together on the couch of gold.

Hungry, they bring out food.
The warriors eat their fill.
They who were lean before can grow fat now.

Day breaks blue-gleaming
the sun is like a glowing coal.
The day shines yellow and the pure sun soars across the sky.
The son of Kan Mirgan
yearns to go back to the land where he was born.

Kan Mirgan's son cries aloud:
'To go there I must have a horse!'
There is no warrior's stallion for him.
He must wait
before he rides back to the lands and waters of his home.

Moons change
years goes by.
From a mountain-pass a fiery stallion runs up to the *yurta*
a black-brown stallion with a silver bridle
dragging its reins of twisted silk along the ground.
Arrows stick from the great quiver like a wooded hill.
All that a valiant warrior needs
is on the horse.
The mighty stallion runs to the golden post.

Kan Mirgan's son leaps out from the *yurta* –
the boy is nine years old –
he lays his hand upon the stallion's neck
leads it by the silken halter
binds it to the golden post.

Katai Mos gives a shout.
He calls together all his people
has all his herds brought in
orders a feast to be got ready.
He kills a whole herd of brown horses for this meal
for this great feast a whole grey herd is killed.
Katai Mos gives the boy a name.
The warrior cries:
'With Kan Mirgan for father

with Kan Areg as his mother
this boy's name shall be
Kureldei Mirgan of the black-brown silver-maned stallion
and his sister's name shall be
Kumus Areg.'
Kureldei, the warrior born, springs up from his seat.
He falls at the feet of Katai Mos.
Rising, he kisses the old man on his mouth.

Kureldei yearns to go back to the lands and waters of his home.
The good Kezil Dyibak goes inside her *yurta*.
The woman takes a robe with eagle wings
out of a golden coffer
places it in Kumus Areg's hands.
The girl drapes the garment round her body
fastens it firmly with nine knots.

The warrior Kureldei Mirgan mounts his black-brown horse.
In the robe with eagle-wings Kumus Areg flies across the air
the sky sounds with the beating of her wings.
The stallion runs across the steppe
the boy beats it with his whip across the flanks
pulls sharply on the bridle
till the corners of its mouth are slit.
The horse's hoofs are light
run lightly as a wild beast's paws.
The stallion flies ahead like an eagle with strong wings
covers a whole month's journey in one day
and in seven days a journey for a year.
The warrior must ride long
but I need little time to tell the tale.
Kumus Areg flies eagle-winged
along the sky.

The warrior comes to the lands and waters of his home.
He stands on the high mountain
looks down on all the level lands.
He sees the white sea flowing
sees the *yurta* where no warrior lives
all overgrown with wormwood
overrun with weeds.

The golden post still stands before the *yurta*.
Kureldei Mirgan rides down
he binds his stallion to the golden post.

Kumus Areg comes with him to the place.
Brother and sister have no bread
no food of any kind.
The warrior leaps upon his horse
rides into the mountains hunting.
In the rich grass six elks stand grazing.
The warrior draws his bow
lets fly an arrow
pierces the six elks through with that one shot.
He hangs three elks on either side of his great horse
then rides back home.
Out of the hides he builds himself a *yurta*
from the elks' meat the warrior carves a meal.

That night brother and sister sleep in peace.
When the day breaks
when the sun rises through the blue-gleaming morning
like a glowing coal
Kureldei Mirgan rides out to hunt wild beasts.
He rides up to the black mountain
looks round him on all sides.
The warrior sees a black rock standing in his path
a larch-tree growing from the rock.
Seven black warriors stand upon its crest.
On that black rock
stands One who is black from head to foot
whose liver is all black.
The warrior cannot tell
whether this Black One is a living man.
Kureldei Mirgan takes out a spade-shaped arrow
draws the bow-string back
till it has passed nine notches on the bow.
Standing he shoots
the arrow pierces that black form.
A door swings open in the rock.

From the black rock's heart endless herds stream out
and countless people.
Kureldei Mirgan looks on them all
the warrior sees his people and his herds.
He drives them to the lands and waters of his home.

The warrior builds himself a *yurta*
builds a store-room to the *yurta*
he makes the *yurta* large
the storeroom of great length.
He kills a whole herd of brown horses
for a great feast a whole grey herd is killed.

The people sit and feast.
All who were hungry eat their fill
those who were lean can grow fat now.
The warrior's people feast
till the cauldron's steam has no more savour for them.
They have so many clothes
that mended garments are not seen on any man.

No warrior dare
come shouting challenges to Kureldei Mirgan
no *aina*[6] would dare plague him with ill-health.
My way has brought me to this place.

He has gone his way.
The valiant warrior Kureldei Mirgan
still lives in his own land.

6. An evil spirit, inhabiting the lower layers of the earth.

The golden sea-otter

from *Kutune Shirka*

Wakarpa

The Ainu of the northern island of Japan are famous as a small and technologically backward culture in contrast to the developed civilization of Japan. The 'hairy' Ainu, as they have been called, have often been despised as a primitive and retarded group, and by now have largely died out or become assimilated with Japanese society. Their language is, it seems, unrelated to any other and the Ainu have thus for long presented a puzzle to ethnology.

They have, however, a rich tradition of oral literature, including stories, songs, ballads, and various kinds of longer narrative poem. Among these *Kutune Shirka*, 'the Ainu epic', is the longest and most celebrated. It was first recorded in the 1920s and consists of around 6,000 lines in all.

Kutune Shirka was intoned rather than sung, and was usually performed by a man (occasionally by an old woman). The reciter held a stick which he used to emphasize the double stress in each of the lines. The poem was recited either in connection with a religious ceremony or at some time of leisure – for instance while waiting for fish to bite at sea or around the fire at home on a winter night.

On the occasion when it was written down the reciter of *Kutune Shirka* was an old blind man named Wakarpa. He must in some sense then be regarded as the author of this version of the poem at least, though how far he was responsible for the overall plot and expression is unclear. He himself asserted that he had merely repeated the poem as he had heard it, but evidence on comparable situations elsewhere (Yugoslavia, for instance) suggests that this assertion does not preclude his having played some part in the composition of this particular version of the narrative.

The basic story of the poem, which is narrated in the first person, concerns someone who is brought up in a castle and then hears about a golden sea-otter. He emerges for the first time from his castle and catches the otter, to the anger of his brother. Later the people of Ishkar try to recover the otter through a number of battles in which they are unsuccessful.

The opening episodes of the poem are given here, in Arthur Waley's translation.

I

My foster-brother and foster-sister –
They it was who brought me up,
And so we lived.
In a castle magically built –
There I grew up.
There was a great pile of treasure
That rose like a cliff, and on top
Lay hand-guards in twos and threes,
Fit for the sword of a chieftain,
And when in twos and threes
Their tassels swayed,
There was a bright gleam on the wall,
So beautiful, so lovely!
In front of the treasure-stand,
On a seat of my own,
On my high seat I grew up.
And by it, to the left,
Was my white-wood bed, so marvellous
In the beauty of its shape.
Who was first reared in it
That it should have been made so lovely?
I did not know, but my thoughts
Were full of wonder.
And all this time
On my high seat I did nothing
But carve patterns upon treasures,
Figures upon sword-sheaths.
That was what I was bent on –
On that and nothing else.
Now it happened at this time
Some stray talk reached me
By roundabout ways

That at the mouth of the Ishkar
A golden sea-otter
Was diving for its food,
And that the Man of Ishkar
To near villages
Had sent news flying,
To far off villages
News had been brought,
And this was what it said:
To whoever can dive into the sea
And bring back the Golden Otter
I will give my sister,
And all the treasure that is mine
Tied up in one bundle
Shall go with her as her dowry!
And because it was so,
From near villages and far villages
The chieftains have come crowding
To the River-Mouth of Ishkar,
And there they had set up
A great row of booths.

It was news of this,
Some stray talk of it,
That reached my ears
And one day I heard my sister's voice –
The lovely ring of her voice,
And this was what she was saying:
'Come now, you heroes that I tend,
Be sure that you pay no heed
To tales such as this.
It is a thing that happened long ago,
And now at the ebb of time
Has happened again;
No more and no less.'
And while my sister spoke
She fretted and fidgeted,
Moving her legs this way and that.
All this troubled me

When I turned it over in my mind.
But still, I carved my treasures,
Graved patterns on my sword
And so, I passed my time.

II

There came a night
When I could not get to sleep,
The god that lives under beds
Prodded me from below;
The god that lives in the beams
Stared at me from above,
Prodded and stared so hard
That as I lay on my bed
I tossed this way and that.
Why was I like this?
I could not make it out.
My brother and sister on their pillows
Were snoring loud,
Snoring both together.
Suddenly, there on my bed,
I stretched myself, and at one bound
I was up on my feet.
I went to the treasure-pile,
I fumbled about in it
And pulled out a basket,
A basket finely lacquered,
The cords that bound it
One after another I untied;
I tilted off the cover.
I plunged my hand into the basket;
An embroidered coat,
A graven belt-sword,
A belt clasped with gold,
A little golden helmet –
All of them together
I tumbled out.
The embroidered coat

I thrust myself into,
The golden clasped belt
I wound about me.
The cords of the little helmet
I tied for myself,
So that it sat firm on my head.
The graven sword
I thrust through my belt.
And though I tell it of myself,
I looked splendid as a god,
Splendid as a great god
Returning in glory.
And there upon the mat,
Though I had never seen them,
I copied deeds of battle, deeds of war,
Spreading my shoulders, whirling round and round.
Then I went out at the door,
And saw what in all my life
Never once yet I had seen –
What it was like outside my home,
Outside the house where I was reared.
So this was our Castle!
Never could I have guessed
How beautiful it was.
The fencing done long ago
Standing so crooked;
The new fencing
So high and straight.
The old fencing like a black cloud,
The new fencing like a white cloud.
They stretched around the castle
Like a great mass of cloud –
So pleasant, so lovely!
The crossbars laid on top
Zigzagged as the fence ran.
The stakes below –
Were swallowed deep in the earth.
In the tie-holes below
Rats had made their nest.

In the tie-holes above
Little birds had made their nest;
Here and there, with spaces between,
The holes were patches of black.
And when the wind blew into them
There was a lovely music
Like the voices of small birds.
Across the hillside, across the shore
Many zigzag paths
Elbowed their way.
The marks of digging-sticks far off
Showed faintly black;
The marks of sickles far off
Showed faintly white.
The ways went pleasantly;
They were beautiful, they were lovely.

The way down to the shore,
The hollow of the way,
I followed down, when suddenly
Some god possessed me and from the ground I trod
A wind carried me high into the air;
High above the path to seaward.
And brought me to a harbour,
Close to a harbour on the shore.
And coming from the sea
A pleasant breeze blew on me and the face of the sea
Was wrinkled like a reed-mat.
And on it the sea-birds
Tucking their heads under their tails,
Bobbing up their heads from under their tails
Called to one another
With sweet voices across the sea.
Over long stretches of sand
I strode, and as I went
The god that possessed me
Thundered in the sky above,
And swiftly along the shore-way
Hurried me to the village of Ishkar,

Near to Ishkar he carried me.
And the castle of Ishkar,
How beautifully it was built!
And under the white foam of the waves
(What they had said was true)
The golden sea-otter
Suddenly, like the glint of a sword,
Flashed above the breakers of the sea.
And there in the shore-road,
In the middle of the wide road
Was a watch-tower marvellously built
With a ladder leading up to it.
Then in the castle
There was a noise and stir.
Suddenly as when light comes at dawn
A woman came out from the castle.
I thought she would surely be beautiful –
The woman of the story I had heard.
But she had straight hair,
Reddish hair cut short
Half way down her long chin.
With nothing beautiful about her
But the jewels she wore.
It was a hideous woman that came out
And climbed up the ladder,
And sat down in the high tower.
I saw that at the mouth of the Ishkar
Were many booths in a row.
From the first of them came a sound
And an Ainu came out;
But if indeed an Ainu,
More splendid than any I had known.
With a new moon and a full moon
His coat was blazoned,
And his hat with the same.
It was a fine man that came out of the booth.
He held his hands high
And towards the woman on the tower
Many times did homage.

The ugly woman
Laughed in scorn of him,
And thrust out her chin.
I had never seen him before
But who else could he be
Than the young Man of the East?

The golden sea-otter
Glinted like a sword;
Then the suck of the tide
Caught it and pulled it down.
Once to seaward
With outstretched hand
The young man pursued it;
Once to landward
With outstretched hand
The man made after it;
Then fell panting upon the rocks.
The Ugly Woman
Mocking at him
Wagged her long chin.
'How hateful she is!' I thought.
Then from a booth at the far end
A sound came
And one stepped out,
Who, though I had never seen him,
I knew to be from Repunshir,
The Man of the Far Island.
He too raised his hands
Towards the woman on the tower
And did homage many times.
The Ugly Woman
Once more turned her face
Towards the harbour, towards the shore
And saw the Man of Repunshir
Going after the golden otter.
Twice he chased it to seaward
With outstretched hand,
Twice to landward with outstretched hand;

Then fell panting upon the rocks.
'I was wrong about him,' I thought.
The Ugly woman
Mocking at him
Wagged her long chin.
Then from the booth that was in the middle
Of that long row of booths
Again there came a noise
And a man came out,
If man not god one could call him,
For he was clothed from head to foot
In chain of gold,
In magic armour of gold,
So cased and folded
That I wondered he could lift his sword.
But many times more marvellous
Than all his trappings
Was that hero's face.
He raised his hands
And towards the tower
Did homage many times.
And now once again
The golden sea-otter
Sank with the suck of the tide.
Three times to seaward
With outstretched hand
He followed after it.
Three times to landward
With outstretched hand
The man, if man he was,
Chased it before him,
So that I was lost in wonder.
But just as dawn broke
He too, the Man of the Little Island,
Was cast upon the shore.
'I was wrong about him,' I thought.
The golden sea-otter
Under the foam of the waves
Was sucked in by the tide,

And I in my turn
Plunged into the surf.
Out to the breakers of the open sea.
It slipped from my hand,
But nothing daunted
I dived again like a sea-bird
And with one foot trod upon it.
It looked and saw what I was,
And so far from fearing me
It came up and floated between my arms
Like a water-bird floating.
Then seizing it by the throat
Up into the sky
Like a bird that had grown arms
Up into the sky I soared,
Straight back towards my castle
Swiftly I sped.
And soon, just as it had been,
I saw my home,
The castle of Shinutapka
Standing like a tall bowl,
With the ground-mist half way up it,
Binding it round.
At the beauty of the castle
Great was my wonder.
I was near now; gently I pulled aside
The hanging door-flap.
My foster-brother,
My foster-sister
Were snoring loud and long.
All this had been in the night-time,
But now in the castle
Day had opened wide.
I threw down the golden otter
On top of the baskets and trays,
The vessels of sacrifice,
And on my high bed,
The bed made for me
I flung myself down.

Tip-of-the-Single-Feather

Velema

This poem forms one of the group of 'true songs' or 'epic chants' which are regarded as the most serious and sustained of the various categories of Fijian oral literature. These poems depict the heroic deeds of warriors and chiefs belonging to the legendary kingdom of Flight-of-the-Chiefs, from whom the present chiefs and their subjects believe themselves to be descended. The setting of the poems is a far-off, heroic, and marvellous world where miracles are commonplace, feats of strength and daring accomplished every day, and even the minutiae of verbal exchange and etiquette are imbued with an air of wonder and grandeur.

The composer of these poems is said to commune with the ancestors, for they not only grant him the powers of artistic composition, but inspire him directly with the words of his song. Many of these ancestors joined personally, it is held, in the battles of the ancient Flight-of-the-Chiefs, and they inspire the poet with the Truth.

Although the poems are felt to be the result of personal inspiration from the ancestors, the poet still composes according to accepted literary conventions. The poem must have particular rhythms and be chanted in a certain musical style. Rhyme occurs frequently and depends on the regular recurrence of the same two vowels at line ends (consonants are disregarded). In 'Tip-of-the-Single-Feather' the lines end consistently in *u-a* (-*ula*, -*uya*, -*uma*, -*ua*, etc.), a stylistic demand which underlies the frequent qualification of personal names with such attributes as *kula* (red or bloody), or *dua* (single or superlative) and helps to illuminate the name of the hero of the present poem (Tip-of-the-Single-Feather, *Vuso-ni-Lawe-Dua*). Repetition and parallelism within lines are also frequent – a feature reproduced in some cases in the translation – and help to create unity throughout the poem. As the translator sums it up, 'though the poet's ecstasy thus [through ancestral inspiration] determines the events of history, his ecstasy is shaped to a strict literary tradition: his father, uncle, or grandfather, whoever has been his mentor, has filled his head with themes suitable for epic songs, with lore about ancient Flight-of-the-Chiefs, with rhythms in archaic language, with metaphors once fresh, now trite through many generations, yet unquestionably marks of the composer's art'.

Each of these 'true poems' is composed for some particular occasion and is thus separate and complete in itself. Thus, though 'Tip-of-the-Single-Feather' shares its setting and style with other similar songs, it is an independent poem, not part of any wider epic cycle. It is translated in its entirety here.

The poem was recorded by the translator in the 1930s in the village of Namuavoivoi in Fiji. Velema, its composer, was a recognized seer and poet. Even as a child his serious yet excitable personality was recognized as a sign of his destiny, and he was chosen to succeed his mother's brother as seer. From him he learnt the techniques for communing with the ancestors: 'he learnt how it felt to speak with them and even let them use his tongue to speak'. At the time the poem here was recorded – one of several – Velema was an old man but still active as seer and poet.

Poems are still composed and performed in Namua-voivoi. Present-day composers no longer sing about the deeds of far-distant ancestors, however, but about the exploits of more recent heroes, in the Second World War and later.

Some of the narrative events may not be immediately clear to the reader and the translator's interpolated explanations following each episode are therefore included with the text, in square brackets.

The background of the story of Tip-of-the-Single-Feather is assumed to be already known to the audience. The initial setting is the village of Flight-of-the-Chiefs which is ruled over by The-Eldest, father of Tip-of-the-Single-Feather. Before the story opens, the warrior hero Curve-of-the-Whale-Tooth has asked The-Eldest, his kinsman, to help him in making a formal gift to the king of Rotuma. The poem opens with their preparations for departure.

The first line is supposed to be chanted by the ancestor who inspired the song.

During one of my sojourns at Flight-of-the-Chiefs –
The-Eldest is calling:
'I am calling Tip-of-the-Single-Feather
Calling him and Curve-of-the-Whale-Tooth.
Listen, Tip-of-the-Single-Feather:
Go bring forth the poplar mast
Which lies felled at the headland of Flight-of-the-Chiefs.'

And Tip-of-the-Single-Feather stands up[1]
And calls upon his age mates.
And they stand up, and they are two hundred.
And Curve-of-the-Whale-Tooth stands up
And calls upon his age mates,
And they number two hundred.
And they race through Flight-of-the-Chiefs.
And they climb to the mountain peak, The-White-Blossom.
And they climb onward to the headland of Flight-of-the-Chiefs
Where the poplar mast lies felled.
Now Tip-of-the-Single-Feather cries:
'Listen, Curve-of-the-Whale-Tooth:
Let yours be the top and mine the base.
And lift up the poplar mast.
Lift it to our shoulders that we may carry it walking upright.'

Now Tip-of-the-Single-Feather says:
'Let our age mates work between us.'
Trees are splintered as they step[2]
Descending from the headland at Flight-of-the-Chiefs.
And they rush past the peak at The-White-Blossom.
They race through Flight-of-the-Chiefs.
And the mast they cast down on the beach at the high water line
And now The-Eldest speaks forth:
'Listen, people of Flight-of-the-Chiefs, all of you:
Go and insert the poplar mast.
When it has been set in its place,

1. It is bad manners to stand in a chief's presence. Standing up thus signifies preparation for action.   2. An example of the gigantic strength of these ancient heroes.

Then let The-Greatest-Prow[3] be launched into the sea.
Thrust it outward so that it will ride the waves.'

[The Eldest instructs Curve-of-the-Whale-Tooth and
Tip-of-the-Single-Feather to bring a felled poplar from the forest
so that it may be used as a mast for the ship, The-Greatest-Prow.
When the poplar has been brought forth, The-Eldest commands
that it be set up in the ship and that the ship be launched.]

And now The-Eldest calls forth;
'All you of Flight-of-the-Chiefs, embark.'
Now the people of Flight-of-the-Chiefs are aboard.
And they heave the halyard.
And they sail upon the open sea.
They are sailing in the sea and one night passes.
They are sailing in the sea and a second night passes.
They are sailing in the sea and it has been one month.
They are sailing in the sea and it has been two months.[4]
Now The-Eldest calls forth:
'Where is Curve-of-the-Whale-Tooth?
Let him come and climb high to look out for land.'
Now Curve-of-the-Whale-Tooth stands up.
And he ascends the poplar mast.
I entered the hole in the masthead.[5]
And watching, I was perched there on the double canoe.
I cast my eyes downward.
And every place was water.
A hurricane was rising on the land.
It enwrapped the headlands at Flight-of-the-Chiefs.
It made the pines lash together
And uprooted the palms at Flight-of-the-Chiefs.
So I called to those below:
'*Isa*,[6] Sir The-Eldest:

3. The-Eldest's boat.   4. These four lines represent a
common device to indicate the passing of time; the audience are made to
live through the events with the heroes.   5. In these poems action is
frequently recounted in the first person (indicated by italics). The person
speaking is always the one most recently mentioned in the narrative –
here Curve-of-the-Whale-Tooth.   6. Conventional exclamation of sur-
prise or despair.

Here is a frightful thing.
A hurricane is rising on the land.
And now it descends to the open sea
And the coral limestone is scattered through the air.'
And now The-Eldest answers:
'This is the wind for our journey.'

[The people of Flight-of-the-Chiefs set out for Rotuma
but sailing is delayed because of uncertain wind. Finally The-
Eldest directs Curve-of-the-Whale-Tooth to climb the mast and
ascertain their whereabouts. Curve-of-the-Whale-Tooth sights an
approaching hurricane. In spite of its frightful violence The-Eldest
calmly decides to sail with it to Rotuma.]

And The-Eldest calls forth:
'Branch-of-the-Red-Nettle,[7] listen then:
Let yours be the mainsheet to control;
You are the true seaman at Flight-of-the-Chiefs.
Listen, Tip-of-the-Single-Feather:
Let yours be the tiller to guide.'
Now the teeth of the hurricane are close by;
Close indeed to crossing the bow.
Now the teeth of the hurricane strike
And the yard and the boom clash together.
But the sailing of the great ship is unconcerned.
A forked oven rises at the bow.
And the wake hums beneath the ship.
Now Tip-of-the-Single-Feather roars:
'The mainsheet, the mainsheet, Branch-of-Red-Nettle!
Indeed I do not mean to yaw.'
And one sail mat is submerged,
And the second sail mat is submerged,
And the third sail mat is submerged,
And the fourth sail mat is submerged.
'Indeed I do not mean to yaw!'
And the fifth sail mat is submerged,
And the sixth sail mat is submerged,
And the seventh sail mat is submerged,

7. One of Flight-of-the-Chiefs' warriors.

And the eighth sail mat is submerged,
And the ninth sail mat is submerged,
And the tenth sail mat is submerged,
And the bow plunges to the second depths
And it wedges into the stone of the ocean floor.
And the people of Flight-of-the-Chiefs flee aftwards,
And together they clamber upward to the stern.

[The-Eldest makes ready for the onslaught of the wind.
He places skilled sailors in key positions so that, when the hurricane
strikes, the well-controlled ship sails swiftly. But Branch-of-the-
Red-Nettle slackens his grip on the mainsheet so that the sail
swings outward and begins to drag in the water. Tip-of-the-Single-
Feather, who is controlling the tiller oar and who wants to take full
advantage of the wind, refuses to tack into the wind. He belabours
Branch-of-the-Red-Nettle, admonishing him to shorten the main-
sheet. But the sail drags more deeply into the water until the
forward point becomes submerged and drags the bow of the
ship to the bottom of the sea where it becomes lodged among the
rocks. Because of the ship's tremendous length the stern still pro-
trudes above water and the men of Flight-of-the-Chiefs find
temporary refuge upon it.]

There is no speaking; they are like mutes.
There they remain, and the land is sorrowfully distant.
And now The-Eldest calls forth:
'Where is Branch-of-the-Red-Nettle?
Let him dive down to our ship's stem.'
And Branch-of-the-Red-Nettle stands up,
And he goes to dive down to the stem of the ship.
I passed by one sail mat; I passed a second;
And I was in pain for want of breath.
Rising I appeared again before the ship's crew.
And now Branch-of-the-Red-Nettle speaks:
'*Isa!* Sir The-Eldest:
Really I did not reach the stem of the ship.'
There they remain, and the land is sorrowfully distant.
And now The-Eldest calls forth:
'Where is Sir Moonlight?[8]

8. A warrior of Flight-of-the-Chiefs.

Let him dive down to the ship's stem.'
And straightway Sir Moonlight dives.
I cast one behind me, and I cast two behind me;
Past three sail mats I dived down,
And I was in pain for want of breath.
Rising I appeared again before the ship's crew.
'And *Isa!* Sir The-Eldest:
Really I did not reach the stem of the ship.'
There they remain, and the land is sorrowfully distant.
And The-Eldest calls forth:
'Where is Fog-of-the-Path?[9]
Let him dive down to the ship's stem.'
And straightway Fog-of-the-Path dives down.
I cast one behind me, and I cast two behind me;
Past three sail mats I dived down,
And I was in pain for want of breath;
Rising I appeared again before the ship's crew.
'*Isa!* Sir The-Eldest:
Really I did not reach the stem of the ship.'
And now The-Eldest calls forth:
'Listen, all you of Flight-of-the-Chiefs;
I am about to uproot my words.[10]
Where is Tip-of-the-Single-Feather?
Let him dive down to the ship's stem.'
And Tip-of-the-Single-Feather stands up.
I prepared to dive down to the stem of the ship.
And now Tip-of-the-Single-Feather speaks:
'Listen, all you of Flight-of-the-Chiefs:
Take some food so that you will be strong,
That the dance at Rotuma will be lively.'[11]
And Tip-of-the-Single-Feather plunges headlong.
One I cast behind me; two I cast behind me;

9. Fog-of-the-Path had the power to create a fog to confuse the approaching enemy.   10. The-Eldest always prefaces a command to Tip-of-the-Single-Feather with this phrase which brings out that his words are of great significance: he is turning to Tip-of-the-Single-Feather, the one who never fails.   11. He is boasting – assuming he will be successful in saving them and reaching Rotuma.

Past three sail mats I dived down;
Past four sail mats I dived down;
Past five sail mats I dived down;
Past six sail mats I dived down;
Past seven sail mats I dived down;
Past eight sail mats I dived down;
Past nine sail mats I dived down;
Past ten sail mats I dived down;
And I was in pain for want of breath;
I but brushed my hands against the stem;
Rising I appeared again before the ship's crew.
And now Tip-of-the Single-Feather speaks:
'The-Eldest, listen then:
In the light of this day we shall die.
It is our custom to gather only on dry land;
Sometimes we fall by the spear, but some of us live on.
Now all of us are forever finished!'

[The people of Flight-of-the-Chiefs are stricken with terror. At length The-Eldest calls upon various members of the crew to attempt to extricate the stern of the ship. All fail until as a last resort Tip-of-the-Single-Feather is called. Bragging, he tells his comrades to prepare for the dance at Rotuma, but just as he reaches the entangled ship's stern his breath is exhausted and he must return again, chagrined before his comrades. Feeling that since he, Flight-of-the-Chiefs' strongman, has failed, the entire company is doomed, Tip-of-the-Single-Feather laments their unhappy fate.]

Now The-Eldest calls forth:
'Sir Kaboa-Who-Stings-Painfully-in-the-Waves,
Dive down to the stem of the ship.'
And this one draws forth his warclub smeared with ashes[12]
And he stands defiant before The-Eldest:
'The-Eldest, you listen then:
I do not know how to loose the stem;
I know only the work of the land!'

12. True ancestral weapons, like Sir Kaboa's, were cleansed with ashes after use in battle.

And now The-Eldest speaks:
'Listen, all you of Flight-of-the-Chiefs:
Prepare yourselves in your patterned barkcloths,
Design your faces with black paint,
It is a bad thing, death without colour.
Now let the muzzle loader be charged;
Now fire forth into the waves
To call Curve-of-the-Whale-Tooth.'[13]
And they fire forth into the waves,
And now Curve-of-the-Whale-Tooth looks down,
And now The-Eldest beckons.
And he beckons with both his arms.
And Curve-of-the-Whale-Tooth descends.
And now Curve-of-the-Whale-Tooth speaks:
'Why do you call me, The-Eldest?'
And now The-Eldest answers:
'Listen, Curve-of-the-Whale-Tooth:
Come, dive down to the stem of our ship.'
And now Curve-of-the-Whale-Tooth says:
'The-Eldest, listen then:
I refuse to dive down to the ship's stem
Even though all on The-Greatest-Prow may die.'
And The-Eldest bursts forth in anger:
'I forbid you to speak, be dumb!
It is I who lay down your laws.'
And now The-Eldest speaks:
'It was because of you, Curve-of-the-Whale-Tooth,
That my canoe was launched.'
And Curve-of-the-Whale-Tooth stands up.
My patterned barkcloth, I drew it forth,
Lightning is at both its ends;
And at its centre is the face of the day.[14]
And the bracelets of striped conch shell, he dons both of them.
And now Curve-of-the-Whale-Tooth dives down.
I cast one behind me; I cast two behind me;

13. Curve-of-the-Whale-Tooth was so far away, on the mast, that he did not realize the danger and had to be signalled to by a gunshot. 14. The sun.

Past three sail mats I dived down;
Past four sail mats I dived down;
Past five sail mats I dived down;
Past six sail mats I dived down;
Past seven sail mats I dived down;
Past eight sail mats I dived down;
Past nine sail mats I dived down;
Past ten sail mats I dived down;
There at the ship's bow I squatted cross-legged.
Then I loosed the stem.
He shoulders the stem of The-Greatest-Prow.
Slowly it comes floating upward.
And The-Greatest-Prow is a floating thing.

[Now that Tip-of-the-Single-Feather has failed, no one else dares attempt. When The-Eldest commands Sir Kaboa to dive, open mutiny is imminent. The-Eldest suggests that they dress in ceremonial regalia which is pleasing to their Ancestors. Now Curve-of-the-Whale-Tooth, who has been standing watch on the top of the mast, is summoned with a cannon shot. At first he refuses to attempt where Tip-of-the-Single-Feather has failed. But he is persuaded that, since the journey is primarily his concern, it is his obligation to resolve the difficulties which have fallen upon the men of Flight-of-the-Chiefs. He dresses himself in a manner pleasing to his Ancestors and succeeds in bringing the ship's bow safely to the surface.]

And now The-Eldest calls forth:
'Listen, all you of Flight-of-the-Chiefs:
Let Curve-of-the-Whale-Tooth pull out the bowsprit;
Let the people of Flight-of-the-Chiefs heave the halyard;
Let Tip-of-the-Single-Feather pay out the mast stays.'
And Curve-of-the-Whale-Tooth chants:
'Lift up the stem of The-Greatest-Prow,
And place it on my shoulder; let it be carried upwards.'
And he inserts the bowsprit in his girdle,
And he walks leisurely aftwards with both arms swinging.[15]

15. A mark of his boasting – swinging arms while walking is a prerogative of chiefs.

And the people of Flight-of-the-Chiefs haul, leaning on the
    halyard.
And Tip-of-the-Single-Feather pays out the mast stays,
But he decides to break firewood for kindling:[16]
'I'll not pay out the stays; I'll tie them fast.'
And Curve-of-the-Whale-Tooth is short of his goal.
And they tug in different directions, those two.
Tip-of-the-Single-Feather is pulling to death,
Curve-of-the-Whale-Tooth is pulling to death,
And his girdle of white horse-tail breaks,
And now his barkcloth tears to shreds.
And the poplar mast is broken in two.
Now Curve-of-the-Whale-Tooth charges forth,
And he lunges to the region below deck and lies down and snores.
And now The-Eldest roars forth in anger:
'For what do you wait, you people of Flight-of-the-Chiefs?
I will kill whoever shirks his duty!'
And now The-Eldest speaks:
'Listen, Tip-of-the-Single-Feather:
I announce your penalty,
You shall scull the ship so that we can reach Rotuma today!'
And Tip-of-the-Single-Feather stands up.
I brought forth one sculling oar.
'*Lean once upon the oar; lean twice upon the oar.*'[17]
It broke on the third down stroke.
I plied ten sculling oars together.
'*Lean once upon the oar; lean twice upon the oar.*'
And the passage of the boat was swift
So that we anchored at Rotuma before the sunset.
And now The-Eldest calls forth:
'Listen Tip-of-the-Single-Feather:
Again I announce your penalty.
Carry forth the anchor of the double canoe.'
And Tip-of-the-Single-Feather stands up.

16. An irrelevant act which, because it is the impulsive and
arrogant act of a hero (he can no longer bear to look at Curve-of-the-
Whale-Tooth's triumph), is admired in the poem.   17. Work chant by
Tip-of-the-Single-Feather as he sculls.

And he picks up the anchor of the double canoe.
And with running leaps he wades the shallows at Rotuma.

[They prepare to tack. Curve-of-the-Whale-Tooth performs his task with such arrogance that Tip-of-the-Single-Feather refuses to cooperate. Their conflict brings about the breaking of the mast. Curve-of-the-Whale-Tooth, who is the entrepreneur of the expedition, unable to cope with this new discouragement retreats below the deck and feigns sleep. The-Eldest penalizes Tip-of-the-Single-Feather, orders him to scull the ship to Rotuma. As a further penalty Tip-of-the-Single-Feather is instructed to set the anchor.]

I glanced upwards at the shore.
And King Rotuma was washing his hands and face, stooping there.
I cast down the anchor of the double canoe.
I charged upon King Rotuma.
Upwards I lifted The-Provinces-Bow-Down,[18]
Poised it there, then I chopped with it as though he were firewood.
There King Rotuma was smashed into bits.
I heaped them together there on the beach at the high-water line.
And I shouldered the legs of King Rotuma.
Then I carried them back to the double canoe.
And now Tip-of-the-Single-Feather speaks:
'The-Eldest, listen then:
I have cut some cleats for the poplar mast
So that it may be cleated together, be strong.'
And The-Eldest roars forth:
'For what has King Rotuma been killed!'
And The-Eldest stands up.
I took up ten whale teeth.
I went to bow down before Curve-of-the-Whale-Tooth.
And I descended below the deck of the double canoe.
And now The-Eldest speaks:
'Listen, Curve-of-the-Whale-Tooth:
King Rotuma lies dead,
Struck down by Tip-of-the-Single-Feather.'

18. The name of Tip-of-the-Single-Feather's battle axe.

And Curve-of-the-Whale-Tooth weeps forth.[19]
And now Curve-of-the-Whale-Tooth speaks:
'The-Eldest, listen then:
For what has King Rotuma been killed!
Indeed I have sweated for you and your people;
You speak in the night; I go out in the rain.[20]
I cut the timbers for your double canoe;
Its passenger was my short white pig.
The-Eldest, listen then:
My gift presentation, it shall not be.
Disembark, all of you; let Rotuma be destroyed!'[21]
And The-Eldest stands up.
And now The-Eldest speaks:
'Listen, all you of Flight-of-the-Chiefs:
Our gift presentation shall not occur.
Disembark, all of you; let Rotuma be destroyed!'
And now the people of Flight-of-the-Chiefs stand up.
And they leap through the shallows at Rotuma,
And on the beach at the high water line they poise their clubs.
And the people of Rotuma poise their clubs.
And the people of Flight-of-the-Chiefs ascend the shore.
And the cock is drawn back
And Red-Whale-Tooth[22] fires the cannon,
A hundred are killed and two are wounded.
And now The-Eldest calls forth
That the people of Flight-of-the-Chiefs fall back,
That they retreat through the shallows at Rotuma.
And the cock is drawn back
And Red-Whale-Tooth fires the cannon;
A hundred are killed and two are wounded.
Now The-Eldest is angry there:

19. It is obligatory to weep when informed of a relative's death, whatever one's personal attitude.   20. A complaint about the mismanagement of the expedition, in Curve-of-the-Whale-Tooth's view, after all his personal sacrifices: only the direst necessity would force someone to work at night or in the rain.   21. Rotuma must be destroyed at once for fear of its people attacking Flight-of-the-Chiefs to avenge King Rotuma.   22. A man of Rotuma.

'Can it be that the village at Rotuma is inhabited!'
And now The-Eldest calls forth:
'Where is Branch-of-the-Red-Nettle?
Let him go ashore to reconnoitre.'

[While Tip-of-the-Single-Feather is carrying the anchor to the shore, he sees King Rotuma stooping to wash himself. To vent his jealousy against Curve-of-the-Whale-Tooth he kills King Rotuma and presents the dead man's legs to The-Eldest as cleats to mend the broken mast. Such defilement of the corpse is a deliberate insult to Curve-of-the-Whale-Tooth. No one believes that the mast will actually be mended. The-Eldest is dismayed before Tip-of-the-Single-Feather's arrogance. Bearing a gift of whale teeth, he goes to humiliate himself and beg forgiveness of Curve-of-the-Whale-Tooth who, when he has expressed his grief at the death of a kinsman, realizes that there is no longer a purpose in carrying through his gift presentation; he suggests the destruction of Rotuma to avoid the retributive anger of its inhabitants. The-Eldest orders the attack and the men of Flight-of-the-Chiefs hasten to the beach to present arms to the men of Rotuma. But Red-Whale-Tooth mans the cannon at Rotuma and the men of Flight-of-the-Chiefs are forced to withdraw. The-Eldest chides them with cowardice and sends Branch-of-the-Red-Nettle ashore to engage Rotuma champions in single combat.]

And Branch-of-the-Red-Nettle stands up.
I waded through the shallows at Rotuma.
And now in his thatched house
Wind-of-the-Open-Sea stands up.
And he takes up The-Stingray-Standing-Alone.[23]
And I came quickly outside.
And Branch-of-the-Red-Nettle gives him recognition:
'Look here, King Rotuma.'[24]
And now Wind-of-the-Open-Sea answers:
'My father was struck down yesterday
I think that I shall follow after him.'[25]

23. The name of Wind-of-the-Open-Sea's spear.
24. Wind-of-the-Open-Sea is now king of Rotuma, succeeding his murdered father.   25. Probably implying that he is not afraid of death.

And now Branch-of-the-Red-Nettle speaks:
'Listen, Wind-of-the-Open-Sea:
My name is Branch-of-the-Red-Nettle,
The poisonous nettle of the people at Flight-of-the-Chiefs.'
And now Wind-of-the-Open-Sea answers:
'The nettle, poisonous there at Flight-of-the-Chiefs,
Is a harmless nettle today at Rotuma.'
And he takes up The-Stingray-Standing-Alone.
Then I thrust at Branch-of-the-Red-Nettle.
And the spear pierces him above the breast.
It pins him grounded among the coral rocks.
Bending my head I braced my foot and pulled it loose.
And the people of Flight-of-the-Chiefs drag his corpse through
    the shallows,
And together they clamber into their double canoe.
And The-Eldest calls forth:
'Where is Sir Moonlight?
Let him go to reconnoitre on the shore.'
And Sir Moonlight stands up.
He leaps through the shallows at Rotuma.
And now in his thatched house
Wind-of-the-Open-Sea stands up.
He takes up The-Stingray-Standing-Alone.
Quickly I came outside.
He meets with Sir Moonlight.
And Sir Moonlight gives greeting:
'Look here, King Rotuma.'
And now Wind-of-the-Open-Sea answers:
'My father was struck down yesterday.
I think that I shall follow after him.'
And now Sir Moonlight speaks:
'My name is Sir Moonlight.
The great moon of the people at Flight-of-the-Chiefs.'
And now Wind-of-the-Open-Sea answers:
'The great moon only at Flight-of-the-Chiefs;
It is dark today at Rotuma.'
And he takes up The-Stingray-Standing-Alone.
Then I thrust at Sir Moonlight.
And the spear pierces him above the breast.

It pins him grounded among the coral rocks.
Bending my head I braced my foot and pulled it loose.
And the people of Flight-of-the-Chiefs drag his corpse through
    the shallows.
And together they clamber into their double canoe.
And The-Eldest calls forth:
'Where is Fog-of-the-Path?
Let him go to reconnoitre on the shore.'
Fog-of-the-Path stands up.
He leaps through the shallows at Rotuma.
And now in his thatched house
Wind-of-the-Open-Sea stands up.
And he meets with Fog-of-the-Path.
Fog-of-the-Path gives greeting:
'Look here, King Rotuma.'
And now Wind-of-the-Open-Sea answers:
'Yesterday my father was struck down.
And I think I shall follow after him.'
Now Fog-of-the-Path speaks:
'My name is Fog-of-the-Path,
The mist of the people at Flight-of-the-Chiefs.'
And now Wind-of-the-Open-Sea answers:
'A fog only at Flight-of-the-Chiefs;
Today at Rotuma it is sunny.'
And he takes up The-Stingray-Standing-Alone.
Then I thrust forth at Fog-of-the-Path.
And the spear pierces him above the breast.
It pins him grounded among the coral rocks.
Bending my head I braced my foot and pulled it loose.
And the people of Flight-of-the-Chiefs drag his corpse through
    the shallows.
There is no speaking; they are like mutes.
There they remain and their land is far distant.
Now The-Eldest calls forth:
'Listen, all you of Flight-of-the-Chiefs:
I am about to uproot my words.
Where is Tip-of-the-Single-Feather?
Let him, finally, go to reconnoitre on the shore.'
And Tip-of-the-Single-Feather stands up.

And he unbinds The-Provinces-Bow-Down.
And he leaps through the shallows at Rotuma.
And Tip-of-the-Single-Feather climbs upwards
And casts behind him the shore at Rotuma.
And he ascends to the mountain ridge at Rotuma.
Tip-of-the-Single-Feather uproots the forest.
And the crowns of its trees he kicks to pieces.
And the people of Rotuma retreat.
It is war in the manner of Flight-of-the-Chiefs.
And he lashes to the front and lashes to the back.
Also he lashes to both sides.
And the people of Rotuma are retreating.

[Branch-of-the-Red-Nettle meets Wind-of-the-Open-Sea, son of King Rotuma and is defeated by him. The-Eldest then sends other warriors to engage Wind-of-the-Open-Sea in combat, and they are defeated in turn. At length he calls upon Tip-of-the-Single-Feather who ascends the ridge behind the village and charges heroically down upon it driving back the entire army of Rotuma.]

And now in his thatched house
Wind-of-the-Open-Sea stands up.
He casts down The-Stingray-Standing-Alone.
Then I unbound The-Headland-of-Rotuma[26]
And I came quickly outside.
And Tip-of-the-Single-Feather races forth.
And Tip-of-the-Single-Feather gives greeting:
'Look forth, Wind-of-the-Open-Sea.'
And Wind-of-the-Open-Sea does not speak.
And Tip-of-the-Single-Feather gives greeting.
And Wind-of-the-Open-Sea does not speak.
And now their chests are pressed together.
And now Wind-of-the-Open-Sea speaks:
'Look forth, you Tip-of-the-Single-Feather.
Now we meet well matched, we two.
You are a chief's son at Flight-of-the-Chiefs
And I am a chief's son here at Rotuma.'

26. His battle axe.

And they present arms, those two.
Tip-of-the-Single-Feather poises his axe.
Wind-of-the-Open-Sea poises his axe.
And they strike forth, those two.
And Tip-of-the-Single-Feather misses aim.
And the man of Rotuma smites him.
And they posture defiantly, those two:
Each braces his foot against the other's.
Tip-of-the-Single-Feather raises his club.
Wind-of-the-Open-Sea raises his axe.
And they strike forth, those two.
Wind-of-the-Open-Sea misses aim,
And the man of Flight-of-the-Chiefs smites him.
And they posture defiantly, those two.
Now indeed it is a great battle that they are fighting.
Wind-of-the-Open-Sea is out of breath
And he flees upwards on the stone foundation of his house.
And Wind-of-the-Open-Sea breathes there.
I was looking out to the sea.
My glance struck upon a certain thing.
I knew what it was; I knew it suddenly.
Indeed it was our young men
Who had gone singing for barkcloth at Vuna.
Their Chief is Lemon-of-the-Sea.
And they anchor there at the rednettle tree.
And Lemon-of-the-Sea leaps forth.
And straightway he climbs thence to the shore.
And Lemon-of-the-Sea calls greeting:
'Look forth, Wind-of-the-Open-Sea.'
And Wind-of-the-Open-Sea weeps straightway.[27]
And now Wind-of-the-Open-Sea speaks:
'*Isa lei!*[28] Cousin, Lemon-of-the-Sea:
Yesterday your uncle was killed,
Struck down by Tip-of-the-Single-Feather.'
And they mourn together, those two.
And now Lemon-of-the-Sea speaks forth:

27. It is obligatory for the announcer of a death to weep.
28. A conventional mourning phrase.

'Listen, Wind-of-the-Open-Sea:
It is you who must remain resting
When we meet with Tip-of-the-Single-Feather.'
And Tip-of-the-Single-Feather charges.
And now Lemon-of-the-Sea stands up.
And he takes up his double-barrelled gun.
And both of its bullets are in place.
I held straight the double-barrelled gun.
I drew back its firing hammer.
And the double-barrelled gun is fired.
And one bullet pierces above the breast
And the other pierces the knee-cap.
And now Tip-of-the-Single-Feather's body blossoms.[29]
The Provinces-Bow-Down is cast to the ground.
He throws down The-Wind-of-the-Rain.[30]
I charged upon Lemon-of-the-Sea.
I fixed both of his arms.
Then I grasped Wind-of-the-Open-Sea.
I hurled them both upward to the second sky.
'This is your feast, Watcher-of-the-Land.'[31]
And they crash down at It-Repels-like-Fire.
And now Sir-Watcher-of-the-Land stands up.
I came quickly outside.
And now Watcher-of-the-Land speaks:
'Look forth, Lemon-of-the-Sea.'
Bending down I sucked him empty.
'Look forth, Wind-of-the-Open-Sea.'
Bending down I sucked him empty.
And now Watcher-of-the-Land speaks:
'My nephew, Tip-of-the-Single-Feather,
He always remembers me in every land.'

And the village at Rotuma is destroyed to emptiness.
And now the wild fowl flies upwards in the wild growth there.
And now The-Eldest speaks:

29. i.e. he manifests the physical signs of anger.   30. His
spear.   31. The ancestor at Flight-of-the-Chiefs, who must be given
constant offerings to secure his continued support. His house is It-Repels-
like-Fire.

'Now that the village at Rotuma is destroyed,
Let us return to Flight-of-the-Chiefs;
Go back so that Flight-of-the-Chiefs will be inhabited.'
Nabosulu
Nabusele[32]

       [Wind-of-the-Open-Sea prepares to meet Tip-of-the-Single-Feather. They charge upon each other and present arms defiantly. They fight until Wind-of-the-Open-Sea takes refuge on the foundation of his house. While he is resting there, he sees his cross-cousin, Lemon-of-the-Open-Sea, approaching with the young men of Rotuma. He announces the death of King Rotuma and he and Lemon-of-the-Sea weep ceremonially. When Tip-of-the-Single-Feather charges upon them, after this intermission in the battle, Lemon-of-the-Sea fires upon him and wounds him. Tip-of-the-Single-Feather is angered; instead of attacking them with weapons, which would imply that they were warriors worthy of respect in battle, he attacks them with his bare hands and hurls them through the air and they fall before the house of Watcher-of-the-Land in the village at The-Land's-Beginning. Watcher-of-the-Land devours them and commends Tip-of-the-Single-Feather for always remembering to make sacrificial offerings to him. The men of Flight-of-the-Chiefs continue the destruction of the village at Rotuma and finally return to Flight-of-the-Chiefs.]

---

32. The conventional coda for all 'true songs'.

Ballad of the Hidden Dragon

The *Ballad of the Hidden Dragon* is one of a group of story-tellers' ballads in medieval China in which sung verse alternates with spoken prose narrative. The particular form in which it is cast (*chu-kung-tiao*) became popular in the eleventh century AD.

The ballads were often delivered by professional reciters who had mastered the necessary arts of composition and musical and verbal performance. Story-telling in one form or another was popular among Chinese audiences, many of whom were illiterate. As the translators write: 'Thanks almost entirely to the story-teller the Chinese man in the street gained a surprisingly intimate knowledge of his own literature and history and was rapidly made aware of new ideas.' The *chu-kung-tiao* ballads were also often performed as semi-theatrical shows in entertainment houses and told by professionals who were also often prostitutes. It is perhaps not surprising therefore that love stories are preponderant in this type of ballad and that there is much dwelling on feminine charms and the passion of love.

Chu-kung-tiao literally means 'various modes'. The prime vehicle for advancing the story is prose, expressed in bare and straightforward language and contrasting with the colourful and expansive verse sections which elaborate the story by lyric description. These sung portions consist of a number of different tunes, following each other according to fixed musical rules. Tunes belonging to the same mode (*kung-tiao*) were grouped together into suites each making up a musical unit, for which different words were supplied by different story-tellers, and each ending in a coda. Each suite was also a single prosodic unit with the same rhyme in the prescribed positions throughout the whole suite. In the next suite both the musical mode and the rhyme had to change (unless the two were separated by a prose passage). The whole was delivered as a solo performance, with accompaniment by string instruments or percussion. The complex form of the *chu-kung-tiao* cannot be fully represented in translation (quite apart from the problem of lack of music), but the translators have tried to use a rhythmic language, which they hope 'will suggest a few of the

complicated and varied metric forms of the original. Our trans-
lated song sections are largely sprung rhythm in a stress tetra-
meter: many different kinds of metric feet are used but an attempt
has been made to keep most lines close to four stressed beats . . .
one of the most popular line lengths in *ch'u* metre is four beats . . .
We have used rhyme regularly in the 'codas' and occasionally
throughout the text simply to remind the reader that the original
is rhymed verse.'

Apart from the short epilogue where the story-teller
adds his final comment, the story is told in the third person.
However, the story-teller introduces a number of dialogues and
soliloquies which give an opportunity for conveying mood and
emotion and also help to create individual characters from types.

The *Ballad of the Hidden Dragon*, by an unknown
author, dates back to a text that was written down at the time of the
Chin Dynasty (AD 1115–1234). Out of an original total of twelve
chapters there remain only the first, second, part of the third, most
of the eleventh, and the whole final chapter. The story is about
Liu Chih-yuan, who eventually became emperor during the Later
Han Dynasty (947–50). But the story-teller is little concerned with
the actual historical personage and instead concentrates on the
early years and adventures of Liu Chih-yuan, in the period before
he became emperor – when he was still a 'Hidden Dragon', an
emperor not yet recognized. The first three chapters describe the
sufferings of his family, his father dead in battle and his widowed
mother fleeing from famine with her two small sons and later re-
marrying. Liu Chih-yuan leaves home, having quarrelled with his
half-brothers, and meets and marries a village girl, Li San-niang.
He is forced to leave her soon after his marriage, and marries as his
second wife the daughter of a military leader. After various ad-
ventures and a successful career as a soldier, he is finally reunited
with his first wife and with his own family.

The extracts here describe his early poverty-stricken
wanderings and his first meeting with San-niang, followed by the
final sections where, after an interval of many years, Liu Chih-
yuan is reunited with his family and San-niang is recognized as his
first wife.

. . .

Each day was like another,
On what day would his destined power show?
One morning, fortune will come
And then his fame will spread through China and barbarian lands.
But now he is the priceless jade from Ching-shan,
Still untouched by Pien Ho's hands.[1]
And just as the flood dragon can hide
In the shallow seep of a horse's hoofprint,
So his destiny awaits auspicious clouds and rainbow arcs.

He went his way lacking money,
So on the road he suffered trials and hunger.
While travelling he fixed his eyes [upon the distant view].
Suddenly saw a village and its fallow-land
Not three miles off.
His steps then seemed to make him fly.
Once there, he looked at all the farmsteads
With their fine fat fields.
Then coming nearer to the high road, he found a newly opened
        inn,
With its signpole thrust aslant above its picket fence . . .

. . . The next day, he said good-bye to the innkeeper and wandered
from one village to the next, drifting as would fallen flower petals
or poplar-cotton curls.

The Hidden Dragon, whose time had not yet come,
Passed the night in a wine-shop.
When the day was breaking, he bade good-bye to Ch'i-weng
To set out once again across the land.
But when he thought about his future
He felt more and more in doubt.
For after all where could he go?

Wending and winding was the road as he set out
And it was just the first of Spring.
Willow fluff dancing in the wind, falling petals flying in the air,
Orioles chasing butterflies winging slowly past.

1. A legendary connoisseur of jade.

Suddenly he is close to a village.
The elms and sophoras touch one another with their branches.
In the shadow of the trees he rested for a time.

You could only see scattered cow-sheds at the rear of the farmyard and simple houses facing south. Hemp was spread on the tender green grass and the *yeh-ku* shone amidst the moss. Tired Chi-yuan slept. In the sophora shadow he slept so deeply he knew nothing. From the compound an old man came, leaning upon a bamboo stick and, when he reached the trees, he saw beneath them the man sleeping on the ground.

Then came the old one out of the compound.
I suppose he was the most respected man in all his clan.
Most orderly his clothes and well made up:
In his hand he held a bamboo staff.
Into the fields he went
Away from the village for half a mile perhaps,
Where wind blew the grain in waves as far as the eye could see.

Suddenly, he is startled;
In the sophora shadow he sees a purple mist, a crimson glow,
Before his eyes a golden dragon plays with a priceless pearl.
And still the vision lingers and covers the Emperor,
Who lay sound asleep and snored like thunder.
While about his face shone all the auspices of kingship.

(Coda)
The old man, moved, sighed for what future would bring.
Within the hour, this homeless man would doubtless leave
Yet far in the future this Hidden Dragon would be king.

The old man said with a sigh: 'One day this man will certainly be honoured though I have not yet got what manner of honour it will be.' He waited for a while and the youth awoke. Whereupon the old one asked him his name and native place, for he hoped to make a friend of him. Chih-yuan answered him.

The old man inquired
And the Hidden Dragon could not refuse him.
He longed to speak of his hardships,
He brooded on his misfortunes once again –

A stream of tears flowed down his cheek.
Then he sobbed and finally
Clasped his hands and began to speak.
'I want to tell you my life story.
But I am so poor I wear only a hempen singlet,
Who will believe me if I speak of honoured ancestors?
Yet once our family fame and heritage were glorious.
For centuries my forebears served constantly at court.
My father died in the battle ranks
And when the end of T'ang had come
And chaos raised the frontier battle beacons,
My mother took my younger brother and me
And all of us left our native place.

Haggard and hungry – suffering, shivering,
How do men survive starvation and cold?
In Yang-p'an village we met a good man
Who asked my mother to be his wife.
She bore him two sons. But when they'd grown,
They proved worthless.
Chin-erh and Chao-erh are their names.
They lent their ears to gossip
And quarrelled with me angrily over what they heard.
Always, we were at each other's throats.
They mocked me for my surname was not theirs.
Should a full-grown man bear taunts from children?
Sore at heart I left my home,
And though I know not how, my legs
Have brought me to your compound.
Where you, good sir, have been so courteous.'

　　　　(Coda)
Once they lived in Ying-chou, in the district of Chin-ch'eng,
But savage wars and chaos stole their land away.
Now, even to speak his family name
Pains him deeply, pricks his shame.
Poor, homeless Liu Chih-yuan who begs his food each day.

　　　　When the old man heard his words, he asked him once
again: 'If you dislike being poor and without a family, I own many

fields in this village, but I have few labourers. Won't you work for me, so we may help each other for six months or a year?' Chih-yuan went with him and when they had entered the village, they asked one Wang, the scribe, to write them up a contract . . . Li's daughter was called San-niang and, when she burned incense that evening, she saw a golden snake several inches long in the moonlight which crawled towards the western chamber.

She was just a country maid,
Yet beautiful beyond compare.
Not Lo-fu, Hsi-shih, nor Ta-chi[2]
Had ever been as beautiful as she.
She was fifteen, just the age when girls begin to dress their hair
And she as yet was not betrothed.
Willow-leaf brows, skin of the peach, and a cherry mouth.
Her flesh was transparent jade, her waist slender
And she knew how to walk in her golden-lotus shoes.

Everything she wore fit handsomely
And her silk clothes were touched with golden threads.
Each evening it was her wont to burn
Incense to the bright, pale moon:
This night she was frightened.
For on the floor, in a shaft of golden light
She clearly saw a little snake, seven inches long,
Go straight to the western hall
The door of which was left ajar.

This lovely girl went swiftly to the room
Where on the wall a lamp was dimly winking.
With a golden pin she raised the wick
And brought the light up blazing bright.
On an earthen bed there lay a youth
Seven feet tall and fair of face.
His imperial body was awesome as a god's,
His eyes were closed and he soundly slept.
Never had San-niang witnessed such a thing.

Red glow and violet mist covered his body,
And the aura showed his good fortune was inexhaustible.

2. Three famous Chinese beauties.

The little snake wriggled in and out his nostrils.
San-niang was delighted:

'Once a soothsayer said that I'd know fame,
That I would become an Emperor's wife,
That I would be Empress and marry a noble man.
Surely this night bears out the prophet's words.
In these last days of the house of T'ang
Some cannot tell the Imperial Dragon from a common snake,
But an Emperor-to-be has found our compound good
So I must straightway pay him my respects.

      (Coda)
"Who cannot recognize a pearl remains poor."
If I reject the auspicious sign
Will Chao-yang palace[3] ever be mine?'

      Thereupon San-niang took the ornamented silver pin
from her hair and broke it in half. When the Hidden Dragon awoke,
with both hands she passed it to him. When he saw San-niang in
the light of her lamp, he was startled and said: 'I am a poor man
and grateful to your father who was kind to me. But I am a hired
hand on your farm, so leave here quickly, please. If your brothers
and their wives knew you were here I would surely be in trouble.'
San-niang replied with a smile: 'Sir, you need not be afraid, I come
a-purpose to make your acquaintance.'

Then the Hidden Dragon knew surprise,
Quickly he leaped from his earthen bed.
Politely he bowed and asked:
'What is the reason, Madam,
You come here deep in the night?
Please, leave the western chamber soon,
It were better for me if you did,
For if the old one knew of it
I would surely be in trouble.'

San-niang was unabashed.
'I came to present myself to the Emperor,' said she.

     3. Chao-yang Palace, literally Bright and Shining Palace,
traditionally belonged to the Empress.

'I look towards the time when he will live
In palaces and wander through royal parks.'
Then in a low voice she said to him:
'Sir, fear nothing.
The day I saw you come to our compound
I knew you were no mean or common man.
First, let us announce our betrothal
And then we'll wed.'
Then breaking her silver pin
She gave one half to Liu Chih-yuan.

      (Coda)
'Though we are not wed, let me share my pin with you.
When you are Emperor we'll live together as man and wife.
As Princess Yueh-ch'ang did with Hsu Te-yen,[4]
Let me pledge to you my life.'

      Liu Chih-yuan could not refuse the pin but other than
      this nothing passed between them . . .

      [San-niang and the Hidden Dragon are married, but
after their marriage the two are forced to separate.]

. . .

When yin and yang first parted to form Heaven and Earth
The separation was very hard,
But do not imagine it was more difficult
Than what this husband and wife did now.
Tonight they cannot bear to leave each other.
Let us exaggerate a little –
They were like Su Hsiao-ch'ing with her student Shuang Chien
      in the post house when she saw him to the River Ch'ien-
      t'ang.[5]

      4. Princess Yueh-ch'ang and Hsu Te-yen broke a bronze
mirror in two as pledge of their love. They were separated for long but
finally, by the help of the two mirror halves, were reunited and lived in
love till death.　　5. This refers to the legendary love of a sing-song girl
and a student, who were forced to part but were finally reunited and
married.

They were as Hsu, the *tu-wei*, surrounded by Sui troops giving
    his half of the mirror to Princess Yueh-ch'ang at Huang-p'o.
They were like the Hegemon leaving his mistress Yu at K'e-hsia.
Like the Cowherd and the Spinning Maid parting after the
    seventh evening of the seventh month.[6]
And the rain and clouds parted as they did
When the beloved goddess of Wu-shan left Sung Yu in his grief.[7]

'If sold, my robe of figured silk can furnish money for your trip,'
    said San-niang.
Her generosity is as great as the mountain.
A moment before she had let down her cloud of black hair
And cut off a lock of it with the axe.
She hands it now to young Liu saying:
'Remember often tonight's love.'
Should you recall examples from the past
Of such affectionate partings
I think no grief in all the world
Could be compared with theirs.
Her pain was so great, again and again the tear pearls fell.
The earth was mourning, Heaven was plunged in sorrow,
The sun itself gave no light.
If Buddha of the Eternal Smile were witness, he too would frown.

      (Coda)
A mandarin duck driven from its mate,
Lien-li trees cut asunder,
Uncaring Hung-hsin and Hung-i have made
The lonely *luan* bird and solitary phoenix separate.

      [The Hidden Dragon undergoes various adventures
(related mainly in the lost portions of the ballad) and is forced to
marry the daughter of a military dignitary, Lady Yueh. In one of
the last episodes of the poem San-niang is captured by bandits. An
expedition is sent to rescue her.]

      6. A myth based on the union of the constellations of the
Herdboy and Spinning Damsel, supposed to occur on the seventh day
of the seventh lunar month. The lovers in the stars could meet only once a
year.   7. Clouds and rain symbolize sexual relationship. The allusion is
to a famous sensual poem (The Goddess) from the third century BC.

. . .

Hung-chao[8] grew wrathful,
Wheeled his charger, and even with the ground he swung his
    sword.
From a distance, before his flags, the bandit watched him scorn-
    fully.
He seized his *fang-t'ien* halberd, two feet wide,
And flung it as his challenge towards the riders of the other side.
The battle drums rumbled, two armies raised their battle cries,
And the reek of violence touched the skies.

Swords were raised and sparks were struck from them;
Halberds thrust – and in the pear-blossom – flashes danced.
Back and forth ten times the battle surged;
Then one reckless hero,
Roaring as a tiger roars,
(Even a Naga could not have dodged him)
Stretched forth his ape-like arms
And grasping his rival's girdle of jade
He snatched him from his saddle.

> Ten times they met before one of the warriors found an
opening. In the midst of combat he dodged his enemy's weapon
and grasping the tuft atop the other's helmet he dragged him side-
ways. Then he clutched the borders of his armoured coat and with
his other hand seized him by the jade belt and lifted him clear of his
decorated saddle. Both the armies stood and watched astounded.

> > The defeated one is like a yellow oriole
> > Whose golden wings beat heavy in the drenching rain.
> > The victorious one like the white egret
> > Whose jade feathers grow lighter in the blowing wind.
> > Who was the man seized alive?

The bandit was courageous, where would one find his match?
He captured Hung-chao, living, and dragged him back to his
    ranks.
In his hand he held his icicle – halberd level,
Wheeled his horse about and rode back out.

> 8. One of Liu Chih-yuan's warriors, sent to rescue San-
niang.

As imposing and fierce as an enraged Lu Pu[9]
Again, he appeared before the troops and cried:
'You, Yen-wei, hear my words;
Don't be like this mindless wretch
Don't wait for me to beat you in a fight!

The proverb does not lie which says:
"Who hates must have an object
As debt must have its creditor!"
You must have your strict commands –
And I don't care if you live or die –
But in the name of humanity and right I'd send you back
And trouble you to relay just one speech.
Tell this to Liu, the *an-fu*, say:
"Come forth yourself in person and carry back your wife!" '

When Yen-wei heard it
His eyes grew wide and flashed.
When he shouted at the bandit.
Anger and hatred dripped like blood from his face and beard.
On his horse he flew to seize his enemy.

Both these angry men feed their madness –
Each struts his bravery, skill, and heroic mien –
They clash in final battle on their mounts.
Alarm sounds of the ornamented trumpets
Trouble the heavens with their din.
The frantic thunders of war drums
Stun the earth with their sound.
The dust is trampled up and dirt rains down from everywhere.
Where arms struck each other, white sparks glanced,

Where divine weapons whirled, cold lightning danced.
Halberds' points struck one another,
For the moment nothing matters but to win or die!
None cares that in a trice he might be covered by the Yellow
    Springs.[10]

9. Lu Pu, a historical personality who lived during the
Eastern Han period (AD 25–220), was Lieutenant and adopted son of
Tung Cho, but subsequently became disgusted by the latter's tyranny
and helped to kill him.   10. The Chinese Hades.

Long they fought but there was neither victory nor defeat.

> (Coda)

You could not tell which was the stronger.
Then for a while they rested before their ranks
And leant on their ornamented saddles atop their horses' heaving
> flanks.

In their battle to the finish, the military arts of both were equal. Eyes as sharp as the bandit's are rare on the earth. Deft hands like Yen-wei's are hard to find anywhere. Fifty times they clashed but there was neither victor nor victim. Each returned to his side to rest. But alas! Kuo Yen-wei became too reckless. He deployed his troops before their banners and tried again to carry off the lady and take her back to headquarters. The troops once more waved their ornamented flags, soldiers beat a flourish on the war drums.

The rest over, strength recovered, the duel began again.
The hands holding the swords returned to their work.

Both generals rested a while
But then Kuo deployed his troops.
Alas! His heart had grown too hasty!
In furious irritation he dashed for another mount
To measure again his bravery and ardour.

As he hurried to his beast, he saw a messenger;
The man was tottering with fear
And quickly stuttered out his report.
His mouth spoke a terrible disaster!
'Five hundred of our soldiers are on the brink of defeat!'

> (Coda)
> Kuo Yen-wei's courage drained away.
> Straight north of them a dust-cloud seemed to boil
> > and sway
> And another squad of wild horsemen galloped up.
>
> Watching from afar they could distinguish nothing
> But guessed that the bandit's reinforcements had
> > arrived.
> Looking closer
> It proved to be the nine-district-*an-fu*'s cohorts!

In the shade of two hundred ornamented flags – gifts of the Emperor, in the crowd of three hundred long silver lances issued by the Son of Heaven, in the glitter of the armour and surrounded by his bodyguards the Emperor-to-be arrived! The golden baldachin was fluttering in the wind, but it could not cast a shade upon the Splendid Emperor. Yen-wei hurriedly jumped from his horse and greeting his sovereign reported Hung-chao's defeat. Chih-yuan was moved and rode his steed forth in person to call the bandit out.

> As soon as the rebels saw him
> They threw down their arms and dismounted their
>   saddles,
> Lifted their helmets, cast off their armour,
> And hastily knelt before his horse.

When the ruler saw that they had submitted, he asked: 'Who are you?' And the two men answered: 'We are not the leaders, there is another who commands our army.' They shouted towards their main force announcing the ruler's arrival and his desire to be seen. One man from the bandits' army rode out.

Thereupon the bandits told their captain all:
'Their commander-in-chief has arrived from Ping-chou,
He wants to meet his enemy's chief.
Do not refuse him!'
When they had thus spoken, the flags and pennons parted to
    make way.
One man rode his charger forth
And all his troops were puzzled.
None said a thing but each was guessing silently –
Their chief held only his silk whip
And shouted his salutations to the ruler:

'Have you been well since we saw each other last?
When I've come close enough, *an-fu*
Fix your eyes on me –
When you recognize my face, you'll be surprised.'
He slid from his priceless saddle,
Threw down his sword,
Dropped bow and arrows
And shed his armoured robe and helmet.

(Coda)
Forward came Liu Chih-yuan, his face filled with delight
'Forgive my failure to welcome you first,
I will now set that right . . .'
And the Emperor-to-be bowed down.
It was a jade column or a golden mountain kneeling before a
    thief!

> The nine districts *an-fu*
> Must be the bandit's relative!
> If this were not so
> Why would he bow?

> And how were they related? Those were Liu Chih-
yuan's half-brothers, Mu-jung Yen-ch'ao and Mu-jung Yen-chin!
They walked forward supporting an old lady: 'This is your mother!
Today we discovered that our brother is an honoured official and
we came especially to congratulate you. We did not know that we
had seized your wife San-niang.' Full of joy, Chih-yuan greeted his
brothers and his wife and dispatched a man to Hsiao-li-ts'un com-
pound to fetch Li San-weng. His sisters-in-law he sent to his head-
quarters in Ping-chou and then he ordered his officers to arrange a
feast. Lady Yueh herself respectfully offered the golden head-dress
and rainbow robe to San-niang. San-niang, however, refused them.

Then, during the feast
San-niang made clear why she did this:
'Hear me, little sister, I will tell you why.
I it was who first married our *an-fu*,
But we have been these thirteen years apart.
You it was, good, virtuous lady
Who urged him on to fame and wealth.

Today I speak my gratitude to you
My lady, for treating me with such esteem
That you received and did not reject me.
Thanks to you my wishes are fulfilled.
Now I am united with my son,
I am content to be your servant –
Even as your slave I could not hope to cancel out my debt –
Why should I wish to be the leading wife
And demand the golden head-dress and rainbow robe?

(Coda)
I have always led a simple rustic life
So were I given the phoenix robe
I'd know not how to wear it nor how to play first wife.'

. . .

The golden head-dress and rainbow robe
Ten times they handed one another.
Then the son, with folded hands, knelt beside his mother:
'I can never forget, good lady,
That for almost thirteen years
You have cared for me so well
That my own flesh and blood could not have been kinder.
I thank you for your gentleness and generosity.

I hardly expected to save my mother from the fiery pit;
I can scarce imagine her as my father's wife
Much less imagine you as his second spouse.'
Lady Yueh asked, smiling:
'How to disperse these doubts and difficulties?
I admire your mother's faithfulness –
Of old or today who has seen her equal?

(Coda)
Why speak of first and second wives?
She'll be my older sister. We will share
A single mouth to breath the air!'

When San-niang saw the Lady Yueh's sincerity, she
accepted at last the golden head-dress and the rainbow robe, but she
felt uneasy in her mind.

Full of joy yet she sighs and groans
Recalling how she suffered in the village.
'Today my husband is highly placed,
But though he now has fame and fortune
There lacks one thing which makes all others incomplete.

Now I hate my brothers and their wives
With an even greater hate!
For they cut off all my hair and spoilt it.
Now, no matter how we may wish it, I've no future.

He whose lot is grief
Is destined never to be rich or honoured.'

(Coda)
A man of iron would be moved to tears
To see her look at the head-dress on its golden tray.
Only hair too short for the smallest pigtail
Had been left by her sister-in-law's shears.

She would like to put the golden head-dress on her
head, but alas! her hair had been ruined and reached only to her
brow. She could hardly gather it together, how then could she pin
the golden head-dress on? San-niang turned to her family: 'I have
one wish – I would like Heaven to tell me my fortune.'

With these words San-niang stood up:
'I wish to speak to all my family;
Please bear with my awkward address
For I am village born and reared
And somewhat ill at ease with ceremony.
To begin with, it was my departed father
Who asked our ruler to be my spouse.
Because of an idle quarrel with my brothers
My husband and I left each other in grief
And for thirteen years I'd no news of him.

My life was hard, I was badly used
Yet I was supposed to be content.
How could I hope that a day would come
When young Liu would be mighty and honoured,
When he would be ruler of nine districts?
Now I know "when the bitterest dregs have been swallowed
Everything else tastes sweet".

So it was said in olden times and is true still.
But how *can* I wear this golden head-dress?
I must ask Heaven to tell me its will –
If my destiny is to be great,
When three times I have combed my hair
Let it be as it was before!'

(Coda)
Say not Heaven has no gods!
They showed her she was to be honoured by men –
As the comb touched her hair it grew long again!

Reverently San-niang asked Heaven's portent: 'If it is [my lot] to become the Emperor's first wife, let my hair grow long again as soon as I touch it with the comb. If gods agree I am only to be the Emperor's second wife, let my hair remain as it is now.' Her words finished, three times she combed her hair and in a twinkling it swept the ground. All cried out: 'A miracle!' Li San-niang put on the golden head-dress – Liu Chih-yuan's hopes were fulfilled.

All generals and officers, all ministers and men
Cried out around the table
Then ceased their drinking from the golden cups
And whispered quietly.
Each saying to another:
'San-niang is faithfulness itself!'
'She loyally awaited her husband's return!'
'From her, history's faithful wives have much to learn!'
. . .

(Coda)
Destinies all have ripened, each moves toward his fate.
Kin and brother here foregather,
Toast their reunion and drink . . .

Brothers and wives are met again . . .
The dragon, the Tiger and their ministers now join forces.

Now that the family was reunited
The banqueting began again.
Music sounded all about.
The *an-fu* looked to Heaven with reverence and thought,
(Must not one whose family is united
Thank the gods for his good fortune?)

The nobleman has found his fate: he has won fame and wealth.
He has taken back his wife. They share the joy of their reunion.
He has even joined again his mother and his brothers.

And in a while his fame will grow more splendid still,
For he will use the Emperor's 'We'
And then ascend the golden throne.

(Coda)
I was asked to make a new tale from the old.
For this worthy, intelligent assembly
I was happy to unfold
The story of Liu Chih-yuan
From the beginning to the end
And with absolutely nothing left untold.

ACKNOWLEDGEMENTS

Thanks are due to the following for permission to reproduce poems and selections in this book:

Gond
V. Elwin and S. Hivale, *Folk Songs of the Maikal Hills* (Oxford University Press, Madras, 1944) and *Songs of the Forest. The Folk Poetry of the Gonds* (Allen & Unwin, London, 1935)

Mongol
Professor C. R. Bawden for translating all poems in this section

Malay
R. J. Wilkinson and R. O. Winstedt, *Pantun Melayu* (Malaya Publishing House, Singapore, 1957)

R. O. Winstedt, *The Malay Magician* and *The Malays: A Cultural History* (Routledge & Kegan Paul, London, 1951 and 1958) and *A History of Classical Malay Literature* (Oxford University Press, Kuala Lumpur, 1969)

Somali
M. F. Abdillahi and B. W. Andrzejewski, 'The Life of 'Ilmi Bowndheri, A Somali Oral Poet who is Said to have Died of Love' (*Journal of the Folklore Institute*, 4, 2/3, 1967)

B. W. Andrzejewski, 'Poetry in Somali Society' (*New Society*, 1, 25, 21 March 1963) and 'The Art of the Miniature in Somali Poetry' (*African Language Review*, 6, 1967) and 'The Roobdoon of Sheik Aqib Abdullahi Jama' (*African Language Studies*, 11, 1970)

B. W. Andrzejewski and I. M. Lewis, *Somali Poetry: An Introduction* (Clarendon Press, Oxford, 1964)

Hassan Sheikh Mumin, *Leopard among Women. Shabeelnagood, a Somali Play* translated by B. W. Andrzejewski (Oxford University Press, London, 1974)

Zulu

T. Cope, *Izibongo. Zulu Praise Poems* (Clarendon Press, Oxford, 1968)

C. and W. Leslau, *African Poems and Love Songs* (Peter Pauper Press, New York, 1970)

Dr David K. Rycroft, unpublished translations

B. G. M. Sundkler, *Bantu Prophets in South Africa*, 2nd edition (Oxford University Press, London, 1961)

H. Tracey, '*Lalela Zulu*' *100 Zulu Lyrics* (African Music Society, Johannesburg, *c*. 1948)

B. W. Vilakazi, 'The Conception and Development of Poetry in Zulu' (*Bantu Studies*, 2, 1938)

Yoruba

B. King, *Introduction to Nigerian Literature* (University of Lagos and Evans Brothers Ltd, Lagos, 1971)

J. A. Adediji, 'The Origin of the Yoruba Masque Theatre: The Use of Ifa Divination Corpus as Historical Evidence'; R. G. Armstrong, V. Olayemi and B. Adu (eds.), 'Ekiti Traditional Dirge of Lt-Col. Adekunle Fajuyi's Funeral'; O. Ogunba, 'The Poetic Content and Form of Yoruba Occasional Festival Songs', (*African Notes*, University of Ibadan, 6/1, 1970; 5/2, 1969; 6/2, 1971)

B. Awe, 'Yoruba Oriki as a Historical Source'
S. A. Babalola, *The Content and Form of Yoruba Ijala* (Clarendon Press, Oxford, 1966)

U. Beier, *African Poetry* and *Yoruba Poetry* (Cambridge University Press, 1966 and 1970); 'Yoruba Vocal Music' (*African Music*, 1, 3, 1956); 'Transition without Tears' (*Encounter*, 15, 4 October, 1960)

U. Beir and B. Gbadamosi, *The Moon Cannot Fight. Yoruba Children's Poems* (Mbari publications, Caxton Press, Ibadan)

E. L. Lasebikan, 'The Tonal Structure and Form of Yoruba Poetry' (*Présence africaine*, 8/10, 1956)

Irish

J. Greenway, *American Folk Songs of Protest* (University of Pennsylvania Press, Philadelphia, 1953)

Frank O'Connor, *Kings, Lords and Commoners. An Anthology from the Irish* (Macmillan, London, 1961 and A. D. Peters & Co. Ltd)

Pueblo

N. Barnes, *American Indian Love Lyrics* (Macmillan, New York, 1925)

K. Kennedy, 'Zuni rituals' (*Poetry*, Chicago, 50, 1937)

Eskimo

D. Freuchen, *Peter Freuchen's Book of the Eskimos* (Barker, London, 1962)

K. Rasmussen, *Intellectual Culture of the Hudson Bay Eskimos; Intellectual Culture of the Copper Eskimos; The Netsilik Eskimos. Social Life and Spiritual Culture* (Nordisk Forlag, Copenhagen, 1930; 1932; 1931)

Hawaiian

M. W. Beckwith, *The Kumulipo. A Hawaiian Creation Chant* (University of Chicago Press, Chicago, 1951)

K. Luomala, *Voices on the Wind: Polynesian Myths and Chants* (Bishop Museum Press, Honolulu, 1955)

S. H. Elbert and N. Mahoe, *Na Mele o Hawai'i Nei: 101 Hawaiian Songs* (University of Hawaii Press, Honolulu, 1907)

M. K. Pukui and A. L. Korn, *The Echo of our Song, Chants and Poems of the Hawaiians* (University Press of Hawaii, Honolulu, 1973)

Maori

A. Alpers, *Legends of the South Seas* (John Murray, London, 1970)
A. Armstrong, *Maori Games and Hakas* (A. H. and A. W. Reed, Wellington, 1964)

Aborigine

R. M. Berndt, *Djanggawul* (Routledge & Kegan Paul, 1952) and 'A Wonguri-Mandjikai Song Cycle of the Moon-Bone' (*Oceania*, Vol. XIX, No. 1, 1948)

C. H. Berndt, 'Expressions of Grief Among Aboriginal Women' and 'A Drama of North-Eastern Arnhem Land' (*Oceania*, Vol. XX, No. 4, 1950 and Vol. XXII, Nos. 3-4, 1952)

M. Jacobs, *The Anthropologist Looks at Myth* (American Folklore Society, University of Texas Press, Austin, 1966)

English

T. E. Cheney, *Mormon Songs from the Rocky Mountains* (American Folklore Society, University of Texas Press, Austin and London, 1968)

E. Fowke, *Lumbering Songs from the Northern Woods* (American Folklore Society, University of Texas Press, Austin and London, 1970)

J. G. Greenway, *American Folk Songs of Protest* (University of Pennsylvania Press, Philadelphia, 1953)

G. Irwin, *American Tramp and Underworld Slang* (Scholartis Press, London, 1931)

B. Jackson, *Wake Up Dead Man: Afro-American Worksongs from Texas Prisons* (Harvard University Press, Cambridge, 1972)

J. Lennon and P. McCartney, *Golden Beatles* Book I (Northern Songs Ltd, 1966)

A. L. Lloyd, *Come all Ye Bold Miners. Ballads and Songs of the Coalfields* and *Folk Song in England* (Laurence & Wishart, London, 1952 and 1967)

A. L. Lloyd, *Corn on the Cob. Popular and Traditional Poetry of the USA* (Fore Publications, London, 1945)

P. Oliver, *Blues Fell this Morning* (Cassell, London, 1960)

I. and P. Opie, *The Lore and Language of Schoolchildren* (Oxford University Press, London, 1967)

Epic and Narrative

M. Alexander, *Beowulf* (Penguin Books Ltd, 1973)

N. Cohn, *Gold Khan* (Secker & Warburg, London, 1946)

M. Doleželová-Velingerova and J. I. Crump, *Ballad of the Hidden Dragon (Liu Chih-yüan chu-kung-tiao)* (Clarendon Press, Oxford, 1971)

Geoffrey Lewis, *The Book of Dede Korkut* (Penguin Books Ltd, 1974)

R. Fitzgerald, *The Odyssey. A Modern Verse Translation* (Heinemann, London, 1962)

Professor C. R. Bawden for his translation of *Zong Belegt Baatar*

B. H. Quain, *The Flight of the Chiefs. Epic Poetry of Fiji* (J. J. Augustin, New York, 1942)

SOURCES OF POEMS

Gond

'The arrow of desire', 'Blue calf', 'Be not proud of your sweet body', 'The bride's farewell', 'Debt', 'The depths of sorrow', 'Easy as a bat', 'The ever-touring Englishmen . . .', 'Flowers', 'Flute player', 'Let me go', 'Like ripples on the water', 'Longing', 'Love and music', 'Love songs', 'My cobra girl', 'My heart burns for him', 'My love is playing . . .', 'The new wife', 'O girl, you torment me . . .', 'O faithless thorn', Old age', 'Once I played and danced in my parents' kingdom', 'Pearly beads', 'Red beauty', 'The right true end', 'She is not for me', 'Song of longing', 'This earthen body', 'Tonight at least, my sinner', 'Water-girl', 'The well', 'What matter?', 'What is man's body?', 'Who can tell?' from *Folk Songs of the Maikal Hills* by V. Elwin and S. Hivale (Oxford University Press, Madras, 1944)

'About to die', 'Come laugh with me', 'Come to me', 'A conceited man', 'Dear as the moon', 'Death', 'Elephants may parade before your house', 'A man's need', 'In my dreams I searched for you', 'The roadmenders' song', 'Moon of the earth', 'O little well', 'The shattering of love', 'Shoes are made to fit the feet . . .', 'Sleeper rise', 'So close should be our love', 'Song of poverty', 'The stars are thundering', 'There is no rest . . .' from *Songs of the Forest. The Folk Poetry of the Gonds* by S. Hivale and V. Elwin (Allen & Unwin, London, 1935)

Mongol

All poems in this section are original translations by Professor C. R. Bawden

Malay

'Invitation to a spirit', 'Of Iron am I', 'May I be beautiful', 'Tin-ore' from *Malay Magic* by W. W. Skeat (Macmillan, London, 1900)

'And tomorrow wend our ways . . .', '*Ave atque vale*', 'A battle of similes', 'The coming of love', 'The disdainful mistress', 'Entwined', 'In the heart of the hills . . .', 'Invitation', 'Jealousy', 'Kisses', 'A little cheat!', 'The lost', 'The lover's prayer', 'The loves of the birds', 'Open the door', 'The opium den', 'O that my love were in my arms', 'Parting', 'Parting at dawn', 'Red ants', 'Remember thou me', 'Sick unto death of love', 'Take up the pen', 'Taunt', 'Unique among girls', 'You drop a pearl . . .' from *Pantun Melayu* by R. J.Wilkinson and R. O. Winstedt (Malaya Publishing House, Singapore, 1957)

'Sri Rama's raiment' from *Malay Literature*, Part II by R. O. Winstedt (FMS Government Press, Kuala Lumpur, 1923)

'A bully', 'Dawn', 'Or ever God created Adam', 'Regret', 'Sanctimony', '. . . Till the sea runs dry' from *Malay Literature* Part I by R. J. Wilkinson (FMS Government Press, Kuala Lumpur, 1924)

'I, lord of all mortals', 'Invocation before the rice harvest', 'Om', from *The Malay Magician* by R. O. Winstedt (Routledge & Kegan Paul, London, 1951)

'Breakers over the sea', 'Love charms', 'The meaning of love', 'Music', 'Song of a sick child', 'Storm at sea', 'White as a paper a-sail in the air' from *The Malays* by R. O. Winstedt (Routledge & Kegan Paul, London, 1958, 5th edition)

'Two young maids', 'Wind' from *A History of Classical Malay Literature* by R. O. Winstedt (Oxford University Press, Kuala Lumpur, 1969)

Somali

'As camels who have become thirsty . . .', from 'The Life of 'Ilmi Bowndheri' by M. F. Abdillahi and B. W. Andrzejewski (*Journal of the Folklore Institute*, 4, 2/3, 1967)

'A denunciation', 'The Suez crisis', 'To a dictatorial Sultan' from 'Poetry in Somali Society' by B. W. Andrzejewski (*New Society*, 1, 25, 21 March 1963)

Modern love poems from 'The Art of the Miniature in Somali Poetry' by B. W. Andrzejewski (*African Language Review*, 6, 1967) 'Prayer for rain' from 'The Roobdoon of Sheikh Aqib Abdullahi

Jama' by B. W. Andrzejewski (*African Language Studies*, 11, 1970) 'The best dance', 'An elder's reproof to his wife', 'Fortitude', 'Independence', 'Lament for a dead lover', 'The limits of sub-mission', 'Modern love poems', 'Our country is divided', 'Poet's lament on the death of his wife', 'A woman sings of her love' from *Somali Poetry* by B. W. Andrzejewski and I. M. Lewis (Clarendon Press, Oxford, 1964)

'Colonialism' from 'The Development of the Genre *Heello* in Modern Somali Poetry' by J. W. Johnson (M.Phil. Thesis, 767, No. 267366, University of London, 1971)

'Battle pledge', 'Modern love poems', 'To a faithless friend', 'To a friend going on a journey' from *A Tree for Poverty* by M. Laurence (Eagle Press, Nairobi, 1954)

'Women and men' from *Leopard among Women* by Hassan Sheikh Mumin (Oxford University Press, London, 1974)

Zulu
'Praises of Henry Francis Fynn', 'Senzangakhona', 'Shaka' from *Izibongo* by T. Cope (Clarendon Press, Oxford, 1968)

'Baboon' from *African Poems and Love Songs* by C. and W. Leslau (Peter Pauper Press, New York, 1970)

'I am the beginning', 'Let Zulu be heard . . .' from *The Theology of a South African Messiah* by G. C. Oosthuizen (Brill, Leiden, 1967)

'Teasing song', 'War song', 'Work song', 'You are lying, O missionary . . .' from unpublished translations by Dr David K. Rycroft

'Dance hymn', 'The springtime of the earth' from *Bantu Prophets in South Africa* by B. G. M. Sundkler (Oxford University Press, London, 1961)

'Come in', 'Home', 'I thought you loved me', 'Jojina, my love', 'Lament for Mafukuzela', 'Lucky lion!', 'My money! O, my money!', 'Old age', 'Satan is following me . . .', 'Take off your hat . . .', 'Those were the days . . .', 'Was it all worth while?' from *Lalela Zulu* by H. Tracey (African Music Society, Johannesburg, *c.* 1948)

'Praise of a train' from 'The Conception and Development of Poetry in Zulu' by B. W. Vilakazi (*Bantu Studies*, 2, 1938)

'Dove's song in winter' from 'The Oral and Written Literature in Nguni' by B. W. Vilakazi (D.Litt. Thesis, unpublished, University of Witwatersrand, 1945)

Yoruba

'Ifa' from 'The Origin of the Yoruba Masque Theatre' by J. A. Adediji (*African Notes*, University of Ibadan, 6/1, 1970)

'Death killed the rich' from 'Odu of Ifa' by W. Abimbola (unpublished typescript, University of Ibadan, 1966)

'Dirge for Fajuyi' from 'Ekiti Traditional Dirge of Lt-Col. Adekunle Fajuyi 's Funeral' by R. G. Armstrong, V. Olayemi and B. Adu (*African Notes*, University of Ibadan, 5/2, 1969)

'Praise of Ibikunle' from 'Yoruba Oriki as a Historical Source' by B. Awe (unpublished paper, Lagos, 1969)

'Salute to the elephant' from *The Content and Form of Yoruba Ijala* by S. A. Babalola (Clarendon Press, Oxford, 1966)

'Mayor of Lagos' from 'Yoruba Vocal Music' by U. Beier (*African Music*, 1, 3, 1956)

'Election songs' from 'Transition without Tears' by U. Beier (*Encounter*, 15, 4 October 1960)

'Kob antelope' from *African Poetry* by U. Beier (Cambridge University Press, 1966)

'Alajire', 'Eshu, the god of fate', 'Hunger', 'Leopard', 'Let the dead depart in peace', 'The lying Muslims', 'Obatala, the creator', 'Oracle: *Iwori wotura*', 'Oshun, the river goddess', 'Praises of the king of Oyo', 'Python', 'Quarrel', 'The time of creation has come', 'Wisdom is the finest beauty of a person . . .', 'Women' from *Yoruba Poetry* by U. Beier (Cambridge University Press, 1970)

'Hunger', 'Praise of a child', 'Song of abuse' from *The Moon Cannot Fight* by U. Beier and B. Gbadamosi (Mbari publications, Caxton Press, Ibadan)

'Tiger' from *Introduction to Nigerian Literature* by B. King (University of Lagos and Evans Brothers Ltd, Lagos, 1971)

'Variety' from 'The tonal structure of Yoruba poetry' by E. Lase-bikan (Présence africaine 8/10, 1956)

'Money! money!' from 'The Poetic Content and Form of Yoruba Occasional Festival Songs' by O. Ogunba (*African Notes*, 6/2, 1971)

'Characteristic features of Yoruba oral poetry', by O. O. Olatunji (Ph.D. Thesis, University of Ibadan, 1970)

Irish

'Are ye right there, Michael?', from *Best Irish Songs of Percy French* (Wolfe Publishing Co., London, 1971)

'No Irish need apply' from *American Folk Songs of Protest* by J. Greenway (University of Pennsylvania Press, Philadelphia, 1953)

'The moon behind the hill', 'No place so grand' from *The Mercier Book of Old Irish Street Ballads* by J. N. Healy (Mercier Press, Cork, 1969)

'Ballinderry' from *The Third Book of Irish Ballads* by M. Jolliffe (Mercier Press, 1970)

'The Dream' from *Folksongs Sung in Ulster* by R. Morton (Mercier Press, 1970)

'The Green Autumn Stubble', 'St Kevin' from *The First Book of Irish Ballads* by D. D. O'Keefe (Mercier Press, 1968)

'A fragrant prayer', 'Hell', 'A hundred thousand welcomes', 'I place myself', 'O king of the world', 'A low prayer, a high prayer', 'The merry jovial beggar', 'Thoughts of God', 'Thanksgiving after Communion', 'O Virgin', 'Welcome O great Mary', 'When your eyes . . .' from *The Religious Songs of Connacht* by Douglas Hyde (Fisher Unwin, London, 1906)

'My grief on the sea', 'Ringleted youth of my love' from *Love Songs of Connacht* by Douglas Hyde (Gill & Son, Dublin, 1893)

'Cushendall', 'From a faction song' from *Popular Rhymes and Sayings of Ireland* by J. J. Marshall (Tyrone Printing Co. Ltd, Dungannon, 1931)

'Belfast linen' from 'Picking up the Linen Threads' by B. Messenger (*Journal of the Folklore Institute*, 9, 1, 1972)

'From a beggarman's song', 'From a lament for Una', 'How well for the birds . . .' from *Kings, Lords and Commoners* by Frank O'Connor (Macmillan, London, 1961)

'A new song on the taxes' from *Irish Street Ballads* by C. O. Lochlainn (Three Candles Press, Dublin, 1939)

'Lullaby, O men from the fields' from *Song-Writers of Ireland* by C. O. Lochlainn (Three Candles Press, Dublin, 1969)

'In memoriam', 'The ould orange flute', 'The wearing of the green' from *Songs and Recitations of Ireland* (Coiste Foillseacháin Náisiunta, Cork, 1971)

'I know where I'm going . . .' from Elsie O'Docoling

'Lisnagade' from *The Standard Orange Song Book* (Armagh, 1848)
'Famine song', 'Must I go bound?' from Agnes Finnegan?
'I once loved a boy' from *Walton's New Treasury of Irish Songs and Ballads*, Part I (Walton's Musical Instrument Galleries, Dublin, 1968)

Pueblo

'Corn-grinding song', 'The sunrise call', 'Sunset song' from *American Indian Love Lyrics* by N. Barnes (Macmillan, New York, 1925)

'Our earth mother' from 'Zuni ritual poetry' by R. Bunzel (47th Annual Report, Bureau of American Ethnology, Smithsonian Institute, Washington, US Government Printing Office, 1932)

'Butterfly maidens', 'The cloud-flower lullaby', 'Corn-blossom maidens', 'Flute song', 'Now from the east', 'The rainbow', 'Song of the blue-corn dance', 'Yellow butterflies' from *The Indians' Book* by N. Curtis (Harper & Bros., New York, 1907)

'The earthquake', 'The songs', 'The taboo woman' from 'Zuni rituals' by K. Kennedy (*Poetry*, 50, 1937)

'The cloud-flower lullaby', 'Dead on the war path', 'Disillusion', 'I wonder how my home is', 'Lost love', 'Prayer for a long life', 'Rain magic song', 'Rains for the harvest', 'Regret and refusal', 'Scalp dance song', 'Shadows', 'Song of the sky loom', 'Songs in the turtle dance at Santa Clara', 'Uru-tu-sendo's song', 'The willows by the water side' from *Songs of the Tewa* by H. J. Spinden (Exposition of Indian Tribal Arts, New York, 1933)

Eskimo

'I should be ashamed', 'The mother's song', 'The old man's song' from *Peter Freuchen's Book of the Eskimos* by D. Freuchen (Barker, London, 1962)

'Accusation', 'The ageing hunger', 'Bear hunting', 'I am but a little woman . . .', 'Morning prayer', 'Musk oxen', 'Remembering', 'Solitary song', 'Spirit song', 'Walrus hunting' from *Across Arctic America* by K. Rasmussen (Putnam, New York, 1927)

'Song of joy' from *Intellectual Culture of the Hudson Bay Eskimos* by K. Rasmussen (Nordisk Forlag, Gyldendalske Boghandel, Copenhagen, 1930)

'The gull', 'Invocation', 'It is hard to catch trout', 'The joy of a singer', 'Mocking song against Qaqortingneq', 'My breath', 'The song of the trout fisher' from *The Netsilik Eskimos* by K. Rasmussen (Nordisk Forlag, Gyldendalske Boghandel, Copenhagen, 1931)

'Dead man's song, dreamed by one who is alive', 'Hunger', 'Hymn to the air spirit', 'Men's impotence', 'Song of the caribou, musk oxen, women, and men who would be manly', 'The sun and the moon and the fear of loneliness' from *Intellectual Culture of the Copper Eskimos* by K. Rasmussen (Nordisk Forlag, Gyldendalske Boghandel, Copenhagen, 1932)

'Darkened in the soul', 'Great grief came over me', 'Song of Sukkaartik', 'Take your accusation back!' from *The Ammassilik Eskimo* by W. Thalbitzer (2nd Vol., Meddelelser om Grønland Bd 40, Copenhagen, 1923)

'Personal song' from *Leadership and Law among the Eskimos of the Keewatin District North-west Territories* by G. Van den Steenhoven (Excelsior, Rijswijk, 1962)

Hawaiian

'The beloved's image', 'Cold and Heat', 'Laieikawai's lament after her husband's death', 'Love by the water-reeds' from *Hawaiian Romance of Laieikawai* by M. W. Beckwith (33rd Annual Report of Bureau of American Ethnology, 1918)

'The Kumulipo' from *The Kumulipo* by M. W. Beckwith (University of Chicago Press, Chicago, 1951)

'Altar prayers', 'Anklet song', 'Fathomless is my love', 'The Kona

Sea', 'Love is a shark', 'O thirsty wind', 'Praise song for King Kalakaua', 'The rain', 'The rainbow stands red . . .', 'Resemblance', 'Song', 'The water of Kane' from *Unwritten Literature of Hawaii* by N. B. Emerson (Bureau of American Ethnology, Bulletin 38, Washington, 1909)

'Albatross', 'The glory of Hanalei is its heavy rain', 'Hilo Hana-kahi, rain rustling *lehua*', 'I'm going to California', 'My sweetheart in the rippling hills of sand . . .', 'Puna's fragrant glades' from *Na Mele o Hawai'i Nei* by S. H. Elbert and N. Mahoe (University of Hawaii Press, Honolulu, 1970)

'Ending' from *Voices on the Wind* by K. Luomala (Bishop Museum Press, Honolulu, 1955)

'O Kane, O Lono of the blue sea . . .', 'Prayer of the fishing net', 'Prayer on making a canoe' from *Hawaiian Antiquities* by D. Malo, trans. N. B. Emerson (Hawaiian Gazette, 1903)

'Behold', 'The leper', 'Piano at evening', 'Sure a poor man' from *The Echo of our Song, Chants and Poems of the Hawaiians* by M. K. Pukui and A. L. Korn (University of Hawaii Press, Honolulu, 1973)

'Born was the island', 'Invocation for a storm', 'The ocean is like a wreath', 'Old creation chant', 'The sea! O the sea!', 'A skilful spearman!', 'A stormy day' from *Fornander Collection of Hawaiian Antiquities and Folk-lore* ed. by T. G. Thrum (Bishop Museum Mem, 4–6, Honolulu, 1916)

Maori

'Chant to Io' from *Legends of the South Seas* by A. Alpers (John Murray, London, 1970)

'O beautiful calm', 'Oh, how my love with a whirling power . . .' from *Polynesian Literature* by J. C. Andersen (Thomas Avery & Sons, New Plymouth, 1946)

'Canoe-hauling chant', 'Government!', 'Ruaumoko – the earth-quake god', 'We object . . .' from *Maori Games and Hakas* by A. Armstrong (A. H. and A. W. Reed, Wellington, 1964)

'The breeze is blowing . . .', 'Fishing song' from *Maori Action Songs* by A. Armstrong and R. Ngata (A. H. and A. W. Reed, Wellington, 1960)

'Hitler, frothy-mouth', 'Lament for Apirana Ngata', 'Seaweed, seaweed', 'A sentinel's song' from *Maori Poetry* by B. Mitcalfe (Victoria University Press, Wellington, 1974)

'Lament', 'Lament for Taramoana', 'Lullaby', 'A mourning song for Rangiaho', 'Song of despair', 'A song of sickness' from *Poetry of the Maori* by B. Mitcalfe (Paul's Book Arcade, Hamilton and Auckland, 1961)

'The mist over Pukehina' from *Traditions and Superstitions of the New Zealanders* by E. Shortland (Brown, Green & Longmans, London, 1854)

'The creation', 'The six periods of creation' from *Te Ika a Maui, or New Zealand and its Inhabitants* by Richard Taylor (Wertheim & Macintosh, London, 1855)

'Landfall' from *The Story of New Zealand* by A. S. Thomson (London, 1859)

'The creation of man', 'Dirge sung at death', 'Disturb me not', 'Give me my infant now . . .', 'Love dirge', 'Song of longing', 'Whispering ghosts of the west' from *The Ancient History of the Maori* by John White (G. Didsbury, Wellington, 1887–90)

Aborigine

Songs 1, 4, 6, 7, 8, 10, 11, 12, 18, 21, 22, 24, 27, 30, 33, 51, 57, 67, 84, 92, 135, 144, 166, 172, 174, 182 from *Djanggawul* by R. M. Berndt (Routledge & Kegan Paul, 1952)

'The birds', 'The Evening Star', 'New Moon' from 'A Wonguri-Mandjikai Song-Cycle of the Moon-Bone' by R. Berndt (*Oceania*, 1948, Vol. XIX, No. 1)

'All you others eat', 'The blowflies buzz . . .' from 'Expressions of Grief among Aboriginal Women' by C. H. Berndt (*Oceania*, Vol. XX, No. 4, 1950)

'Sail at the mast head' from 'A Drama of North-Eastern Arnhem Land' by C. H. Berndt (*Oceania*, 1952, Vol. XXII, Nos. 3–4)

'Snails', 'Yellow cloud' from 'The Wuradilagu Song-Cycle of North-Eastern Arnhem Land' in *The Anthropologist Looks at Myth* by M. Jacobs (American Folklore Society, University of Texas Press, Austin, 1966)

English

'Have courage, my boy, to say no!' from *Mormon Songs from the Rocky Mountains* by T. E. Cheney (American Folklore Society, University of Texas Press, Austin, 1968)

'The Lake of the Caogama' from *Lumbering Songs from the Northern Woods* by E. Fowke (American Folklore Society, University of Texas Press, Austin, 1970)

'O God of Bethel' from *Congregational Praise* (Independent Press of Congregational Union of England and Wales, London, 1951)

'Jeff Buckner', 'Jesus Christ', 'Plane wreck at Los Gatos', 'Two hoboes' from *American Folk Songs of Protest* by J. Greenway (University of Pennsylvania Press, Philadelphia, 1953)

'Ballad of the D-Day Dodgers' from *Ballads of World War II* by Hamish Hamilton (Lili Marleen Club of Glasgow, 1950)

'Song of a Hebrew' from *Jazz Poems* by A. Hollo (Vista Books, London, 1963)

'Chain gang blues' from *Negro Verse* by A. Hollo (Vista Books, London, 1964)

'The preacher and the slave', 'They can't do that' from *American Tramp and Underworld Slang* by G. Irwin (Scholartis Press, London, 1931)

'If you see my mother . . .' from *Wake Up Dead Man* by B. Jackson (Harvard University Press, Cambridge, 1972)

'Drill man blues' from *Coal Dust on the Fiddle* by G. Korson (University of Pennsylvania Press, Philadelphia, 1943)

'Eleanor Rigby', 'For No One' from *Golden Beatles* Book I by J. Lennon and P. McCartney (Northern Songs Ltd, 1966)

'I'll have a collier for my sweetheart', 'The Donibristle Moss Moran disaster' from *Come all Ye Bold Miners* by A. L. Lloyd (Laurence & Wishart, London, 1952)

'Robens' promised land' from *Folk Song in England* by A. L. Lloyd (Laurence & Wishart, London, 1967)

'Down in the valley', 'To the pines' from *Corn on the Cob. Popular and Traditional Poetry of the USA* by A. L. Lloyd (Fore publications, London, 1945)

'Bow down your head and cry', 'The peeler's lament' from *Cowboy*

Songs and other Frontier Ballads by J. and A. Lomax (Macmillan, New York, 1925)

'Judgement day' from *The Negro and his Songs* by H. W. Odum and G. B. Johnson (University of North Carolina Press, Chapel Hill, 1925)

'Dey got each and de udder's man', 'I's gonna shine' from *Negro Workaday Songs* by H. W. Odum and G. B. Johnson (University of North Carolina Press, Chapel Hill, 1926)

'I'm through with you', 'I work all day long for you' from *Blues Fell This Morning* by P. Oliver (Cassell, London, 1960)

'1952', 'Salome', 'School dinners' from *The Lore and Language of Schoolchildren* by I. and P. Opie (Oxford University Press, London, 1967)

'Pastures of plenty' from *Woody Guthrie Folk Songs* by P. Seeger (Ludlow Music Inc., New York, 1963)

Epic and Narrative

'Beowulf's fight with Grendel's mother' from *Beowulf* trans. by M. Alexander (Penguin Books Ltd, 1973)

Zong Belegt Baatar an unpublished translation by Professor C. R. Bawden

'Blood Marksman and Kureldei the Marksman' from *Gold Khan* by N. Cohn (Secker & Warburg, London, 1946)

Ballad of the Hidden Dragon from *Ballad of the Hidden Dragon* by M. Doleželová-Velingerova and J. I. Crump (Clarendon Press, Oxford, 1971)

'The story of Bamsi Beyrek of the grey horse' from *The Book of Dede Korkut* trans. by Geoffrey Lewis (Penguin Books Ltd, 1974)

'New coasts and Poseidon's son' from *The Odyssey* trans. by R. Fitzgerald (Doubleday, New York, 1961 and Heinemann, London, 1962)

'Tip-of-the-Single-Feather' from *The Flight of the Chiefs* by B. H. Quain (J. J. Augustin, New York, 1942)

'The golden sea-otter' from *Kutune Shirka* by A. Waley (*Botteghe oscure*, 7, 1951)

INDEX OF TITLES AND FIRST LINES

First lines in italics

A battle of similes, 94
About to die, 33
Above, above, 289
A bully, 93
Accusation, 248
A child is like a rare bird, 168
A cigarette, 65
A cigarette my girl is smoking, 78
A conceited man, 32
A creature to pet and spoil, 161
A denunciation, 102
A fragrant prayer, 178
A fragrant prayer on the air, 178
After these words the Weather-Great prince, 408
Ah blessed plant! ah lucky creeper!, 79
Ah, look at all the lonely people, 385
Ah my daughter, my grandchild!, 351
Ah, the blowfly is whining there, its maggots are eating the flesh, 350
A hundred thousand welcomes, 176
A hundred thousand welcomes, thou Body of the Lord, 176
Alajire, 151
Alajire, we ask you to be patient, 151
Alas! I am seized by the shark, great shark, 281
Albatross, 282
A little cheat, 90
'Alkinoos, king and admiration of men', 390
All night from the roof of the chieftain, 90
All round about the door of your house, 210
All you others, eat, 351
All you young men an' maidens come an' listen to my song, 194
A low prayer, a high prayer, 180
A low prayer, a high prayer, I send through space, 180
Altar prayers, 269

Although I leave Braglu, I am close to it, 328
A man's need, 20
A mourning song for Rangiaho, 310
And tomorrow we wend our ways, 89
An elder's reproof to his wife, 105
A new song on the taxes, 194
Anklet song, 277
A query, a question, 268
'Are ye right there, Michael?', 196
Are you glad?, 67
As camels who have become thirsty . . . the poet's lament, 108
*As camels who have become thirsty after they have been grazing in the Haud
    for a long time*, 108
A sentinel's song, 302
As in a pot the milk turns sour, 25
A skilful spearman!, 277
A song of sickness, 314
As red as a starling's his peepers, 93
As the sunlight in the sky, 56
A stormy day, 274
A stream flowing steadily over a stone does not wet its core, 105
At Glendalough lived a young saint, 192
A tree I know where a love-bird's lighted, 96
At Su K'wa K'e there used to bloom a flower, 210
At the time when the earth became hot, 260
Ave atque vale, 91
Awake, O rain, O sun, O night, 270
A woman in childbirth, fainting with cruel pain, 106
A woman sings of her love, 107
A wonderful occupation, 247
Ayaiyaja, 247

Baboon, 134
Ballad of the D-Day Dodgers, 376
Ballad of the Hidden Dragon, 493
Ballinderry, 190
Battle pledge, 101
Bear hunting, 239
Beautiful, lo, the summer clouds, 218
Behold, 289
Belfast linen, 200
Benediction for the felt, 43
Benediction for the tent, 46

Be not proud of your sweet body, 32
Be not proud of your sweet body, 32
Beowulf's fight with Grendel's mother, 407
Big breakers roll over the sea, 91
Blood Marksman and Kureldei the Marksman, 445
Blossom is in her hair, 23
Blue calf, 28
Blue calf tethered, 28
Born was the island, 259
Born was the island, 259
Bow down your head and cry, 365
Brass and parrot feathers, 150
Breakers over the sea, 91
Broken the pot, there's still the jar, 92
Butterflies flutter and flit o'er the bay, 78
Butterfly maidens, 215

Canoe-hauling chant, 311
Chain gang blues, 360
Chant to Io, 297
Child of death, 152
Children's poems, 167, 382
Cold and heat, 278
Colonialism, 117
Come in, 141
Come laugh with me, 20
Come to me, 20
Cool in summer's heat, 23
Corn-blossom maidens, 214
Corn-blossom maidens, 214
Corn-grinding song, 221
Could I remove the stones from the river?, 30
Cushendall, 200

Dance hymn, 141
Darkened in the soul, 252
Dawn, 85
Dead man's song, dreamed by one who is alive, 233
Dead on the warpath, 212
Dear as the moon, 17
Death, 33
Death killed the rich, 158
Death killed the rich, 158

Death will make entry into your body which is so beautiful, 33
Debt, 35
Dekunle, handsome man, hail!, 154
Dey got each and de udder's man, 361
Dirge for Fajuyi, 154
Dirge sung at death, 303
Disillusion, 211
Disturb me not, 301
Disturb me not, O buoyant youths!, 301
Doves flit by in their flocks of thousands, 96
Dove's song in winter, 139
Down in the jungle, 382
Down in the valley, 369
Down in the valley, 369
Drill man blues, 370

Each day was like another, 495
Eager to breathe out, 249
Easy as a bat, 27
Eleanor Rigby, 385
Election songs, 160
Elephants may parade before your house, 33
Ending, 270
Entwined, 79
Eshu, the god of fate, 150
Eshu turns right into wrong, wrong into right, 150
Eulogy to the bow and arrow, 45
Eyaya-eya, 237

Famine song, 186
Fathomless is my love, 280
Fear was about me, 231
Fishing song, 313
Flowers, 23
Flute player, 26
Flute song, 216
For no one, 384
For the cultural campaign, 56
Fortitude, 107
Fragrant the grasses of high Kane-hoa, 277
Freedom and dignity have reached us, 119
From a beggarman's song, 184
From a faction song, 200

From a lament from Una, 184
From a satirical poem about drink, 53
From the conception the increase, 294
From the north-west a cloud has come up, 58

Gentle hunter, 163
Gently! Gently! Gently!, 275
Give me my infant now, 302
Glorious it is to see, 230
Glorious Virgin, heavenly vision, 175
Go, let us go my friends, go home, 138
Good night to thee, Fair Goddess, 223
Go on, thou noisy one!, 134
Government!, 314
Grant a canoe that shall be swift as a fish!, 289
Great grief came over me, 248
Great grief came over me, 248
Grew in Hades, 295

Hail, fathers, hail!, 216
Hark to the rumble of the earthquake god!, 299
Have courage, my boy, to say no!, 375
He comes from the house as lightning flickers in the sky, 26
He could hit a blade of grass with his spear, 277
He had no friend, 33
He has annihilated the enemies!, 134
He is patient, 149
He is walking in the road, 32
He lives in the outer land, 445
Hell, 175
Hell whose rains and cold appeal, 175
Here I stand, 232
Her red cloth is like the lightning, 18
He talks and talks, 26
He wears a beard to let us see that he is pure within, 93
He who is my master, 69
Hey, young bride!, 140
High-placed above me the branches quiver, 91
High towers the grass where once we'd meet and wander, 78
Hilo, Hanakahi, rain rustling *lehua*, 284
Hilo, Hanakahi, rain rustling lehua, 284
His teeth are white as curds, 22
Hitler, frothy-mouth, 311

Hitler, frothy-mouth, wooden-head, 311
Home, 138
How well for the birds, 181
How well for the birds that can rise in their flight, 181
How young I was, 31
Hunger (*Fear was about me*), 231
Hunger (*Hunger is beating me*), 167
Hunger (*Hunger makes a person lie down*), 166
Hunger is beating me, 167
Hunger makes a person lie down, 166
Hungry and thirsty we break these stones in the heat of the sun, 35
Hymn to the air spirit, 232

I, a blue wolf, 70
I am blessing two, not one, 159
I am but a little woman, 239
I am but a little woman, 239
I am filled with joy, 233
I am greeting you, Mayor of Lagos, 164
I am the beginning, 142
I arrive where an unknown earth is under my feet, 300
Ibikunle! the Lord of his Quarters, 153
I could not sleep, 240
I draw a deep breath, 243
I dwell on the misty steppe, 68
Ifa, 159
Ifa divination was performed for Tiger, 157
Ifa speaks in parables, 159
If it's rice-grain, say it's rice-grain, 96
If of a beetle you'd make game, 95
If there's no wick within the lamp, 89
If you, O Aynabo, my fleet and fiery horse, 101
If you see my mother, 363
If you see my mother, partner, tell her to pray for me, 363
If you smoke a cigarette, 65
If you stay to school dinners, 382
I have grown old, 254
I have no more a golden store – this sets the world a-scorning, 181
I heard the songs, 219
I know where I'm going, 189
I know where I'm going, 189
I lie in the darkness, as the dead shades gather, 307
I'll have a collier for my sweetheart, 372

I, lord of all mortals!, 80
I'm a decent boy just landed, 187
I'm going to California, 285
I'm going to California, 285
I'm through with you, 383
In a mean abode on the Shankill Road, 200
Independence, 199
In memoriam, 193
In my dreams I searched for you, 25
In Puna's fragrant glades, 282
In San Juan I wonder how my home is, 211
In Shaka's days we lived well, 136
In sunlight raindrops look like dew, 94
In the County Tyrone, near the town of Dungannon, 198
In the heart of the hills, 78
In the heart of the hills, the rain unabated, 78
In the name of Allah, the Merciful, the Compassionate!, 81
In the name of God, the merciful, the compassionate!, 81
In the north the cloud flower blossoms, 213
Invitation, 89
Invitation to a spirit, 82
Invocation, 253
Invocation before the rice harvest, 87
Invocation for a storm, 274
Io dwelt within the breathing-space of immensity, 297
I once loved a boy, 188
I once loved a boy and a bonny, bonny boy, 188
I place myself, 177
I place myself at the edge of Thy grace, 177
I rise up from rest, 236
It's gonna shine, 361
It's gonna shine, 361
I shall dance, I have hope, 141
I should be ashamed, 237
I shouted day and night, 142
I sit beneath the throne of Allah!, 80
I spied a bear, 239
I thought you loved me, 135
I thought you loved me, 135
It is a time of hunger, 236
It is hard to catch a trout, 247
It is so still in the house, 236
It's a mighty hard road that my poor hands have hoed, 379

It sleeps by day!, 138
I used to be a drill man, 370
I watched last night the rising moon, upon a foreign strand, 186
I weep for my loved one, 304
I went down to the river, poor boy, 365
I went to a foreign land to work for money, 285
I will sing a song, 244
I will visit, 252
I wonder how my home is, 211
Iwori wotura, 157
I work all day long for you, 362
I work all day long for you, until the sun go down, 362

Jealousy, 78
Jeff Buckner, 360
Jesus Christ, 380
Jesus Christ was a man that travelled through the land, 380
Jojina, my love, 136
Judgement day, 361
Jump over the wall and come to me, 20
Just as eventide draws near, 301

Ka-la-kaua, a great name, 273
Kisses, 88
Kob antelope, 161

Laieikawai's lament after her husband's death, 278
Lament, 307
Lament for a dead lover, 107
Lament for Apirana Ngata, 317
Lament for Mafukuzela, 138
Lament for Taramoana, 305
Land earth-root, 253
Landfall, 300
*Last night I had a dream bad 'cess to my dreaming I thought I was stand-
     ing at the 'Labour Borue'*, 201
Leaf of lehua *and* noni-*tint, the Kona Sea*, 273
Leopard, 163
Let me go, 29
Let me proceed by this way!, 311
Let's paddle, dear, by yonder fort, 89
Let the dead depart in peace, 160
Let us come in to worship Jehovah, 141

Let us sing of it ever and long, 253
Let Zulu be heard, 142
Like a she-camel with a large bell, 107
Like ripples on the water, 26
Like the yu'ub wood bell tied to gelded camels that are running away, 104
Liquor, you turn us into kings, 36
Lisnagade, 198
Listen to the call of the muezzin, it calls people to prayer, 102
Lo, alas, I look and seek, 241
Long ago how fine was everything!, 211
Long ago in the north, 212
Long had passed the hour of midnight, 85
Long-haired preachers come out every night, 366
Longing, 21
Look where the mist, 305
Lost love, 210
Love and music, 26
Love by the water-reeds, 279
Love charm, 81
Love dirge, 303
Love is a shark, 281
Lover of mine, if upland you journey, 91
Love songs, 18
Lucky lion!, 138
Lullaby, 316
Lullaby. O men from the fields, 203

Mafukuzela, Rain-giving clouds, 139
Many days of sorrow, many nights of woe, 360
Many women call on me to sleep with them, 310
May His Body make me safer, 179
May I be beautiful, 79
Mayor of Lagos, 164
Mbuyazi of the Bay!, 132
Men's impotence, 235
Menzi son of Ndaba, 129
Ministers who've sold the King, 67
Misty and dim, a bush in the wilds of Kapa'a, 276
Mocking song against Qaqortingneq, 249
Modern love poems, 110
Money! Money!, 165
Money! Money!, 165
Moon of the earth, 17

Morning prayer, 236
Music, 80
Musk oxen, 240
Must I go bound?, 191
Must I go bound and you go free, 191
My breath, 244
My cobra girl, 23
My foster-brother and foster-sister, 464
My grief on the sea, 183
My grief on the sea, 183
My heart burns for him, 21
My homestead's with lightning aflame, 92
My ketch must lead into the fray, 88
My little breath, under the willows by the water side we used to sit, 209
My Lord, what a morning when de stars begin to fall, 361
My love is playing, 26
My love is playing on a fiddle, 26
My madman bathes in the golden tank, 28
My money! O, my money!, 135
My money! O, my money!, 135
My mother said I must not have a collier, 372
My Nkosi you loved me, 142
My sweetheart in the rippling hills of sand, 281
My sweetheart in the rippling hills of sand, 281

Neap-tide and the ebbing days slide, 314
New coasts and Poseidon's son, 389
New Moon, 353
Next after comes Coyote, Stretched-out-in Dew, 212
1952, 382
No bird, no fabled fowl it is, 90
Nobody will quarrel with the woodcock, 167
No Irish need apply, 187
No place so grand, 184
Now from the east, 216
Now from the east, 216
Now the New Moon is hanging, having cast away his bone, 353
Now you depart, and though your way may lead, 102

Obatala, the creator, 149
O beautiful calm, 308
O beautiful calm, 308
O brother, as you've given me so much, 28

Och! What will we do for linen?, 200
O come, my body is alone, come laugh with me, come talk with me, 20
O deep-blue sea, O God Uli!, 270
Odyssey, 389
O elephant, possessor of a savings-basket full of money, 161
O faithless thorn, 22
O faithless thorn, 22
Of Iron am I, 81
Oft do I return, 242
O girl, you torment me, 19
O girl, you torment me, you are so deceiving, 19
O goddess Laka!, 269
O God of Bethel, 381
O God of Bethel, by whose hand, 381
Oh! Dublin sure there is no doubtin', 184
Oh, how my love, 309
Oh, how my love with a whirling power, 309
Oh, now we're leaving home, me boys; to Ottawa we're going', 374
Oh! 'tis pretty to be in Ballinderry, 190
Oh, you are a kilt which a young dandy set out to choose, 107
O Jojina, my love, I always miss you, 136
O Kane, O Ku-ka-Pao, 259
O Kane, O Lono of the blue sea, 271
O Kane, O Lono of the blue sea, 271
O King of the world, 180
O King of the world, 180
Old age, 31, 134
Old age has come, my head is shaking, 31
Old creation chant, 259
O little well, 24
O little well, you give no water, 24
Om, 86
O men from the fields, 203
O men, the beautiful world is going to be spoiled, 115
Om! Virgin goddess Mahadevi! Om!, 86
O my comrade, it is cold, 278
O my sinner, les us spend this night together, 27
O my son, 305
O my son, born on a winter's morn, 316
O my soul be patient, she is very beautiful, 27
Once I played and danced in my parents' kingdom, 31
Once upon a time, 430
One day you'll have to go to the City of the Dead, 33

Only the air-spirits know, 229
On the isle of Penang there is 'stablished a city, 90
On the twenty-sixth of August, our fatal moss gave way, 371
O our Mother the Earth, O our Father the Sky, 208
O Paddy dear, and did you hear the news that's going around, 185
Open the door, 96
O Piano I heard at evening, 286
Oracle: *Iwori wotura*, 157
Or ever God created Adam, 90
Oshun, the river goddess, 160
O sleeper rise, if thou would'st see, 17
O swan, come slowly from the sky, 18
O that my love were in my arms, 95
O the praties are so small, 186
Our country is divided, 103
Our earth mother, 220
Our tarin' Dan O'Connell, sure he was a mighty man, 200
Over and over again to people, 103
Over there in your fields you have, 208
O Virgin, 175
O water-girl! with tinkling anklets, 22
O you hollow-cheeked offspring, 134
O you who come to me – alas!, 278

Parting, 78
Parting at dawn: *Three pantuns*, 88
Pastures of plenty, 379
Peace be unto you, Penglima Lenggang Laut!, 82
Peace be with you, O Tin-Ore, 83
Pearly beads, 19
Perhaps – well, 235
Personal song, 236
Piano at evening, 286
Plane wreck at Los Gatos, 378
Plashes the tree-trunk lost in the river, 96
Poet's lament on the death of his wife, 104
Praise of a child, 168
Praise of a train, 134
Praise of Ibikunle, 153
Praises of Henry Francis Fynn, 132
Parises of the King of Oyo, 152
Praise song for King Kalakaua, 273
Prayer for rain, 113

Prayer of the fishing net, 270
Prayer on making a canoe, 289
Prince Sumiya, 58
Pull in the net!, 313
Puna's fragrant glades, 282
Python, 163

Quarrel, 167

Railroad look so pretty, 367
Rain all over the cornfields, 215
Rain magic song, 209
Rains for the harvest, 208
Raja, my heart is mad for you, 21
Ready we stand in San Juan town, 209
Red ants, 79
Red ants in a bamboo – the passion, 79
Red beauty, 18
Regret, 90
Regret and refusal, 210
Remembering, 243
Remember thou me, 96
Resemblance, 280
Ringleted youth of my love, 182
Ringleted youth of my love, 182
Rise! arise! arise!, 222
Rising fondly before me, 279
Robens' promised land, 373
Rory and Liam are dead and gone, 193
Ruaumoko – the earthquake god, 299
Rust destroys the wheat, 30

Sail at the mast head, 352
St Kevin, 192
Salome, 382
Salome was a dancer, 382
Salute to the elephant, 161
Sanctimony, 93
Satan is following me, 139
Satan is following me, 139
Say father, say mother, 139
Scalp dance song, 212
School dinners, 382

Seaweed, seaweed, 317
Seaweed, seaweed, drifting, drifting, 317
Seeing its corners, it is square, 43
Seeking, earnestly seeking in the gloom, 298
See the headlands yonder stand, 303
See two passenger trains, Lawd, 361
See! yonder hill the bitterns seek, 88
Senzangakhona, 129
Shadows, 210
Shaka, 126
She goes with her pot for water, 35
She had no business doin' it, but she came out o' the East, 363
She is not for me, 27
She is teck'wi, 219
She truly needs good character, 166
Shine on me, moon, 302
Shine, O sun! tenderly on my skin, 303
Shoes are made to fit the feet, 24
Shoes are made to fit the feet, 24
Sick unto death of love, 96
Siilenboor, 63
Since, when you die, delight, 110
Sleeper rise, 17
Slowly the muddy pool becomes a river, 160
Snails, 349
So close should be our love, 21
Solitary song, 229
Something was whispered, 229
Song, 276
Song of abuse, 167
Song of a Hebrew, 383
Song of a sick child, 97
Song of caribou, musk oxen, women, and men who would be manly, 230
Song of despair, 304
Song of joy, 251
Song of longing, 30, 31
Song of poverty, 18
Song of Sukkaartik, the assistant spirit, 253
Song of the blue-corn dance, 218
Song of the sky loom, 208
Songs from the Djanggawul cycle, 328
Songs in the turtle dance at Santa Clara, 212
Soul of my child, Princess Splendid, 87

Sound of snails – crying, 349
Spirit song, 252
Sri Rama's raiment, 83
Stop there, old one, within your haven, 317
Storm at sea, 86
Sunset song, 223
Sure a poor man, 285
Swaggering prince, 163

Take a golden comb, 34
Take off your hat, 137
Take off your hat, 137
Take up the pen, 88
Take up the pen and write a text, 88
Take your accusation back!, 251
Taking between them, 45
Taunt, 93
Teasing song, 140
Thanksgiving after Communion, 179
That our earth mother may wrap herself, 220
That somebody, my own special one, 210
That song there I borrow, 251
The ageing hunter, 241
The arrow of desire, 22
The beloved's image, 279
The best dance, 108
The best dance is the dance of the eastern clans, 108
The birds, 352
The birds saw the people walking along, 352
The blowflies buzz, 350
The body perishes, the heart stays young, 134
The breeze is blowing, 318
The breeze is blowing, 318
The bride's farewell: Two songs, 28
The British, the Ethiopians, and the Italians are squabbling, 103
The cloud-flower lullaby, 213
The cloud-piles o'er Kona's sea whet my joy, 280
The colonialist governments, 117
The creation, 295
The creation of man, 298
The crops are all in and the peaches are rottening, 378
The darkness presses all around!, 315
The dawning sun, 63

The day breaks, your mind aches, 384
The depths of sorrow, 34
The depths of sorrow in tears have not been measured, 34
The disdainful mistress, 89
The Donibristle Moss Moran disaster, 371
The dream, 201
The earthquake, 218
The-Eldest is calling, 475
The ends of the hibiscus burgeon, 97
The Evening Star, 354
The ever-touring Englishmen, 35
The ever-touring Englishmen have built their bungalows, 35
The fruit was atop the shelf, 90
The glory of Hanalei is its heavy rain, 283
The glory of Hanalei is its heavy rain, 283
The golden sea-otter, 463
The great fool, 140
The great sea, 251
The green autumn stubble, 191
The gull, 241
The gull, it is said, 241
The iwa flies heavy to nest in the brush, 279
The joy of a singer, 247
The Kona sea, 273
The Kumulipo: A creation chant, 260
The Lake of the Caogama, 374
The leper, 287
The light of the four Suns, five Moons, 79
The limits of submission, 103
The lost, 91
The lover's prayer, 96
The loves of the birds, 92
The lying Muslims, 159
The mangoes grow in clusters, 21
The meaning of love, 92
The merry jovial beggar, 181
The mist over Pukehina, 305
The moon behind the hill, 186
The mother's song, 236
The Muslims are still lying, 159
The new wife, 30
The ocean is like a wreath, 275
The old man's song, 254

The one who does not love me, 167

The opium den, 93

The ould Orange flute, 198

The Palm tree grows in the far bush, 160

The peeler's lament, 363

The pointed clouds have become fixed in the heaven, 274

The preacher and the slave, 366

The rainbow, 217

The rainbow stands red . . . A tiring song, 277

The rainbow stands red o'er the ocean, 277

There is a halo round the moon, 35

There is a young Muslim Chinese, 93

There is drink fermented, 53

There is fear in, 229

There is no rest, 25

There is no rest for her, and sleep has left her bed, 25

There was an earthquake, 218

The right true end, 28

The roadmenders' song, 35

The sail at the mast head dips from side to side, 352

The sea! O the sea!, 284

The sea! O the sea!, 284

The shattering of love, 25

The six periods of creation, 294

The song of the trout fisher, 242

The songs, 219

The speckled horse, 64

The speckled horse is bucking, 64

The springtime of the earth, 143

The springtime of the earth has come, 143

The stars are thundering, 24

The stars are thundering in the sky, 24

The story of Bamsi Beyrek of the grey horse, 413

The Suez crisis, 115

The sugar-cane is just a cubit high, 18

The sun and the moon and fear of loneliness, 229

The sunrise call, 222

The taboo woman, 219

The time has come for us to part, 383

The time of creation has come, 159

The tiny ant at night you would be seeking, 89

The vicissitudes of the world, O Olaad, are like the clouds of the seasons, 106

The water of Kane, 268

The wearing of the green, 185
The well: Two songs, 23
The white, orphaned camel kid, 66
The white, orphaned camel kid, 66
The willows by the water side, 209
The wind and the rain are beating down, 25
The 'word' of an antelope caught in a trap, 68
The 'word' of a watch-dog, 69
The 'word' of a wolf encircled by the hunt, 70
They can't do that, 368
They hanged Jeff Buckner from a sycamore tree, 360
The young flute player, 26
The young viper grows as it sits, 126
This being a fair and peaceful day, 46
This earthen body, 34
This truly wonderful steed, 51
This very day, a little while ago, you lived, 212
This way from the North, 221
Those were the days, 136
Thoughts of God, 176
Three songs from the Moon-Bone cycle, 352
Tiger, 157
. . . Till the sea runs dry, 90
Tin-ore, 83
Tip-of-the-Single-Feather, 473
Title of a swift horse, 51
To a dictatorial sultan, 106
To a faithless friend, 106
To a friend going on a journey, 102
To kill a bat is easy, 27
Tonight at least, my sinner, 27
Toroi Bandi, 67
To the pines, 376
To the pines, to the pines, 376
To you this little village is as dear as the moon, 17
Trousers first of ancient fabric, 83
Two hoboes, 367
Two young maids, 92
Two young maids of beauty fair, 92

Under my thoughts may I God-thoughts find, 176
Unique among girls, 78
Up and up soars the Evening Star, hanging there in the sky, 354

Uru-tu-sendo's song, 223

Variety: Why do we grunble?, 164
Voices lifted high in singing, 80

Walrus hunting, 240
War song, 134
Was it all worth while?, 137
Water-girl, 22
We are croaking as does the frog, 316
Welcome O great Mary, 178
Welcome thou of high estate, 178
We object, 316
We're the D-Day Dodgers, out in Italy, 376
What is man's body?, 34
What is man's body? It is a spark from the fire, 34
What matter?, 36
What on earth! I fear and tremble!, 252
What will become of Hawaii?, 287
When stubble lands were greening you came among the stooks, 191
When the rain drums loud on the leaf, 280
When Toroi Bandi was alive, 67
When your eyes, 179
When your eyes shall be closing, your mouth be opening, 179
When you've just been jugged by an upright judge, 368
Where are the hands and feet, 302
While we are at peace, 282
Whispering ghosts of the west, 300
Whispering ghosts of the west, 300
White as paper a-sail in the air, 91
White as paper a-sail in the air, 91
Who can tell?, 35
'Who will pay for the milk I gave you?', 29
Why do we grumble because a tree is bent, 164
Wind, 86
Wind searching as a sieve of brass, 86
Wind would tear a man's shroud, 86
Wisdom is the finest beauty of a person, 156
Wisdom is the finest beauty of a person, 156
With his tusk-like fierce moustaches and double-pointed beard, 93
Women, 166
Women and men, 116
Women have no share in the encampments of this world, 116

Working is another way of praying, 383
Work song, 140
Would God that I and my darling, 184

Yai-yai-yai, 240
Ye brave bold men of 'Cotia, 373
Ye fog that creeps there in the uplands, 274
Yellow butterflies, 214
Yellow butterflies, 214
Yellow cloud, 350
Yellow cloud rising up from that fighting, from the people playing and
   throwing spears, 350
Ye Protestants of Ulster, I pray you join with me, 198
Yiya wo!, 137
Yonder comes the dawn, 223
Yonder, yonder see the fair rainbow, 217
You are coming very slowly, why do you delay, 23
You are lying, O missionary, 141
You are lying, O missionary, 141
You can make a tidy leaf-pot out of sarai leaves, 20
You drop a pearl, 89
You drop a pearl, 'twill keep its hue, 89
You have brought pearly beads, 19
You may talk of Columbus's sailing, 196
Young Una, you were a rose in a garden, 184
You play the flute, 21
Your body might have come from the loins of a prince, 17
You've started today on life's journey, 375
You were the fence standing between our land and the descendants of Ali,
   107
You who give sustenance to your creatures, O God, 113

Zong Belegt Baatar, 430

INDEX OF AUTHORS

Abse, Dannie, 383
Ajukutooq, 253
Akjartoq, 243
Aleqaajik, 248
Alohikea, Alfred, 283
Apolebieji, Odeniyi, 161
Arnatkoak, 236
Arowa, Omobayode, 154
Arrabey, Salaan, 106
Aua, 236, 239, 240
Avane, 241

Beddo, Frank, 360
Bohem, Nugent, 198
Boucicault, Dion, 185
Bowndheri, Ilmi, 108

Casey, Peter, 181
Colum, Padraic, 203
Costello, Tomas, 184
Crummy, Biddy, 178
Cussrooee, Biddy, 183

De Brun, Padraig, 193
Djalparmiwi, 350
Djurberaui, 351
Doddridge, Philip, 381

Ferguson, J., 371
French, Percy, 196

Gavan, Lennox, 374
Guthrie, Woody, 378, 379, 380

Haad, Siraad, 107

Hassan, Mahammed Abdille, 102
Hauroa, Matangi, 307
Herea, Te Heuheu, 310
Hill, Joe, 366
Hilton, L. M., 375
Homer, 389

Igjugarjuk, 240
Ikinilik, 242

Jama, Sheikh Aqib Abdullahi, 113
Jigmed, Chimediin, 53, 56

Ka-ʻehu, 287
Kaiama, 276
Kalola, 280
Kavanghongevah, 216
Keaulumoku, 260
Kerehoma, Rarawa, 302
Kittaararter, 251
Kivkarjuk, 239
Koianimptiwa, 214
Korkut, Dede, 413
Kuapakaa, 275
Kunene, Raymond Mazisi, 140, 141

Lahpu, 215
Lele-io-Hoku, 282
Lennon, John, 384, 385
Liagarang, 349, 350
Likelike, Princess, 281
Liliʻu-o-ka-lani, Princess, 282
Logan, John, 381

McCartney, Paul, 384, 385
Magogo, Princess, 140
Makere, 305
Masahongva, 214, 216
Masaveimah, 216
Mavimbela, 135
Maze, Mack, 363
Mossman, Bina, 285
Mumin, Hassan Sheikh, 116
Muuse, Abdillaahi, 105

Nakasuk, 241, 253
Napa, 252
Ngata, Apirana, 311
Nihoniho, Tuta, 314
Nohomaiterangi, 316
Nuur, Faarah, 103

O'Gallagher, Alice, 178
Oliver, William, 372
Orpingalik, 244

Palea, 286
Paraone, Tiwai, 297
Paulinaoq, 233
Piuvkaq, 247, 249
Pukui, Mary Kawena, 289

Purdom, George, 373

Qarshe, Cabdullaahi, 117

Rangiaho, 304
Reedy, Arnold, 317

Sandag, 68, 69, 70
Shembe, Isaiah, 141, 142, 143
Sizemore, George, 370

Tangikuku, Hine, 314
Tatana, Hannah, 317
Te-whaka-io-roa, 302
Tu-kehu, 308, 309
Turei, Mohi, 299

Ugaas, Raage, 104
Utahania, 248
Uvavnuk, 251
Uvlunuaq, 237

Velema, 473

Wakarpa, 463
Wetea, 308, 309